DATE DUE

GAYLORD			PRINTED IN U.S.A.

*Joe R. and Teresa Lozano Long Series
in Latin American and Latino Art and Culture*

REMEMBERING THE HACIENDA

Religion, Authority, and
Social Change in Highland Ecuador

BY BARRY J. LYONS

UNIVERSITY OF TEXAS PRESS, AUSTIN

Requests for permission to reproduce material from this work should be sent to: Permissions, University of Texas Press, P.O. Box 7819, Austin, TX 78713-7819
www.utexas.edu/utpress/about/bpermission.html

⊗ The paper used in this book meets the minimum requirements of ANSI/NISO z39.48-1992 (R1997) (Permanence of Paper).

LIBRARY OF CONGRESS CATALOGING-IN-PUBLICATION DATA

Lyons, Barry J. (Barry Jay), 1958–
Remembering the hacienda : religion, authority, and social change in highland Ecuador / by Barry J. Lyons.—1st ed.
    p.   cm. — (Joe R. and Teresa Lozano Long series in Latin American and Latino art and culture)
  Includes bibliographical references and index.
  ISBN-13: 978-0-292-71339-0 (cl. : alk. paper)
  ISBN-10: 0-292-71339-8
  ISBN-13: 978-0-292-71439-7 (pbk. : alk. paper)
  ISBN-10: 0-292-71439-4
    1. Monjas Corral Hacienda (Ecuador)—History.   2. Haciendas—Ecuador—Case studies.   3. Agricultural laborers—Ecuador—Pangor River Watershed—Social conditions.   4. Church lands—Ecuador—Pangor River Watershed—History.   5. Indians of South America—Ecuador—Pangor River Watershed—Social conditions.   6. Catholic Church—Ecuador—Pangor River Watershed—History.   7. Social change—Ecuador—Pangor River Watershed.   8. Pangor River Watershed (Ecuador)—Social conditions.   I. Title.   II. Series.
  HD1471.E22P365 2006
    333.2—dc22
                                                              2006017298

Dedication
   To
   Donald and Rosalyn Lyons, my parents;
   Mercedes, who shared so much of this with me;
   and
   the people of Monjas Corral-Tepeyac Bajo, who made it possible

A

   Donald y Rosalyn Lyons, mis padres;
   Mercedes, quien compartió mucho de esto conmigo;
   y
   la gente de Monjas Corral-Tepeyac Bajo, quienes lo hicieron posible
   Dioselopague nishpami yupaychani.

CONTENTS

ACKNOWLEDGMENTS   ix

PART ONE: INTRODUCTION   1

   1. *Introduction*   3

   2. *A History of Pangor and Monjas Corral*   27

PART TWO: SOCIETY AND RESISTANCE   71

   3. *Hacienda Society and the Base of the Triangle*   73

   4. *Saint Rose's Blessings*   100

   5. *Reciprocity and Resistance*   125

PART THREE: RESPECT AND AUTHORITY   165

   6. *Disobedience and Respect: Two Accounts*   167

   7. *Respect, Authority, and Discipline*   216

PART FOUR: THE LEGACY OF THE HACIENDA   257

   8. *The Demise of the Hacienda*   259

   9. *Liberation Theology and Ethnic Resurgence*   279

NOTES   311

BIBLIOGRAPHY   321

INDEX   341

ACKNOWLEDGMENTS

I began to learn about rural Ecuador before I ever decided to be an anthropologist. To the U.S. Peace Corps I owe my first introduction to Ecuador in 1981, and to the people of the town I call San Ramón de Bolívar—above all the Guizado Medrano family—my first and most profound lessons in Ecuadorian culture. San Ramón and the Guizado Medrano household remain my Ecuadorian home.

It was also in San Ramón that my curiosity was piqued by stories of the old-time muleteers' trips over the mountains to a place called Pangor. My decision ultimately to conduct fieldwork in Pangor had something to do with the comforting thought that "home" was just on the other side of the mountains.

Manuel Guizado, now my father-in-law, accompanied me on my first trip to Pangor, and Dina Medrano, my mother-in-law, spent a good deal of time helping my wife, Mercedes, and me in Riobamba and Pangor. We have been lucky to have my brother-in-law, Prof. Luis Guizado, and his family living in Riobamba since 1992. Luis aided me in archival research and in many other ways. Janéth Núñez Guizado also provided invaluable assistance in 1991–1992.

Some of my greatest debts are of course to the many people in Pangor who welcomed me as an anthropologist into their communities and homes. I cannot name them all individually, but I would like to thank collectively the communities of Achín, Ajospamba, Baraspamba, Guangopud, La Florida, Pinipala, San Vicente–Cachipamba, Tepeyac Alto, Tepeyac Gatazo, and the Centro Poblado. I was proud to have Tepeyac Bajo as my "home" community in Pangor. Avelino Shagñay, Jacoba Sayay, and their family brought me into their household for the first year and more of my fieldwork, kept me happy and well fed, and gave me my deepest insights into indigenous lives. Miguel Guailla and Rosa Yuquilema were helpful friends and neighbors during my last year of fieldwork. I am grateful also to Manuel Yépez, Joaquina Niamo, Alberto Yumbo, José María Pillajo, Andrés Yépez, Agustín Choca, Margarita Yépez, Gabriel Niamo, Rosa Condo, José Amancha, Luis Amancha, Pedro Guailla, Manuel Miñarcaja, Olmedo Yuquilema, Fermina Yuquilema, and many others. To them all I can only say an Ecuadorian "Dioselopague" (May God repay them) for their hospitality.

Sister María Luisa Urquieta probably did more than any other person to help me gain a favorable reception both in Pangor and in Riobamba church circles. I will always be grateful for her friendship and admire her dedication to a life of service.

Other members of the Equipo Misionero Itinerante, especially Father Carlos Vera and Sofía Rosero, became friends. The same is true of a number of other pastoral agents beyond the Equipo. I think with a special fondness of Father Michel Alexandre, a man of great integrity and human warmth, and Sister Charo Hallo, whose friendly interest in my own religious tradition encouraged me to host a memorable Seder in Pesach of 1992.

Among the graduates and students of the Centro de Formación Indígena in Riobamba who have honored me with their trust and whose conversation is always invigorating, I would like to mention in particular Delfín Tenesaca, Esteban Tenesaca, Carlos Amboya, and Maximiliano Asadobay.

The bishop of Riobamba, Mons. Víctor Corral Mantilla, encouraged me in my project, permitted me to participate regularly in various church events at the diocese level, and, together with Mons. Agustín Bravo and Father Estuardo Gallegos, allowed me access to the diocese archives. In the archive of the bishopric, Eliza Velata and Patricia Auquilla provided cheerful company and assistance. I am also grateful for the friendship and insights that Víctor Alejandro Campaña offered from early on.

I was lucky to be able to share some of the joys, trials, and intellectual excitement of fieldwork with Rebecca Tolen and Elise Nyborg-Christensen, both of whose research in Chimborazo overlapped my own. In Quito, Felipe Monar, Aida Albiño, and the Arroyo family were very generous with their hospitality.

I benefited greatly from the assistance and advice of Dr. Segundo Moreno Yánez, chair of Anthropology at the Universidad Católica in Quito. Dr. Francisco Carrión and Dr. Xavier Izko kindly arranged for my affiliation with the Facultad Latinoamericana de Ciencias Sociales in Quito during the last year or so of my research in Ecuador. I would also like to thank the Instituto Nacional de Patrimonio Cultural for authorizing the research. Among

Ecuadorianists in the United States, Frank Salomon and Norman Whitten Jr. both gave helpful advice at the outset of my fieldwork.

Ing. Bayardo Ulloa, Arq. Franklin Cárdenas, Dr. Alfonso Chávez, Miss Piedad Zurita, and others at the Casa de la Cultura in Riobamba facilitated my use of the historical archive under their care. Father Gabriel Barriga in Cajabamba, Sisters Heroína and María José in Sicalpa, and Father Luis Curipoma in Pallatanga all kindly permitted me to look through parish archives. The secretary of the Pangor *tenencia política* (civil parish authority), Eduardo Guamantaqui, allowed me to examine documents in the archive under his responsibility. Father Guillermo Jiménez always gave Mercedes and me a gracious welcome at the Monastery of San Alfonso in Riobamba, where we examined the Redemptorist chronicles.

Other people in Ecuador who have generously shared their perspectives, advice, and information with me include Baltazar Asadobay, Manolo Barreno, Mons. Agustín Bravo, Lic. Ciro Cazar, Sister Isabel Fonseca, Lic. Rafael García, Lic. Carlos Moreno, Rafael Murillo, Dr. Lautaro Ojeda, Rosa Pagalo, Dra. Isabel Robalino, Ing. Luis Rodríguez, Dr. Vicente Soria, and Lic. Delfín Tenesaca, the former parish priest of Pangor.

My advisors at the University of Michigan, Bruce Mannheim and Sherry Ortner, were extraordinarily generous with their time, encouragement, and constructive criticism throughout my graduate career and have continued to provide advice and support whenever I have needed it. A number of others have read or listened to me talk about parts of this manuscript and offered valuable comments: Marietta Baba, Ruth Behar, Sueann Caulfield, David Frye, Carol Greenhouse, Tanya Gulevich, Lisa Gurr, John Hamer, Pat Heck, David Holmberg, Rosalyn Lyons, Bill Mitchell, Rosario Montoya, Gananath Obeyesekere, Richard O'Connor, Sherry Ortner, Celeste Ray, John Robb, Chris Schmit-Nowara, Rebecca Scott, Krista Van Vleet, Mae Wallace, and Scott Wilson, as well as the University of Texas Press's two anonymous reviewers and the anonymous reviewers of two journal articles based on this book. I am also grateful for the advice and support of Theresa May, for Kathy Bork's skillful copyediting, and for the professionalism of other members of the editorial staff at the University of Texas Press. Chris Fairchild provided expert assistance with illustrations. Marilyn Moore and Xia Wu cheerfully helped with clerical tasks.

My other intellectual debts will become apparent through my citations, but I would like to acknowledge one in particular here. I wrote much of this book in critical dialogue with James Scott's work, both drawing on and critiquing it. I have found Scott's eloquence, passion, and intellectual rigor an inspiring model and a challenge, and critique here is a kind of tribute.

Among friends who have given moral support are Bryan Duckham, Adam

Eigner, Janise Hurtig, Peter Kassis, Charo Montoya, John Robb, Steve Rubenstein, Kathryn Stern, and Karin Tice. Raina O'Neill taught me a lot about hope, dignity, and the meaning of writing as a vocation.

My deepest and most long-term debts are to my family. My parents, Donald and Rosalyn Lyons, have encouraged and supported me materially, intellectually, and emotionally. Their own wide-ranging interest in the world and respect for people from every background have shaped my own outlook. My wife, Mercedes Guizado, accompanied me in Pangor, aided in interviewing and archival research, and continually helps me in my efforts to understand Ecuadorian society and culture. She has given me crucial advice, moral support, and a necessary push more than once and took over the bulk of our common responsibilities while I wrote. I cannot say that our two children have always facilitated my writing, but Daniel and Michael have been good company, and I do believe that some of what I have learned as their father has found its way into the lines that follow.

My fieldwork in Ecuador from 1989 to 1992 was partly financed by a Social Science Research Council and American Council of Learned Societies International Doctoral Research Fellowship. The University of the South supported subsequent trips in 1995, 1996, and 1998 through Faculty Research Grants. The Harry Frank Guggenheim Foundation, the Woodrow Wilson National Fellowship Foundation, the Charlotte W. Newcombe Foundation, and the Department of Anthropology and Rackham Graduate School of the University of Michigan all provided fellowship support for writing in 1993–1994. Wayne State University (WSU) supported subsequent writing stints through College of Liberal Arts Research and Inquiry Grants in 2001 and 2003 and a sabbatical semester in 2002. The WSU Humanities Center provided a Small Grant for work on illustrations in 2005.

The story and song text at the end of Chapter 5 are reprinted from *Anthropology and Humanism* 24, no. 1, with the permission of the American Anthropological Association, Arlington, Virginia. Chapter 9 is based on my article "Religion, Authority, and Identity: Intergenerational Politics, Ethnic Resurgence, and Respect in Chimborazo, Ecuador," published in *Latin American Research Review* 36, no. 1.

The Instituto Geográfico Militar (Quito) kindly gave permission to use portions of its "Mapa Físico" and "Sicalpa" maps as the basis for Figures 3 and 9, respectively.

PART ONE

Introduction

CHAPTER I

Introduction

HACIENDAS, LIBERATION THEOLOGY, AND RESPECT

In much of Latin America, large landed estates called haciendas dominated the countryside from the colonial period through the mid-twentieth century. Peasant laborers lived and worked on these estates in serflike conditions. In the Ecuadorian Andes, most hacienda laborers were Quichua-speaking indigenous people, or Runa, who grew their own food on hacienda land and were obligated to work for the landlords in return.[1] Landlords' control over the Runa was reinforced by the latter's lack of economic alternatives, political power, or easy access to the legal system.

Violence was a familiar feature of life on haciendas. An anthropologist described the everyday use of whips on an Ecuadorian hacienda in the 1960s:

> On horseback and equipped with whips, . . . the mayordomos and mayorales [stewards and overseers] regulate all the day's activities. The threat of the whip, usually snapped at their legs, urges the peons on to work. The peons are warned of the approaching mayordomos by the stream of . . . insults from the supervisors and . . . they usually artfully leap away from the cracking whip. . . . All the while they . . . engage in verbal interplay with their supervisors. . . . A kind of oral battle ensues wherein insults, frequently disguised as jokes in order to avoid open hostility, are hurled between peons and overseers. [CRESPI 1968:194]

Imagine also listening to a man of around sixty in 1992 as he describes how he was punished as a youth for skinning a sheep incorrectly. It is a quiet evening in his house; we are sitting on stools between the cooking fire and the door, having finished a supper of potato soup served by his wife. He was in charge of pasturing the hacienda sheep, and one died, he says. He was supposed to skin it but was inexperienced and damaged the hide. The steward whipped him. The lash, he stresses, had three "buttons." I do not understand the significance of this, so he gets up and takes down an old riding whip hanging on the wall. He makes three loops in the leather strip, representing three knots, three "buttons," increasing the lash's impact. Then he pushes up his pants leg, indicating his calf. "It tore off the skin!" he says. His voice nearly breaks with, it seems to me, the memory of his pain, his powerlessness, and the injustice of the punishment.

His wife has been sitting by the fire, listening. She asks him what his mistake was in skinning the sheep. He explains again: he had begun at the wrong end. She punctuates his explanation with a short laugh, shaking her head at the same time.

In Ecuador, as elsewhere in Latin America, the state carried out an agrarian reform in the 1960s and the 1970s. Wage labor largely replaced the old serflike labor regime, and peasants gained title to some hacienda lands. Yet, large estates still survive in some areas, and land conflict between peasant villages and those estates continues to be an important political issue. Even where peasants now own the land, the old hacienda system has had an enduring impact on rural society, religion, and politics.

This book addresses some large questions about how indigenous peasants experienced, responded to, and remember conditions on a hacienda. How did people who were harshly oppressed and exploited make sense of their situation and of the forces that governed their world? In what ways did they resist their oppression, and in what ways were some of them co-opted or induced to accept an oppressive system? What role did religion play in how people viewed the world, in resistance, or in teaching people to accept oppression? And after an oppressive system ends, how do people remember it, what legacies does it leave, and how do these memories continue to shape their lives?

I had long wondered about such questions, but I did not set out to study the hacienda system when I began my research in 1989. I wanted mainly to study the contemporary relationship between indigenous people and the Catholic Church. Beginning in the 1960s, in the wake of Vatican II and the Cuban Revolution, some sectors within the Catholic Church in Latin America undertook a radical transformation symbolized by the phrase, "liberation theology." The church had been intimately tied to conservative, wealthy elites. Sectors identified with liberation theology attempted to reposition the church as an ally of the poor in struggles for social justice. In place of the traditional emphasis on priestly authority, the sacraments, and the saints, they encouraged the poor to take the Bible into their own hands and interpret it in the light of their own experiences of poverty and oppression. Theologians and pastoral agents understood the Bible as a call for liberation from sinful social structures.

I was interested in what Runa responses to this institutional transformation might reveal about indigenous culture and its relationship with non-indigenous influences. Did Runa villagers embrace liberation theology and find in it a reflection of their own views of the world? Or did they find it culturally alien? Did liberation theology newly awaken them to a sense of their human dignity, as some accounts suggested? Or did preexisting traditions of resistance to oppression shape their experience of liberation theology in more complex ways?

To explore these questions, I spent three years in the parish of Pangor, in Chimborazo province, from 1989 to 1992, and made shorter visits to Pangor in 1995, 1996, 1998, and 2003. Chimborazo is one of the most heavily indigenous provinces in Ecuador, a center of the contemporary indigenous political movement, and the leading stronghold of liberation theology in Ecuador. The bishop from 1954 to 1985, Leonidas Proaño, was attacked by some and praised by others as the "bishop of the Indians." He took to wearing a peasant poncho in place of the princely soutane worn by previous bishops and carried out his own land reform on church-owned estates in the 1960s. The church owned a hacienda in Pangor called Monjas Corral. Bishop Proaño stopped renting out the hacienda to wealthy landowners and rebaptized it "Tepeyac," after the mountain where a humble indigenous man encountered the dark-skinned Virgin of Guadalupe in early colonial Mexico. Proaño turned some of the hacienda lands over to the Runa who lived and labored on the estate. They formed the community of Tepeyac Bajo, the village that hosted me during my fieldwork.

The continuing influence of liberation theology in Tepeyac Bajo was obvious from the beginning of my stay; the legacy of the hacienda era was apparent in more subtle ways. During my first week in Tepeyac Bajo, villagers met in their chapel to study the Bible, guided by a lay Quichua missionary from another parish. These meetings culminated in a Mass said by the current bishop of the diocese. In his homily, the bishop reminded villagers of the racial abuse and economic exploitation they still suffered. When one of them got on a bus, other passengers might say, as though to an animal, "You, Indian, to the back!" When they arrived in town with potatoes to sell in the market, they were offered an unfairly low price. The bishop called on his listeners to demand respect for their dignity as children of God. "No, brother," he suggested they answer those who abused them. "We are children of God by baptism like you, and therefore we are your brothers. You can't treat me that way."

"Respect," or *respeto*, was a prominent theme in discussions that week. At one point, I was asked to introduce myself to the assembled villagers and tell them why I had come. I explained that one purpose of anthropology was to encourage respect among people of different cultures. As a researcher in the village, I would not be criticizing their way of life, let alone trying to change their religion. Instead, I wanted to learn about their culture and, ultimately, convey my understanding to others in a way that would help others respect them.

A catechist from a neighboring village then stood up and commented approvingly on my remarks about respect. He talked about the ways indigenous people are often not respected by other Ecuadorians. He went on to talk about the need for respect in contexts that I had not anticipated my comments might evoke—respectful behavior among Runa and their respect for their own communal authorities. I began to suspect that, by chance, I had used a word that meant more to my listeners than I had known. I was well aware of the racism indigenous people suffered and expected them to value respect in interethnic relations, but I would have to find out why the catechist saw fit to raise the issue of respect within the village.

Other discussions that week revealed that *respeto* referred to an important local moral value that villagers perceived was in crisis. In the religious meetings, they pondered how the Bible could help them teach children to respect their parents, and they lamented the recent decline in respect. I later learned that this sense of crisis was deeply rooted in the historical changes of the past several decades. Until the mid-1980s, youths learned and earned respect by sponsoring religious feasts, but no one sponsored feasts any more. Villagers in their forties and older recalled the hacienda era as a time of respect—even though, as they bitterly noted, landlords and their delegates did not treat Runa laborers with much respect.

As I became increasingly aware of these connections between past and present and delved more deeply into villagers' memories of the hacienda, I became more and more fascinated with the hacienda as something to be understood in its own right, not only as a prelude to the present. I supplemented what I learned from villagers' accounts by searching archives in neighboring towns and Quito for documents that would help me trace the history of the hacienda and the region. The result is this study, which focuses mainly on the hacienda era while also discussing the contemporary village and liberation theology in the light of local history.

My account focuses on Monjas Corral and its successor community, Tepeyac Bajo. It would be artificial and misleading, however, to draw inflexible lines around Monjas Corral as my unit of analysis. The estate was not the seat of an isolated society and culture. Hacienda residents sometimes moved from one estate to another, and many Pangor residents were migrants from the central Chimborazo basin. Many of my informants therefore had experience of various haciendas, and this is reflected in their oral accounts and my analysis.

Anthropologists study large questions about human experience by looking closely at particular places, places that always have their own idiosyncrasies. Monjas Corral was not necessarily a "typical" hacienda—there may be no such thing. Latin American haciendas varied widely in size (with some smaller, some much larger than Monjas Corral), in concentrating on different crops or livestock, in private versus institutional ownership, and in specific land tenure and labor arrangements (e.g., direct management by landlords versus sharecropping). They also varied in the origins and culture of the resident labor force, in landlords' origins and outlook, and in the ways broader political and economic contexts influenced the strategies of residents and landlords. I try to indicate how each of these factors affected the experience of residents of Monjas Corral.[2]

I write in part for my colleagues in anthropology and related disciplines. Anthropologists have written very little about haciendas anywhere in Latin America (especially in English) and not much about liberation theology, either. I will try to show that this case has a good deal to teach us about the workings of a system of domination; about the nature of religion, authority, resistance, and violence under such a system; and about the processes of religious change and ethnic resurgence. At the same time, I hope to share my fascination with these questions and with rural Ecuador with a broad audience, including students and others who may be new to anthropology. I do not believe that complex arguments require impenetrable prose, or that intellectual sophistication is best demonstrated by only addressing those already familiar with a discipline's theoretical traditions and terms. I will be satisfied if this book is judged as both a good introduction to its topics and a contribution to scholarly knowledge and understanding.

STUDYING CULTURE, PAST AND PRESENT

What does it mean to study how Runa experienced and responded to the hacienda system or how they relate to the Catholic Church today? How do I go about weaving together archival information, informants' accounts, and fieldwork observations to answer such questions, and what sort of generalization counts as a satisfying answer? As an anthropologist, I assume that social processes are also cultural processes: the ways people relate to other people and understand these relationships give rise to shared patterns of symbols and meanings, and, reciprocally, these shared meanings shape social relationships. Readers new to anthropology will already be familiar with the concept of culture, which has become commonplace in political discourse and even everyday conversation, but it is worth reviewing how anthropologists approach culture and its implications for this analysis.

First, to speak of "patterns of symbols and meanings" or, more metaphorically, "webs of significance" (Geertz 1973:5), is to indicate that culture is not simply a collection of disparate, separate elements. Instead, its elements are interconnected. In approaches centered on "actors" and "practice," anthropologists speak of "dispositions," habitual ways of responding to the world, that are "transposed" from one situation or domain to another (Bourdieu 1977). While different approaches variously emphasize cognitive models, symbolic meanings, learned physical responses, or other sorts of mental and embodied "stuff" seen to generate behavior, the main point here is that this stuff shows some degree of consistency and coherence from one situation to another and one person to another within the same society.

For example, suppose I notice that, when Pangor farmers pray before planting, they often say they will share food with others, implying that God and the saints expect this in return for making the crops grow. I can expect that this same assumption about the divine may be operative in other contexts as well and may have been so in the past, if people tell me they used to pray in the same way. I might look for it in the ways people celebrated saints' feasts or wondered about their landlords' harvests. Part of the anthropologist's task, then, is to discover these patterns, to find the assumptions (or dispositions, models, etc.) that underlie them, and to work out how these assumptions hang together—how they link up more or less coherently with other assumptions as people apply them in various activities and domains.

While this notion of culture as a socially shared, more or less integrated system of meanings has filtered out of anthropology and into common usage, anthropologists have become increasingly concerned with the analytic costs (and political dangers) of insufficiently nuanced interpretations of the concept. Some of our anthropological forebears and some nonanthropologists who have taken up the concept to think about identities and group conflicts have tended to exaggerate the degree to which the members of a culturally defined population uniformly share an integrated, internally consistent culture. One implication is an image of the world as composed of self-contained groups and societies, each one with "its" culture and with impermeable boundaries. In the Andes, Runa would all share a fully coherent Runa culture, mestizos (nonindigenous Spanish speakers) would all share mestizo culture, and the ethnic and racial distinction between them would prevent mestizo influences from affecting different Runa differently or introducing disparate, inconsistent strands into Runa culture. Such a model makes it difficult to imagine how cultural change can occur, and especially how it can occur without disrupting the presumed uniformity and integration of the culture. Thus, a further implication of exaggerating the shared and integrated nature of culture is either that culture does not change—Runa have simply maintained the same culture over the centuries, as tourist brochures sometimes suggest—or that cultural change is equivalent to the loss of a group's own culture, leading to either a state of cultural "disorganization" or replacement by someone else's culture.

Such assumptions overlook the fact that groups and societies have long influenced one another across permeable and historically constructed, shifting boundaries. Viewing culture as a fixed whole, they also miss a sense of people as *active* participants in cultural processes. People do not only "have" or "lose" culture; they engage with cultural symbols and scenarios, interpret them, make choices, rework and modify them in coming to terms with the world and pursuing their goals. As individuals negotiate the complexities of social life, the embodied dispositions and culturally shaped desires that come to the forefront in one domain may generate behavior that seems inconsistent with the ideas they express in another context. Furthermore, even in what cosmopolitan readers might view as a relatively homogeneous little village, differences in gender, age, social status, and individual biographies are associated with different patterns of socialization and different versions of a theoretically shared cultural repertoire. Class and ethnic divisions and conflicts within society as a whole imply tensions among different cultural strands and sometimes radically opposed interpretations of society.[3]

Hacienda Runa could sometimes honor the owner of a neighboring hacienda by asking him to sponsor a child's baptism and, at other times, speak of landlords in general as having sold their souls to the devil. It would be a mistake to expect to find "the indigenous view of landlords" or "the indigenous experience of the hacienda," in the sense of a single, all-encompassing, perfectly coherent view. The same is true of "the indigenous view of liberation theology."

Instead, what one can expect to find are multiple strands, a repertoire of possibilities, an ongoing dialogue among competing views with varying degrees of coherence and elaboration. This book presents an interpretation of that dialogue in an attempt to understand how Runa have responded to the possibilities open to them under the hacienda and since.

Reconstructing the past from oral accounts gathered decades later is a tricky matter, and even more so when one is attempting to reconstruct not only events but meanings, not only what people now say about the past but the way people thought about their lives in the past. Memories are not frozen representations of the past but change in a continual dialogue with the present. Tepeyac Bajo elders' anxieties about respect today, for example, shape the ways they talk about respect in the hacienda era. At one level, this book is all about the present: it reports how former hacienda residents remember the hacienda today. Some of my colleagues have gone further, to suggest that a study like this can *only* be about the present—that oral memory is too oriented to contemporary contexts to serve as genuine evidence about what the past was "really" like.

My response is that anthropologists with access to oral histories have a responsibility to the past, especially when those oral accounts concern institutions and transformations of major historical import, such as haciendas and their demise. Very few mid-twentieth century anthropologists were able to gain access and carry out fieldwork on functioning haciendas. The few full-length ethnographies of Andean haciendas on the eve of or during agrarian reform do provide some rich material on social structures, land and labor, and other matters (Crespi 1968; Mangin 1954; Skar 1981). Oriented by theoretical concerns and ethnographic conventions different from those that shape this study, however, they rarely offer direct quotations of hacienda residents' own words or a close sense of differently positioned residents' perspectives and subjective experience.

Along with these few contemporary ethnographies and retrospective oral accounts of the sort I gathered, written records are the other main source of information on haciendas. Unfortunately, peasants on haciendas could rarely write. Documents almost always reveal the perspectives and concerns of elites more directly than those of peasants or other groups that anthropologists have traditionally worked with.

I do cite archival documents extensively in some parts of this book. Yet, written records must be interpreted with as much caution as other sorts of evidence. This point was brought home to me forcefully when I read some pages of an old hacienda account book to the oldest living Monjas Corral resident, José María Pillajo, in 1995. Tayta José reacted angrily to the steward's claim that he had lent money and sold meat on credit at laborers' request. These were lies that bosses used to cheat the laborers, he said.

While hacienda residents mainly show up in judicial archives and estate records in their role as laborers, oral accounts allow us to place the landlord-laborer relationship in the broader context of residents' whole social and cultural world. To rule these accounts out categorically as evidence about the past would unnecessarily put a severe limitation on our understanding. Anthropologists who live with the subjects of oral accounts are in a position to assess how current circumstances shape those accounts and discern how the accounts still speak about the past. I do not mean to brush aside the difficulties of this endeavor but mean only to say that those difficulties are worth confronting.

One strategy I have used in interpreting oral accounts is to pay close attention to the nuances of language for clues as to how perspectives from different historical periods are embedded within an account. In interviewing informants, I took care to ask what they remembered their elders and other hacienda residents saying as well as asking about their own experiences. I use and compare multiple accounts from different informants who vary in their perspectives, gender, current religious outlook, age, and other features. I think of this as a kind of triangulation: we gain a better sense of a point distant in time by viewing it from different angles.

Finally, a holistic approach to the hacienda—that is, an approach that attempts to grasp hacienda society as a complex set of relationships, not just the landlord-laborer relationship, and that places that relationship within a broad cultural framework—yields a rich sense of context. Combined with an ethnographic examination of the present, that sense of context can help in assessing how oral accounts reflect both past and present. In this book I discuss posthacienda changes and the contemporary role of memories and analyze the hacienda, so readers themselves can make that assessment. All that said, even the ethnography of the present produces uncertain and partial knowledge at best, as postmodernists have stressed. One can only try.

AUTONOMY, RESISTANCE, AND HEGEMONY

In the course of this study, I engage successively and jointly with three overarching themes: autonomy, resistance (together with the related concept of reciprocity), and hegemony. These themes are ultimately intertwined, but each one emerges out of a distinct body of ethnographic and theoretical literature and offers a distinct angle on the hacienda and its aftermath.

Autonomy

From the late 1950s through the 1970s, scholarship on Latin American haciendas tended to emphasize peons' dependence and lack of autonomy vis-à-vis their landlord. Eric Wolf and Sidney Mintz set the tone in a classic article analyzing haciendas and plantations ([1957] 1977). Wolf and Mintz distinguished the two types primarily as a matter of their access to markets and capital: hacienda landlords used limited capital to supply small-scale markets, whereas plantations were more capital intensive and supplied large-scale (often European) markets. As a result of their limited capital and markets, haciendas could not pay sufficient wages to attract and retain laborers; instead, they relied on a series of "binding mechanisms." These included monopolizing landownership to deprive peasants of alternatives, granting laborers access to land and other resources they could use to subsist on, indebting them, developing relationships of mutual service, and reinforcing all these bonds through coercion. Workers became psychologically as well as economically dependent on the landlord, a symbolic "father" who disbursed "favors" to his "children" and "mediate[d] between them and the outside world." Only in passing did Wolf and Mintz acknowledge horizontal "relationships which spring up among the hacienda workers," giving these relationships no analytic attention, in sharp contrast to the consciousness of common condition, marital alliances, ritual kinship, and union organization they recognized among plantation workers ([1957] 1977:41–44, 57–58; see also Keith 1977).

In research on Andean haciendas, a geometric image crystallized a similar view: the "open triangle," or "triangle without a base" (see Figure 1). With the landlord at the top, the vertical legs of the triangle represent his relationship with individual peasants. The missing base of the triangle represents the absence of horizontal relationships among peasants, both within the estate and beyond its boundaries. Deprived of any autonomy, they competed with each other for the landlord's favor (see Thurner's review of this literature, 1993:43–44).

Some scholars writing in the 1960s and the 1970s were especially interested in the rise of peasant leagues and unions. They understood the base of the triangle to refer specifically to formal organizations that enhanced class solidarity and used the model to conceptualize "political mobilization" where such organizations had previously been absent, not to deny the existence of informal horizontal relationships (e.g., Tullis 1970; Whyte and Alberti 1976).[4]

Nonetheless, especially as combined with Wolf and Mintz's model, the image easily lent itself to a view of hacienda peasants' (premobilization) social life as emptied and flattened under the weight of landlord domination. If one imagines the landlord as holding all power and control over resources, nothing seems left that could have animated horizontal social relationships

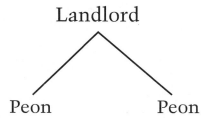

FIGURE 1. *The triangle without a base. Adapted from Tullis 1970:42.*

—let alone any autonomous vertical relationships among peasants. A more recent Freudian analysis of paternalism on Cuzco-area haciendas based on these models exemplifies this view (Anrup 1990). While stressing that peons referred to the landlord as *tayta,* or "father," the study makes no attempt to explore hacienda residents' family dynamics and their relationship to other *taytas* besides the landlord. *Tayta* is actually an everyday term of respect among Runa, but the author appears to assume that only their relationship with the landlord was psychologically significant.

Certainly, indigenous political history in areas of hacienda domination can be summarized as a loss of local political autonomy and authority and only very recent recovery. In much of highland Ecuador, the position of native chiefs became so compromised under Spanish rule and communal autonomy so vitiated that indigenous commoners fled to haciendas as a better alternative. It was extremely difficult for them, as hacienda peons, to organize themselves collectively and openly without the landlord's approval. Only in the twentieth century did former hacienda communities like Tepeyac Bajo gain legal and territorial autonomy, and with it the ability to pursue their collective interests routinely in direct negotiations with other organizations and the state.

Yet, when we look more closely at indigenous people's lives on haciendas, another dimension emerges. Galo Ramón has shown that, as people resettled on haciendas, they re-created a web of social ties and a zone of partial autonomy (1987). Wolf and Mintz viewed peasants' need for land as binding them to the landlord, but hacienda residents' rights to use farmland and pastures formed the material basis for an autonomous economic and social life. In some areas—though I would not say this of twentieth-century Pangor haciendas—landlords' control over land and labor was rather tenuous; thus, Juan Martínez Alier could characterize "the history of *haciendas*" as "the history of how landowners attempted to get something out of the Indians who were occupying *hacienda* lands" (1977:142; see also Webster 1981).

Large upland pastoral haciendas found it especially difficult to control their scattered and mobile labor force of herders (Maltby 1980), but as we shall see, farming as well as herding could sustain autonomous social networks.

Hacienda residents parlayed their access to hacienda resources into relationships of exchange and mutual aid with peasants in neighboring communities—sometimes to landlords' dismay, as when hacienda residents incorporated neighbors' animals into their own flocks on hacienda pastures (Guerrero 1991:279–285; Mallon 1983:77–78; Martínez Alier 1977). Residents' kinship ties and *compadrazgo* (ritual kinship) within and beyond the estate counterbalanced their subordination to the landlord (Crespi 1968:95–120, 205, 315–373; Guerrero 1991:162–170). As for hacienda peons' debt to the estate, another one of Wolf and Mintz's "binding mechanisms," Bauer (1979), Ramón Valarezo (1987), and Guerrero (1991) interpret it less as a sign of their bondage than of their ability to pressure landlords into disbursing money and goods. These reinterpretations add up to a picture of a much more vital, self-assertive, and autonomous social world among hacienda residents than that suggested by the classic images of debt peonage, binding mechanisms, paternalism, and a triangle without a base (see also Thurner 1993). Orlove and Custred, emphasizing the flexibility and range of links among households, put it this way: "[P]easants in the Andes create their world rather than passively and impotently inheriting a tragic past that offers them no choice but to continue it" (1980:54).

I already knew that Pangor Runa maintained wide-ranging networks of mutual aid and exchange before I ever went to Pangor. I had been a Peace Corps volunteer in the early 1980s in San Ramón,[5] a mestizo village on the other side of a mountain range from Pangor. Villagers there warmly recalled old practices of mutual visiting and exchange between the two regions and Pangoreños' occasional participation in the maize (corn) harvest. My research in Pangor confirmed the economic and cultural significance of these ties and others for Pangor hacienda residents. Hacienda Runa constructed a richly meaningful social world on and beyond their estates, based on both horizontal ties among peers and asymmetrical and vertical relationships structured by kinship, age, gender, and fiesta sponsorship. Within this social world, they sustained a critical understanding of the hacienda, exerted pressure from below on Runa overseers, and sometimes found support in conflicts with landlords and their agents.

At the same time, it would be a mistake to exaggerate the autonomy of Runa social and cultural life or to idealize it as a realm of pure solidarity, insulated from larger structures of oppression. Landlords and hacienda administrators regulated relations among neighbors, spouses, and different generations within the resident community. They also supported and made use of the fiesta system and the authority relations associated with it. The complexity of Runa social life thus provided openings for cultural influences across ethnic and class boundaries.

While scholarship oriented by concepts of paternalism and the open triangle tended to overlook everyday social ties among peasants and, thus, to underestimate the autonomy and vitality of their social world, it correctly recognized that the absence of formal organization weakened peasants' autonomy and ability to pursue their collective interests. Informal social networks helped sustain everyday, spontaneous resistance, but communal structures or class-based organizations could build local unity, link peasants to more encompassing levels of organization, facilitate flows of information about larger political contexts, and channel struggles over hacienda working conditions or land reform in qualitatively different ways. Monjas Corral residents seem to have kept their distance from outside organizations during the initial stages of agrarian reform—not because of any dependency on paternalistic overlords but because of understandable suspicions. Had they developed and used ties to such organizations to gain a better understanding of provincial and national political processes, they might well have come through the land reform period with title to a larger and better portion of the former estate than they ended up with.

In the course of agrarian reform, the people of Monjas Corral, like other former hacienda residents all over the highlands, did constitute themselves as a legally recognized community. Today, they meet in a weekly assembly to discuss matters of common interest and work together one or two days a week maintaining village paths, clearing irrigation ditches, and planting potatoes or trees on communal land. Along with thousands of similar highland communities, they participate in parish-level, provincial, and national federations. These organizations make up the strongest mass-based social movement in Ecuador and perhaps the strongest indigenous movement in Latin America.

Leaders of the national indigenous confederation CONAIE (Confederación de Nacionalidades Indígenas del Ecuador) called for indigenous people around the country to mobilize in June 1990 in support of a series of demands on the government concerning land, economic policy, indigenous cultural rights, and other issues. Pangor Runa gathered in village assemblies and intervillage meetings and talked about their long history of oppression and the president's refusal to meet with their national leaders. They responded by blocking the highway that runs through the parish, holding their products from town markets, and joining in a mass demonstration in the provincial

capital. Hundreds of thousands of other indigenous people staged similar actions in other highland regions, essentially shutting down the country for a
week. This first national indigenous *levantamiento*, or "uprising," marked
the emergence of the indigenous movement as a force that presidents ignore
at their peril.

This book does not delve into the development of this national movement
and its struggles since 1990 (see Almeida et al. 1992; Pallares 2002). Instead,
it offers a long-term historical context and some insights into the local-
level dramas that underpin the movement. Pangor Runa's bitter memories
of racial oppression and economic exploitation under the hacienda sharpen
their perspective on current inequalities and help fuel their commitment to
organized, collective struggle. Trying to make sense of their continued experience of poverty and racism after the demise of the hacienda, they sometimes say things like, "We are still oppressed [*llakichishka*]; only now instead
of the hacienda, they oppress us through inflation, low prices for our products, bad government, the whole economic system."

The particular struggles have changed, and so have the organizational
forms through which Pangor's indigenous people fight back. Still, contemporary villagers draw on some organizational forms and cultural practices
inherited from the hacienda, reworking and adapting these inherited forms
to negotiate intravillage tensions, strengthen communal authority, and reinforce ethnic solidarity. As members of an official community, they certainly maintain an expanded autonomy and more direct engagement with
the state and other institutions as compared with the hacienda period. Then,
people relied on informal social networks to confront the harsh conditions
of hacienda life. Now, they also look to formal organizations to defend their
interests in issues ranging from local utilities projects or cattle rustling to
national economic policies or proposals for a free-trade area of the Americas.

Resistance and Reciprocity

During my work as a Peace Corps volunteer in San Ramón, I was struck
by the continual flows of small gifts I saw among kin and neighbors and
the strong obligation that people seemed to feel to respond to others' material needs and desires. This strong sense of obligation sometimes clashed
with my own assumptions—rooted in my upbringing in a very individualistic, capitalist society—that people are obligated to fulfill only commitments
they have freely chosen. As a beginning graduate student in the mid-1980s,
I learned that this sort of gift giving and sense of obligation was a classic
theme in anthropology, usually treated under the concept of "reciprocity,"

since gifts tend to flow back and forth and imply mutual obligation (Mauss 1990; Sahlins 1972).

I also learned that reciprocity was a very prominent theme in Andeanist anthropology. In addition to looking at more or less symmetric exchanges among social equals, scholars had analyzed how the Inca state gave gifts to conquered peoples and their lords to draw them into unequal relationships. These relationships added up to a system of redistribution, meaning that "gifts" and services flowed into and out from a central point, in this case, the state (Murra 1962, 1978). Some Andeanists (e.g., Wachtel 1977:83) claimed that these gifts kept Inca subjects from experiencing the relationship as exploitative. Similarly, contemporary wealthy peasants used asymmetric reciprocity to legitimate the exploitation of poorer peasants, as hacienda landlords did to legitimate the exploitation of hacienda laborers (see, e.g., Orlove 1974).

This work on reciprocity and redistribution as legitimation struck me as overlooking something that loomed large in my own experience. I had heard over and over again from sharecroppers in San Ramón about exploitative sharecropping arrangements that they had to negotiate and maintain through the ostensible exchange of "favors" and "gifts." They described these arrangements as a denial and a perversion of reciprocity. The contrast between the everyday flow of gifts and favors among poorer peasants and what they viewed as the greediness, stinginess, and lack of human consideration on the part of wealthier villagers led them to develop a complex moral critique of the "rich" that associated their behavior, ultimately, with the devil. If public appearances of reciprocity among rich and poor "masked" domination (Orlove 1974:316), the poor that I knew did not seem in any way taken in by the disguise but only more embittered by it.

My teachers eventually directed me to the work of James Scott, a political scientist specializing in Southeast Asia. In fieldwork in a Malaysian village, Scott found a gap similar to what I observed in San Ramón between official representations and the critical discourses that subordinates develop in autonomous social spaces away from their overlords' gaze (1985). Reviewing accounts from around the world, he argues that such gaps were the normal condition of colonial, slaveholding, and peasant societies (1990). Scott also shows that peasants' attachment to a "moral economy" rooted in reciprocity and guaranteeing basic subsistence has often generated resistance to the claims of landlords and the state. Focusing at first on open rebellions (1976), he later turned his attention to everyday forms of covert, often anonymous, resistance (1985).

Scott defines resistance as "act(s) by member(s) of a subordinate class that is or are *intended* either to mitigate or deny claims . . . made on that class by superordinate classes . . . or to advance its own claims . . . vis-à-vis those superordinate classes." He argues that repression makes open, collective resistance rare, and the general absence of such collective resistance has misled scholars into viewing peasants as passively accepting their condition. Covert, individual acts of resistance are less risky, and their ubiquity is a better guide to peasant attitudes. Furthermore, unorganized, individual, but ubiquitous acts of resistance have sometimes had powerful historical consequences. For these reasons, Scott's definition of resistance includes "both individual and collective acts." He also makes clear that his definition encompasses "ideological resistance that challenge[s] the dominant definition of the situation and assert[s] different standards of justice and equity," such as criticism of elite individuals' moral character and behavior (1985:290; original emphasis). While Scott's definition and his work on resistance focus on class relations, he considers issues of dignity and respect as well as control over labor and surplus production to be central to those relations (1985:236–240; idem 1990:22–23).

Scott's first two books focus on peasant resistance to the erosion of a traditional "moral economy" as agriculture becomes commercialized and market-oriented landlords intensify their demands on peasants or ignore customary obligations of paternalistic care. Erick Langer has found cases of Andean haciendas that seem to fit this scheme. A wave of agrarian capitalism swept over Latin America beginning in the late nineteenth century, and peasants in Chuquisaca, Bolivia, staged strikes in response to entrepreneurial landlords' attempts to reduce their traditional prerogatives (Langer 1985, 1989). On the other hand, an overly mechanical application of Scott's (1976) model risks oversimplifying Andean history by dividing it neatly into "before" and "after" commercialization and idealizing an earlier period of supposed harmony among landlords and peasants. Andean peasants have, in fact, suffered a series of successive waves or cycles of state impositions since the Incas and of commercialization since the sixteenth century (Larson 1991).

I did find considerable resentment toward landlords and resistance on the part of Monjas Corral residents. Unfortunately, the limited evidence available concerning particular landlords' economic strategies and temporal fluctuations in resistance allows only a tentative assessment of whether residents were responding to an erosion of the moral economy associated with broader historical trends. The formal abolition of debt peonage in 1918—a liberal government measure to "modernize" labor relations and free up labor for the booming lowlands export economy—may have indirectly led Monjas Corral renters to treat laborers less "generously." In addition, several renters put laborers to work on capital improvements to the estate or increased agricultural production. At least one drafted laborers into service on another commercial enterprise off the estate. All of these measures may have exemplified general regional tendencies associated with closer ties to lowlands markets, and they could have intensified tensions over renters' labor demands.

On the other hand, notably lacking in the accounts I gathered in the 1990s was any memory of an earlier period when landlords (owners or renters) were more generous, any subjective sense of the erosion of an earlier moral economy. Former hacienda residents did have clear ideas about how decent landlords should have behaved and a well-developed critical discourse about how landlords generally violated those expectations. In part, as Scott (1976) suggests, their expectations arose from the insecurity of peasant agriculture and peasants' reliance on reciprocity and redistribution as social insurance. In part, as Scott also suggests, they were associated with universal human needs for respect and dignity (1985, 1990), and as Mauss (1990) suggests, with the common notion that labor services are a kind of gift. Landlords themselves found it a useful strategy occasionally to display their generosity, thereby reinforcing the expectations that they violated at other times (see Scott 1985:335–340).

Finally, Runa's moral expectations and their critique of landlords arose from the particular ways they developed and maintained a moral economy and a cosmology (an understanding of the universe) founded on reciprocity in their social, economic, and religious life. A principal objective of Part Two of this book is developing a rich understanding of this critique and its grounding in everyday life and cosmology.

In the wave of resistance studies Scott's work helped inspire, social scientists have applied the concept of resistance to many sorts of relations beyond class, including gender, race, and ethnic difference. Yet, relations structured by different axes often crosscut one another in complex ways that make resistance itself ambiguous and ambivalent. As Abu-Lughod notes, "resisting at one level may catch people up [in webs of power] at other levels" (1990:53). This leads us to the related question of hegemony, the third general theme that runs through this book.

Hegemony

Broadly, the question of hegemony concerns whether and how people come to participate in, accept, and support structures or systems of rule, inequality, and exploitation. The concept of hegemony was developed by the Italian Marxist Antonio Gramsci in the 1920s and the 1930s in his attempts to

understand the stability of capitalism in Western Europe and lay the theoretical bases for an effective revolutionary strategy (1971). Since the 1970s,
anthropologists and others have widely adapted the concept to analyze the
relationship between culture and power in many other contexts.

What Gramsci meant by "hegemony" is, at times, uncertain and variable (Anderson 1976–1977), and scholars differ in the ways they have interpreted and adapted the term. In one meaning, hegemony refers to the intellectual and moral leadership that a ruling group exercises over allied groups
or classes. These groups identify with and accept the prestige, values, and
outlook of the leading group, consenting to its leadership and joining it in a
ruling coalition, or "hegemonic bloc." Hegemony in this sense is contrasted
with the domination that rulers exercise over subordinate classes through
coercion (see, e.g., Kurtz 1996).

Scholars have also commonly used the term *hegemony* to refer to the role
of ideas, meanings, and culture throughout society, and especially among
subordinate classes, in perpetuating inequality. Used in this sense, the term
is often qualified as "ideological" or "cultural" hegemony and is close to
"false consciousness" and "mystification," which refer to ideas that blind
people to their real class interests. The concept of ideological hegemony suggests that ruling groups and the "traditional intellectuals" who serve them
promulgate ideas that lead subordinates to "consent" to the existing order
in some sense. Hacienda-era priests, for example, preached obedience to authority, and their sermons influenced Runa's worldview. Likewise, indigenous people seem to have internalized some racist associations between
European physical features and inherent superiority and beauty. Nonetheless, I argue that the concept of ideological hegemony, like false consciousness, focuses too narrowly on ideas alone and leads to an unhelpful analytic
separation between "what people believe and value" and "what society is
really like."

Thus, I follow others (Hall 1988; Mitchell 1990; Roseberry 1994) in understanding "hegemony" as a deeply material and social as well as a cultural
concept. In this sense, hegemony refers to practices, relationships, and
meanings that establish or maintain domination on a broader basis than
simple coercion while not precluding coercion. The great advantage of the
term thus is that it invites us to consider not simply ideas and meanings but
ideas in practice. It directs our attention to patterns of alliance and division
among social classes as well as the ideas and identities that shape and reflect
those patterns, and to material transactions together with the way people interpret those transactions as fair or unjust.[6]

Note that this definition does not imply the absence of any conflict. Indeed, Roseberry (1994) has written of hegemony as providing a "language of contention," a framework within which conflicts are understood and pursued. The definition does suggest that hegemony shapes conflicts in ways that ultimately stabilize inequality.

Here I come back to reciprocity, redistribution, and moral economy. For all the endemic conflict over levels of redistribution and labor demands, did hacienda landlords gain a measure of acquiescence on the part of residents through displays of "generosity"? Scott makes several points that are pertinent here: "[T]he euphemization of property relations . . . is *always* the focus of symbolic manipulation, struggle, and conflict. We must not view these patterns as *merely* a ploy, a mystification, as dust thrown in the eyes of subordinate classes" (1985:308–309; original emphasis). A "hegemonic ideology," he goes on, should not be seen as created and promulgated purely from the top down; "it is always the creation of prior struggle and compromises that are continually being tested and modified" (1985:336n). Moreover, these struggles and compromises have a material dimension, entailing real concessions on the part of the elite. "The struggle of subordinate classes, in other words, helps determine what kind of compromise will make consent possible" (1985:338n).

Scott develops these points in the course of an argument largely directed *against* the concept of hegemony, which he interprets in purely ideological terms. However, they are compatible with a broader concept of hegemony that encompasses social processes, conflicts, and material concessions. I do not claim that hacienda landlords secured a very strong hegemony at the level of relations of production and exchange; resentments were endemic and coercion ever-present. It appears to have been very difficult for landlords and laborers to reach a stable compromise both sides could live with. Having cautioned earlier against oversimplified constructions of "the indigenous experience of the hacienda," however, I do not want to limit the picture to resentments, resistance, and coercion. As Scott suggests, landlords faced with a recalcitrant labor force sometimes made material concessions. To the extent they did so, those concessions sometimes reduced friction and resistance. Some hacienda residents probably did occasionally experience landlords as generous and viewed some features of the hacienda system as beneficial, such as access to abundant land on Monjas Corral.

Along with redistribution and reciprocity, another, less often described, dimension of social relationships in the Andes is what I call the "respect complex." This is a set of understandings, practices, and relationships centered around moral regulation, elder-junior hierarchies, and notions of "respect." This term, borrowed from Spanish into Quichua as *respeto* (noun) and *respetana* (verb), pervades oral accounts of the hacienda era. Young couples gained respect by sponsoring fiestas under the guidance of Runa elders who were often hacienda overseers. Elders and hacienda authorities worked together to maintain moral order, resolve conflicts, and instill respect in their juniors through ritual discipline. In an Easter ritual of confession and purification, for example, overseers and elders gave their subordinates three lashes "in the name of the Father, the Son, and the Holy Ghost" and then blessed them. Force and religious meanings were intimately intertwined in local understandings of how ritual discipline reshaped subjectivities.

Most scholars writing on power and domination, whether within a Gramscian framework or otherwise, treat coercion and persuasion as opposite and interchangeable ways rulers can gain subordinates' compliance. This includes Scott, in his influential model distinguishing the "public transcripts" that subordinates perform under duress from their "hidden transcripts" of dissent and resistance; Scott argues that the coercion underlying the public performance precludes any true persuasion (1990). The respect complex forces a reconsideration of such oppositions. Rather than approaching persuasion and coercion as separate strategies, I find it more fruitful to explore their interrelation. This requires examining the politics of discipline associated with the labor regime together with discipline that regulated relationships among Runa themselves. This approach reveals *respeto* as simultaneously an aspect of hacienda hegemony, a strand in Runa culture and social relations, and a "language of contention" between hacienda bosses and variously positioned hacienda residents.

As the discussions in the village chapel my first week in Tepeyac Bajo indicated, *respeto* remains a language of contention, taken up and reworked in new struggles and projects. Indigenous Catholic activists and mestizo priests appeal to respect for elders to argue for ethnic and religious loyalty. Activists and ordinary villagers draw on memories of hacienda-era discipline in developing models of community authority and "indigenous law." Villagers of different generations and stances invoke respect in varying ways as they respond to the Bible and liberation theology. Out of this complex interaction between past and present, a distinctive local modernity is emerging.

These approaches to autonomy, resistance, and hegemony will help us see how indigenous people have actively engaged with landlords, priests, the state, and others in ways that have both reshaped and been shaped by indigenous culture, society, and identity. Indigenous people have not been passively dominated or unilaterally "awakened" by stronger outside forces. They have often found ways to press their own agendas and resisted the demands and projects of others at odds with those agendas. Yet, they have not only resisted external forces, and especially not as a monolithic group. Indigenous people have interacted with others in complexly differentiated ways influenced by age, gender, and social status within their communities. These differences have allowed for loyalties as well as resentments toward nonindigenous others, cooperation as well as resistance, and cultural flows across ethnic boundaries.

PLAN OF THE BOOK

Chapter 2 completes this introductory part of the book by describing Pangor and its history from pre-Inca times. To dispel images of timeless Indians, this chapter stresses the ways indigenous people have participated in regional history and been shaped by it. I consider how hacienda formation, migration, and ethnic transformation in Pangor may have influenced local historical consciousness. Finally, the chapter assesses how church ownership of Monjas Corral, renters' strategies, and regional and national political and economic history affected life on the estate.

Parts Two and Three focus on the hacienda era. The three chapters in Part Two, "Society and Resistance," emphasize the autonomy of hacienda residents' social life, their critical perspective toward landlords, and their resistance. Chapter 3 uses the image of a triangle *with* a base as a first approximation to survey hacienda social relations, both vertical and horizontal. Chapter 4 focuses on the ritual expression of reciprocity in religious fiestas and agricultural rites, showing how these practices generated both an implicit theology of agricultural production and a hierarchy of authority and respect. Chapter 5 examines how Runa applied expectations of reciprocity in judging and responding to landlords' behavior.

Part Three explores respect and authority, ritual discipline, and the contested meanings of violence on the hacienda. Chapter 6 presents two life histories as an entrée into individual attitudes and strategic postures toward hacienda authority. Chapter 7 analyzes the respect complex, critiques Scott's (1990) model of domination and hidden transcripts, and develops an alternative approach to hegemony.

Finally, Part Four, "The Legacy of the Hacienda," brings the story up to the beginning of the twenty-first century with an emphasis on how the hacienda past continues to inform the present. Chapter 8 explores the ambivalent relationship between villagers and the Catholic Church during the agrarian reform, questioning the common narrative according to which indigenous peasants were passive until liberation theology opened their eyes. This chapter also describes transformations in local political organization and religious life in the aftermath of land reform. Finally, in Chapter 9, I show how villagers' relationship with the past and with the Catholic Church influences contemporary local religion, community politics, and ethnic revitalization.

TRANSLATIONS, NAMES, AND CITATION CONVENTIONS

In general, I try to give fairly close, conservative translations, and I indicate even small omissions with ellipses. The translations are somewhat freer and looser—though maybe more faithful to the spirit of the original in some ways—in the life histories in Chapter 6. I provide Quichua or Spanish words in parentheses or brackets when the original wording is ambiguous, difficult to translate, or of special interest for Andeanists. Some fuller citations, Quichua texts of many citations, and discussions of specific translation issues may be found in Lyons (1994b).

Representing speech on paper is a challenge. Rhythm, tone, and patterns of repetitive elaboration, even pauses and "ums" and "ahs," carry a good deal of meaning in a face-to-face context, but these are either difficult to convey on paper or tiresome to the reader. Talk is often more like poetry than like prose—the distinction itself is an artifact of Western literary tradition—and at times I follow Tedlock's suggestion of using poetry-style broken lines and other devices (1983:3–61). I also indicate pauses by repeated commas—two (,,) for brief pauses, three (,,,) for somewhat longer pauses. I reserve the ellipsis (. . .) for places where I have cut words.

Spanish and Quichua diminutives pervade rural highland Ecuadorian speech. The Spanish diminutive, frequently used in Quichua as well, is the suffix -ito or -ita. The Quichua diminutive is wawa, which as a noun means "baby" or "child." In some cases, I retain the original words in diminutive; in others, I use "little" (e.g., taytito as "little father"). The use of "little" may sometimes strike the reader as odd; it should be understood as expressing a sort of affectionate regard or deference. Where four or five diminutives occur in rapid succession, I do not feel compelled to translate every one; the repeated diminutive would call undue attention to something that is locally unremarkable.

To make the etymology clear, I generally retain the Spanish spelling of loan words used in Quichua. This does not mean that these words are not "really" Quichua. Some of them have evidently been in the language for centuries, as attested by the retention of an /h/ in some loan words whose h has become silent in modern Spanish. At least from the speaker's point of view, such words are just as much a part of the mother tongue as any words from the native pre-Inca Puruhá language that entered local Quichua centuries ago and whose origin is long forgotten.

Yet, this is not necessarily the case for *every* Spanish word incorporated into Quichua conversation. Unlike Puruhá, Spanish is a living language and a part of Quichua speakers' social environment, and Quichua speakers do sometimes switch back and forth between Quichua and Spanish. Many Latin Americanists write every Spanish word incorporated into the speech of indigenous language speakers according to the orthographic conventions of the indigenous language, implying that the word is being used as a word in the indigenous language, not Spanish. This practice may be more faithful to speakers' pronunciation, but it seems to me to suggest a more closed linguistic environment than may be the case. Here, it would imply that every Spanish-origin word is thoroughly "Quichuacized," that Quichua speakers think of it as only a Quichua word with no connection to Spanish. In other words, this convention seems to erect an artificial boundary, sealing off the two languages from each other despite the loans, in a way that misrepresents the ethnographic reality. A Quichua speaker using a Spanish-origin word may be simultaneously speaking Quichua and Spanish, in the sense that the word's meanings for speaker and addressee are shaped by prior experiences of its use in both Quichua and Spanish conversations. Since cultural influences across ethnic boundaries are part of my argument, I choose to write Spanish-origin words in a way that does not obscure their origin.

Otherwise, my orthographic conventions for Quichua are a compromise between a faithful representation of local Pangor or Chimborazo forms and accessibility to the reader. I adopt the *k* and *w* from the current standardized Quichua alphabet, except for words with a long history of being spelled in other ways in Spanish-language documents and scholarship, such as *huasi-cama* (not *wasikama*).

The phonetic reading of letters used is generally similar to standard Latin American Spanish, with the following modifications:

g—Always hard, as in English 'get'. E.g., *kangi*.

h—At the beginning of some Spanish loan words where it is now silent such as *hacienda*, *habas*, and *horno*, pronounced in Quichua like an English *h*.

k—When followed by a vowel, same as in English. At the end of words or before another consonant, somewhere between a velar Spanish *j* sound and an English *k*; occasionally voiced. E.g., *ñukanchik*, *shamukpi*, *chairik*.

kh—An often strongly aspirated *k* sound, in *khipu* 'overseer'.

ll—As in Ecuadorian highland Spanish, pronounced like the *s* in the English *leisure*.

r—As in Ecuadorian rural highland Spanish, intermediate between a trill and the highland *ll*.

s—Like the Spanish or English unvoiced *s*, with the exception of some loan words, where it is voiced in Quichua as /z/ (e.g., *casi, casarana* [<*casarse*], *casuna* [<*hacer caso*]).

sh—As in English.

ts—As in English *tsetse*.

w—As in English; the diphthong *aw* is pronounced like *ow* in the English *cow*.

z—As in English.

Stress in Quichua falls on the penultimate syllable of the word, unless otherwise indicated by an accent mark.

For readers who do not speak Spanish, the pronunciation of the most important place names used here is roughly as follows:

Monjas Corral: **Moan**-hahss Core-**all**
Tepeyac Bajo: Teh-pay-**yoc Bah**-ho
Pangor: Pahn-**gore**
Chimborazo: Chim-bore-**ahss**-so

Unless otherwise specified, informants named in this book should be assumed to be former Monjas Corral residents. Following my informants' wishes, I generally use the true names of individuals and communities. The exceptions are Andrés Castillo, Armando Guerrero, José Krueger, María Lema, Ignacio Lara, Lorena López, and Agustín Paca.

One final note on my citation conventions. I cite archival documents with an asterisk and an abbreviated title and date, for example, "*Gallegos-Barba 1873," and list these documents in a separate section of the Bibliography under these abbreviated titles.

CHAPTER 2

A History of Pangor and Monjas Corral

IMAGINING INDIANS

When I was a Peace Corps volunteer in a village in central Ecuador in the early 1980s, I sometimes gazed over the rolling corn and wheat fields and up toward the high mountains a few miles to the east. The village was in the Chimbo River valley, with mountain chains on either side. Rising above the fields were folds of velvety green where the mountains were forested, and then yellow-brown slopes of grass and craggy rock peaks. In late afternoon, as the sun descended behind me, it accented the contours of the slopes and peaks with a warm reddish light and deep shadows. With the same wanderlust that brought me from a suburban U.S. upbringing to Ecuador in the first place, I would wonder what was on the other side of those beautiful mountains.

Older villagers told me that they used to load up their horses and travel over the mountains. It was a steep hike, and on a traveler's first trip, the mountains would grow angry at the unfamiliar trespasser, they said. Strong winds would blow, or a thick fog might descend. But the people on the other side, in Pangor, would receive travelers warmly and give them potatoes to take home in exchange for their corn or wheat.

The mountains marked a linguistic and ethnic boundary as well as a boundary between corn and wheat country and potato country. The people in "my" village spoke Spanish and thought of themselves as "white" or mestizo. The people they used to trade with in Pangor were *indígenas*, "indigenous people" or "Indians." The indigenous language, Quichua, was the Ecuadorian version of the Inca language. When I came back to Ecuador as an anthropologist, I decided I wanted to carry out my research in Pangor.

I had entered the Peace Corps to get to know a culture different from my own, and I had certainly done so in the Chimbo valley. Yet, I still envied my Peace Corps friends who had had the chance to learn Quichua in indigenous villages in Chimborazo province, on the Pangor side of those mountains. A fascination with cultural differences later drew me to anthropology.

As an anthropologist, I learned that this fascination can be a source of pitfalls as well as insights. It is all too easy to romanticize cultural differences, to project our own yearnings or fears onto "exotic" others. We imagine that their world is simpler or purer, a place set apart, where time stands still. In both the United States and the Andes, common discourses and images have cast Indians as figures from a mythical past. These images deny Indians a history in the sense of changes that they have helped shape.

My first real encounter with Ecuadorian indigenous people came when I wandered out of a Peace Corps training center in Chimborazo province one Sunday in 1981. Walking along the cobblestone road, I came to a dirt road that branched off and decided to see where it would lead me. A scrap of embroidered cloth on the ground caught my eye, and then I found a broken silver earring of the sort indigenous women wear. I fantasized about the possible archaeological significance of these items. I somehow felt as though the ground and the air around me were saturated with the past and I was walking back in time. Eventually, I found myself in a quiet village plaza, a packed-earth yard with a little church on one side, a well, and a small store. Twenty minutes later, villagers carrying hoes on their shoulders filed into the plaza, returning from a communal work party in which, they told me, they had been cleaning irrigation ditches.

Soon, I was surrounded by a crowd of people curious to learn about me and my language. Young men asked me in Spanish how to say "I love you" in English, and as the young women behind them laughed, they reciprocated by teaching me the words in Quichua. The village president thanked me effusively for visiting the village, took me into the store, and gave me a drink.[1] It was a "*National Geographic*" experience.

But my perceptions were shaken when I noticed that one woman, under her indigenous-style shawl, was wearing a tee shirt depicting John Travolta, who had recently made a hit in the United States with the movie *Saturday Night Fever*. The tee shirt momentarily broke the spell of the exotic, allowing me to see that these people were my contemporaries, no matter how far from my home and how differently from me they lived. This chapter is meant to have an effect similar to that John Travolta tee shirt—to dispel some of the distorted assumptions associated with exoticism and with common perceptions of Indians. I hope to do this by sketching how indigenous people have

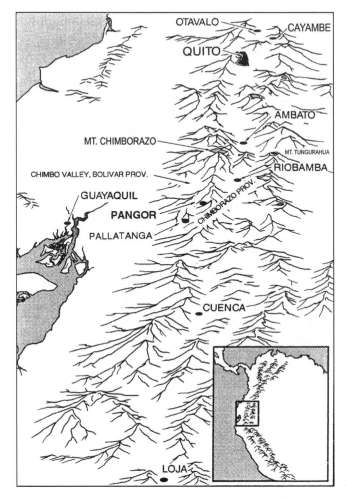

FIGURE 2. *Northwestern South America. Adapted from Weismantel (1988:42).*
Used with permission.

participated in history and how powerful historical forces have reshaped
their lives. An imagined trip to Pangor will introduce the geographical setting for this history and highlight some of the features that easily play into
North American or European imaginings of the exotic. A foreign traveler's
visit to Ecuador might start in Quito, the capital. Quito is located in the
northern Ecuadorian Andes on a broad plain between two mountain chains
(see Figure 2). These parallel chains, or cordilleras, run from north of Quito to
southern Ecuador. Between the two great mountain chains are smaller hills,

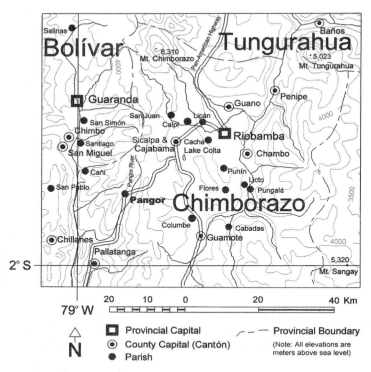

FIGURE 3. *The Chimbo and Riobamba basins*

mountains, and valleys. Knots of high mountains join the two chains, dividing the whole region into a series of basins. Likewise, smaller chains split off from or run alongside the main north-south chains in some places, marking off other basins such as the Chimbo River valley.

From Quito, it is a three-and-a-half-hour bus trip on the Pan-American Highway south to Riobamba, the capital of Chimborazo province (see Figure 3). Tourists are commonly drawn here (as I was) by Chimborazo's status as one of the most heavily indigenous provinces of Ecuador. Riobamba, like most highland towns, is predominantly mestizo, but around it and to the south is a central basin densely populated with mainly Quichua-speaking people.

Another half hour past Riobamba are the twin towns of Cajabamba and Sicalpa, where Riobamba was located in the colonial period. (Riobamba was rebuilt at its present site after an earthquake destroyed the town in 1797; Burgos Guevara 1997:344.) Cajabamba and Sicalpa are small, quiet towns today, but they come alive once a week on market day, when indigenous people from surrounding villages come in to buy and sell animals and grains and to purchase products brought by traders from other places. The two towns together form the administrative center of the *cantón*, or county, of Colta, which encompasses Pangor.

Just past Cajabamba, at marshy Lake Colta, a branch of the highway veers off to the west and winds its way up the western cordillera (Figure 4). There is a breathtaking view of Lake Colta, plains and hills around it covered with a patchwork of fields and grasslands, and of high mountain chains and snow-capped peaks surrounding the basin. A bus might take twenty or thirty minutes to climb from the valley floor, at about thirty-three hundred meters above sea level, to the pass at about forty-two hundred meters. Along the road, barley gives way to potatoes and then to tufts of grass. Eventually, the slope becomes nearly level. As the road winds through the pass, the view of the central basin is lost, and then one emerges at the top of the outer slopes, overlooking a narrow valley. The Pangor River, at first little more than a stream, flows down the center of the valley. The road follows the valley down to the south and gently westward, and the changes in scenery are reversed. At the top are mostly empty grasslands. A few minutes later, a few cows or horses appear, perhaps a herd of sheep.

FIGURE 4. *Church of Balbanera, by Lake Colta, built by Spaniards in 1534*

FIGURE 5.   *View up the Pangor valley toward Monjas Corral from Ajospamba, with town of Pangor (lower left), Pan-American Highway*

In another five minutes, the bus passes a cluster of houses nestled at the foot of high mountains. Cultivated fields also appear, at first almost lost in the expanses of grass, but by about thirty-four hundred meters largely replacing the grass. The crops that are adapted to this altitude and the cold nights that go with it include potatoes, other Andean tubers, and fava beans. The ecological zone at about three thousand to thirty-two hundred meters and higher, where bunchy grass is the natural vegetation, is known as the *páramo*.

As one continues down, barley complements the potato fields. The bus passes by a cluster of houses around a church, just down the hill from the road to the left: the town of Pangor (Figure 5). A bit later and lower, maize and wheat begin to predominate.

About eighty minutes down from the pass, one reaches the town of Pallatanga, center of a subtropical region at twelve hundred to fifteen hundred meters. Pallatanga's climate is suitable for temperate-climate crops like beans, maize, and peas as well as tropical fruits and sugarcane; in Inca and early colonial times, cotton was also grown. The terrain is flatter from Pallatanga on down; soon the bus will leave the Andean foothills altogether and speed across the flat Guayas basin, passing by banana groves, sugarcane fields, and rice fields. This study focuses on the high end of the Pangor basin, an area of steep slopes covered by *páramo* grass and potato fields. To the south-southwest is the gradual descent down the valley to Pallatanga. To the northeast is the pass leading to the central basin. The valley itself runs through the western cordillera, and high mountains overlook it on each side, west and east. Beyond those mountains to the west and northwest is the Chimbo River valley of Bolívar province, the maize region where I was a Peace Corps volunteer.

Tourists looking out the windows of a bus at the thatched-roof huts in the upper Pangor basin might easily imagine themselves to be in a place where time has stood still for centuries. If the bus stops to pick up local people, the tourists may hear them speaking the Inca language. Local women's dress— dark wraparound skirts and shawls held in place with a large pin—does show continuities with Inca-period dress (Figure 6). A man walking behind a cow along the road or a child herding a flock of sheep may remind the tourist that some things did change in the sixteenth century, when Spanish invaders and settlers brought those animals to the Americas. But anyone who identifies innovation with computers, industry, and mechanized agriculture will be tempted to view the scene as one of an essentially static society. Tourists who notice the newer houses made of cement block with corrugated metal roofs, the signs telling teachers and government officials where to turn off from the highway to get to village schoolhouses, and the electricity lines put up in the 1990s might suppose that only recently have the winds of modernity begun to change this society.

Tourists have not been the only ones prone to view rural, Indian society as static. Many scholars, Ecuadorian intellectuals, and other city dwellers have also done so, especially before the upsurge in the 1990s of indigenous political activism shook up such perceptions. Some thought that the Conquest was a kind of knockout blow that left Indians prostrate, unable to defend themselves or to be more than a dead weight on Ecuadorian society over the next four and a half centuries (see Salomon's critique, 1988:95). In another version, Indian prostration resulted from the combination of bondage on haciendas and a degrading religion, Catholicism in name but superstition and drunkenness in substance. Leonidas Proaño, bishop of Riobamba, saw an image of Indians' role in history in the story of the Good Samaritan: they were the man beaten and left for dead at the side of the road. He described church-sponsored radio and literacy programs in the 1960s as having helped Indians finally "awaken from their centuries-long slumber" (1989:87).

Still another form of denying indigenous participation in history, almost the opposite view of this image of Indians as immobilized by their bondage,

FIGURE 6.   *Woman spinning wool in Tepeyac Bajo, 1991*

focuses on high, mountainous areas like the upper Pangor basin. The slow, winding climb to Pangor from the more densely populated central basin; the expanses of almost empty *páramo;* the steep mountain slopes; the thick, damp fog that often blankets the slopes in the rainy season; and the strong winds in the dry season all combine to give the impression of an isolated, inhospitable, wild place. Indigenous folklore itself associates the high mountains with wildness. It is easy to imagine that "pure," unconquered Indians and Indian culture might have taken refuge in such a place (see Aguirre Beltrán 1967; Poole 1994; Silverblatt 1987).

Since the 1980s, scholars working at the intersection of anthropology and history have shown how misguided it is to view any society, and certainly

Andean society, as unchanging. It is not that "traditional" peoples have just begun to awaken and enter the arenas where history is made. Rather, people in places like Pangor have always participated in making their history. Scholars have also shown that such places have long been connected to broader regional and even intercontinental economic and political systems (Salomon 1988; Wolf 1982). These scholars' work makes it possible to sketch a history of the Pangor area set in a regional context.

Pangor did sometimes serve as a refuge for people fleeing mistreatment and land scarcity in the central basin, but it was not isolated from the effects of colonialism and the hacienda system. Those effects were mediated by indigenous agency, indigenous people's responses. In Pangor as elsewhere, indigenous resistance to burdensome colonial tribute exactions contributed to the development of the hacienda system. Autonomous indigenous villages resisted, sometimes successfully, the loss of land to haciendas. Indigenous people settling on haciendas actively negotiated the terms of their subordination, and hacienda residents sometimes fled or protested abusive treatment.

At the same time, the story I shall tell is more complex than a romantic tale of indigenous people resisting oppression and defending their cultural identity. Andean society was stratified before the arrival of the Spaniards, and indigenous nobles sometimes collaborated with Spanish colonialism. Indigenous people incorporated Catholicism into their world view and social relations. Andean and European colonial notions and practices of authority interacted to form a complex hybrid.

Marx famously remarked that people make their own history, but not under conditions of their own choosing. Along with indigenous agency, we shall also consider how the state, colonial elites, landlords, and economic and geographic factors all shaped the development of the hacienda system and the experience of Monjas Corral's residents.

Marx's aphorism can be interpreted to refer to "history" in another sense, too, as people's subjective knowledge of how the past led to the present. People form their own understandings of history and their place in history, but not under conditions they fully control. Thus, another aim of this chapter is to indicate how local patterns and processes of land use, migration, and ethnic transformation shaped Pangor hacienda residents' historical consciousness, especially their sense of how they and their ancestors came to be hacienda residents.

Despite the important changes in indigenous cultures and identities over the last five hundred years, I retain the term "indigenous people" as a general category and a gloss on the Spanish term *indígenas,* used by

Quichua-speaking people when they are speaking in Spanish. While the term foregrounds the continuities between indigenous people today and their pre-Columbian ancestors, it should be clear that contemporary indigenous culture and identity are not wholly "indigenous" in the literal sense, that is, autochthonous or identical to pre-Columbian cultures and identities. As an ethnic-racial label, the word *indígena* (indigenous) takes its meaning from a conceptual opposition to other terms such as "white," "Spanish," or mestizo (mixed). In that sense, there were no indigenous people before the Spanish invasion, but only Puruhaes, Chimbos, and other peoples. By the same token, these peoples would never have become "Indians" but for Columbus's geographical confusion of the Americas with India. Because the Spanish cognate *indios* has taken on pejorative connotations, I reserve the term "Indian" for contexts in which I am focusing on *perceptions* of "Indians" and for translating *indio.*

PANGOR AND THE NORTHERN ANDES BEFORE THE SPANISH INVASION

Before the northward expansion of the Inca state encompassed what is now Ecuador in the late fifteenth century, northern Andean peoples were organized into small-scale, local chiefdoms—nonstate societies with hereditary leadership. Despite their small scale, these chiefdoms were strongly stratified societies. Chiefs had a good deal of power to settle disputes, enforce moral norms, and punish wrongdoers. They had multiple wives and servants, and they could call on the agricultural labor of the whole community. Chiefs had special claims over high *páramo* lands: a portion of the game hunted in the *páramo* was given to them in tribute, and some employed specialist hunters (Ramón Valarezo 1987:52; Salomon 1986a:83, 125–131, 138–139).

Chiefs' authority was partly based on redistribution. Their control over labor and long-distance trade gave them a surplus that they "generously" redistributed among their subjects. When a chief's subjects came to work in his maize fields, he provided food and drink to make it a festive occasion. Pre-colonial chiefs did not control land as private property; land was not a commodity that they could buy and sell at the expense of their people's right to farm it (Salomon 1986a:125–131, 138–139).

The people of neighboring chiefdoms seem to have shared a sense of common ethnic identity within the major basins that roughly constitute today's provinces. The Puruhá people lived in the area of the modern province of Chimborazo and the Chimbo people in Bolívar province. Pallatanga seems to have been part of the Chimbo ethnic area—it was included in Chimbo-area jurisdictions in the early colonial period (Cabildo de Quito [1577] 1991:252; Espinoza Soriano 1988:149–151)—and a 1581 report by Miguel de Cantos, the *corregidor*, or governor, of Chimbo, lists Pangor as an appendage of Palla-tanga. Six "*ayllos*," or localized descent groups of 150 to 300 people, each with its own chief, made up the population based in the Pallatanga district. Some of these groups and their chiefs' authority evidently extended up the Pangor valley; Cantos refers to "the Indians . . . in Pangor, subject to Palla-tanga" ([1581] 1991:303–308). He also mentions a group of Puruhaes in the upper-middle Pangor basin ([1581] 1991:308).[2] Thus both peoples may have had a presence in precolonial Pangor and Pallatanga. The cooperative re-lationships through which twentieth-century villagers in the Chimbo val-ley and Pangor exchanged corn and potatoes probably had precolonial roots. Puruhá households and chiefdoms in the central basin, for example, may have obtained cotton, coca, and fruits from Chimbo partners in the warmer areas of lower Pangor and Pallatanga (see Salomon 1986a).

The upper Pangor basin itself, however, was probably only sparsely popu-lated and cultivated in pre-Inca times. The fertility of high *páramo* land is hard to maintain year after year, while the tough *páramo* grass makes clearing new land a very difficult task. No large domestic animal whose manure might maintain fertility existed in the northern Andes before the Incas introduced llamas. Chiefs and others based at lower altitudes might have used the *páramo* for hunting deer and rabbit (Salomon 1986a:38, 73–74, cf. 194; Ramón Valarezo 1987:51–57). Settlement in the Pangor basin was probably concentrated at middle and lower levels.[3]

The Incas conquered the Puruhá and Chimbo areas in the last decades of the fifteenth century. The Inca state aggregated local chiefdoms into larger units, creating additional levels of chiefly hierarchy. The paramount leader was responsible for supplying laborers to the state for a set period; after one group of laborers completed its turn, another took its place. Each of the com-ponent units similarly rendered tribute in the form of rotating service to the paramount chief (Salomon 1986a:193–195; idem 1986b:92, 109; Espinoza Soriano 1988:170–171).

The Incas also resettled people according to the central Andean "archi-pelago" model, so that each ethnic group had direct access to different zones rather than trading with other groups. Thus Puruhaes from Xunxi who pre-viously might have traded with Chimbo households for fruit were now sent to the central Chimbo valley and Pallatanga to cultivate it themselves. Puru-haes from Guayllabamba were settled in an enclave in Pallatanga to produce cotton. A group of people from Pangor, conversely, appears to have been resettled in Punín, in the center of the Puruhá country (Espinoza Soriano

1988:175; Haro Alvear 1977:36; Moreno Yánez 1981:109; Paz Maldonado [1582] 1991:321; Salomon 1986a:192–201).

Resettlement also occurred on a larger geographic scale: the Incas brought people from what is now Peru and Bolivia to Ecuador, and vice versa. Both the Chimbo and the Puruhá areas received substantial contingents of settlers from the south (Espinoza Soriano 1988:170–176; Moreno 1981). A group of Chachapoya people from northeastern Peru apparently came to Pallatanga (Cantos [1581] 1991:304; Salomon 1986a:158–160, 194). Thus, ethnic Chimbo natives now shared Pallatanga with resettled Puruhaes and others.

The Inca state, like the aboriginal chiefs, primarily demanded labor and services rather than products. The state was responsible for providing the raw materials and supplying the basic needs of the laborers in its service. These principles helped ensure local subsistence even though the state expropriated a surplus. The state, like an Andean chief, also redistributed a portion of the wealth it captured back to its subjects, in the form of gifts of fine cloth and products from distant regions. Despite the profound changes the Inca state introduced, redistribution remained the basis of authority (Murra 1962, 1978; Wachtel 1977:62–73, 80–81).

What the Spanish invaders encountered in 1532 was thus anything but a homogeneous society of simple "Indians." The Inca empire was a complex, highly stratified society—like Spain itself in that respect—but one that operated on different principles. Divisions within Andean society played an important role in the origins of Spanish colonialism. The Inca state was still consolidating its rule in the northern Andes, and it was weakened by a dynastic civil war just then coming to an end. The Spaniards found allies among chiefs who had been on the losing side or were resentful of the Inca presence altogether. The alliances and divisions of the invasion period continued to be active forces in local politics for some decades into the colonial period. The relationship between chiefs and their subjects also played an important role in colonial politics and eventually in the development of the hacienda system.

SPANISH COLONIALISM AND THE DEVELOPMENT OF HACIENDAS
Indigenous Chiefdoms under Colonial Rule

Much of colonial history and the development of the hacienda can be understood in terms of the interests and struggles of four different sorts of actors: the Spanish Crown; the local colonial elite; indigenous chiefs; and indigenous commoners. The Spanish Crown depended on the local colonial elite—

Spanish settlers and their descendants—to staff the colonial administration, indoctrinate the natives, suppress any uprisings, send tribute to Spain, and develop enterprises such as textile workshops that contributed to the colonial economy and, ultimately, to the royal coffers. At the same time, the Crown competed with the local elite for control over indigenous labor and the wealth it could produce. The Crown had a long-term interest in preserving indigenous communities with land so that they could produce tribute and counterbalance the local Spanish elite. As long as indigenous communities remained intact and politically autonomous, the colonial elite depended on the state for access to indigenous labor, thus inhibiting any tendencies toward independence from Spain. On the other hand, the Crown was not averse to selling land to Spanish settlers when it was severely short of cash and it judged that indigenous communities did not need the land.

Spaniards who had come to live temporarily or permanently in the Andes and their descendants had several sources of livelihood and wealth. Those with positions in the colonial administration could enrich themselves by taking a portion of the indigenous tribute they collected, exploiting indigenous subjects' labor, or using their power in other ways to extort wealth from their subjects. Many Spaniards in the Audiencia of Quito (roughly modern Ecuador) set up textile workshops (*obrajes*) that supplied clothing for the mining centers in the south-central Andes. Colonial settlers also developed sheep and cattle ranches and agricultural estates, often linked to *obrajes*. Control over land was not initially the main source of wealth for settlers, but land became a valuable commodity and a way to control indigenous peasant labor.

Indigenous chiefs, for their part, were already middlemen between their people and the state in the Inca period. Spanish colonialism presented them with a new set of pressures and opportunities. Some initially welcomed the opportunity to free themselves from the Incas and recover lost resources. By the last decades of the sixteenth century, however, the alliances between Spaniards and local chiefdoms were strained. A growing Spanish population and a reorganized colonial administration exacted heavy tribute in labor, goods, and, eventually, money; forced the resettlement of dispersed populations in towns to facilitate control; and began to expropriate indigenous lands. The chiefs themselves, termed "caciques" in the colonial period, were placed in a deeply contradictory position.

On the one hand, caciques were hereditary lords with an internal legitimacy based on kinship and redistribution. Recurrent Spanish complaints against the chiefs' participation in drinking fests with their people suggest that they continued to play an active role in rituals of reciprocity and redistribution. Some caciques organized commercial operations such as community textile workshops in order to satisfy Spanish tribute demands in a relatively painless way. They often acted to defend their people's interests against colonial abuses and sued Spaniards who tried to usurp communal lands. On the other hand, the colonists relied on the local native rulers as intermediaries with the subject population. Chiefs were responsible for collecting tribute from their subjects and supplying laborers to the colonists, and colonial tribute and labor demands became increasingly burdensome as compared with the Inca period. A cacique who failed to supply his people's quota of tribute and labor could be punished harshly.

Some chiefs also took advantage of the new opportunities for amassing wealth that the colonial economy offered by privatizing community lands, developing their own agricultural or livestock enterprises, or selling off land to Spaniards. Spaniards sometimes manipulated the selection of chiefs to ensure the chiefs' cooperation. Chiefs themselves sometimes adopted Spanish dress and other Spanish symbols of status, and marital alliances were common between chiefly families and Spaniards or mestizos. Such alliances were an important avenue for the transfer of land to mestizo hands. In some areas of the Andes, the caciques were eventually incorporated into the local Spanish-mestizo elite. While some chiefs participated in indigenous uprisings, in other cases, rebels attacked native chiefs along with Spanish officials and landowners, and chiefs sometimes helped suppress uprisings (Borchart de Moreno 1980; Larson and Harris 1995; Martínez F. 1990; Moreno Yánez 1985:394–396; Moreno Yánez 1989:116ff; Ramón Valarezo 1987:233f; Rasnake 1988:107–148; Spalding 1973:596; Spalding 1974:80–82, 172–176; Spalding 1984; Stern 1982:38, 134; Stern 1983; Wachtel 1977:129–131).

Indigenous commoners were individually the least empowered of these four sorts of actors and subject to exploitation by each of the others. They nonetheless found room to maneuver between the conflicting interests of the other three. Commoners sometimes joined with their caciques in defending community lands, re-creating Andean cultural practices, seeking ways to meet or reduce tribute burdens, and resisting the encroachments and abuses of Spanish settlers and colonial officials. At other times, they appealed to the Crown for protection against abusive caciques and local Spaniards. In still other cases, and crucially for the development of the hacienda, they found that local Spaniards could help them hide from their caciques and from Spanish colonial officials, thereby allowing them to evade or reduce their tribute. Finally, none of these groups were monolithic, and indigenous commoners could also take advantage, for example, of the competition for labor among Spanish landowners. We shall see examples of each of these strategies in the history of the Pangor area.

Early colonial policies accommodated the interests of the Crown and Spanish settlers through two institutions, the encomienda and the mita. The encomienda consisted of a group of indigenous people placed under the authority of a Spaniard, the *encomendero*. The *encomendero* received tribute from the caciques, retained a portion, and passed the rest up the administrative hierarchy on its way to Spain. The *encomendero*'s other main responsibility was to arrange for the religious instruction of his charges. The first *encomenderos* were the conquistadors and their heirs; they were joined by later settlers and religious orders.

The mita was an adaptation of the Incaic system of rotating labor to meet Spanish colonial needs. Every year, in theory, one-fifth of the adult indigenous men who were subject to native chiefs and possessed rights to communal land were assigned to mita service. After a year, they were to go home and be relieved by another contingent. Spanish colonists used mita laborers, or *mitayos*, in mines, textile workshops, public works, domestic service, and agriculture and herding. The colonists obtained the right to a set number of *mitayos* according to their political influence in the regional governing bodies. The employer owed the laborers a small wage, a good part of which was directly recycled back to the colonial authorities as tribute payment (Pérez Tamayo 1947).

The encomienda and colonial mita represented a compromise between the Crown's interest in maintaining control and receiving tribute and Spanish settlers' wish for access to indigenous wealth and labor. It was, however an unstable compromise. The clashing interests and actions of these parties and of indigenous caciques and commoners were to lead eventually to the growth of haciendas.

From Chiefdoms to Haciendas

Heavy tribute demands were one of several factors that contributed to the breakdown of native communities and their replacement by haciendas. Spanish colonial tribute was theoretically set at the same levels as Inca-period tribute or less, but local practice consistently overrode legal theory. Moreover, there was a crucial difference between Inca and Spanish tribute. The Inca state had mainly demanded labor and assumed the risks of poor weather or other conditions that affected harvests on state lands. The Spaniards, in contrast, demanded fixed quantities of goods. Even a community that could normally meet its assessment without difficulty could be overburdened when a poor harvest or other problems arose.

The same was true when tribute was later fixed in monetary terms, with the added difficulty that money could be secured only by selling goods or labor outside of the community. The Riobamba area was an important center of textile workshops for this purpose. In the second half of the eighteenth century, however, the South American market for textiles from the Audiencia of Quito shrank considerably. Meanwhile, the drain of money from the colony to Spain in the form of tribute for the Crown continued and, indeed, intensified. In 1776, a group of Riobamba chiefs petitioned for a return to tribute in kind, pleading that they were now unable to sell their textiles to pay their tribute. Unfortunately, the Crown had no interest in accumulating unmarketable textiles (Contreras 1987:18–27).

Demographic decline of indigenous communities was both a symptom and a cause of further difficulties from early on. Epidemic diseases from Europe periodically swept through the Americas, devastating indigenous populations that had little immunity. Heavy tribute burdens and the loss of land and other resources to colonists taxed community members' ability to feed themselves and their children. Forced labor sometimes took people out of their communities for long or permanent service at a great distance. In 1549, for example, Quito authorities ordered about fifty men from Pallatanga to go mine gold in southern Ecuador (Pérez Tamayo 1947:213–217). In the late seventeenth century, a substantial group of Pangor natives was taken to Guayaquil (Haro Alvear 1977:261). Around the same time, the *encomendera* of Pangor took people belonging to two middle Pangor valley communities to Riobamba for her personal service. Most of them evidently stayed on in the city even after completing their period of service, and others from home joined them. They probably had lower tribute assessments and no obligation to perform mita service there, because they were natives of another jurisdiction (at that time Pangor was still part of the *corregimiento* of Chimbo; Bonnett 1992:106–107; *Cacicazgos 1730s; Moreno Yánez 1985:44–45).

Many native Andeans fled their home communities in order to evade the mita and other forms of oppression. Some went to urban centers, others to remote areas not firmly under Spanish control, still others to rural areas far away from their caciques or local Spaniards to whom they had been subject. As early as 1538, the cabildo (municipal governing body) of Quito commissioned an official to hunt down such fugitives, offering a reward for each one recaptured (Pérez Tamayo 1947:335).

While some chiefs initially benefited by recruiting and sheltering migrants from other regions, the decline in locally rooted subject population was ultimately fatal for many chiefdoms (Powers 1995). Tribute and mita assessments were slow to adjust to declining population. As the population base shrank, the burden of tribute and mita obligations grew heavier on those who remained (Bonnett 1992:104–105). Ever-heavier exactions only increased the incentives to flee, creating a vicious circle.

While population was in effect squeezed out of the chiefdoms, the developing haciendas pressured and induced people to remain outside. Landowners often retained *mitayos* for an extended period beyond the one-year mita service, thereby converting them into long-term resident laborers. Under a system known as *concertaje*, a laborer, or *concierto*, would be tied by debt to his employer. In some cases, the debt consisted of fines for animals lost or injured under the *mitayo*'s care, inflated charges for goods forced on the laborer, and other similarly arbitrary impositions. Whatever the source, the debt allowed the landowner legally to retain the laborer until the debt was paid or worked off. Given low salaries, the *mitayo*'s continued tribute obligations, and the continued imposition of fines and other charges, this point might never come (Juan and Ulloa [1747] 1990:297–298, 300–301; Oberem 1981:313–317; Peña Montenegro [1668] 1985:164–165).

The use of debt as a mechanism of coercion is a well-documented fact: laborers were sometimes able to bring their protests to the attention of the authorities (see, e.g., Pérez Tamayo 1947:101–109). Recent scholarship, however, has pointed to another, traditionally neglected, side to "debt peonage." At least in some cases, laborers voluntarily received advances from landowners in the form of food, clothing, or contributions for ritual expenses. The landowner might never intend or expect the laborer to repay the debt, but, rather than coercion, the debt represented a process of negotiation of the terms under which the laborer would stay on. That laborers were sometimes able to negotiate these terms is confirmed by the complaint of Gen. Juan José Flores, Ecuador's first president and a large landowner himself, that haciendas sometimes "seduced" Indian *conciertos* away from each other (Espinosa 1984:161–162).

Ramón Valarezo has argued that laborers also attached themselves to haciendas as a way to undo the *reducciones*, the forced resettlement in towns. He shows that the *reducciones* forced people to maintain two residences, one in town and one near their fields, and to travel frequently between the two. As haciendas expanded at the expense of indigenous lands and built up a permanent resident labor force, they also provided people with the opportunity to resettle in what had been their ancestral home. The price was working for the hacienda, but the new *conciertos* were also granted land to work for their subsistence. Hacienda labor was part of a negotiated arrangement rather than a term of mita service not subject to the same kind of negotiation and that would take the laborer away from his fields and animals (Ramón Valarezo 1987:219–220; see also Powers 1995).

With limited, uncertain markets for their production and limited capital, hacienda landlords were loath to make substantial, continuing monetary investments in their labor force in the form of attractive wages. Having ample access to land, they found it more advantageous to allow their laborers to produce their own subsistence (Wolf and Mintz [1957] 1977). The use of a plot of land was thus one of the main incentives, along with the transfers registered as debt, that haciendas offered to secure permanent resident laborers. Both native people who had long been farming the same or nearby land and *forasteros*, migrants from other places, were drawn to settle on haciendas by the possibility of re-creating a partly autonomous livelihood on hacienda land.

A seventeenth-century bishop of Quito summed up some of the factors that pushed people to leave their native communities and resettle on haciendas:

> The Indians flee from their towns and go to other provinces, where the Spaniards, in order to make use of them, hide them; so that the *encomenderos* come to lose their tribute payments. . . . [T]hose who receive in their ranches the Indians . . . are careful to treat them well, so that they remain on their haciendas . . . [The Indians] flee from the . . . abuses that they suffer . . . on the part of the *corregidores*, the priests, the caciques, and the *encomenderos* themselves . . . They rarely or never flee and leave their lands, without being pushed to it by . . . mistreatment . . . , and even then they leave with great pain and sorrow. (PEÑA MONTENEGRO [1668] 1985:153–154)

While tribute and mistreatment at the hands of civil and ecclesiastical authorities pushed indigenous people to seek shelter on haciendas, then, the demand for their labor and the possibility of moving again allowed indigenous fugitives some bargaining power. At the same time, the bishop denounced hacendados who imposed arbitrary fines in order to convert *mitayo* laborers into debt peons (Peña Montenegro [1668] 1985:164–165). Indigenous people thus became permanent resident laborers on haciendas through a combination of coercion and choice, fraud and negotiation.

As of about 1700, a good number of the Pangor-area natives who had previously been taken to Riobamba now lived as indebted laborers on various haciendas somewhere in the region. Their cacique, pressed to complete the mita contingent required of him, obtained an order for their renewed *reducción*; we do not know how successful he was in implementing it. He also tried to reduce his mita assessment by petitioning for some of his subjects to be stricken from the rolls. Over the next several decades, he and other local caciques engaged in a series of disputes with another leading cacique for control over their subjects. Pangor caciques were evidently finding it difficult to keep enough people under their authority to fulfill their quota of *mitayos* and tribute for the colonists (*Cacicazgos 1730s).

The colonial elite obtained land in a number of ways. Many of the conquistadors secured land grants on the heels of the Conquest; these served
as one basis for later expansion. Some *encomenderos* also converted their
authority over people into landownership (Salazar de Villasante [c. 1570–
1571] 1991:71–83). Periodically, in the so-called *composiciones de tierras*, the
Crown sold legal titles to lands that colonists had illegally bought or simply
taken over. Some male colonists built up their landholdings through marriage to daughters of chiefly families that claimed former communal lands
as private property. Religious institutions commonly gained land through
donations (Borchart de Moreno 1980; Ramón Valarezo 1987:144–165).

The origins of the hacienda Monjas Corral, in the upper Pangor basin,
lie in the late seventeenth and early eighteenth centuries—the same period
when Pangor-area chiefdoms seem to have entered into a crisis (Figure 7). The
Convent of the Nuns of the Immaculate Conception in Riobamba owned a
cattle ranch in Rumipamba, the precursor of the hacienda, by 1686. The nuns
sold the ranch, including one hundred head of cattle, to Sgt. Blas Romero of
Riobamba in that year. Romero expanded the ranch by buying another six
and a half *caballerías* (possibly about seventy hectares) of contiguous land
from Lorenzo Pasto of Pallatanga. Pasto's name suggests membership in a
local chiefly family.[4] He might have needed money to pay his people's tribute
assessment, or he might have been pursuing his individual economic interests (*Rumipamba 1704).

In 1704, the convent bought back the ranch, now with 162 head of cattle.
The reacquisition also included the rights to four *mitayos* from Pangor
chiefdoms.

In these early years, the estate seems to have been managed exclusively
as a cattle ranch—that is how the land title refers to it, and in both the 1686
and the 1704 transactions, its price was specified in direct proportion to the
number of cattle (*Rumipamba 1704).

The 1704 land title names no other haciendas bordering Rumipamba and
is very ambiguous about the estate's boundaries. The Pangor cacique, Andrés
Zárate, and his subjects still maintained control over extensive lands in the
middle and upper parts of the basin, as attested by decrees they obtained from
the Crown in defense of their lands in 1695 and 1713. One of the sites named
in the 1713 decree, Llallapata, probably refers to an area that would later be
attached to Monjas Corral (*Despojo 1862).

Spanish colonists continued to form and expand haciendas in the Pangor
area during the course of the eighteenth century. In contrast to the vague
definition of the boundaries of Rumipamba in 1704, a will defining the
boundaries of the neighboring hacienda of Guangopud at the end of the
same century names other haciendas bordering it on every side (*Testa-

FIGURE 7.   *Section of Monjas Corral*

mento 1792). Nonetheless, the descendants of Andrés Zárate's people farmed and grazed cattle on their own land well into the 1800s; nineteenth-century documents refer to them as *indígenas* or *socios* (members) of the *común* (community) of Pangor. They numbered 166 in 1843, compared to 213 indigenous people who lived on haciendas in the middle and upper parts of the Pangor basin (*Pangor 1836–1856:62v–66). The hacienda system was certainly well entrenched by the end of the eighteenth century, although haciendas still jostled with indigenous communities.

The seventeenth and eighteenth centuries were also a period of ethnic transformation and reconstitution. One aspect of this transformation was the replacement of local indigenous languages such as Puruhá by Quichua, the lingua franca of the Inca empire. Quichua seems to have already carried a special prestige in the Puruhá area in the early colonial period (Paz Maldonado [1582] 1991:321). The colonial church further promoted the use of Quichua over native local languages in religious indoctrination (Moreno Yánez 1989:132–133). Colonial policies also contributed to an ethnic reconstitution by defining a generic category of "indigenous" people who paid tribute and were subject to different laws from Spaniards and mestizos.

The social upheavals associated with the breakdown of chiefdoms and resettlement in haciendas further transformed identities. Some chiefdoms and the identities associated with them persisted into the nineteenth century, but in much of the highlands, migration and resettlement reshaped identity on a massive scale. In the Cayambe region in northern Ecuador (see Figure 2), *forasteros* amounted to almost one-half of the indigenous population in 1720. Almost all of them were *conciertos* on haciendas. Hacienda laborers of *forastero* and local origin rose up together in 1777, grouped by hacienda, and attacked important local caciques (Ramón Valarezo 1987:107–111, 223, 230–235).

Evidence from southern Ecuador indicates that intermarriage between local natives and migrants was common. Differential tribute and mita burdens provided an incentive for such couples and their offspring to identify themselves as migrants (Pérez Tamayo 1947:338–340).

In the Riobamba region itself, there was likewise a massive influx of migrants from other regions. The Puruhá language disappeared in the seventeenth (or possibly the eighteenth) century (Burgos Guevara 1997:348; Schroder 1984:54), and the term "Puruhá" dropped from usage as an ethnic designation.[5] Today in Chimborazo, as throughout highland Ecuador, the Quichua language is one of the main markers of indigenous or Runa ethnicity. Within this broad ethnic category, some local identities did persist or reemerge, linked to hacienda communities, to surviving autonomous communities, and to larger regional groupings.

While Puruhaes and Chimbos were being transformed into Runa, other social categories were also coming into being or changing. I have been referring to the colonial elite a bit loosely as "Spaniards and their descendants" or "Spanish colonists," but many of the first Spanish invaders took indigenous wives or concubines. Their offspring were the first generation of mestizos. Unions among mestizos, Spaniards, and indigenous people resulted in growing numbers of mestizos. The term *mestizo* originally meant "mixed" or "hybrid," and that is still its standard translation. In social practice, however, its meaning in relation to other categories such as *blanco* ("white") and indigenous gradually became much more complex. At the elite level, wealthy descendants of the conquistadors often claimed purely Spanish lineage and called themselves *blancos*, thereby suppressing the memory of early colonial mixing and reserving the term mestizo for those of lesser social status. The line between *blanco* and mestizo, clear in principle, became much harder to draw in practice (and by the late twentieth century, the two terms could be used almost as synonyms).

At more humble social levels, indigenous individuals and families, especially in urban areas, could sometimes pass into the mestizo category by adopting cultural signs of a mestizo identity (Moreno Yánez 1989:135). Conversely, consensual unions and sexual abuse of indigenous women by Spanish or mestizo landowners, priests, and others resulted in offspring who might be treated as indigenous.

Racial categories thus referred to social and legal distinctions, not to a full and objective reckoning of bloodlines. A case from several decades after Independence underscores this point. In 1853, the Pangor parish priest recorded the marriage of José Manuel Benites and Antonia Villalba, identifying the groom as "white" and the bride as "indigenous." This was not the only case of a mixed-race marriage, but something else makes this one particularly instructive. The white groom and the indigenous bride were such close relatives that they required a special dispensation from the archbishop to marry! Clearly, "white" and "indigenous" could not have signified pure ancestries (*Pangor 1836–1856:39v & insert 39–40).

While these social categories were developing, divisions were also growing between South America–born whites (*criollos*, creoles) or mestizos and new Spanish arrivals, especially those come to take up posts in the colonial administration. Resentments against the new arrivals and the Crown itself intensified in the later 1700s, when administrative reforms increased the drain of indigenous tribute to Spain. The flight of indigenous people from the chiefdoms to haciendas represented a victory for the local colonial elite in its struggle with the Crown for control over indigenous labor and resources. Independence in 1822 solidified and extended that victory. The creole and mestizo elite could now manage the state to advance their interests without interference from the Crown. As we shall see, they would still have to contend with indigenous actions and responses.

HACIENDAS AND INDIGENOUS PEOPLE FROM INDEPENDENCE TO LAND REFORM
Ecuador, Pangor, and Monjas Corral, 1822–1879

The nineteenth-century Ecuadorian state was closely tied to the landowning elite and the Catholic Church hierarchy. Indigenous tribute, *concertaje*, and the elite's ownership of large estates all survived the turbulence of Independence. In the aftermath of Independence, the state created a rural police force and reinforced coercive debt peonage. *Conciertos* still fled excessively harsh conditions, however, and landowners continued to compete for laborers, which allowed laborers some room for negotiating their conditions of servitude.

During the first several decades after Independence, the highland commercial economy suffered from the devastation of war and post-Independence political instability. While exports from the coastal lowlands gradually recovered, the market for highlands agricultural products was quite restricted through the middle nineteenth century (Contreras 1987; cf. Marchán Romero 1984). The highland economy was relatively isolated from the coast during this period. These conditions did not provide much impetus for the further expansion of haciendas in the highlands generally.

Local history, however, does not necessarily follow the same rhythm or direction as regional and national history. As long as mules were the primary means of transport, Pangor's location on the outer slopes gave it an advantage over the central highland basins in the supply of potatoes, meat, or cheese to the coast. The valley itself continued to be an important muleteers' route between the highlands and the coast. These conditions may have made Pangor-area land attractive to members of the provincial elite.

There are indications of continuing pressures on indigenous communal lands in the mid-nineteenth century. In 1843, the Ecuadorian government instituted the sale of supposedly empty, unused lands (*tierras baldías*) in order to pay its foreign debt (Acosta 1994:59). This policy allowed a provincial aristocrat, Ignacio Lizarzaburu, to form two extensive haciendas in the middle and lower Pangor basin (*Fianza 1881). Around the same time, the indigenous *común* of Pangor entered into a legal battle over lands and boundaries with the hacienda Llalla and/or Monjas Corral (*Despojo 1862:16).

The hacienda Rumipamba came to be known as Monjas Corral sometime in the first half of the nineteenth century. The estate had a succession of owners from 1792 to 1879. In 1852, owner Vicente Barba annexed to Monjas Corral the neighboring hacienda of Llalla. The two were owned, rented, and managed together until the 1960s, with the name Monjas Corral serving for the whole (*Barba-Cárdenas 1879; *Prot/EP 1851–1853:187).

A local census conducted by the parish priest in 1843, the only document of its kind available for the entire hacienda period, sheds some light on Monjas Corral and Llalla at that point (*Pangor 1836–1856:60v–64v). The steward of Llalla was married to an indigenous woman whose surname, Llamuca, suggests descent from an important eighteenth-century chiefly family (*Cacicazgos 1730s). The Llamuca family played an important role in the religious life of the hacienda and the parish. The priest's 1843 list of *fundadores*, or life-long fiesta supervisors, names the Llalla steward himself as *fundador* of one fiesta; this role was, in reality, held by couples, and he may have inherited it through his wife. A Catalina Llamuca was *fundadora* of two celebrations, and members of the related Titushunta family oversaw another. Perhaps the local fiesta system developed partly out of the old ritual roles of chiefly families (cf. Rasnake 1988:120, 131, 168–170). The intermarriage between the Llamuca family and the steward also suggests one avenue by which hacienda bosses could have become familiar with the ways chiefs maintained authority through redistribution. Aside from the steward's family, the resident population of Monjas Corral and Llalla consisted of fifty-eight people: fourteen married couples and their children, including a three-generational extended family and six single or widowed men and women.

Economic and political developments intensified the pressures on highland indigenous communities and hacienda laborers in the last four decades of the nineteenth century. In the 1860s and the 1870s, the regime of Gabriel García Moreno conscripted indigenous men to work on the roads joining the highlands to the coast. The increasing possibilities for marketing highland products on the coast, where the export economy was booming, created incentives for highland landowners to expand their landholdings and labor force. While indigenous tribute was abolished just before García Moreno's presidency, he imposed other fiscal burdens that pushed more indigenous people into servitude on haciendas (Fuentealba M. 1990:55; Van Aken 1981:455–456).

Powerful whites continued to covet indigenous lands in Pangor in the 1860s. Bruno Dávalos, a two-time provincial governor, attempted to acquire communal lands by claiming they were empty (*baldías*). The indigenous occupants successfully defended their lands (*Pangor 1863; Castillo Jácome [c. 1942]:237). What eventually became of the *común* of Pangor is not clear, however. I did not come across any documents referring to it after this period. In the 1990s, most of the surnames of community leaders mentioned in the 1860s documents could be found among mestizos in the town of Pangor and the mestizo community of Baraspamba, just up the mountains from the town and bordering Monjas Corral to the southwest. Perhaps they are descendants of the *común* members.

As for Pangor-area hacienda residents, the evidence suggests a pattern of migration. Over the four decades from 1843 to 1881, the family composition of Monjas Corral and Llalla changed considerably. Only four surnames represented on the priest's 1843 census still appear on an 1881 list of male hacienda laborers. In 1843, only six of seventeen adult men have one of these surnames; in 1881, nine of eighteen. Six adult male surnames present in 1843 disappeared in the interval, while six new surnames appeared (*Conciertos 1881; *Pangor 1836–1856:64r–64v).

Two processes could account for this instability in male surnames. One is intermarriage between haciendas and residence on the woman's natal hacienda. Men from Monjas Corral might have relocated matrilocally (to the wife's home estate) if they judged that another hacienda offered better working conditions or more ample land for farming and keeping animals. Second, individuals and families bound by *concertaje* might have fled from Monjas Corral to other estates or to the coast. Such flight was not uncommon in the region, and one man is actually listed in 1881 as a fugitive from Monjas Corral (*Conciertos 1881).

Whether through marriage or flight, the general regional trend in the twentieth century was migration from the central basin to the Pangor area and from Pangor to Pallatanga and the coast. Almost all families in the Pangor area today trace their origins back some generations to the central basin, while many have relatives who have relocated in Pallatanga and farther west. Families left the central basin because of land scarcity and other pressures on hacienda laborers, while Pangor's low population density and agricultural fertility made it a favorable refuge. Their descendants often left Pangor out of dissatisfaction with conditions on haciendas there and in search of better conditions in the historically underpopulated subtropics and coast. Rates of flow no doubt varied locally and over time; oral histories suggest that the last two or three decades prior to the land reform (i.e., from the 1930s or the 1940s) were a period of high turnover on Monjas Corral. In a long-term view, the upper Pangor valley has historically been a way station in multigenerational sequences of migration from the central basin on to the Pallatanga area and the coast. The 1843–1881 data hint that this pattern was already in place by that time.

This pattern of migration, together with other factors, shaped local historical consciousness in an important way. Haciendas seem to have formed particularly early in the colonial period in parts of the central Riobamba basin, including the area around Colta and a little to the south, where migrants to Pangor generally came from (Borchart de Moreno 1988:504), perhaps weakening local memories of ancestral indigenous ownership of the land. Migrants from the central basin were even less likely to view Pangor lands as ancestrally theirs. A memory of ancestral ownership and dispossession by haciendas may well have been perpetuated among descendants of the *común* of Pangor or other local formerly autonomous communities. Monjas

Corral residents probably interacted with these people in town or when the hacienda called on neighbors to aid in the harvest or cattle roundups. But none of the six surnames of *común* leaders in the 1860s are found on an 1887 list of twenty-three Monjas Corral laborers (*Inventario 1887). My guess is that *común* members and their descendants gradually became mestizos (and perhaps tended to avoid intermarriage with hacienda residents). This ethnic distinction would have compounded the effects of migration in keeping indigenous hacienda residents from identifying with the ancestral owners of the land.

The long history of hacienda presence in Pangor, and specifically of Monjas Corral itself, further contributed to a sense that haciendas had always been part of the landscape. In the 1990s, elderly men born on Monjas Corral could list the names of the men who had rented the estate going back to the turn of the century. Asked what they had heard about how the church had come to own the estate, they said a childless widow, Manuela Ávalos, had owned Monjas Corral and Guangopud and willed both to the church on her death. (This version is contradicted by the archival record of the church's purchase of Monjas Corral in 1880, unless it refers to an earlier period of church ownership.[6]) They did not know how Ávalos had acquired her property, and as for the origins of haciendas more generally, they said it was only in recent years that they had learned that indigenous people once owned all the land and had been dispossessed by whites of foreign ancestry.

The record of a ten-year legal battle between Vicente Barba and his son-in-law Pacífico Gallegos over the ownership and management of Monjas Corral offers a further glimpse at the estate during the García Moreno period. An inventory of the estate describes its physical condition in 1873. Five buildings were clustered at the administrative center of the hacienda—three two-room houses, a hut, and a manger. They are described as made of earth with straw roofs, very old, and falling into ruin. The main house had a veranda with three wooden pillars on carved stone bases. In front of this house was a small cobblestone patio with an old stone cross and a stone font. Laborers probably periodically gathered there in the morning to receive orders, and other administrative and ritual functions would have been carried out in this space. One room of one of the structures evidently served as a chapel: there were four prints representing saints as well as a statue of Saint Rose of Lima, the patron saint of the hacienda. The structures also served for storage: in one was a pile of lime, in another a few old hoes, plowshares, and other tools (*Gallegos-Barba 1873:17v–18).

Barba had been using the hacienda for agriculture as well as livestock raising. The official carrying out the inventory observed four potato fields, seed potatoes, a field of fava beans, and three piles of cut barley awaiting threshing. Livestock continued to be important, however, as it always would be in Monjas Corral: 279 cows and 62 horses, mules, and burros were enumerated (*Gallegos-Barba 1873:18–20).

According to a traditional view in the literature, Latin American elites viewed hacienda ownership mainly as a source of prestige, and they did not cultivate the land efficiently with a view to profit. The Barba-Gallegos dispute hints at the social meaning of landownership in describing a "custom the Indians have of doing the *entradas*." Around Palm Sunday, hacienda residents would bring mules or horses loaded with firewood and charcoal for the landowner to his home in Riobamba. The term *entrada* (entrance), together with the association with Palm Sunday, suggests that their arrival might have had some ritual meaning. Any time hacienda residents had to bring goods to the landowner in town, the act expressed recognition of his authority over them. This authority was especially highlighted when, as Gallegos claimed, the Indians gathered the firewood and charcoal at their own expense and used their own animals to convey them. Gallegos said he had received ten loads of firewood from Monjas Corral in 1874, as well as others from other estates he owned. One can imagine that, in the eyes of Riobamba's townspeople, the trains of Indians arriving with horses and mules at the houses of their masters on Palm Sunday represented a display of each landowner's power and wealth (*Gallegos-Barba 1873:79–80v).

Of course, firewood and charcoal are also for burning. The courtroom dispute over the *entradas* focused on their monetary rather than prestige value. Whatever else the hacienda was, for its owners (and, later, its renters) it was certainly a source of products that could be used or sold. Recent scholarship on Latin American haciendas has revised the picture of landowners as economically apathetic and shows that it was not a fundamental lack of interest in the economic potential of the land so much as limited markets and capital that tended to restrict investment in increased production in some periods.

Defending the management of Monjas Corral in 1873–1874, Pacífico Gallegos listed several "notable improvements" he said his associate and trustee Prudencio Granizo had made: "the considerable increase in cattle and horses, the cultivation and clearing of several pieces of land that [were] not . . . worked before, . . . and . . . the increase . . . of a number of arms [laborers] which are the principal basis for the good maintenance and progress of an estate" (*Gallegos-Barba 1873:70–70v). Granizo added that he had established a small cheese-making shop "with the object of taming the cattle" (*Gallegos-Barba 1873:71). Given the difficulties of transporting milk from

Monjas Corral to town, presumably, there had not been any point in regularly milking the hacienda cows; now that the milk could be made into cheese on the estate, they would become accustomed to regular milking. Gallegos claimed to have invested more than three hundred pesos in the hacienda for tools, seeds, and money and goods to distribute to the laborers (*suplimentos* and *socorros*; see Chapter 5). (For comparison's sake, a single cow was worth ten to twenty pesos.)

Barba disputed these claims of a dramatic improvement in the management of the estate, but both sides were in essential agreement that careful management was important to enhance the hacienda's value and profits. Irrigation ditches should be constructed and maintained; land should be cultivated; pastures should be separated with fences or ditches; animals should be rounded up every month and branded; and most important, as Gallegos indicated, the labor force should be increased (*Gallegos-Barba 1873:71, 74, 75v, 79, 81–84).

All of these measures to maintain and improve the estate depended on the force of manual labor, augmented only by hand tools and draft animals. Hacienda landlords in many areas seem to have faced a chronic shortage of labor from the beginnings of the system until the mid-twentieth century. Labor was perpetually scarce in the upper Pangor basin; the cold, the fog, the strong winds, and the tough *páramo* grass that had to be hoed by hand in order to cultivate a new field all kept the population density lower than in the central Chimborazo basin.

Hacienda landlords in Pangor thus had a strong interest in inducing laborers to settle on the estate, keeping them there, and squeezing as much labor out of the residents as possible. This need for labor could be a source of bargaining strength for laborers, especially when they were moving to a new home, and, given low population densities, landlords could offer ample access to land. On the other hand, landlords' demand for labor was also a persistent source of conflict, clashing with laborers' need for time to attend to their own crops and animals. In 1864, three Pangor hacienda residents complained to a Riobamba judge that they had been "mistreated . . . by the steward . . . and the administrator . . . for having missed work just one day because we had to plant our cornfields to support our family . . . and as the assigned tasks [*tareas*] are too heavy we are not able to finish in one day . . . and we are fed up with continual mistreatment . . . and . . . the steward's wife [has been] making threats to kill us" (*Iñacoto 1864).

Former hacienda laborers I spoke with more than a century later voiced the same grievances: excessive piecework tasks, lack of time to tend the family crops, and bitter conflicts with stewards over labor demands.

Monjas Corral under Church Ownership, 1880–1962

LOCAL AND NATIONAL HISTORIES   In 1880, the Diocese of Riobamba acquired Monjas Corral for fourteen thousand pesos. The sale included 300 head of cattle, 50 horses and mules, 225 sheep, tools, a couple of potato fields already planted—and the debts of eighteen laborers (*Cárdenas-Diócesis 1880). For the next eighty years, the diocese rented out the hacienda, its fields, pastures, animals, and resident labor force, together with other estates in its possession, to members of the provincial landed elite (Figure 8). Technically, the diocesan seminary owned the estates, and the rent helped pay for the education of seminary students in the local minor seminary and the major seminary in Quito.

Archival records and former laborers' accounts indicate the names of successive hacienda renters (Table 1). Unfortunately, none of the renters or stewards were still alive during my fieldwork. The Riobamba diocese's historical archive contains rental contracts, inventories, and even a few hacienda account books from the first four decades of church ownership, but I found fewer inventories and no account books from more recent rental periods. Longtime hacienda residents provided some details on individual renters, but the turnover in the hacienda resident population and the deaths of some longtime residents prior to my research limited the historical depth of most of the accounts I obtained. These limitations prevent a detailed examination of the management of the estate under different renters that might elucidate long-term trends.

The first two decades of church ownership were clouded by an expensive legal battle with Manuela Barba, Vicente Barba's daughter and Pacífico Gallegos's wife, who retained a lien on the estate. For much of the 1890s, the estate was in some sort of trusteeship as a result of the lawsuit (*Barba-Cárdenas 1879; *Cárdenas-Diócesis 1880; *Legajo 2 bis 1881–1909; *Proaño 1917). Manuela Barba and her sons were also political enemies of the church and gave money, support, and top military leadership to a revolutionary liberal movement that viewed the church's wealth and power as an obstacle to progress (Castillo Jácome [c. 1942]:153, 161, 290; Maldonado y Basabe 1930: 116). After triumphing in 1895, the liberals separated church and state and expropriated some of the church's landholdings.

Historians have traditionally interpreted the Liberal Revolution as representing the ascendancy of the coastal commercial elite over highland landowning interests tied to the church. Recent scholarship has shown that both liberal and conservative alliances were quite complex, spanning the regional division and reflecting factional conflicts within the highland elite. The most

TABLE I. *Renters of Hacienda Monjas Corral, 1881–1961*

Rental Period	Renter(s)	Annual Rent (No. of Haciendas Included in Rental)[a]
1881–1885	Miguel and Manuel Lizarzaburu[1]	1,000 pesos (2)
1885–1887	?	1,500 pesos (2)[b]
1887–?	Reinaldo García	500 pesos (1)
1889–1894, possibly again ?–1898	Under trusteeship because of Manuela Barba lawsuit	
1894–?	Antonio Mosquera	1,800 sucres[c] (6)
1898–?	Reinaldo García	
?–1902	Manuel García (?) (possible trustee before Mosquera and/or subrenter or associate of Mosquera or Reinaldo García)	
1903–1909	Domingo Cordovez Maure Leandro Barba (subrenter?)[d]	4,000 sucres (6)
1910–1916	Aurelio Cordovez Ricaurte	6,100 sucres (6)
1917–1918	Aurelio Cordovez Ricaurte (rental contract expired but retains control)	
1918–1925	Vicente Guevara	7,700 sucres (6)
1926–1934	Vicente Guevara	14,000 sucres (6)
1935 (Jan.–Apr.)	Vicente Guevara (deceased 1935)	14,000 sucres (6)
1935–1940	Guevara family (Carmen Merino and sons)	14,000 sucres (6)
1941–1947	Guevara family (Carmen Merino and sons)	25,000 sucres (6)
1948–1954	Antonio Santillán and Guillermo Novillo	67,000 sucres (2)
1955–1961	Carlos Arturo León	80,000 sucres (?)[e] (1)

SOURCES: *Fianza 1881; *Lizarzaburu to Bishop 1885; *Arrendamiento 1885; *Rivadeneira al Vicario 188–; *Legajo 2 bis 1881–1909; *Arrendamiento 1902; *Arrendamiento 1909; *Arrendamiento 1918; *Arrendamiento 1924; *Arrendamiento 1931; *Arrendamiento 1938; *Bases 1954; *Cons. Gub. 1939–1947, 10/8/47; *Terminación 1955;*V. de Guevara al Obispo n.d.

[a] Monjas Corral and Llalla are counted here as one hacienda, rented separately (1), together with Hacienda Colta–La Merced (2), or together with five other estates (6).
[b] Both names on rental contract, but only Miguel's name appears in later documents.
[c] Sucres were instituted as the national currency in 1884; 1 sucre = 1.25 pesos (in late nineteenth century) (*Comparación 1886; O'Connor 1997:46).
[d] No document linking Barba to Monjas Corral located, but two oral histories name him as renter immediately before Aurelio Cordovez.
[e] Dates and minimum bid set by Curia in *Bases 1954. Rental contract not located.

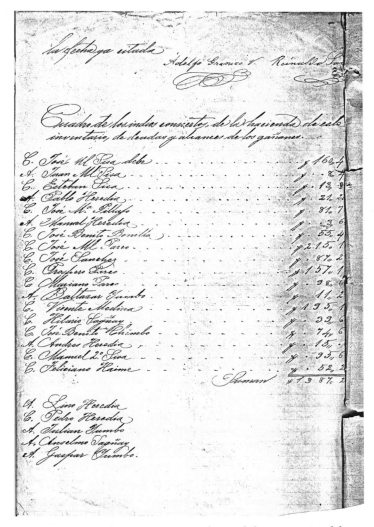

FIGURE 8. *Monjas Corral* conciertos, arrimados, *and their respective debts, as inventoried for rental in 1887 (*Inventario 1887)*

aristocratic, wealthy sector of the local landowning class was generally conservative, but some landowners, such as the Gallegos-Barba family, supported the liberals.

Indigenous people from parts of the central Chimborazo basin also joined the revolutionary liberal armies. Pangor Runa witnessed an important battle in the upper Pangor basin, gave refuge to fleeing soldiers in their huts, and seem to have viewed the liberals as pro-indigenous. They apparently did not take any active part in the fighting, though. Historians do not yet fully understand the social causes and implications of the Liberal Revolution in the highlands. While the church and allied factions lost power, highland landowners remained influential even at the national level and still dominated the highland provinces.

The liberal regime did render the diocese's hold over its haciendas somewhat tenuous. At times, the bishop of Riobamba had to send instructions for the rental of the estates from exile in Peru. Renter Aurelio Cordovez claimed in 1919 that his political influence had protected the estates from expropriation by the liberal government. Cordovez himself retained control of Monjas Corral after his contract expired, only handing it back when the bishop agreed to sell him all the estate's cattle.[7]

The diocese rented out the estates for the next thirty years (1918–1947) to a single family, the Guevaras. Vicente Guevara seems to have maintained a generally cordial relationship with leading church officials, who considered him a virtuous Catholic gentleman (*Flores and Izurieta to Obispo 1937). After his death in 1935, the diocese continued renting the estates to his widow and sons. Former laborers' accounts indicate that the Guevara sons administered Monjas Corral one at a time, by turns.

The beginning of the Guevara period on Monjas Corral coincided with the most significant piece of liberal legislation directly affecting the hacienda system, the abolition of *concertaje* in 1918. More precisely, the law eliminated the coercive supports of debt peonage, so that laborers could no longer be imprisoned for debt and legally forced to work for their creditor. Consonant with the interests of the coastal elite, this allowed more laborers to leave the highlands for the coast.

The law probably also made it easier for laborers to move from one hacienda to another, perhaps enhancing their bargaining power. Despite the legal change, however, landlords and stewards still used coercion to retain laborers in Pangor. When a family decided to leave a hacienda, according to oral histories, they had to keep their decision secret, load their possessions on horses and mules at night, and be gone by the next morning. Even after that, in one or two incidents, the Monjas Corral steward later encountered and attacked fugitive laborers on mountain paths. The steward murdered the laborer in one such encounter (JMP 9/2/1992; AYu 6/13/95). Perhaps with the removal of legal coercion, some stewards sought to retain laborers by cultivating a fearsome personal reputation.

The abolition of *concertaje* may have also made landlords (landowners or renters) less willing to disburse grain, money, or other goods to laborers, now that debt would no longer bind the laborer to the estate. Hacienda rental contracts up to 1918 stipulated that the church would reimburse the renter for such advances up to a set amount that presumably securely bound the *concierto* (*Arrendamiento 1885; *Arrendamiento 1918). This provision reflected the church's interest in increasing the labor force and hence the value of the rental. The provision disappeared from contracts after 1918. My informants, whose memories would obviously mostly pertain to the post-1918 period, said that disbursements on Monjas Corral were minimal. Archival evidence supports this picture, at least for the last rental period: the steward did not even maintain an accounting of disbursements and residents' work, and the renter more or less admitted never having paid the laborers until forced to by legal action near the end of the rental (*Liquidaciones 1961:June 2, June 6).

The abolition of *concertaje* probably made it harder for the church to hold renters legally accountable for maintaining or increasing the labor force. Contracts up to 1918 required renters to reimburse the church for any decline in laborers' collective debt and to hand back the estate with the same number of *conciertos*. Again, these provisions disappeared from later contracts, replaced by vaguer injunctions to maintain the labor force and obey national labor laws.

The change may not have had much effect on Monjas Corral right away: the long contracts awarded the Guevaras and their repeated renewals would have made it in their own interest to maintain the labor force, just as it remained in the interest of private landowners in underpopulated areas like Pangor to do so. When the time approached to give up the estate, however, renters may have been tempted to intensify their exploitation of the hacienda residents even past the point at which some would be driven to flee the estate.

In early 1947, the Guevaras still hoped to renew their rental, but then they had some clashes with church officials and probably suspected they would lose the contract. A delegate sent by a church body to visit Monjas Corral and hacienda Colta-Merced that May reported that about 40 peons (adult laborers) had abandoned the estates. Lifelong Monjas Corral resident Reinaldo Sisa's account suggests that the Guevara son who was administering Monjas Corral adopted a vindictive attitude toward the hacienda residents once it was clear the contract would not be renewed and contemplated making off with the hacienda residents' livestock (see Chapter 6; *Cons. Gub. 1939–1947:2/5, 4/10, 5/17, 5/28, 1947).

The abolition of *concertaje* changed the formal definition of the landlord-laborer relationship. Under debt peonage, laborers' usufruct plots were, in legal terms, only an incidental benefit in lieu of higher pay. These plots now became central to the definition. Hacienda residents were obligated to work for the hacienda because they lived on and farmed hacienda land. They were legally entitled to a nominal wage, but it was not always paid. The plots ceded to residents were long known as *huasipungos*; from 1918 on, legislation and scholarship refer to the labor system as *huasipungaje* instead of *concertaje*, and the laborers themselves as *huasipungueros* rather than *conciertos*. It is symptomatic of the lack of fundamental change this entailed, however, that hacienda account books and laborers in Pangor continued to use the term *concierto* until the 1960s agrarian reform (*Tepeyac 1964).

The highland economy went through ups and downs during the Cordovez and Guevara periods. At the beginning of the century, the government completed construction of a railroad line running through the central highland basins and veering west from southern Chimborazo down to the coast. The railroad linked the highlands more closely to the booming coastal economy, especially stimulating highland potato production between 1910 and 1930 (Trujillo León 1986:81). The increase in the rent paid by the Cordovezes for the six church-owned estates, as compared with the rent during the Mosquera period (see Table 1), may be a reflection of the improved possibilities for marketing hacienda products on the coast.

The situation was reversed when international prices for cacao and other coastal exports dropped sharply from the late 1920s through the early 1930s. Prices for highlands agricultural and livestock production fell in a chain reaction. Some landowners seem to have responded by increasing the pressure on resident laborers and neighboring autonomous communities to provide free or low-paid labor. Indigenous people in some areas of northern Ecuador and Chimborazo put up strong resistance, linking up with urban-based socialist and communist organizations (Almeida Vinueza 1990:177–179).[8]

Falling agricultural prices help explain the church's willingness to extend Guevara's rental contract in 1931 with no increase in the rent. The extension to 1940 was advantageous for the Guevara family, as prices began to recover in the mid-1930s. Soon after, World War II and the postwar international economy provided a renewed stimulus for coastal exports and coastal demand for highland products. These trends were reflected in a large increase in the Guevaras' rent in 1941 and then a dramatic jump in what Antonio Santillán and Guillermo Novillo paid beginning in 1948. In the 1950s, urbanization in the highlands as well as on the coast increased demand for dairy and other products. The church raised the rent again for the last renter, Carlos Arturo León.

León's rental period, from 1955 through 1961, coincided with important changes in the Ecuadorian highland economy and politics. These changes set the stage for fundamental transformations in the relationship between landlords and hacienda residents. In parts of northern Ecuador, growing urban demand for dairy products encouraged landlords to switch from agriculture to dairy operations. This switch and the adoption of agricultural machinery reduced landlords' need for labor. Landlords in those areas also increasingly chose to use valley lands for irrigated pastures planted with high-quality grasses. As they restricted or relocated *huasipungos* from valley lands apt for irrigated pastures, conflicts with laborers sometimes intensified. Some laborers joined in a national movement for land reform focused on the demand for title to *huasipungo* plots.

These regional economic and political trends converged with national and international developments to lead to land reform in the 1960s (Barsky 1988; Guerrero 1983). The Cuban Revolution aroused fears of communism among national elites and in the U.S. government, which called for reform as an alternative to revolution. The Catholic Church added its endorsement of social progress and land reform in Vatican II. Modernizing dairy landlords, who no longer needed so much labor, were prepared to relinquish hillside land to *huasipungueros* and employ wage labor, as long as they could keep prime valley land.

This was the solution promoted by the 1964 agrarian reform law. Actual outcomes on each hacienda during the ensuing decades varied according to the local ecological and market conditions for dairy production, the interest and ability of landlords to make this transition, and the pressures hacienda residents were able to apply.

Monjas Corral had always been primarily a livestock enterprise, supplemented by potatoes and other crops, and it is not clear if renters increased its dairy production in the 1950s. The completion of the road from Cajabamba through Pangor to Pallatanga in 1952 (Tufiño 1987:7) may have actually stimulated Monjas Corral renters to intensify agricultural production. León used a tractor to help increase potato cultivation, and with it, demands on laborers to work in the planting, weeding, and harvest.

Bishop Proaño had been talking about turning over church lands to indigenous peasants as part of a project of "incorporating the Indian into civilized life" since at least 1956 (Gavilanes del Castillo 1992:126–127). He decided to cease renting out Monjas Corral after the expiration of León's contract on January 1, 1962. This was the end of the "classic" hacienda period for Monjas Corral—the period I shall be considering in the next two parts of this book—though some neighboring estates continued to operate much as before for another decade or two. Management of Monjas Corral passed into the hands of administrators appointed by the bishop, inaugurating a period of experimentation, transition, and land reform. Proaño eventually turned over most of the estate to the resident laborers and others.

THE CHURCH, RENTERS, AND LABORERS   Having offered a chronological overview of the period of church ownership and rental of Monjas Corral, I shift now to a more analytical discussion of the same period. What difference did church ownership make in the management of the estate? How did the church decide whom to rent to, and what kind of people were the renters? What did the church ask for in the rental contracts? Did it make or mandate capital investments in the hacienda that entailed demands on residents' labor? In what ways was renters' treatment of hacienda residents a consideration in church decisions and rental contracts?

Father Agustín Bravo, a longtime priest in the diocese who rose to become Bishop Proaño's vicar-general and an in-house historian and archivist, once told me that bishops before Proaño never visited the haciendas they owned and did not know their value. As a result, individuals with close personal ties to the bishops were able to obtain the rentals cheaply and make a good profit while the diocese benefited very little.

This picture is quite plausible in some respects. Personal connections have always counted for a great deal at every level of Ecuadorian society. Prior to Proaño, bishops generally came from aristocratic families, had a leading role in local high society, and even had relatives or family friends among potential hacienda renters. The long rental periods and renewals conceded to the Cordovezes (1903–1916) and the Guevara family (1918–1947) also suggest that something other than impersonal, competitive bidding underlay the selection of renters.

The men who rented the diocese's haciendas exemplified the close connections between the landowning elite, the church, and the state. The first renters, the Lizarzaburu brothers (1881–1885), belonged to a family that owned two neighboring Pangor haciendas. The two brothers alternated with each other and another Lizarzaburu in the provincial governorship for most of the 1880s. A kinsman of Aurelio Cordovez became bishop of Riobamba during Cordovez's rental period (*Cordovez to Vicario 1919). Cordovez's family had a long-term relationship with the bishopric; he and his brothers collected rents and tithes for the diocese in the 1890s (*Arrendamiento 1895; *Colecturías 1893–1908). The Cordovez family was also active in local politics; two of their number briefly occupied the provincial governorship in the twentieth century. Carlos Arturo León, the last renter, held the top political offices of Colta county (which includes Pangor) at various points and was also president of the provincial landowners' association (the Centro Agrícola) in 1961. Bishops from aristocratic backgrounds themselves probably felt quite comfortable with such individuals, and they may have felt it was in the church's political interests to treat these renters favorably (Castillo Jácome [c. 1942]:237, 296–297, 420; *Cordovez to Secretario 1918; *Fianza 1881; Maldonado y Basabe 1930:24; Sylva Charvet 1986:51).

The case of the Guevaras in particular supports Bravo's point. In 1937, several years before their third contract was due to expire, Vicente Guevara's widow proposed to renew it for another seven years in her and her sons' names and offered to raise the rent from 14,000 sucres to 25,000 sucres. The bishop appointed a commission to study her proposal. In their report, they reminded the bishop of his strict obligation under church law "to keep a careful watch . . . over [the seminary's] possessions, on whose proper, conscientious, and forward-looking administration depends the future of a diocese." The commissioners raised several financial issues: the sucre had lost over half its value and agricultural commodities had tripled in price in the past six years; seminary expenses had increased; and the bishopric's budget was very tight. They concluded that accepting a rent of 25,000 sucres would "cause enormous damage to the interests of the bishopric." They also recommended a rental period of no more than three years unless the rent was pegged to the dollar. Another would-be renter offered to pay 30,000 sucres, yet the bishop accepted the Guevaras' offer of 25,000 sucres for an additional seven years, apparently without any open bidding. When this period was finally nearing its end, the bishopric prepared for a dramatic increase in revenues, setting the minimum bid at 30,000 sucres for Monjas Corral alone—just one of the six estates the Guevaras had been renting for S/.25,000. The Guevaras were certainly paying far less than market value (*Arrendamiento 1938; *Junta Admin. 1937; *Flores and Izurieta to Obispo 1937; *Romero to Ordóñez 1937; see also *Dueñas to Ordóñez 1942; *Dueñas to Ordóñez 1944).

On the other hand, documents from other periods give the impression of a church more fully willing and able to defend its financial interests. The church sometimes formally solicited bids for the rental, and would-be renters competed in their offers of higher rents or investments in the estate (e.g., *Bucheli to Obispo 1917; *Cabezas to Vicario 1917; *Guevara to Vicario 1917; *León and Dávalos to Vicario 1917). In 1881, the Lizarzaburu brothers won the rental of Monjas Corral and another estate in open, face-to-face bidding in which their agent and a competitor progressively raised their offers of capital improvements. Four years later, Miguel Lizarzaburu was in debt and unable to keep up with the rental payments. He asked for an early dissolution of the contract, complaining that the haciendas did not produce enough to pay the rent. The bishop did not personally visit the properties, but he sent a delegate to inspect them. During the ensuing negotiations, Lizarzaburu complained bitterly that the delegate had underestimated the cost of the new alfalfa and potato fields, irrigated pastures, and irrigation ditches he was leaving (*Comparación 1886; *Fianza 1881; *Lizarzaburu to Bishop 1885; *Observaciones 1886).

By comparison with landowners in other provinces farther north, twentieth-century landowners in Chimborazo province were generally slow to invest in technological change (Schroder 1984; Sylva Charvet 1986). They did nonetheless view haciendas as profit-making enterprises and sometimes did invest in them. The Lizarzaburu period (1881–1885) exemplifies the interest the diocese showed in investments that would raise the value of the rental. In their winning bid, the Lizarzaburus offered to plant alfalfa and increase the number of cattle and horses on Monjas Corral. They employed about sixteen hundred man-days in digging new irrigation canals and ditches around improved pastures, with the agreement and reimbursement of the diocese (*Arreglo 1886; *Comparación 1886; *Fianza 1881; *Lizarzaburu to Vicario 1881; *Observaciones 1886). In 1947, after considerable study and discussion, church officials decided to demand that the next renter construct additional irrigation canals. It is true that lack of direct church control made it difficult to ensure that capital improvements were actually made: arguing for charging higher rent in lieu of capital improvements, the bishop noted that renters tended to promise improvements and then not fulfill their promises (*Cons. Gub. 1939–1947:5/17, 5/28, 1947)

The hacienda renters themselves were entrepreneurs as well as wealthy landowners; renting the hacienda was an investment. Jorge Trujillo has found that wealthy, well-connected liberals who rented haciendas that had been expropriated by the liberal state in the early twentieth century tended to intensify their exploitation of hacienda laborers in order to raise production for coastal markets (1986:75). Despite the factional and ideological differences between liberal renters of state-owned haciendas and those who rented church-owned estates (more likely conservatives), it seems likely that renters of whatever persuasion were a self-selected group with a relatively strong commercial orientation.

The Cordovez family apparently subrented Monjas Corral in the first decade of the twentieth century to a Leandro Barba. Barba owned or rented a sugar mill in Pallatanga as well. He forced Monjas Corral people to work in the sugar mill and to take cane alcohol and sugar blocks on horseback up to Cajabamba for sale in the highlands (JMP 9/2/1992; RS 9/14/1992). Aurelio Cordovez was known for breeding imported cattle stock, at least later on his own properties. One of the Guevaras was a prominent businessman and banker (Castillo Jácome [c. 1942]:272, 288). The penultimate renters turned Monjas Corral back to the church with potato fields assessed at 61,000 sucres—almost their yearly rent for Monjas Corral and Colta-Merced (*Terminación 1955). Carlos Arturo León periodically brought a tractor and laborers from his own hacienda to Monjas Corral, where he again increased potato cultivation.

The limitations I have mentioned in the archival and oral records do not allow me to define in much more detail the economic strategies of each renter and their implications for the hacienda-laborer relationship. Two informants with a long enough family history on the hacienda to know mentioned the Leandro Barba period in the early 1900s as particularly bad in that work in the sugar mill and conveying loads to Cajabamba forced hacienda residents to neglect their own animals and subsistence plots. Practically every rental period, however, is remembered as bad.

When I tried to elicit information on the specific strategies or policies of each renter, the responses generally began with the phrase, "Just the same . . ." There is one steward who was notoriously cruel, Ignacio Lara. He administered Monjas Corral at some point in the Guevara period (according to one informant) and again in the late 1950s under León. It was during his periods of employment that the exodus of Monjas Corral residents intensified, and his abuses provoked protests in 1961 (see Chapter 8).

To the extent church officials before Proaño thought about the indigenous people living on church estates, it seems to have been primarily in economic terms. Until *concertaje* was legally abolished, rental contracts contained some very specific provisions concerning the labor force. It is instructive to compare these provisions to those concerning livestock.

The first rental contract set the tone for subsequent contracts. At the beginning and end of each rental period, an inventory was made of everything of value on the hacienda: buildings, unharvested fields, potatoes in storage, tools, livestock, and indebted laborers. The two inventories were compared when the renter turned the hacienda back to the diocese. With respect to such things as potatoes in storage or in the fields, the renter was obligated to make up for any deficit with a cash payment. The hacienda's cattle, horses, and sheep were a more important part of its basic value, and in this case, the renter was legally committed to returning the hacienda with the same number and classes of animals that he received it with. The language of the contract is almost the same with respect to *conciertos:* "The renter has the obligation to return the same number of *conciertos* with their respective debts on the haciendas of Monjas-Corral and Colta, replenishing others located on them [on the haciendas], until the number of absent ones is reached."

As with livestock, whose numbers some contracts obligated the renter to increase, the diocese was interested in expanding the labor force. In the first contract, the diocese agreed to reimburse the renter for advances to new *conciertos* as long as they were young and healthy. Finally, the diocese included this stipulation: "The renter may not, for any reason, take the *conciertos* . . . to sugar mill haciendas to employ them in labors there, nor may he send them on trips to the subtropical brush or the coast, and if he does so, he will pay the debts of all those *conciertos* who should die for that reason, and, in addition, other *conciertos* to replace the dead ones." Working conditions in sugar mills were hazardous, and tropical diseases such as malaria were common in the lowlands. The diocese was thus protecting its investment (*Fianza 1881).

Rental contracts after 1918 did call on renters to treat laborers well, or, as one contract put it, with "Christian charity." The most specific was probably that prepared in 1954 under Bishop Proaño, which incorporated these provisions:

> The renter must commit himself to respect the rights that the permanent laborers . . . have to their *huasipungos* and assigned plots, paying them the minimum legal salary, . . . giving them good treatment, respecting and keeping the days of religious precept [i.e., Catholic holidays], and, in general, paying all of the compensation in the forms established by the law and the labor authorities. . . . It will be expressly prohibited for the renter to make use of the laborers . . . for work extraneous to the service of [the estate], except for the case of the servants that the renters of Monjas-Corral and La Merced must send, one every two months, by turns, . . . for service in the episcopal palace. (*BASES 1954:IV)

The provision requiring renters to send hacienda residents for a month's service in the episcopal palace (the bishop's residence and office building) was a long-standing feature of these contracts. (Oral histories indicate that they were usually sent from La Merced, not Monjas Corral.) This provision would have provided an opportunity for bishops to learn firsthand about conditions on the haciendas and whether renters were abiding by their commitment to pay legal salaries. More research might be enlightening, but I have not turned up any evidence that bishops actually availed themselves of this opportunity, possibly excepting Proaño.

In monthly (sometimes biweekly) meetings from February to October 1947 to discuss the rentals, church officials' discussions focused on the feasibility of capital improvements and on what the church could charge for rent. Despite the church's interest in maintaining the labor force, the minutes of these meetings give no indication that considerations of how the current renters treated hacienda residents or how prospective renters might do so entered into their decisions (*Cons. Gub. 1947). It is not surprising, then, that contractual provisions for good treatment often remained a dead letter.

Rental contracts before and after 1918 also obligated renters to ensure that hacienda residents received religious instruction. Some contracts gave the renter general responsibility for the "morality of the peons." These provisions referred in practice to weekly early morning prayer and instruction sessions (the *doctrina*) and to the renter's support of the authority of the *regidor*, a liaison between hacienda residents and the parish priest. Private haciendas, however, also generally maintained the same institutions of early morning prayer sessions and *regidores*; their existence on Monjas Corral was not a function of church ownership.[9]

High church officials' attitude toward the residents of church-owned haciendas surely reflected their generally elite background, but it also expressed the dominant theological outlook of the period prior to Vatican II. One Riobamba bishop said of his flock, "They are poor in worldly treasures, but what does it matter as long as they are rich in the priceless treasures of faith?" (*de la Torre 1924). Another noted, "This life of ours will vanish like smoke" (*Ordóñez 1936);[10] thus, what mattered was shepherding the flock through the sacraments that would get souls to heaven. As long as church-owned haciendas yielded the money to train priests as effective shepherds, they were fulfilling their role.

CONCLUSION

This overview of the interactions of indigenous villagers, Andean chiefs, Inca and Spanish conquerors and settlers, state officials, landlords, and others over five centuries has several implications for understanding the hacienda system and twentieth-century Monjas Corral. First, I have noted that precolonial Andean society was strongly stratified, and chiefly authority persisted into the colonial period. Reciprocity and redistribution were central principles of pre-Andean social life through which peasant cultivators gained access to the products of other zones and chiefs and Inca rulers bolstered their authority. Hacienda landlords thus made use of practices of discipline and redistribution partly rooted in Andean culture. At the same time, hacienda residents applied their expectations of reciprocity and redistribution when making claims on landlords and judged them critically when they violated those expectations.

The hacienda system itself, as a negotiated arrangement that accommodated some of landlords' and residents' interests, contributed to the persistence of reciprocity and redistribution as principles of Runa social life and moral judgment. Colonialism had transformed land into private property, allowed local elites to form haciendas, and squeezed indigenous people out of the communities where they had rights to communal land. On haciendas, however, they regained access to land and other resources as part of the tense "pact" by which they negotiated their livelihood under conditions of subordination. Hacienda Runa re-created a partly autonomous sphere of production and exchange, coexisting with the production of crops and livestock under the hacienda's management and control. Runa household production, using hacienda resources and Runa labor, was necessary for the reproduction of the hacienda's labor force, but at the same time, it competed with the hacienda for resources and especially labor time. This tense coexistence of different spheres of production within the hacienda helped sustain varying interpretations of the hacienda-laborer relationship, with Runa bringing their experiences of reciprocity in their own production and exchange relations to bear critically on landlords' behavior.

I cannot confidently fit Monjas Corral into a standard general narrative of increasing agricultural commercialization and intensified exploitation and resistance. That would require more detailed data on the estate as an economic enterprise and a broader historical study of Chimborazo haciendas' place in the regional economy since the late nineteenth century. Pangor's location on the outer western slopes may have encouraged landlords to intensify the production of potatoes and other products for the coast beginning in the García Moreno period or even earlier. The abolition of *concertaje* in 1918 probably made landowners and especially renters less inclined to disburse goods or money that could be counted as debt. The church sometimes promoted capital improvements on Monjas Corral that would have entailed demands on residents' labor, and the church did not significantly restrict renters' exploitation of resident laborers. Renters themselves treated the hacienda as a commercial enterprise, although, again, the limited data do not indicate that their exploitation of the laborers necessarily became worse over time.

At any rate, former Monjas Corral laborers themselves do not narrate local history as a progressive erosion of an earlier moral economy. They recall conditions as always having been bad or as having fluctuated cyclically with the comings and goings of the most notorious steward. Nor apparently did Pangor hacienda residents preserve a widespread memory of indigenous ancestral ownership of the land. The upper Pangor basin itself was probably only sparsely settled at most in precolonial times, and the descendants of upper-middle Pangor basin natives seem to have become mestizos. Migrants to Pangor haciendas tended to be from haciendas in the central basin, and their descendants in Pangor seem generally to have viewed haciendas as long-established, if not eternal, facts of life. Hacienda-era historical narratives, then, did not criticize landlords as violating expectations that were traditionally honored, as the moral-economy school posits, or critique the hacienda system itself as based on an original dispossession, as more recent indigenous political discourses do. It was, instead, in their semiautonomous social relations and religious life that hacienda Runa sustained a critique of the hacienda and a basis for resistance. We now turn to a closer examination of hacienda society and religion.

PART TWO

Society and Resistance

CHAPTER 3

Hacienda Society and the Base
of the Triangle

THE HACIENDA AS A SOCIAL SETTING

This chapter offers an overview of hacienda Monjas Corral, focusing on its spatial, administrative, and especially social organization in the 1880–1960 period. Haciendas are easy to describe as a type of formal organization with the landowner at the top of the chain of command and various categories of laborers at the bottom. They have also been described as a distinctive sort of economic enterprise: compared with plantations, haciendas minimize capital expenditures, aim at self-sufficiency, use semifree (rather than slave or purely wage) labor, and are more oriented to local or regional rather than long-distance markets (Wolf and Mintz [1957] 1977). Scholars have given less attention to understanding the hacienda as the setting for a web of social relationships.

Despite their subservient position in the chain of command, indigenous people living on haciendas collectively created a complex society that spanned hacienda boundaries. Social ties among kin and friends enhanced hacienda Runa's economic security and their room to maneuver vis-à-vis the landlord. Hacienda residents' rights to use hacienda land and other resources were a material basis for an autonomous domain in which they exchanged labor and goods as an everyday expression of social relationships. These ties also had an important moral dimension. Hacienda Runa worshiped in ways that recognized and deepened such ties, and they maintained a sense of identity that sometimes reinforced horizontal solidarity as well as vertical hierarchy.

In this chapter, the image of hacienda residents' social networks as the base of the triangle serves to focus attention on some of the relatively horizontal and relatively autonomous aspects of residents' social life. In many ways, peasant social networks provided a counterweight to their subordination to the hacienda. At the same time, indigenous social life was not purely horizontal and autonomous, nor did all vertical relationships work in exactly the same way. The image of a triangle *with* a base, pointing to both vertical and horizontal social relationships, is simply a useful first approximation.

This chapter first sketches the physical layout, the formal organization, and the social hierarchy that characterized hacienda Monjas Corral and other haciendas in the area. Then, in the bulk of the chapter, I describe the social world of hacienda Runa with an emphasis on the more or less horizontal, more or less autonomous "base of the triangle."

THE SOCIAL ORGANIZATION OF SPACE

As words naming key social institutions often do, the word *hacienda* has a complex set of meanings. First, it refers to the entire land area owned as a unit, together with everything and everyone living on it: the hacienda Monjas Corral, hacienda Guangopud, and so on. In this sense, the hacienda was at once a property, a spatial area, and a social entity. More narrowly, the hacienda was an administrative structure and economic enterprise aimed at producing a profit for the owner or renter. Thus, we can speak of "the hacienda" in opposition to "the community" or "the laborers." The indigenous people living within the confines of the hacienda provided labor for that enterprise, but their interests often clashed with the interests of the hacienda as an enterprise. In local usage, the resident community of hacienda times is referred to simply as "the people" (*gente*, a Spanish word adopted into Quichua). Finally, *hacienda* in Spanish or Quichua can also refer to the administrative and ritual center of the estate—physically, a central cluster of buildings and yards. For the sake of clarity, I will not use the term "hacienda" by itself in this sense.

Monjas Corral covered a broad slice of the upper Pangor basin, from the western heights bordering on Bolívar province across to the eastern rim of the basin (Figure 9). The Pangor River runs south down the middle of this area, dividing what was historically Llalla on the west from the historical core of Monjas Corral proper on the east. Starting at about thirty-five hundred meters above sea level at the northern border of the estate, the river drops about three hundred meters over the five kilometers to the southern border. The four thousand meter–high ridges and peaks marking the borders of the basin and, historically, of the estate are four to five kilometers to the west of the river and two to four kilometers to the east. In all, the estate comprised about three thousand hectares (thirty square kilometers).

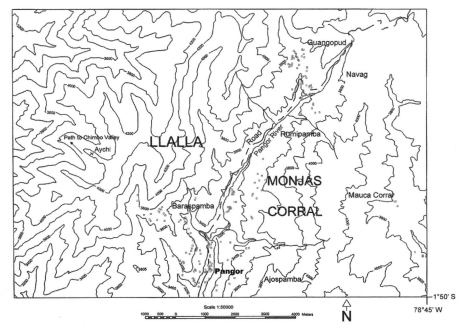

FIGURE 9.   *Monjas Corral and the upper Pangor Basin. Squares represent dwellings seen in 1960 aerial photographs. Based on I.G.M. 1969. Used with permission.*

In the southern and middle area of the hacienda, the land rises from the river relatively slowly and gently for about a kilometer to the east. The administrative and ritual center of the hacienda was located in this part, toward the southern end. It consisted of a cluster of buildings, along with the space around them. An 1873 inventory describes three two-room houses, a hut, and a manger, all with earthen walls and straw roofs. A small courtyard in front of the main house was paved with stones and had a stone cross and font (*Gallegos-Barba 1873:17v–18). New houses were built in subsequent years, but later documents and oral histories give no indication of any major architectural innovations until the 1960s, after the diocese took over direct control of the estate from the last renter.

These buildings and outdoor spaces served a variety of purposes. Owners, renters, and stewards slept in the main house when they were on the estate. Hoes, yokes, and other tools, as well as seed potatoes and hacienda products, were stored in one or two rooms of the houses. One room served as a chapel where hacienda residents received religious instruction, prayed, and worshiped the patron saint. The yards between and around the houses also served as a gathering place where laborers received orders, were disciplined, and celebrated fiestas. This area was thus the ritual center for the resident community as well as the enterprise. I will refer to these buildings and the associated space as the "hacienda house," the "central hacienda complex," the "hacienda yard," or some such term.

In the same general area of the estate were corrals for hacienda animals and pastures for those horses, oxen, and milk cows that were kept in the valley. The hacienda (as an enterprise) cultivated alfalfa, potatoes, and other products in the same area, as well as a little barley in a small, flat area of Llalla, near the river.

The land rises steeply from the river along most of its western bank. In the southwest, about a kilometer back from the river—a half hour's rigorous walk up to the first crest and behind—is an area where the slopes are gentle enough for cultivation or dwellings. At least one early renter planted potatoes in this area (*Legajo 2 bis 1881–1909). Farther up on both the eastern and the western sides are extensive *páramos*, upland meadows where hacienda livestock roamed.

At least in the last decades of the hacienda period, most of the resident families built their huts on the eastern side of the river, in an area from near the central complex to a couple of kilometers up the valley. A few families also lived in the hills in the southwest. Hacienda residents planted potatoes, other tubers, and fava beans around their huts and in other parts of the estate for their own subsistence. They also maintained herds of cattle and sheep in the *páramo*.

Hacienda spatial organization clearly reflected social hierarchy. The central hacienda complex and the enterprise's most intensively used pastures and fields occupied some of the choicest valley land. Administrative, disciplinary, and ritual functions were all concentrated at the center, under the control and supervision of hacienda bosses. At the same time, resident laborers' dwellings and plots occupied relatively good land, and former laborers told me they were free to build their huts and plant their crops anywhere they wished. Monjas Corral's relatively fertile land and extensive pastures were the main benefits the estate offered to attract and retain resident laborers.

LANDLORDS, STEWARDS, AND LABORERS: ADMINISTRATIVE STRUCTURE AND SOCIAL HIERARCHY

The administrative structure and duties of people on the hacienda may be summarized as follows:

1. Owner (Diocese of Riobamba)
2. Renter (*arrendatario, amo*), sometimes his wife
3. Steward (mayordomo), sometimes his wife, here termed "steward-ess," and assistants
4. Resident full-time laborers (*concierto gente*):
   a. Overseer (Sp. *mayoral*, Q. *khipu*)
   b. Cowhands (*vaqueros*), possibly shepherd (*ovejero*)
   c. Field hands (*labranza*)
5. Other members of resident households with rotational, part-time, or occasional duties and sometimes providing voluntary labor (*arrimados, ayuda, huasicamas,* other)
6. Nonresident part-time or occasional laborers (sharecroppers, *ayuda* labor, aid in harvest)

Let me elaborate on each of these categories. As described in the last chapter, the Diocese of Riobamba purchased Monjas Corral in 1880. From 1881 to 1961, the diocese rented out the hacienda, together with several others it owned in the province, generally for seven-year periods. The rental included the livestock on the hacienda and the right to the land and the labor of those living on it. In the management of the estate, Monjas Corral renters occupied roughly the same structural position as the owners of private estates. Within contractual constraints, they made basic decisions about economic strategies, held a good deal of power over the lives of hacienda residents, and imparted orders through their hired subordinates. Like most of the provincial elite, renters owned houses in Riobamba or other towns in the central basin. Several renters were drawn from the core of the provincial elite, a small group of aristocratic families who claimed to be of pure Spanish descent.

Renters probably spent less time on the estate than the owners of neighboring private haciendas, some of whom seem to have lived much of the time on their estates, and, unlike ownership, rental periods expired. As a result, renters probably had a less personal relationship generally with hacienda residents than that between private owners and "their" hacienda residents. However, the Guevara family's long (thirty-year) rental period and, conversely, the occasional sale of privately owned haciendas soften this distinction. Pangor Quichua speakers have adopted the Spanish word *amo*, with connotations of "boss," "master," or "lord," to refer to renters and private owners alike. I use the word *landlord* to refer to both.

The renter hired a steward (mayordomo) to live on the hacienda. The steward was responsible for the day-to-day administration of the hacienda and the supervision of labor. The class and ethnic background of the stewards varied somewhat within the broad mestizo category. They were commonly mestizos from Riobamba or smaller market towns. As mestizos, they spoke Spanish as their first language, but they had to be fluent in Quichua in order to supervise the indigenous labor force.

The steward's wife lived with him on the hacienda and oversaw female laborers performing rotational service in the hacienda house. In addition, during some periods, the steward was accompanied by other mestizo assistants. The steward Ignacio Lara brought two nephews to assist him on the hacienda, and some oral accounts refer to the three collectively as "stewards."

The indigenous families that resided on the hacienda formed the core of the labor force. Up to 1918, the relationship was legally defined by the contractual commitment of an adult male member of each household who had received an advance to work for the estate over a specified period of time. As part of this arrangement, the hacienda also granted the *concierto* land to live on and farm and the right to use hacienda pastures, firewood, and other resources. After 1918, this access to land and other hacienda resources became the formal basis of the relationship between households and the hacienda. The name of one household member, generally an adult male who headed the household, would be inscribed in the hacienda account books as the person to whom this access was granted and who owed full-time labor in return. Hacienda residents continued to use the word *concierto* to refer to this status.

The full-time work week was four days, possibly, in some periods, five. The laborer served the hacienda as field hand, cowhand, or overseer. When the named laborer was ill or otherwise occupied, households might send another member or find someone else to work as a substitute, but this could be a point of angry contention. Oral histories tell of stewards rejecting women or youths as substitutes on the grounds they could not work as hard or as skillfully.

Monjas Corral renters and stewards selected one full-time laborer to serve as overseer. The overseer aided the steward in planning and supervising daily labors and received a salary in addition to normal usufruct rights.[1] This tended to be a long-term position; the same overseer might serve for a couple of decades or more.

One or two cowhands were responsible for herding the cattle in the *páramos*, counting them, and recovering any strays from neighboring haciendas, with the aid of the neighboring cowhands. Late nineteenth-century hacienda account books show the cowhand as receiving a salary, but it is not clear whether this accurately represents reality then or later. During some periods, the hacienda may have also assigned the task of herding hacienda sheep as a particular household's long-term duty, though some informants indicated that this duty was rotated among households.

The rest of the full-time laborers worked as field hands. They plowed, weeded, harvested, or did whatever other tasks the steward and overseer assigned them. For each workday or completed task (*tarea*), they received a *raya*, or mark in the hacienda account book. Theoretically, each *raya* corresponded to a small daily wage, but this was often more an accounting theory than a real transfer of cash.

In addition to regular daily labors, the field hands also performed a variety of rotating duties. The most burdensome was to serve as house servant, or *huasicama* (Q., house caretaker) for a six-week turn. Each household actually had to supply three laborers when its turn came: a man, his wife, and a teenaged or adult offspring, relative, or someone else hired at their expense. During the six-week period, they lived in the hacienda house. Their tasks included caring for horses, milk cows, and oxen; cleaning the stables; chopping wood and making charcoal to sell in Cajabamba on behalf of the steward; buying food in the market for the steward's family; watching over the hacienda's irrigated pastures at night to keep other residents from surreptitiously grazing their livestock there; and, in the case of the women, grinding flour, cooking, bringing food to the steward in the fields, washing clothes, and so forth.

Another rotational duty during the harvest period (April–August) was to watch over the piles of harvested potatoes in the fields to prevent pilfering. This meant staying outside by the potatoes through the cold night. The person assigned to this duty was responsible for any shortfall.

Every week, the steward ordered a laborer to take firewood, cheese, and eggs to the renter in town. This task was termed *acude*, the laborer who performed it, the *acudero*. Field hands could also be charged with occasional duties such as going to meet the renter at the train station near Cajabamba and accompanying him back to the hacienda on horseback. (The road from Cajabamba through Pangor to Pallatanga was completed only in 1952; Tufiño 1987:7.)

Other household members besides the full-time laborer had to perform services on a rotational basis. In addition to house service, young women helped milk hacienda cows, while young men or women took the household's turn herding hacienda sheep. Informants also remember being ordered to spin wool for the hacienda and, as children, to watch over pigs through the night as they rooted in and fertilized hacienda fields. Furthermore, the *tareas* that full-time laborers were ordered to complete each day were often too demanding for them to complete alone. A *tarea* was theoretically one man-day's work, but in practice other members of the household sometimes had to work alongside the full-time laborer.

Households sometimes included recently married offspring or other adults who did not have access to land in their own right. Adults living in this way as subordinate members of a *concierto* household were called *arrimados*. Evading the full labor requirements of the hacienda by not farming land independently, they were able to help farm the household plot. They also did sometimes work in hacienda labors in order to earn *rayas* for monetary pay. If *arrimados* owned animals in their own right, however, they were required to provide one or two days of labor each week in exchange for pasture. This sort of labor was termed *ayuda*.

I have not been able to trace in detail the population history of Monjas Corral under church ownership and rental, but documents from the beginning and end of the period give a rough idea of the number of resident households. The diocese's 1880 title refers to the debts of eighteen laborers, some of them probably *arrimados* (*Cárdenas-Diócesis 1880). An 1887 list names fourteen *conciertos* and nine *arrimados* (*Inventario 1887). An account book from 1964, not long after the last rental, lists the same total number of male laborers, twenty-three (*Tepeyac 1964), and the next year, sixteen men and one widow were officially recognized as having given full-time labor service (*IERAC 1965). The number of resident households and full-time laborers probably fluctuated between the low and the high teens.

In addition to the resident labor force, people living on the margins of the hacienda also contributed labor to the enterprise. Some kept animals in hacienda pastures in exchange for *ayuda* labor. In a more conflictive version of something similar, the hacienda steward or overseer sometimes caught neighbors poaching hacienda resources. Guangopud residents frequently crossed the border to gather firewood. If the steward or overseer caught them, he would take an article of clothing or tools from them as security and demand labor for its return. In addition, residents of the town of Pangor and the neighboring mestizo hamlet of Baraspamba sometimes entered into sharecropping arrangements with the hacienda: the hacienda provided land and seed and received half of the harvest.[2] In addition, renters sometimes invited people from Baraspamba or the town to aid in harvests or animal roundups in return for food, drink, and/or monetary or in-kind compensation. I did not study these relationships, focusing, instead, on the experience of the former hacienda residents who hosted me during my fieldwork.

Such was the formal hierarchy of work roles. Overlaid on and in addition to this structure, vertical elder-junior relationships organized hacienda life.

The term "elders" is broad and relative, but the preeminent indigenous elders were those who filled two religious offices. The *regidor* and the *fundador*, together with their wives, supervised and helped sponsor important annual religious fiestas. They sat at the top of a hierarchy of prestige and authority based on distinctions between permanent officers and rotating annual sponsors, between major or repeated annual sponsors and those who had undertaken fewer or more minor burdens of sponsorship, and between sponsors and those who had never sponsored a fiesta and were therefore not considered full adults. The positions of *regidor* and *fundador* sometimes coincided in the same man. It was also common for the hacienda overseer to hold at least one of these positions.

Among kin, similarly, elders held authority over juniors. *Regidores, fundadores,* and others, speaking as "elders," taught children to respect their parents, godchildren to respect godparents, and younger siblings to respect older siblings. Notions of respect permeated vertical (and, in some ways, horizontal) relationships at every level of hacienda society.

Both classic and more recent accounts of hacienda paternalism depict each laborer as isolated from others in a dyadic, vertical relationship with hacienda bosses (Wolf and Mintz [1957] 1977; Anrup 1990). Yet overseers and *fundadores* mediated the relationship between landlords and other residents, and other hierarchical relationships also existed among hacienda Runa. A crucial question is the degree to which landlords' power shaped and penetrated the hierarchy among hacienda residents.

In some ways, the vertical relationships among hacienda residents reinforced and mirrored the relationship between landlord and laborers. Overseers were named for their ability to transmit and enforce landlords' demands, and they were sometimes harsh and abusive in doing so. The *regidor's* or *fundador's* relationship with the divine enhanced the overseer's authority when these positions coincided. Norms of respect and disciplinary practices between parents and children, elders and juniors, I shall argue, helped prepare hacienda residents to respect landlords.

In other ways, these different vertical relationships operated at cross-purposes. Overseers were subject to pressures from kin and community *not* to enforce all of their bosses' orders. *Arrimados'* dependent ties to *conciertos* shielded the former from the hacienda's labor demands. The perceived generosity of *fundadores* and their relationship to the divine modeled notions of authority that hacienda residents drew on in judging hacienda bosses critically. Hacienda Runa in conflict with current landlords occasionally obtained crucial advice and aid from *former* renters and other powerful individuals. Even vertical relationships, then, could create spaces of autonomy

and resistance. This is even more true of the (comparatively) horizontal relationships to which we now turn.

KIN, *COMPADRES*, AND RUNA SOLDIERS:
THE BASE OF THE TRIANGLE
Kin, Compadres, *and Friends*

Given migration from hacienda to hacienda and to the coastal lowlands, one
might imagine that the hacienda labor force consisted of an assortment of
families with no kinship or other significant links between them, and with
weak and unstable ties beyond the hacienda. The reality was quite different.
Hacienda residents cultivated various sorts of social ties that transcended
hacienda boundaries, and when they migrated, they preferred to move to a
hacienda where they had friends or kin. Having settled on a hacienda, they
and enough of their offspring tended to stay long enough to build up significant coalitions of kin and friends on the same hacienda. Pangor-area hacienda communities were small enough for a single person's descendants to
make up a significant proportion of the labor force in just a generation or
two. On at least two occasions on Monjas Corral, groups of brothers banded
together to openly challenge the stewards—the Yumbo brothers around 1940
and the Amanchas in 1961. These haciendas were large enough to allow for
some marriage within the hacienda but, at the same time, too small for that
to be the universal marriage pattern, given avoidance of cousin marriage.
Thus, households were tied through marriages both to other households on
the same hacienda and to people on other haciendas in the area.

A sample kinship chart will help illustrate these patterns. Patrilateral,
matrilateral, and affinal kinship (kinship through fathers, mothers, and
spouses, respectively) can all create significant bonds in Pangor. In Figure 10,
I have traced some (not all) of José María Pillajo's family connections on
Monjas Corral and elsewhere. Tayta José's paternal grandfather was originally from the Quito area; he married a Monjas Corral woman and settled
down on the hacienda. On his mother's side, Tayta José was descended from
one of four Heredia brothers, members of a numerous family group on Monjas Corral from at least the late nineteenth century. His mother's mother was
a Condo, a surname traceable to the central valley but with numerous representatives in Ajospamba, a neighboring hacienda, in the twentieth century.
In the generation immediately preceding his own, Tayta José had two married aunts (FZ and MZ) who continued to live on Monjas Corral as adults,
together with their husbands and at least some of their descendants (Tayta
José's cousins). Through his mother's sister Dolores's marriage and his sister

Martina's marriage, he was linked to the Sisa family group, which had long-standing roots on Monjas Corral and probably the most common surname during the early-middle decades of the twentieth century.

Tayta José was married to the sister of Ángel María Guailla, who became overseer of the hacienda as well as *fundador;* Ángel María's wife was also a relative through the Heredia brothers. Tayta José's link to Ángel María's son Segundo Ángel—who also became overseer and served with his wife as *fundadores*—was reinforced by two other marriages: Tayta José's sister Rosa married Segundo's brother Roberto; and his wife's (and his adopted) granddaughter Elisa married Segundo's wife's brother Mariano. Through his affinal links to the Guaillas, Tayta José was also linked to the six Amancha Guailla brothers (and at least one sister) who came of age as laborers on Monjas Corral between the 1940s (the oldest) and the early 1960s.

So much for Tayta José's kinship links to others on the hacienda. It is also worth mentioning that he named as his best friends on the hacienda several of the five Yumbo brothers, though they were not his kin. One of the five was overseer for a time; their one sister was also married to Mariano Niamo, long-time overseer and religious authority.

In Figure 10, I have also put some of Tayta José's ties beyond the hacienda. Through his wife, he was linked to members of the Guailla family who remained in the central basin. Through his father's sister Estefa, he had numerous cousins on Ajospamba. Finally, his siblings Segundo and Rosa both left Monjas Corral for the subtropical region near Pallatanga. A more complete chart would show even denser webs of kinship both within and beyond Monjas Corral.

In addition to kinship in the strict sense, Ecuadorians also recognize a sort of spiritual kinship based on the sponsorship of life-cycle sacraments. As elsewhere in Latin America and the Roman Catholic world, this has been a very important way for people to create or strengthen social bonds. The man and woman who sponsor the baptism of another couple's child, for example, not only become the child's godparents, but the two couples also become "co-parents" (*compadres,* or, in the feminine, *comadres*). Sponsorship involves bearing some of the ceremonial expenses, participating in the church ritual, and contributing to or hosting the ensuing celebration. Godparenthood further entails enduring obligations of material support and moral guidance from godparent to godchild and gratitude and respect from godchild to godparent. *Compadrazgo,* the relationship between co-parents, is considered a sacred, lifelong tie of mutual support and respect. The couples must always greet each other as *compadre* or *comadre;* they periodically visit each other and exchange gifts; and a severe incest taboo between *compadres*

Through Wife

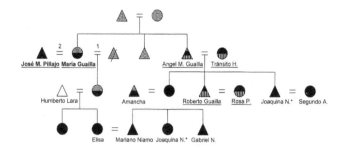

Through Siblings

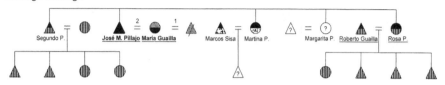

Through Father

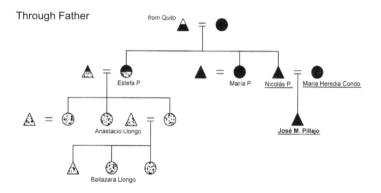

Through Mother

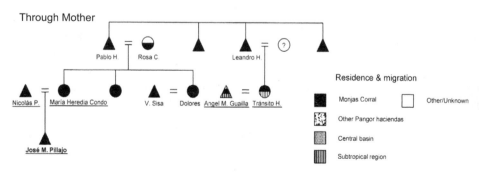

FIGURE 10. *José María Pillajo's kin. The names of individuals who appear more than once are underlined.*

minimizes the potential for sexual jealousies. Pangor Runa also often extend *compadrazgo*-like treatment to the immediate kin of their *compadres* and godchildren.

Compadrazgo can be established both horizontally and vertically, that is, between social equals and unequals. In the case of unequals, it is generally the socially inferior parents who ask a wealthier or more powerful couple to sponsor their child's baptism or other sacrament. The relative frequency of horizontal versus vertical *compadrazgo* has varied in different Catholic societies and historical periods. *Compadrazgo* is such an important bond that the balance between horizontal and vertical *compadrazgo* is a good indication of more general patterns (Mintz and Wolf 1967).

The two most important occasions for godparenthood in Pangor were marriage and baptism. One might imagine that paternalistic landlords would be called on to sponsor laborers' weddings. As a rule, however, the groom's parents sponsored the wedding, sacralizing their own relationship with their son and new daughter-in-law rather than extending *compadrazgo* outward or up the social ladder. The immediate, practical significance of this was that it created an obligation on the part of the new couple to live with the groom's parents for the first year or two, working with and "serving" them in return for their sponsorship. This could be burdensome for the daughter-in-law, but it also counterbalanced the pressure from the hacienda for the young couple to enter the rolls soon after marriage as a new *concierto* household with full-time labor obligations to the estate. Indeed, it may have contributed to the young couple's maneuverability vis-à-vis the hacienda by providing them with time to accumulate some resources under the older couple's tutelage and to consider their options. After this period, they not infrequently chose to move and become *conciertos* on another estate, sometimes the wife's home estate.

As for baptism, the evidence from Pangor is mixed. Andrés Castillo and his wife, Lorena López, mid–twentieth century owners of Guangopud, apparently did become godparents to a number of laborers on their estate. Oral accounts tell of López's treating her godchildren generously, especially after Castillo's death, even possibly distributing land titles to some of them. On the other hand, in all my interviews no one ever referred to any of the renters or stewards of Monjas Corral as godparents or *compadres*. The relatively temporary and distant relationship of renters to laborers, as compared with resident owners (together with the intensely conflictive relationship between stewards and laborers), may account for the difference between the two haciendas. Reinaldo Sisa of Monjas Corral did have Carlos Gallegos—owner of Chiquicaz in the central valley and of a small ranch by Guangopud—sponsor one of his children's baptism. Still, it is noteworthy that Gallegos, while a member of the provincial elite, had no role in Monjas Corral itself. This relationship would have potentially strengthened Tayta Reinaldo's position in a conflict with the hacienda renters or stewards, providing him with a source of aid, advice, or refuge.

I did not systematically gather data on *compadrazgo* ties, but the information I did obtain indicates that laborers on both Monjas Corral and privately owned estates such as Guangopud frequently looked to each other and to others of relatively humble social status to sponsor their children's baptism. Andrés Yépez, a migrant to Monjas Corral from a privately owned estate in the central basin, explained that the father's parents, as sponsors of the couple's wedding, thereby gained a claim to sponsor the first-born child's baptism as well. Rosa Condo, who continued to live with her husband's parents on Monjas Corral for two decades after her marriage, said that they were the godparents of all her children.

More commonly, after the first child, the couple found sponsors among others on the same hacienda with whom they otherwise had no close kinship link or other people outside the hacienda. Tayta Andrés claimed to have close to twenty godchildren, most of them from the hacienda he lived on before coming to Monjas Corral. Alberto Yumbo, who grew up on Guangopud and married into Monjas Corral, told me he had twelve godchildren. He spoke of his acceptance of the role of godparent as simply following in the footsteps of his parents, who similarly had godchildren and *compadres*. Several informants also mentioned that, when Pangor hacienda laborers sponsored a religious feast for Carnival or a local patron saint, they typically invited and feasted their *compadres* from other haciendas in Pangor and the central basin. *Compadres* outside the hacienda could be indigenous or mestizo: besides other hacienda laborers, some informants mentioned Cajabamba townspeople or mestizo peasant farmers in the central basin or Bolívar province as *compadres*.

Pangor people also constructed various other forms of fictive kinship on the model of *compadrazgo* and biological kinship. Runa midwives—often the mother-in-law or mother of the woman giving birth, sometimes a neighbor—performed rites combining elements of Catholic baptism with indigenous practices. The midwife was considered a "true *comadre*" (*comadre legítima*); the term "blood *comadre*" (*comadre sangre*) was used for midwives as well as for baptismal sponsors. Other forms of unofficial *compadrazgo* were customary between people in Pangor and people in Bolívar province.

Joaquina Niamo recalled a special friendship her father, Mariano Niamo, maintained with two laborers on Lupaxí, another Pangor hacienda. All three were named Mariano, and they chose to take this as a bond between them:

"Let's drink together, name mates (Sp. *tocayos*)," they would say when they encountered each other in Pangor.

This playful relationship could be a source of serious mutual aid. One night when Joaquina was a young girl, her father's name mates came to help him and the family load their things on horseback and move to Lupaxí, where they said working conditions would be better. The family would have moved, she said, but for her resistance to leaving home. She went on to describe another sort of fictive kinship one of these Marianos established later with her first husband: this man and her husband took to greeting one another as "my father" and "my son." She herself maintains a similar relationship as fictive "mother" to someone in Ajospamba.

Economic Ties

The hacienda's control over land and other resources and its redistribution practices contributed to whatever legitimate authority landlords could gain in laborers' eyes. It is therefore crucial to note that laborers' autonomous social networks also had an important economic dimension that balanced and reduced their dependence on the hacienda.

Pangor Runa strongly value working together among kin and neighbors in the fields, particularly in harvest labor, when the hosts share a portion of the harvest with the harvesters. Informants said that kin and others commonly cooperated in planting and other agricultural labors in hacienda times, as they did during my fieldwork in the 1990s. The host and beneficiary of the day's labor was expected to express his gratitude by providing a good meal to the helpers.

In addition to exchanging labor, households also cooperated in dealing with the risks inherent in agriculture. During the planting or growing season, friends and relatives customarily designated rows of their fields for each other to harvest. Someone whose own field yielded a poor harvest still received some of the harvest of other fields.

Livestock were also important in the household economy. A young or impoverished couple often started or increased their herd of cattle or sheep by asking a wealthier friend or relative to place a female animal under their care. The couple then had the right to keep one of every two calves or lambs born to the animal during the time they cared for it. As a young man, José Pillajo built up his sheep herd in this way with the aid of an older friend, Vicente Yumbo. From beyond the hacienda, as well, indigenous people in parts of the central basin where pasture was scarcer sometimes arranged to put their animals under the care of friends in Monjas Corral. In some hacienda regions, similar practices were sometimes a source of conflict, with landlords attempting to deny free access to pastures for animals belonging to nonresidents; I have not heard stories of such conflicts in Pangor.

As we turn now to economic relations transcending hacienda boundaries, the forms of vertical exchange merit special attention. "Vertical exchange" here refers to exchange between areas at different altitudes that produce different goods; such exchange has been vital throughout the Andes since pre-Columbian times (Murra 1975). Roque Espinosa has suggested that sets of ecologically complementary haciendas amassed by single owners offered *conciertos* access to the resources of different zones, including the western lowlands. Espinosa specifically cites the haciendas belonging to the Riobamba church in the late nineteenth century as an example of these sets (1984). While he offers no direct evidence for the role of sets of haciendas in *conciertos'* household economies, his supposition is reasonable on the face of it. If it were true—especially if the hacienda directly mediated access to the products of other zones through redistribution, in the mode of pre-Columbian Andean chiefs and the Inca state—this could have substantially enhanced landowners' or renters' legitimacy as generous patrons.

In fact, however, the available late nineteenth-century Monjas Corral account books, which carefully note (and, if anything, exaggerate) hacienda disbursements to the laborers, provide no indication that renters distributed any product besides barley from other zones. The Riobamba church did not actually own any haciendas down from Monjas Corral on the western outer slopes or lowlands. When individual Monjas Corral renters did own properties in the lowlands, it was more of a misfortune than an opportunity for the laborers. Leandro Barba, who subrented Monjas Corral probably in the first decade of the twentieth century, also owned or rented a sugar mill in the Pallatanga area. He is remembered as a "terribly cruel" renter who forced Monjas Corral laborers to go work in the sugar mill and to drive mules with contraband cane alcohol from Pallatanga to Cajabamba, leaving their own plots and animals abandoned (see also Weismantel 1988:67).

Although most of Monjas Corral is too high for barley, and the best barley land was cultivated by the hacienda, laborers did apparently plant some barley on their subsistence plots. Lower-altitude areas on the inner slopes and central valley are more favorable for barley, however. Monjas Corral was generally rented out together with Colta–La Merced, a barley-producing hacienda, and landlords often had their own barley-producing haciendas in the central basin as well. They sometimes took Monjas Corral's laborers to these other haciendas to aid in the barley harvest and gave them a sack of barley each to take home.

Much more prominent in contemporary oral memory, however, is another form of interzonal articulation: the exchange of potatoes for maize and other products with people from the Chimbo valley in Bolívar province. The hacienda did have a modest role in allowing for this exchange. One informant mentioned that Monjas Corral's residents used potatoes from the *socorro*, a sack of potatoes disbursed annually by the hacienda to each household, to take on their trips to the maize region. He also said that the landlords gave the laborers leave for the month of November to go and exchange potatoes (or sometimes labor) for grain in the maize region (RS 6/15/95). In addition, landlords evidently did nothing to prevent people from Bolívar province from visiting their Pangor friends to engage in such exchanges.

People in Pangor as well as Bolívar recall these exchanges with a remarkable nostalgia and mutual affection—especially remarkable given the ethnic boundary between the two regions. (Indeed, a few people from both sides continue occasionally to make the trip with horses over the mountains to this day, despite the greater convenience of motor transport to local market towns.) In addition to the important material benefits to both parties, what accounts for the nostalgia and affection is the manner and context in which these exchanges were carried out. A sack of potatoes was conventionally exchanged for a sack of maize, but the transaction was far from a simple impersonal act of barter. I experienced some of the warmth that surrounded these exchanges when I visited Reinaldo Sisa for the first time in his house together with my wife, Mercedes, who is from the maize region. I had not yet met Tayta Reinaldo, but he had heard from others about Mercedes: he greeted her as *comadre* and asked after her family. Later, he told us that, years before, when she was a little girl, he had visited her house around All Souls' Day, at the beginning of November. For this holiday, rural Ecuadorians customarily bake "bread babies" by pressing the dough into a mold in the form of a baby. Mercedes's family, he said with a chuckle, presented him with a bread baby to be his "godchild," thereby establishing *compadrazgo*. (My father-in-law confirms the custom.) On our second visit, Tayta Reinaldo (Dioselopague) served us potatoes with roasted guinea pig, as befits a *compadrazgo* relationship.

More generally, at any time of year, either side could establish a *compadrazgo* tie simply by addressing the other as *"compadre."* Mercedes's father recalls that visitors from Pangor would present their hosts with gifts of roasted guinea pig along with a sack of potatoes, saying as they did so, "Have this [Sírvase], *compadre."* The hosts were then obligated to respond as *compadres*. Sorting through the maize they had in storage, they selected some of the best, biggest ears to fill a sack, just as they would to give to any kind of *compadre*. In addition to maize, they might also give their visitors other specialties of the region, such as wheat tortillas filled with cheese.

Their relationship with Chimbo valley people linked Pangor Runa to other zones as well. Many Chimbo-area villagers worked as muleteers during the dry season (around May through August). The muleteers traveled down to the coastal lowlands and then up to Pangor, bringing tropical products such as plantains, semirefined sugar (*panela*), and sugarcane liquor (*trago* or *aguardiente*). For these products, as for maize, the Pangoreños gave them potatoes in return.

Finally, I should note that Pangor hacienda residents regularly attended the weekly market in Sicalpa and Cajabamba. (To my knowledge, there were no hacienda stores on Pangor haciendas, as have been described for some haciendas elsewhere in Latin America.) The trip to the market town was an occasion for socializing and drinking with people from other haciendas as well as marketing, thereby reinforcing laborers' ties beyond their own hacienda.

The Morality of Reciprocity

These various sorts of ties that hacienda laborers cultivated with each other and beyond the hacienda are significant not only because they counterbalanced laborers' material dependence on the landlords. These exchanges took the general form that anthropologists have termed "reciprocity" or "gift" exchange—an exchange of goods and services that expresses and sustains a sense of mutual obligation in an ongoing relationship. Reciprocity has long permeated Andean life in a number of ways beyond its functions in vertical exchange. At one level, it sets the "rules of the game" that villagers follow in mobilizing labor and pursuing their material interests—what they have to give a particular kinsman in return for help with the harvest, or how to approach an older acquaintance to ask for a calf to raise (Mayer 2002:105–142). Participating in this "game" involves partly calculated moves, but it is also a kind of sensory and emotional experience, one periodically intensified on festive occasions through the flow of food and drink: "A reciprocal bond with another is the moment he patiently returns to you, lightheaded, . . . holding a sticky shot glass in a jostling crowd, . . . waiting for you to stop laughing with others to turn to him, drink the shot, and complete the cycle. This is the feeling, both a sensation and a memory, that must be rekindled on the less exuberant occasions when a favor is needed" (Colloredo-Mansfeld 1999:157). As hacienda residents followed or manipulated the "rules" of reciprocity and shared the sensory experience of reciprocity in their exchanges with kin, *compadres*, neighbors, and trading partners, they also sustained their own sense of how people should treat one another, what a good relationship was like.

Reciprocity differs from contractual or market exchange in several ways. First, the transaction is not wholly voluntary—rejecting a gift or failing to reciprocate appropriately risks damaging the relationship. Second, the terms of exchange are not set by an explicit negotiation based on open self-interest (Mauss 1990). Pangoreños did not bargain with Chimbo valley people over whether or not to give a roasted guinea pig or over the hospitality and the stuffed wheat tortillas that they might be given in return. Each side's material interests were best served by displaying generosity, hospitality, and consideration for the other. That way, the immediate transaction would go smoothly, feelings of mutual regard might grow, the visit would be repeated or reciprocated, and the relationship would continue.

Because reciprocity involves long-term hopes as well as short-term calculations, feelings and expectations about social relationships as well as material interests, it lends a distinct moral cast to economic and social life. People should recognize their dependence on one another (and, cosmically, on the divine). They should not be too proud to accept others' help or gifts, as though they did not need anybody and did not wish to be in others' debt. By the same token, they should show gratitude and treat others with generosity and consideration.

Westerners—whose social life is split between the market, where open self-interest prevails, and private relationships, idealized as a realm of purely sentimental and selfless gift exchange—are prone to try to force reciprocity onto one side or the other of this split. On the one hand, we might romanticize reciprocity as pure altruism. On the other, we might dismiss the appearance of spontaneous generosity, goodwill, and moral concern that surrounds reciprocity as a mere pretense that covers up purely calculating, self-interested behavior. Mauss begins his classic analysis by opposing reality to pretense (1990:3). Yet, the thrust of his argument is to transcend these oppositions by showing that reciprocity balances and blends self-interest with an investment in social relationships that is often emotional and moral as well as practical (see Parry 1986). In pointing to the moral ideals that hacienda Runa sustained through reciprocal exchanges, therefore, I am not denying that these exchanges served their material interests.

Nor am I arguing that hacienda Runa or other rural Ecuadorians have always lived up to such ideals. Hypocrisy, manipulation, and conflict can be found among people anywhere, and they exist among Ecuadorian villagers as well. The point is a little more subtle. Even when hacienda residents or villagers today attempt to manipulate each other or evade a request for a favor, the social forms they use refer to those same moral expectations and therefore sustain them as norms. They claim to be oriented to those norms and plead practical inability to meet the request, for example. In the marketplace, the fundamental sins are stealing, forced exchange, lying, and fraud—acts that violate others' autonomy and control over their property and the integrity of contracts. It is not that such acts are virtues in Ecuadorian villages, but of more fundamental concern in local moral discourse are acts that deny people's healthy interdependence—refusing social intercourse, being stingy instead of generous, and failing to give positive consideration to others' needs and desires.[3]

Reciprocity can operate in vertical as well as horizontal relationships. Early colonial chiefs, for example, ceremoniously requested their subjects' labor as though it were a personal favor, and they "generously" distributed food, drink, and other goods to them. Hacienda-era fiesta sponsors similarly received voluntary contributions such as a guinea pig or bottles of alcohol from kin and others, and they gave food and drink to fiesta celebrants. When goods and services flow to and from a central point or figure such as a chief or fiesta sponsor, anthropologists term the pattern "redistribution" (Polanyi 1968:9–18, 148–157). Since each particular transaction that made up the pattern had a personal, giftlike character, we can say that redistribution incorporated reciprocity (Sahlins 1972). Reciprocity in both horizontal and vertical relationships helped sustain generosity and mutual consideration as norms that hacienda Runa applied in judging their overlords.

These moral norms extended to the relationship with the divine as well: reciprocity is an ontology, an understanding of people and the cosmos as inescapably interconnected through flows of energy along lines of "obligation and counterobligation" (Allen 1988:67–94). In the next chapter, I shall elaborate on how religious rituals expressed a theology of agricultural production that shaped Runa understandings of the hacienda. I prepare here for that discussion by mapping the ways hacienda-era religious life reflected and strengthened the base of hacienda residents' social triangle.

Social Networks and the Sacred

In many ways, the hacienda was the basic unit of organization for hacienda-era religious life. The resident community of each hacienda gathered once a week for early-morning prayer sessions in the hacienda chapels. Each hacienda had its own patron saint, whom laborers honored in an annual fiesta, and its own Runa *regidor* and alcaldes, who supervised the fiestas of Carnival and Corpus Christi. During these fiestas, hacienda residents engaged in a series of ritual exchanges with landlords, stewards, and overseers.

Even the ritual occasions that took the hacienda as the basic unit of organization, however, did not revolve only around the vertical relationship with the landlord. The hacienda was a community as well as a hierarchical organization, and fiestas were occasions for intensifying relationships within the resident community. They could also transform and sanctify these relationships, particularly the relationship between the fiesta sponsor and the authority who oversaw the fiesta (the *fundador* or the *regidor*). At one time, indeed, it appears that there were simultaneously two distinct, complementary *fundador* positions on Monjas Corral for the fiesta of the patron saint, reflecting the community's social organization. The lesser *fundador*, Pablo Sisa, symbolically represented the Sisa family group and its cohesion as a group as well as the Sisas' ties to the larger community.

Moreover, the hacienda did not totally encapsulate Runa religious life. Even Carnival, Corpus Christi, and the patron saint's fiesta transcended hacienda boundaries in some ways. In contrast to the classic image of closed corporate communities in which fiesta sponsorship defines community boundaries (Wolf 1955:458), it seems to have been fairly common for someone living on one hacienda to sponsor the fiesta of another hacienda's patron saint. While Saint Rose, for example, had a special responsibility for the crops, animals, and people on Monjas Corral, her reputation as a saint who could work miracles and bestow blessings was sufficient to attract sponsors from surrounding haciendas as well. Sponsors aside, many residents of nearby haciendas would come to the fiesta on Monjas Corral to honor the saint while enjoying the festivities and reinforcing their ties to people on Monjas Corral. They could also do so when the fiesta sponsors brought the image to the church in Pangor for a Mass and associated festivities.[4]

The alcaldes' fiestas, especially Carnival, were concerned in large part with the local hierarchy: Carnival was an occasion for ritual exchanges between hacienda residents and their bosses. Yet, it was also an occasion for friends, neighbors, and *compadres* within and beyond the hacienda to visit one another and renew their ties. Four months later, moreover, the alcaldes were responsible for organizing what we might call war games for Corpus Christi. Bands of indigenous "soldiers" staged a kind of "play" (Q. *pukllay*) that both expressed and spanned hacienda boundaries and that offered an experience potentially threatening to the ethnic hierarchy.

An elderly mestizo informant from the town of Pangor recalled bands of indigenous people, each band from a different hacienda, battling for control of the town plaza. Former Monjas Corral residents did not mention a battle in the town plaza, but this account accords with ethnographers' descriptions from other areas of Ecuador and the central Andes. It is a widespread custom on festive occasions for bands of indigenous people from surrounding villages to ritually "invade" the town plaza and fight each other for control of the plaza. As others have suggested, this custom clearly expresses and reinforces boundaries between communities—in the Pangor case, hacienda communities. At the same time, this play displays a fierceness that has come to be associated broadly with indigenous people and that mestizo townspeople could find threatening. Indeed, one indigenous informant spoke of the "soldiers'" activities as "inspiring fear" (manchachi-k/-shpa; AYu 7/16/92 and 6/17/95).

Several Monjas Corral informants' accounts suggest another dimension to this play not so frequently mentioned in anthropological accounts of ritual battles. The bands of soldiers did not simply represent themselves and their own hacienda communities. The alcaldes invited young men from other haciendas as well as their own hacienda to come and play the role of soldiers. These young men borrowed or rented soldiers' clothing from townspeople. My informants describe the bands of soldiers, perhaps forty or fifty in all, riding about on horseback, marching in lines like military conscripts, and firing off rifles into the air or even at each other across the hills. Each band had a *capitán* who gave orders to the others. In other words, the participants actually "played" at being soldiers.

In addition to the link to "ritual battle" traditions, then, we should also consider this play as an instance of the pan-Andean tradition of festive mimicry or play, sometimes mocking play, with identities not necessarily one's own but with which one is in some way engaged. White priests, lawyers, and foreign tourists are sometimes targets of such mockery. During Carnival or Corpus Christi in Pangor, men also dressed and danced as indigenous women, as *yumbos*, or "wild" Indians from the eastern lowlands, and as birds.

The war play was not an open, explicit representation of an indigenous uprising (it would probably not have been tolerated if it were). One Monjas Corral informant, Alberto Yumbo, spoke of two sides in the play war at Corpus Christi, "Ecuadorians" and "*curuchupas*"; he rather uncertainly identified *curuchupas* as Peruvians. "*Curuchupas*" is, historically, a derogatory name for Eloy Alfaro's conservative enemies. Other, somewhat older, informants clearly identified *curuchupas* as such, and they spoke of Alfaro, the liberal revolutionary leader, as having taken indigenous people's side against the white lords. Given these memories and the social content of the Liberal Revolution, it is possible to see in the bands of indigenous soldiers joined from various haciendas something more than mere play. As so often happens in ritual play, without being fully aware of it, perhaps, people flirted with possibilities that were too serious, too potentially threatening to the social order, to be allowed routine expression in any other form.

Some other important fiestas were not centered on the hacienda at all. Monjas Corral residents participated in various fiestas and pilgrimages outside of the hacienda, reaffirming their connections to a broader world. They would go "visit" the Virgin of Navag in the *páramo* between Pangor and the central basin, the Virgin of Pungalá, on the eastern side of the central basin, or the Señor de la Salud, a reputedly powerful image of Jesus as the Lord of Health, in Santiago, Bolívar province. A particularly important local pilgrimage was that in early June to Aychi, on the edge of Monjas Corral, at the high point of the pass over the mountains between Pangor and the maize region. Pilgrims from both regions would meet on the feast day at Aychi to pay homage to the Virgin of Aychi.

The religious life of Pangor hacienda residents, then, was multifaceted. Hacienda prayer sessions and fiestas did, in some ways, reaffirm the separate identity of each hacienda community and its internal hierarchy. At the same time, religion could express and intensify forms of solidarity among hacienda residents and their connections with others beyond their own hacienda.

Sense of Identity

Indigenous hacienda residents' sense of their own and others' identities emerged out of these patterns of social, economic, and religious life. On one level, people did have a sense of belonging to a particular hacienda community; they were Monjas Corraleños (or Monjaskuna; or Guangopeños, Ajospamba people, and so on). Joaquina Niamo's account of her reluctance to leave Monjas Corral as an adult is revealing both of hacienda residents' sense of proprietorship over hacienda resources and of social boundaries between haciendas. Her husband wanted to move the family to a neighboring hacienda, Ajospamba, but

> I didn't listen. "Why should I go? Husband, bad person, . . . in the hacienda land, they'll stinge [Q. mitsanga] the water, they'll stinge firewood. They'll stinge pasture. They'll stinge the path. Why should I go? Here, the children . . . are growing up. Right here I'll stay, come what may. I won't go."
> BL Who did you think would stinge?

JN The people [gente], the people of that hacienda.

BL The Runa themselves?

JN Sure, among ourselves, the little fellow human beings over there on Ajos. (8/22/1992)

A well-known hacienda-era song, "Gallegos Runa," also suggests that residents of privately owned haciendas sometimes identified with their landlord in opposition to people of other haciendas. The first verse and refrain are as follows:

I'm a Gallegos Runa, ay, caramba![5]	Gallegos runami kani, ¡ay, caramba!
I'm not afraid of anybody, ay, caramba!	Pitapish mana manchani, ¡ay, caramba!
[Refrain]	
I'm a Gallegos Runa.	Gallegos runami kani.

The Gallegos were one of the leading landowning family groups in the province, with several haciendas in Pangor. My host during fieldwork, Avelino Shagñay, explained that the verse evoked scenes of Runa men drinking and boasting belligerently to one another: "I'm not afraid of anybody because, even if I'm put in jail for hurting someone in a fight, my *patrón* [boss] Gallegos will use his influence to get me out."

On the other hand, Runa's identification with their own hacienda community was balanced by migration, intermarriage, and social ties across hacienda boundaries. Gabriel Niamo's account of some of his father's difficulties as overseer offers a counterpoint to his sister Joaquina's comments concerning hacienda resources. The steward demanded that the overseer extract labor by force from neighbors who poached Monjas Corral resources: "From up in Guangopud, . . . they would cross over into this mountain with animals, or for firewood. Then the steward would order him to be harsh, to beat them, to just force them to come out and work. . . . In turn, my late father, 'Why should I do that to the hacienda people, to our own people [propio gente kakpitik]?' he said; he didn't beat them" (6/16/1995). I do not know for certain how Mariano Niamo in fact handled this dilemma as overseer, but his son, at least, assumes that he should have resisted the steward's demands. The thoughts and words that Tayta Gabriel attributes to his father presume a sense of empathy with the laborers on a neighboring hacienda as people essentially in the same boat, members of the same broad moral community.

Ethnic and racial categories reflected and reinforced ambivalent vertical relationships and horizontal solidarities. Pangor Quichua has several terms to refer to nonindigenous ethnic/racial status: *yurak* (literally, "white");

mishu or *nishu,* maybe derived from mestizo; and a pejorative word, *tsala.* As used in Quichua, the word *amo,* "boss" or "lord," also has racial and ethnic connotations, and it was the word I heard most frequently used to refer to non-Runa.

The word *amo* has a complex set of meanings. Paired with *tayta* (father) and used in the diminutive, it has been incorporated into the most common Quichua name for God, Tayta Amito. Even during my fieldwork in the 1990s, Quichua speakers' everyday conversation still occasionally manifested an assumption that *amos* were a fundamentally different and, in some sense, better sort of human being (see Chapter 7).

Until the end of the hacienda period, mestizos expected and forced indigenous people to address them with great deference. Perhaps in an allusion to the Christ Child, hacienda residents addressed landlords as *niño/niña* (Sp. "child"). But deference was required even in the absence of any particular relationship; it was not only the deference of peasant laborers toward their landowner but the deference of one "race" toward another. Deferential formulas often included the word *amo* or *amito,* or a Spanish word with a similar meaning, *patrón* (master, boss), often used in the diminutive. Quichua speakers also used (and still use) some Spanish words that historically referred to aristocratic status to signify nonindigenous racial status, for example, *caballero* ("gentleman") and *señor (señora).*

The alien power that the word *amo* seems to signify, however, is not necessarily benevolent, divine, or morally superior. Like North American parents who tell misbehaving children that a bogeyman will come and get them, indigenous parents in Pangor sometimes hush children who resist going to sleep at night with the warning, "Kuku amo shamunga" (The devil *amo* will come). Two acquaintances from southern Chimborazo told me this practice had taught them from childhood to fear mestizos "in our bones" (JC 7/19/1992). While hacienda residents may have sometimes viewed their landlords as racially superior, they also sometimes viewed them as having a compact with the devil. In either case, any sense of identification with their landlords had to be complicated by the perception that *amos* were fundamentally "other."

The figure of the *kuku amo,* the devil *amo* as bogeyman, brings to mind Mary Weismantel's incisive analysis of similar images of terrifying whites, such as the *pishtaco* of Peruvian and Bolivian folklore, a man who rapes, extracts body fat, and kills. Weismantel shows that, in recounting stories about such figures, indigenous Andeans assert the need to erect boundaries around an autonomous space of safety and solidarity in the face of racialized violence, even when whites are a familiar part of the local social landscape and absolutely closed borders are impossible (2001:6–16). In warning their children about the *kuku amo*, hacienda Runa taught them that comparative safety lay among Runa and not in any bonds they might come to feel with landlords.

On the other hand, Pangor Runa refer to the people of the maize region in Bolívar province not so much as mestizos or *amos* as by the geographic designation *provincia gente* ("province people"). Their language and dress marked *provincia gente* as nonindigenous, but *provincia gente* were anomalous as mestizos: like Runa, they were country people who worked the land, and their trading relationships with Pangoreños were essentially symmetric. If, as Weismantel suggests, Andeans view identity as emerging from social interaction (2001:191–192), perhaps the designation of *provincia gente* was a way of recognizing these common bonds among the people (*gente*) of Pangor haciendas and the Chimbo valley people.

Hacienda residents shared a sense of common racial and ethnic identity as *runa* (Q.), or *indígenas* (Sp.), with Quichua-speaking residents of other haciendas and autonomous communities. In Quichua, *runa* and its plural, *runakuna*, can refer to human beings in general, to an adult man of unspecified ethnicity, or to indigenous people and indigenous men in particular, depending on the context. Mestizos sometimes use the word *runa* as a racial insult, so indigenous people generally avoid the term when speaking in Spanish.[6] Instead, they refer to themselves in Spanish as *indígenas;* older people sometimes use the term *naturales*, from the Spanish colonial designation for "natives."[7]

As we saw in the last chapter, racial and ethnic identities are the product of a complex history involving both state and elite impositions and grassroots responses. Indigenous identity is ambivalent, and has probably long been so to those who bear it, implying social inferiority as well as membership in a culturally distinct moral community. Nonetheless, indigenous hacienda residents' sense of sharing a common ethnic-racial identity with other Runa on the same hacienda, on other haciendas, and in autonomous communities was one way they recognized a broadly "horizontal" dimension to the social triangle—an "us" with whom they shared similar cultural practices, social conditions, and bonds of kinship and friendship.

A related point can be made regarding much of what I have said about the base of the triangle. *Compadrazgo* and saints' feasts had their historical origins as such in European Catholicism; hacienda Runa did not create them out of nothing. The practice of exchange between different ecological zones such as Pangor and the Chimbo valley predated haciendas. Yet, under the conditions set by broad structural forces and bequeathed to them by history, hacienda residents continually re-created a social base in the course of building their families, providing for their subsistence, sharing drinks and laughs with others in town, playing at baptizing bread babies in the maize country, engaging cosmic forces, and finding ways to accommodate, evade, or resist hacienda demands. Again, "triangle" and "base" make for too simple a metaphor if they are taken to imply that the vertical and horizontal dimensions were always separate and distinguishable, that an autonomous indigenous society existed untouched by relations of power. Earlier in this chapter, I took pains to point out the complex links between the hacienda's power structure and the social hierarchy among indigenous residents, and I will return to this theme in later chapters. The metaphor of the triangle or, indeed, the distinction between the "vertical" and the "horizontal," is only useful as a first approximation and as a way of focusing analytic attention on different aspects of society in turn.

The next two chapters analyze both horizontal and vertical dimensions of hacienda society but emphasize the (relatively) horizontal as a source of critique and resistance to power. In Chapter 4, I explore how religious rituals elevated reciprocity and redistribution to cosmic principles governing agricultural production and authority. In Chapter 5, I argue that the same principles informed hacienda residents' critical vision of landlords' behavior and their resistance.

CHAPTER 4

Saint Rose's Blessings

One room in the central administrative complex of the hacienda Monjas Corral served as a chapel. Its main fixture was a framed print about three feet high of a fair-skinned, rosy-cheeked woman cradling a child in her arms. Historians of Latin American church iconography might identify the image as Saint Rose of Lima, who lived in the late sixteenth and early seventeenth centuries and devoted herself to prayer and severe self-mortification (Flores Galindo 1987:203). To the local people, however, she was simply Santa Rosa, their Saint Rose, who appeared one day by the brook that bears her name. She might be referred to with special respect as Mama Virgen Santa Rosa, Mother Virgin Saint Rose, or with affection in the diminutive as *virgencita*. A visitor to the hacienda chapel would probably have found several candles burned down to different degrees in front of the image. Laborers would place them there after rubbing them over their animals to commend the animals to Saint Rose's care and to ask her to make them fertile.

August on Monjas Corral was a month of clear, sunny skies, sometimes freezing nights, and a nearly constant strong wind. The wind made it hard to walk on exposed hilltops and slopes; it could lift a man's heavy wool poncho and blow it up around his head. The sun dried the paths and cultivated fields, turning them to dust that rose up in clouds as one walked. Toward the end of the month, however, the wind began to die down, some days were overcast, and there was even an occasional light shower.

At this point, hacienda residents celebrated a feast to secure Saint Rose's blessings, above all, the fertility of their animals and crops. Fiesta sponsors designated by the *fundadores* hired a priest to say Mass, carried the image in a procession, and supplied abundant food, drink, and entertainment. After the feast, Saint Rose could be depended on to bring rain in September, and people could start planting their potatoes and other crops. Over the next several months, they would lay small piles of seed potatoes in front of the image and ask Saint Rose for her blessing.[1]

Patron saints' feasts and other calendrical religious feasts are an old and widespread feature of Catholic religiosity and a venerable topic of Latin American ethnography. Anthropologists have debated their origins and significance for autonomous, landowning indigenous communities but have given much less attention to their role on haciendas (see Chance and Taylor 1985; Greenberg 1981:1–22). In this chapter, I follow a number of Andeanists who have explored rituals of reciprocity and redistribution among people and sacred beings understood to regenerate fertility (Abercrombie 1998; Allen 1988; Bastien 1978). Festive reciprocity intensified the bonds among hacienda residents. Religious practices and understandings of fertility also legitimated certain kinds of social relations, generating prestige and authority for those who redistributed a portion of their bounty in the fiesta while implying condemnation of those who rejected reciprocity (Cancian 1965; Taussig 1980).

This is not to say the fiesta was a purely autonomous indigenous creation. Historically, Spanish conquerors, administrators, missionaries, and settlers brought the Catholic notion of a saint and patron saints' feasts to the Andes (see Abercrombie 1998:223–258; Christian 1981; Foster 1960). Priests derived some of their income from the fees that fiesta sponsors paid them for saying Mass, and they promoted and attempted to regulate saints' feasts as occasions for instilling church teachings. In some areas where autonomous indigenous villages retained land, mestizos in parish centers imposed heavy fiesta obligations on indigenous villagers as a mechanism for extracting wealth (Burgos Guevara 1997:168–185; M. Harris 1964:25–35). In Pangor, landlords no doubt sometimes brought images of particular saints to their haciendas to establish them as patron saints, and they supported the authority of *fundadores*. The latter were at once the linchpin at the center of cycles of reciprocity and redistribution and crucial intermediaries in the hacienda's power structure.

On the other hand, indigenous people in Pangor, as in other parts of Latin America, developed conceptions of the saints and ways of honoring them that diverged from Catholic orthodoxy. Landlords and priests had only a limited role at most in the selection of *fundadores* and annual fiesta sponsors. Sponsors asked landlords' permission to congregate in the hacienda chapel and yards for the feast, and they paid priests to say Mass in the parish center, but fiestas required no other mestizo presence or supervision. Indeed, landlords and stewards sometimes seem to have absented themselves out of fear that alcohol might embolden laborers inclined to insubordination. Thus, while indigenous Catholicism was never a fully autonomous creation, saints' feasts did constitute a realm of partial autonomy for hacienda residents from the power of landlords and the church and state. Hacienda residents further elaborated their understandings of fertility and divinity in household planting rites, another realm of relative autonomy.

After a general overview of saints and fiestas in Pangor, I will describe the fiesta of Saint Rose and agricultural rites in order to make several points. First, Pangor Runa conceived of their harvests and livestock as gifts received in reciprocal exchange with Saint Rose and other beings. Saint Rose expected homage in the form of candles, prayers, and, most important, the annual fiesta in her honor, all of which manifested an attitude of respect that Pangor Runa talk about as "remembering" or "thinking of" (*yuyarina*) her. In return, she brought the rains and made their fields and animals fertile. Prayers and special, shared meals at planting were, similarly, a form of homage that God and other beings would reciprocate by making the seeds grow and yield a harvest.

Mauss (1990) argues that gifts remain spiritually linked to the donor even when they are in the recipient's hands, and I suggest that one way this is true is that the use to which the recipient puts the gift is often of concern to the giver. Rural Ecuadorian gift-giving etiquette often assumes that people give gifts out of a particular sense of the recipient's needs or desires and with particular intentions in mind. The recipient's failure to fulfill those intentions is a kind of rejection of the gift. For example, when a woman in San Ramón gave her younger half sister some hand-me-down children's clothing for the sister's children to wear and the sister, instead, sold the clothing, the donor commented angrily, "What I give is not good enough for her." Villagers apply the same principle to God: harvesters who let grain be trampled and people who waste food are rejecting God's gift, and God may punish them by leaving them hungry in the future. Those who have argued that reciprocity privileges use values over exchange value (e.g., Taussig 1980) are correct in the sense that gifts come with use intentions attached (see also Lyons 1994b:Chap. 2). This does not mean that gifts should never be passed on to others—some gifts are *meant* to be shared. The divine blessings of agricultural fertility in Pangor were that sort of gift.

While human beings are fully capable of conceiving of deities who give them things without any broader ethical concern for what they do with the bounty, and there are Andean cases of saints whose blessings seem to fall disproportionately on commercial elites (see, e.g., Lagos 1993), that is not how Pangor Runa conceived of Saint Rose's and God's role in agricultural production. Within the fiesta itself, the main way that people gave to Saint Rose was through other people. In planting rites, similarly, the sharing of food was an integral aspect of the homage that God and other beings would "reciprocate" by making the seeds fertile. The prayers that accompanied planting also expressed a broader assumption that God gave people food to satisfy their needs and for them to share generously with others.

In the last part of this chapter, I analyze how the fiesta helped reproduce social hierarchy on the hacienda. Elders and, above all, *fundadores* gained authority by "serving the Virgin" (Saint Rose). Young couples gained a stake in this social hierarchy by undertaking their first fiesta sponsorship, a rite of passage into full, adult personhood.

SERVING THE SAINTS
Saints and Other Beings

In official Catholicism, the saints are persons who lived an exemplary life and have been recognized by the church as capable of interceding with God to secure favors (miracles) for their devotees. The church has also historically promoted a similar devotion to other entities, such as the Sacred Heart of Jesus, a nineteenth-century symbol of resistance to secular liberalism and "modernism" to which the García Moreno regime officially consecrated the nation.

Baltazara Llongo, an elderly woman, told me a story about the image of the Sacred Heart in Ajospamba that displays some of the ways local conceptions of saints depart from orthodox Catholic doctrine. She said her father told her that the image originated in a previous epoch, the age of the Incas. This epoch ended in a cataclysmic "judgment," or "world turning" (*juicio vueltana*), "at the moment of the 12:00 Mass," when the local church and the people inside were buried. In the same judgment, the formerly totally flat land was transformed into the broken, mountainous land it is today.[2] After some time, the image miraculously appeared on top of the ground, and the landowner found it. Recognizing it as a *tayta amito* (a male saint), he took it to the hacienda house and sponsored a Mass for it every year. Eventually, his successor took the saint to Quito, but the saint kept returning to Ajospamba until he finally cut off its toe. He then sent a printed image to Ajospamba to take the place of the original figurine. The landowner also appointed one of the laborers, Mama Baltazara's ancestor, to sponsor the Mass and, in subsequent years, to see to it, as *fundador,* that others sponsored a Mass. Mama Baltazara's family continued to supervise the fiesta as *fundadores* until the agrarian reform (BL 7/24/92).

This story exemplifies several aspects of Pangor Runa's conceptions of saints. In this as in several other local cases, saints' images miraculously appeared or were "born" (*nacerishka*) in the places over whose fertility they now preside. They had a life of their own, especially three-dimensional figurines or statues. While Quichua speakers use the Spanish word *imagen* (image), these images themselves were the saints, or at least living manifestations of the saint, not simply images of a saintly human being. The images' repeated return to the rural places where they first appeared was a common motif in sixteenth-century Spanish apparition stories. William Christian interprets this motif as an expression of tensions between local religion and official church control and between Spaniards' rural livelihoods and their concentrated, urban-style settlement patterns (1981:75–76, 91).

Given the associations between patron saints and agricultural fertility in Pangor, we might interpret the Ajospamba saint's local rootedness and the landowner's forcible removal of the saint as an expression of the tension between agricultural production based on Runa labor and the expropriation of that production by an urban-based landowning class. At the same time, this story appears to grant landowners a significant and primordial role in local fertility as those who first found and recognized the saint, established the fiesta, and appointed the ancestral *fundador*. Perhaps that is not surprising, given *fundadores'* role as intermediaries and the fact the story comes to us from a family of *fundadores*.

Landlords play no role, however, in the story I was told of Saint Rose's appearance on Monjas Corral. She first appeared standing on a rock or pasturing some sheep by a stream on the hacienda. She was then brought into the hacienda chapel to "live" there. Hacienda residents venerated the saint with candles, but one night a mouse knocked over one of the candles, setting the hacienda house on fire. Saint Rose burned with the hacienda house. A white dove, it is said, emerged from the flames and flew up into the sky. After that, Saint Rose appeared to one of the laborers in a dream, saying, "I have not gone away. I am right here, living sadly in the place where the hacienda [house] burned. Make a little portrait for me to dwell in that." This laborer established himself as *fundador* by purchasing the print described above for the saint to inhabit (GN 8/23/92; JN/MY 6/29/1992).[3]

A third case exemplifies how some saints have been fit into long-standing Andean notions of sacred places. Aychi is a rocky mountain in the southwestern corner of Monjas Corral at the highest point on the path between Pangor and Bolívar province, the kind of place that is treated as powerful and sacred throughout much of the Andes. A small rock shrine there is dedicated to the Virgin of Aychi. The Virgin is said to have appeared to a traveler in a dream. Two other rock outcroppings nearby are identified as Tayta Aychi and Wawa Aychi, Father Aychi and Child Aychi. As a mountain, Aychi is or has a living spirit owner, ambiguously identified with one or all three of these, Virgen, Tayta, or Wawa; perhaps the three are different manifestations of the same living mountain. A village bordering Monjas Corral at the base of one of the paths leading up to the mountain houses a figurine of the Virgin of Aychi in its chapel. About a foot tall, the figurine presumably represents or manifests the Virgin as she appeared to the traveler in his dream. Mass is officially said annually in honor of this Virgin; the fiesta in the village is combined with a pilgrimage up to the mountain.

Several people explained to me that God appointed the saints to be his *muchachos*, or "servant boys." Another metaphor compares the relationship between God and the saints to that between a landowner and his stewards.[4] Nonetheless, the saints are seen to have autonomous power to bestow blessings or inflict punishments. *Fundadores* promoted the reputation of their particular saints as both "miraculous" and "punishing." To those who appealed to the saint and honored it through sponsorship, the saint would give blessings of good health, good harvests, healthy and fertile animals, sometimes even a wife or husband to an unmarried devotee. Conversely, the saint might visit some misfortune, such as the death of an animal, on those who evaded or reneged on their ritual obligations. Despite the diversity of origins and place associations, these blessings and punishments do not vary a great deal from saint to saint.[5]

Since numerous ethnographies of religion in the central Andes emphasize mountain lords (e.g., Allen 1988; Bastien 1978), it is worth saying a few words about the role of mountains in Pangor. Aychi seems a bit unusual locally in the degree to which the mountain as such is an object of veneration, almost overshadowing the Virgin. For the most part, only shamanic specialists interact ritually with mountains (*urkukuna*). A few people told me that they invoked mountains at planting, or they were said by others to do so. In general, however, the saints and God, and not the mountains per se, are the focus of both collective and individual or household ritual. Some people indicated to me that this situation predated the 1960s; a local catechist, on the other hand, attributed it to the biblical emphasis of both post–Vatican II Catholicism and Protestantism and the questioning of traditional practices that both have promoted.

Saints and mountains contrast in moral character. Saints may punish someone who evades fiesta sponsorship, but they are essentially benevolent sources of health and fertility. Mountains are more ambivalent, dangerous, and wild figures; they are as likely to be associated with the devil as with God. Mountains are said sometimes to aid in shamanic witchcraft; there are mountains that, when appropriately asked, may kill a person. The mountains are also capable of benevolence and moral authority, and shamans may call on them for aid in curing witchcraft or other afflictions. Agustín Choca attributes his knowledge of healing techniques in part to dreams in which mountain spirits have given him instruction. Some mountains, he insists, are *Dios parte,* servant boys or stewards under God's authority, just like the saints, while others belong to "the other side." Stories circulate of healing séances in which mountain spirits tell about the afterlife and describe, in graphic detail and in a stern tone reminiscent of hacienda-era priests' sermons, how sinners are punished. Only saints, however, not mountains as such, are objects of regular devotion through annual festivals.

Fiestas and Fiesta Sponsorship

Table 2 summarizes the most important local festivals that residents of Monjas Corral and neighboring haciendas regularly participated in as sponsors. The dates of these celebrations mostly follow the standard Catholic calendar.

The positions of religious authority and responsibility associated with fiestas were of two basic kinds. In Pangor, as in other places around Latin America, individual couples annually took on the burden of sponsoring the fiesta as a form of devotion to the saint and service to the community. The generic name for these positions was *prioste.* More unusual is the existence in Pangor (and elsewhere in Chimborazo) of higher, long-term authorities who appointed the *priostes,* termed *fundadores* in the case of the saints' fiestas and *regidores* in the case of Carnival and Corpus Christi. *Fundador* means "founder"; the *fundadores* generally traced their position back through inheritance to the person or couple who initiated the fiesta. They considered themselves servants of the saint; they were the special custodians of the image. They generally served until old age forced them to pass the position on to a younger sibling or to someone in the next generation.

The role of *regidor* was similarly a long-term position, but it differed in some important respects from that of *fundador.* It was not essentially inherited; instead, officially, the *regidor* was appointed by the priest. The *regidor* acted as an intermediary between the priest and the resident community, with responsibility for maintaining standards of upright behavior within the community. For example, the *regidor* was supposed to see to it that young people involved in sexual liaisons promptly married. The *regidor* was aided in these functions by the sponsors he appointed for Carnival and Corpus Christi, who were termed alcaldes. The alcaldes carried a *vara,* or staff of office, during their year of service.[6]

TABLE 2. *Annual Fiestas in the Monjas Corral Area*

Name	Dates	Description
Noche Buena (Christmas Eve), Año Nuevo (New Year's Day)	Dec. 24, Jan. 1	New alcaldes ceremonially inaugurated by priest in church in Pangor
Carnival	Variable, Feb. 3–Mar. 9	Major fiesta, sponsored by alcaldes. Hacienda residents presented gifts to landowners, ate and drank in hacienda yard
Corpus (Corpus Christi)	Variable, May 21–June 24	Alcaldes provided food and drink in hacienda yard
Aychi	ca. June 2	Mass and pilgrimage to mountain shrine
Corazón de Jesús (Sacred Heart)	June 25	Feast of patron saint of haciendas Guangopud and Ajospamba; *fundadores* were Runa hacienda residents
Santiago (St. James)	July 25	Feast of patron saint of town of Pangor, with mestizo *fundadores* from town
Virgen del Rosario	Aug. 28	Feast of patron saint of town of Pangor; mestizo *fundadores* from town
Santa Rosa (St. Rose of Lima)	Aug. 30	Feast of patron saint of Monjas Corral

The prestige and authority associated with all of these positions were partly shared by both members of a married couple. The position of *fundador* was inherited, preferentially, by the eldest offspring without regard to gender and was shared with that person's spouse; the *fundadores* of any particular saint were thus a couple, *fundador* (male) and *fundadora* (female). In Monjas Corral, the last *fundador* acquired the position through marriage to the *fundadora*, then a widow. Sponsors were likewise generally couples, with women taking primary responsibility for food preparation and men for most of the more public functions.

Within the category of *priostes* for saints' feasts, there were generally six roles carrying different levels of material burden and prestige. Accounts are somewhat inconsistent as to the rank order of the lower and intermediate types of sponsorship, but it was roughly as follows, from the least to the most expensive and prestigious:

1. *chamicero* (bonfire sponsor)
2. *toro prioste* (bull sponsor)
3. *albacero* (>*albazo*, a kind of band music played at dawn on fiesta days)
4. *pendonero* (>*pendón*, a banner carried in processions)
5. *sermón prioste/uchu prioste* (sermon sponsor or little sponsor)
6. *jatun priostes* (two couples; big sponsors)

The fiesta of Saint Rose began with several days of ritual visits by the *fundadores* and other people to the house of each *prioste* in turn. The *fundadores* formally blessed the *priostes* and exchanged food and drink with them and the accompanying celebrants. These visits led up to a communal celebration on a Saturday night in the hacienda chapel, where celebrants recited prayers, set candles before the saint's image, and ate and drank. The *chamicero* made a bonfire, contracted a band to play festive music, and supplied fireworks, food, and drink. The *albacero* supplied hot cinnamon water with an infusion of cane alcohol (*canela*).

The next morning, on a Sunday close to the official feast date of August 30, the sponsors carried Saint Rose at the head of a procession down to the town of Pangor and into the church for Mass. The big sponsors (*jatun priostes*) and the little or sermon sponsor (*uchu prioste, sermón prioste*) made prior arrangements with the priest for Mass and paid the bulk of his fee, though all the sponsors contributed. The festivities continued after Mass, sometimes in the town and other years back at the hacienda. The *jatun priostes* contracted a band and costumed dancers. The *toro prioste* brought wild bulls from the *páramo* and contributed an embroidered blanket that was tied onto the back of a bull as a prize for the man who was able to untie and grab it.

On Monday, the sponsors designated for the following year's fiesta carried Saint Rose at the head of a procession back from the town to the hacienda chapel. In Monjas Corral, the festivities continued with more drinking, eating, and music at the sponsors' houses. At the end, the sponsors collected monetary contributions from the celebrants and gave them to the *fundadores* to help offset their costs (Figures 11, 12, and 13).

RECYCLING THE BLESSINGS

Based on oral accounts of fiestas during the hacienda period and up to the mid-1980s (when the system of *fundadores* and sponsors was still function-

FIGURE 11.   *Virgilio Guailla, Gabriel Niamo, and Virgilio Guailla's son with the image of Saint Rose*

ing) and on the ordinary practices of fiestas today, we can reconstruct something of what these fiestas must have been like. The fiesta was an occasion for multiple cycles and levels of reciprocity and redistribution, with food and drink being some of the most important objects of exchange. Andeanist readers will be familiar with some aspects of these festive exchanges of food and drink, which are pervasive and have been sensitively described by Allen (1988) and Colloredo-Mansfeld (1999). I do not assume familiarity on the part of all readers, however, and I want to illustrate both the intensity and complexity of reciprocal exchanges and the central role of *fundadores* in Pangor's fiestas. For this illustration, I focus on the *fundadores'* visits to the sponsors' houses in the first days of the fiesta. The *fundadores* (husband and wife), along with people invited to accompany them, would go to the houses

FIGURE 12. *Procession with the image of Saint Rose*

of the *priostes*, bearing gifts of food. Let us go along in our imagination, then, on one of these visits. I use the present tense to make this description more vivid, but it is a reconstruction of something I did not observe.

> We start at the *fundadores'* house, where a party of people has congregated in the morning. During the whole year, the *fundadores* have been raising animals for this occasion, some to slaughter and cook, others to sell in order to buy other food items. On this morning, some of their relatives, neighbors, and friends have come with guinea pigs, bread, or eggs to help them out. They serve good food and drink to each one. For the visit to the sponsors' house, they prepare a number of *medianos*, or assemblages of food, consisting of pairs of roasted guinea pigs laid down in the form of a cross, chicken, potatoes, eggs, cheese, bread, oranges, fish, and bottles of sugarcane alcohol.
>
> The *fundadores* leave their own house, any small children, and domestic animals in the care of trusted friends for the week. People in the accompanying party help them carry the *medianos*, especially women relatives of the *fundadores*. As the *fundadores* and their party set off, the caretakers say laughingly, "Don't get drunk!" knowing full well they will. The friends may have to go that evening to bring them back from

the *priostes'* house in order for them to rest up for the following day's visit to another pair of *priostes*.

As the *fundadores* approach the sponsors' house, the sponsors walk out to them, greet them, and kneel to receive their blessing. They then invite the *fundadores* into the yard of the house. There, the *medianos* are formally displayed on a table or cloths laid on the ground and presented to the *priostes* as a gift. The *priostes* attend to the visitors with large servings of food brought out from their kitchen. At some point, they present the *fundadores* with a big bowl of food, practically overflowing, and including the head of a guinea pig and a chicken leg. The *fundadores* do not eat this dish themselves but redirect it to someone else who they have ensured is sitting nearby. By accepting the food, this person agrees to sponsor the following year's fiesta.

During the course of the day and into the evening, at any time when food is not being served, most likely, someone is serving cane alcohol to someone else. The *fundadores* offer shot glasses or cups of cane alcohol to the *priostes* and others, the *priostes* to the *fundadores* and others. Other men pull out a bottle or jug and make the rounds with it. When a man with alcohol holds out a shot glass, the recipient takes the glass,

FIGURE 13. *Andrés Yépez serves Vicente Yubaillo a drink.*

holds it up, and, directing himself to someone else nearby, says, "Salud" (Health) or "Uñashun" (Let's drink); after drinking, the recipient returns the glass with thanks to the server. The server gives the next drink to the other person nearby whom the recipient has addressed, who similarly directs the following drink to someone else, and so the server goes from person to person. Each act in the sequence is a statement of one person's esteem for another (whether a sincere statement or not), and someone offered a drink cannot easily refuse without insulting the server and the person who directed the drink to him or her. The recipient does not necessarily have to empty the glass; the server accepts it back with some alcohol still in it, especially from female recipients. Occasionally, a recipient who wishes to express special esteem for the server (or perhaps just wishes to get the server drunk more quickly) says to the server, "Ishki uñashun" (Let's both drink); after drinking, the recipient then holds out the glass for the server to refill, making sure it is good and full before handing it back for the server to drink.

After several hours of this, most of the celebrants, especially the men, are at least tipsy, and some have passed out. The bottles and jugs are only temporarily stowed away, and those who have closed their eyes are shaken awake when the hosts and their assistants bring out more food—first, bowls of soup with meat, then plates piled high with potatoes and guinea pig, perhaps an additional main course, and finally bowls of sweet gruel.

Pastoral agents since the colonial period have been complaining that, for indigenous Andeans, a fiesta just serves as an excuse for a *borrachera*, a mass drinking spree that has no relation to the fiesta's "true" religious meaning. The Synod of Quito in 1594 named the "vice of *borracheras*" as the "principal impediment" to the Christianization of the Indians and directed priests to "preach to the Indians . . . [against] this vice . . . ; and . . . visit their towns . . . on horseback to prevent these gatherings . . . , and they may punish the Indians they find in them, and spill out their chicha [fermented beverage], and break the vessels" (López [1594] 1978:136–137). Three hundred years later, a delegate reported to the bishop of Riobamba that "the fiestas in the villages are an occasion for general drunkenness and many disorders, rather than for religious rites to foster piety" (*Visita 1893). A parish priest lamented in 1915, "They have no . . . celebration without alcohol . . . what measures, what remedies can one take? I've only managed up to now to get them to come without drinking [on the way] to the fiestas." He could bar drunks from Mass, but he could not control drinking after Mass (*Párroco 1915). Pastoral agents voice similar sentiments today.

The view that villagers use a fiesta as an "excuse" for drinking assumes that the exchange and consumption of food and drink among people has nothing to do with their relationship to the saint and God, the ostensible purpose of the fiesta. Yet, for villagers, the two are intimately connected. Mauss noted long ago that, in many cultures, humans stand in for spirits or gods as the recipients of sacrificial gifts (1990:14–18), and this is clearly an aspect of Andean fiestas (Abercrombie 1998:349–350). When the *fundadores* and *priostes* slaughtered animals and prepared food to serve each other and all the guests, spent money on alcohol, and paid for a band, dancers' costumes, and so on to enliven the fiesta, they were, at the same time, serving other people and serving Saint Rose, *sacrificing* to Saint Rose.[7] In anticipation of sponsorship, villagers would designate an animal or field for Saint Rose, promising to use the product to feed celebrants or pay for drink and other expenses. They expected that Saint Rose would then watch over the animal or field with special care and evidently assumed that the saint was pleased by the great feast held in her honor. In return, Saint Rose made the *priostes'* and *fundadores'* herds increase, made their fields fertile, and maintained the agricultural fertility of the area in general so that people could continue to hold fiestas in her honor. As Abercrombie comments of Bolivian Aymara fiestas, participants' own satiation with abundant food and drink "points to the desired return for the sacrifice, which is the gods' help in providing just such plenty" (1998:501n29).

The fiesta thus encapsulated several interlinked cycles or levels of reciprocity. At the most minute level, celebrants carried out innumerable small exchanges of drink with one another. A set of *priostes* made this all possible by providing meals as well as drink, hosting the *fundadores'* visits, and securing a band and other entertainment throughout the days of the fiesta. Each of them had been served many times before as a guest at other fiestas, and now it was their turn to serve the others.

Each *prioste* couple initiated and completed their service through a cycle of reciprocal exchange with the *fundadores*. They may have asked the *fundadores* to name them as *priostes*, accompanying the request with a gift of alcohol. As guests at the previous sponsors' house, they were designated as new *priostes* by receiving the bowl of food redirected into their hands by the *fundadores*. As *priostes*, they in turn hosted the same sort of gathering, receiving the visit of the *fundadores* together with their gifts of food, feeding the *fundadores* and their accompanying party, and providing the food by which the *fundadores* designated the following year's *priostes*.

The *priostes* relied on further cycles of reciprocity within their own social networks for help in bearing the burden of fiesta sponsorship. Women close to the family could be called on to lend a hand in the kitchen. Relatives, friends, and neighbors might bring a gift of a guinea pig, a chicken, a gallon of cane alcohol; the gift, termed a *jucha* (debt), carried with it the obligation to make a similar contribution in return at some time in the future when the donor was a sponsor (see Monaghan 1990).

All of these cycles of reciprocity among human beings were encompassed within the long-term reciprocity between the fiesta celebrants and Saint Rose. The *fundadores* were lifelong servants of Saint Rose, and their ability to set out lavish displays of *medianos* for the sponsors year after year was testimony to Saint Rose's beneficence. Everyone else who participated in the festivities similarly expected her blessings, in accordance with the level of their devotion and their contributions.

Pangor Runa also shared food as a way of pleasing the divine and securing blessings in return when they "entrusted" their seed to God, the Earth, and other divinities in planting. Alberto Yumbo explained this practice, which continues today:

> If you pray to Yayito Dios [Father God], Mamita Virgen María, Allpa Mama [Earth Mother], there will always be some grain to eat. Like this: you call on other people to join you, prepare . . . some peeled corn,[8] slaughter a guinea pig, a sheep, nicely prepare that meat. You talk among wife and husband and say, "We're planting. Children, we're planting now; let's pray to Yaya Dios." . . .
>
> It seems that Yayito Dios thanks that . . . and Dios gives grain. (7/16/1992)

The prayers at planting also make clear that the divine expectation that the gift of food will be shared goes beyond the specific contexts of planting rites and fiestas themselves. Conventional prayer formulas do not simply ask for a good harvest but motivate the request in terms of the family's needs, images of eating together as a family, and the practice of serving food to others: It is you who maintains us, you who feeds us; make this seed grow, give us a harvest, in order for us to give food to other people who visit, to neighbors, to others. Year after year, Pangor Runa thus reaffirm that they are fitting subjects to ask the divine to produce a harvest not as isolated individuals or for unlimited accumulation, but as members of families that need the food, that eat together, and that share food with others.

The same idea runs through stories in which a wandering old man or a hungry beggar turns out to be God, who rewards or punishes people according to their treatment of him. In one story, the stranger appears while a group of people are threshing barley on a hacienda. Rather than welcoming him, they rudely chase him away. The barley catches fire, and the whole harvest turns to ashes. The message is clear: God withdraws his blessings of food when people are stingy.

RESPECTED ELDERS AND INSOLENT BRATS

In the fiesta, these moral and cosmological understandings concerning reciprocity and fertility also generated a hierarchical social order. The fiesta enhanced the prestige of the established couples who were able to sponsor it repeatedly and, above all, of the *fundadores,* who played such a central role in organizing and aiding the sponsors. As an obligation incumbent on recently married couples, fiesta sponsorship also incorporated young people into the community as adult but subordinate members while distinguishing adult persons from those who had not yet sponsored at all. This hierarchy was an integral part of the structure of hacienda authority (as we shall see briefly here and more fully in Chapter 7).

The Authority of Fundadores *and Elders*

The fiesta system allowed relatively wealthy, established hacienda residents to convert wealth to prestige and authority. Young couples started out on a relatively low rung on the ladder of sponsorship. Older, wealthier couples took on more burdensome types of sponsorship and were repeatedly called on to do so. The fiesta had something of a leveling effect within the community, though apparently not a strong enough effect to erase differences in wealth. Monjas Corral's fertility and ample pasturelands allowed some residents the means to sponsor the fiesta repeatedly without being reduced to utter poverty. Their large herds and harvests then ratified not only their own hard work but also the blessings of Saint Rose in repayment for their sponsorship. Established Runa couples who resisted sponsorship were criticized as *gamonales,* a term that elsewhere in the Andes refers to "rich landlords" or "rich exploiters"; "these *gamonales,* they only want to get rich, they don't want to serve the *virgen,*" people would say (JMP 9/2/1992). For those who were willing to redistribute a portion of their wealth in service to the saint and the community, on the other hand, sponsorship brought prestige and greater respect. Respect for elders was a basic assumption of life under the hacienda, and the fiesta supported this assumption (cf. Cancian 1965).

The *fundadores* themselves had substantial expenses every year in connection with the visits to the sponsors' houses. Without the possibility of observing and making a detailed account of their expenses and the contributions they received, one cannot be absolutely certain, but it does seem that they had to make a considerable net outlay. José María Pillajo, a repeated sponsor, said the *fundadores* had to spend more than a sponsor and had to be wealthy in order to bear their costs (JMP 9/2/1992). Even Avelino Shagñay, a catechist whose involvement with liberation theology has sharpened his skepticism about the saints' powers and his critical view of the old fiesta system and the *fundadores*, discounted my suggestion that others' contributions might explain the *fundadores'* ability to bear these costs. He instead recalled the fertility of the land and commented that the *virgen* gave to her devotees (9/4/1992). Thus it seemed that Saint Rose regenerated the wealth of sponsors and *fundadores*. The participation of the wealthier members of the community as sponsors and *fundadores* gave the fiesta a redistributive character.

The *fundadores* were, ideologically, paramount elders (*yuyakkuna*). They ordered people to serve as sponsors, gave them gifts to put them under obligation, arrived at their houses on the first days of the fiesta to bless them and contribute to their expenses, and acted as intermediaries between the hacienda community and its patron saint. They also administered moral guidance and punishment on other occasions (see Chapter 7). People today remember the *fundadores* as big people (*jatun*) who "gave orders" (*mandakkuna*), the analogue, in some sense, of the community presidents of today. The difference is that presidents are not respected as authority was respected in the hacienda period.

Fiesta sponsorship as an idiom of hierarchy also shaped the relationship between the mestizo townspeople of Pangor and hacienda Runa. Indigenous *fundadores* could not typically order mestizo townspeople to sponsor, but the converse was normal. The fiestas of the patron saints of the town were sponsored one day by mestizo sponsors, another day by indigenous sponsors, all of them under the authority of mestizo *fundadores*. Sponsorship of these fiestas, indeed, seems to have carried a special prestige precisely because of the racial associations. Avelino Shagñay says that his father, a laborer on Ajospamba, sponsored the fiesta of Santiago in order to be seen as a "Runa of the town, now 'seen' by the whites. Now, [other people would presumably say,] 'That man is big; one must kneel and greet him formally. And God will help him'" (8/29/92).

Young Couples as Sponsors

If the fiesta was an enactment of fundamental social values, it is not surprising that it also helped define social personhood. Fiesta sponsorship marked the difference between a youth of no account and a full person, an adult with standing among neighbors and peers, someone who had earned the right to be greeted and treated with respect. The idea that someone who had not yet sponsored a fiesta was not a complete person was expressed quite explicitly, in exactly those terms (as it still is): a nonsponsor was not a *persona*. This lack of social standing was one of the sanctions that traditionally obliged young people to take on the burden of sponsorship. Through sponsoring a fiesta one became a person (*persona tukun*).

A person's first fiesta sponsorship normally followed marriage within a few years and was associated with marriage in effecting this transformation. Avelino Shagñay described the connection in this way: "[Fiesta sponsorship] was to become big. To show that you had gotten married, so that the people would respect you. If I don't do that, the people won't respect [me]. That's what the *fundadores* said" (8/29/92). To understand fully the significance of fiesta sponsorship, then, we must examine the symbolic, economic, and political significance of marriage.

In Pangor, marital status is more important than chronological age in determining whether someone is referred to and addressed as a girl or a woman, a boy or a man. Unmarried youths in their twenties might be called by first name only, while even teenagers, at marriage, typically begin to be addressed and referred to as Tayta or Mama, followed by the first name. On a more abstract and general level, the complementary pair is the pan-Andean symbol of completeness. The married couple itself, called *kariwarmi* (male-female) in Pangor, is a common metaphor for completeness and complementarity (see Allen 1988:72–85; Platt 1986).

As a practical matter, marriage was a precondition for autonomy vis-à-vis parents during the hacienda era. Young people lived in their parents' house and were subject to their commands until sometime after marriage. They helped cook, tend to the family's animals, work the family plot, and fulfill the household's obligations to the hacienda. Even today, it is difficult for a single or widowed individual to maintain an independent household with no one else to help with farming, raising animals, cooking, and other tasks. Heavy labor obligations to the hacienda would have made it almost impossible.

This is not to say that marriage brought immediate autonomy. Generally, the groom's parents sponsored the wedding. Partly in repayment for this and the expenses of the celebration, the young husband and wife began their married life with the customary obligation to serve the husband's parents for a period of a year or more. They might also go frequently to the wife's natal home as well, staying for short periods to help the wife's parents with their agricultural and domestic labors.

Obligations to the husband's parents were often particularly burdensome to the new bride. Accounts of the "mean mother-in-law" who had nothing but criticism for her daughter-in-law's cooking or washing are commonplace. Although she did much of the cooking, the daughter-in-law did not have the right to serve the food at mealtime. Instead, the mother-in-law presented the food to each household member as her gift (see Weismantel 1988:26, 134, 171–181).

Eventually, the young couple established a separate household; if they stayed on the same hacienda, they would ask the steward for permission to build a house and for a plot to farm. They would now have more economic autonomy from their natal households—along with direct labor obligations to the hacienda. They would continue to exchange labor and other services with parents, but now on a somewhat more voluntary and balanced basis. They would also now need to exchange labor and services with others around them: labor for planting and harvesting; perhaps borrowed oxen for plowing; a horse, burro, or mule to perform some task on the hacienda; or a female animal to care for in exchange for the rights to half the offspring. They would hope to see the cattle and sheep they started out with begin to multiply into a small herd to match their growing needs as a family. And they might designate a calf or lamb for Saint Rose, knowing that in the near future they would be called on to sponsor the fiesta. They would expect that Saint Rose would look after the animal named for her with special care by protecting the lamb from being eaten by a wolf, keeping the calf from losing its balance on a steep slope. Michael Taussig notes that "marriage everywhere is held to be an especially favorable occasion for opening a cycle of reciprocal exchange" (1980:163, citing Lévi-Strauss 1964:46); *fundadores* in Pangor took the opportunity to bring the couple into a relationship of reciprocity with the saint.

The role that the obligation of fiesta sponsorship played in newly married couples' separation from parental households is not entirely clear. It is possible that newlyweds sometimes sponsored the fiesta while still living in the parental household. In that case, the parents must have borne a good part of the costs on behalf of the young couple, as perhaps a symbolic recognition of the latter's ongoing labor service, but implying further indebtedness and service. In other words, the fiesta might have renewed the debt created by the wedding feast.

Usually, however, it seems that young couples sponsored the fiesta after establishing an independent household. Fiesta sponsorship was a way for the couple to gain Saint Rose's blessings over their labors as a newly autonomous economic unit. They had to sell and slaughter livestock for the fiesta itself, but Saint Rose would repay them by providing bountiful harvests and making their (remaining) animals multiply. The general goodwill and respect that a couple gained through fiesta sponsorship must have allowed them greater access to the labor and services of others. Thus, the efficacy of Saint Rose's blessings can perhaps be interpreted in Durkheimian terms: together with Saint Rose, the community blessed the couple's efforts, providing very practical benefits.

While bringing recognition for the couple as an autonomous unit in the community, however, fiesta sponsorship also entailed continuing deference to the older generation. Through sponsorship, the young couple became members of the community of adults, but subordinate members. Sponsors properly followed a hierarchical order in serving food and drink, giving first to elders and giving them better portions. Young fiesta sponsors recognized the *fundadores'* authority and put themselves under their tutelage.

Fiesta sponsorship was too costly for young couples to carry out without indebting themselves to older, more established members of the community. Alberto Yumbo recalled taking gifts to others who could lend money or utensils and ceremoniously requesting their aid. "Mama Virgen would help you later, you'd say; later, you'd be able to have something." Yet, for a young couple, "it wasn't easy to put on that feast" (7/16/1992).

More broadly, fiesta sponsorship signaled the couple's subordination to a chain of authority that flowed down from the hacienda. Hacienda bosses supported the *fundadores'* authority and apparently viewed fiesta sponsorship as a useful part of the moral education of young laborers. Manuel Yépez said that the steward, overseer, and *fundador* all cooperated in dealing with troublesome young people. "The steward would say, 'Beginning now, you have to do a fiesta. So that you will control yourself. Don't be insolent. Be a *prioste* and follow the *fundador*'" (JN/MY 6/29/1992).

Despite the redistributive character of the fiesta at the upper levels of responsibility, fiesta sponsorship must have sometimes seemed negatively redistributive to young couples without a large herd or other wealth, faced with heavy labor obligations to the hacienda, and pressured by the older generation, with the support of hacienda authority, to serve as sponsors. The people who took their turn in hacienda times now describe their sponsorship with pride, but there is, nonetheless, evidence of ambivalence. Some young couples, pleading economic inability, resisted sponsorship for a time, as José María Pillajo remembered: "They would say, 'We don't have anything. . . . Those who have things, they will do it. They should do it. We don't have . . . money or livestock . . .' That's how some people would beg off" (9/2/1992). The language of this plea, as Tayta José remembers it, did not question that fiesta sponsorship was basically a good thing. Instead, the couple sought to gain time by appealing to the assumption that people should be considerate of one another's situation, and expectations should be commensurate with the ability to bear the costs.

From the perspective of the older generation and, especially, the *fundadores*, however, a young couple needed Saint Rose's blessings in order to build up their wealth. In bestowing her blessings, Saint Rose would take into account their domestic needs, but also their commitment to recycling a portion of the bounty to others and back to the saint. To allow too much time could have threatened these premises. Elders may have also considered it politically and morally risky to allow a young couple who were becoming autonomous from their parents to delay for too long the renewal of their subordination to the older generation as represented by the *fundadores*. Luis Amancha says young couples were obliged to sponsor "so that they would lead their lives serving Saint Rose, so that they would respect their elders" (8/2/1992).

Young people who put off sponsorship were subject to a strong campaign of social pressure. *Fundadores* might compare recalcitrant nonsponsors to dogs:

> "You are without any fiesta. You're good for nothing. A snot-nosed kid [*mocoso*]. An insolent brat [*malcriado*] . . ." they said. . . .
> On the day of the feast, . . . they served drink to those who had put on the fiesta. . . . If someone had not put on the fiesta, they just give him a little bit of food, or maybe they don't serve him any drink at all. They just leave him out. "You are worthless. In this community, in this place, you are a dog," they say. That's how it was in the old days. (AS 8/29/92)

The fiesta itself was a logical occasion for humiliating those who had refused to sponsor. Others told of similar criticism being voiced in the *doctrina*, the weekly early-morning gathering in the hacienda chapel: "This one lives like a dog, without any fiesta, without any obligation" (AYu 7/16/1992).

Other people who had already taken their turn had a stake in maintaining the prestige value of sponsorship by differentiating themselves from nonsponsors (Cancian 1965:135). Two married men in their thirties, the sons of Monjas Corral laborers, told me of their elders' criticisms in 1992, after the old fiesta-sponsorship system had broken down:

> [The old people say] they have more respect, they have already earned their honor . . . They have already done their obligation. . . . The elders

criticize: "He hasn't done any fiesta, any obligation; no, there's no respect," they say. . . .

[The elders praise those who have sponsored fiestas:] "That person is
. . . no longer just some kid with a runny nose. . . . Everybody has seen
. . . them carry the *virgen* [Saint Rose in the procession]. Now they can't
say that person is worthless. . . . That person now has his face washed,"
they say. . . .

They say, "*Pucha!* You, runny-nosed kid, you haven't done even one
fiesta, you don't know anything. Me, I have done it, I have 'earned' Mass
for the *virgen*, for a saint. That's how I am." . . .

They don't say it to our face, but I've heard it. . . . "They don't have
respect, they're ill-behaved upstarts. . . . They don't even know how
to greet a person," they say. "They don't realize anything." (MG-OY
8/10/1992)

Harsh as it was, such criticism rested on the same moral assumptions we
have examined about people, society, and divinity. For example, the image
of the stubborn nonsponsor as a dog was simply the converse of the idea that
sponsorship transformed young people into moral and social persons. With
the hacienda's support, elders constructed the social order as a moral community in which they were the arbiters of social status and moral worth, and
respect reflected moral worth. From their point of view, criticism was meant
to push the target into a proper relationship with elders and the divine. Nonsponsors had not fulfilled an obligation, had not earned respect, had not
served the saint, had not given food and drink and diversion to other people,
had not contributed to maintaining the agricultural fertility on which all depended. They were in debt, and the elders, who were their creditors, had the
right to remind them of it.

Young people might have resented the harsh form of this criticism and
might even have harbored doubts as to whether God or the saint really rewarded sponsorship. Yet, they had little choice but, ultimately, to follow in
their elders' footsteps. Once they had done so, like any burdensome rite of
passage, fiesta sponsorship raised them above their juniors who had not yet
undertaken it. Thus, they acquired a stake in the fiesta system and the *fundadores'* authority. The authority of the *fundadores* underpinned the social
value of the young couple's investment.

A personal account can illustrate some of the more intimate meanings of
sponsorship, even though individual experience surely varied. In the 1960s,
when Virgilio Guailla was a young man, villagers in the Pangor area were in-

creasingly taking advantage of the new possibility of bus travel as well as new freedom from hacienda labor demands to embark on pilgrimages to distant saints' sanctuaries. His account is more concerned with these long-range pilgrimages than with fiesta sponsorship, but it begins with a reflection on the latter, and similar expectations about the saints' help applied in either case.

Virgilio Guailla is the eldest son of the last *fundadora*. He was remembering how the old people adored and served Saint Rose with music and several days of fiesta, and he commented, "It turns out, that is in order to live with a blessing. . . . To this day, we keep and adore her, and all the *tayta amitos*. . . . Because of that, . . . we have a blessing, . . . a little grain, an animal. So I go through life content . . . adoring the *virgencitas*" (VG 6/30/1992). This is his outlook today, but he has not always seen things this way. He told me of his grandfather admonishing him as a youth not to neglect Saint Rose but to view her as a family inheritance:

But I was just a boy without experience yet, and I didn't understand. . . .
    "What will she give? What? She doesn't give anything. They [the elders] just say that with no reason. . . ."
    That's how I thought, a bit not thinking well. (VG 6/30/1992)

What experience led him to change his view?

When I was just married a short time, I didn't have anything. . . . I suffered a lot, . . . with my wife [and] small children. . . . I . . . talked with my wife: "Now that we're married, how will we live? . . . I work, but God doesn't give [a good harvest]. How will we live?"
    I . . . talked . . . with some friends. They said, "No. No one is going to help you. Now you have a wife, you have a family. No one is going to help you.
    "Instead [of looking to humans for aid], . . . let's go to greet the *virgencitas*.
    "People before have gone to the Virgin of Lajas, in Colombia, and then they do very nicely, they do well.
    "The Virgin's, God's, blessing will help you. Let's go to Colombia. Let's go to the Virgin of Azogues, . . . Quinche, the Señor de Gran Poder [Lord of Great Power] [in Quito], the *tayta amito* Señor de la Salud [Lord of Health] in Bolívar province [various popular pilgrimage sites].
    "If you go to all those places, they all will help you.
    "Your father and your mother, now that you're grown, they won't give you anything." (VG 6/30/1992)

Tayta Virgilio was mulling over this advice when the saints appeared to him in his dreams.

> They give a blessing in a dream at night. It's like, they make you dream. You see some beautiful "children," little *señoritas*.[9] . . .
> [They say,] "You be like this: have enormous goodwill [*voluntad*] [toward us, the saints]. Go around visiting the sanctuaries, visiting the Holy Mother Churches . . . asking for God's blessing. And don't think about getting rich. To get rich is not good. Only God's blessing is good. . . ."
> That's how they speak to me at night when they make me dream, these beautiful *señoritas*, appearing in a Holy Mother Church.
> They are not a father [or a] mother, to say, "Here, have some grain," or "Here, take this bread, this fruit." . . . They gradually, slowly—God [Dios] . . . gives a blessing, they do, the *virgencitas*." (VG 6/30/1992)

He summed up his understanding: "[Your parents] won't give you any more. Maybe once in a while, they'll give something, but not more, not for the future. When you go to visit, they'll give you a plate of food. But for a living, for your work [to bear fruit], for grain, animals, you have to ask God. Then God gives. God gives to all of us, every family, every neighbor, because we are all God's children" (VG 6/30/1992).

The saints, then, came into Tayta Virgilio's dreams and his life, replacing his youthful skepticism with the religious quest for their blessings as part of the experience of adulthood. They helped him make the transition from a youth who worked alongside his parents in the fields, helped look after their animals, lived in their house, and ate from their cooking pots to a man with an independent household, responsibilities to a wife and children, and a poor, precarious economic position to start with. Now, instead of looking to his parents to feed and clothe him, he would look to God and the saints to provide by blessing his labor and that of his household, making his crops grow and his animals multiply. While he speaks here of securing these blessings more through pilgrimage than through fiesta sponsorship, Tayta Virgilio did, in fact, participate in the fiesta of Saint Rose as well, even briefly joining his mother and stepfather as *fundadores*.

Extrapolating from Tayta Virgilio's experience, one can draw a schematic, tentative picture of the meaning of fiesta sponsorship for young couples. On the one hand, sponsorship was a material burden imposed on them just as they were starting to build up their resources. At the same time, the *fundadores* helped them assume that burden and promised that Saint Rose would, too. On a larger scale, Saint Rose and God would also now bless their labors, and the community would recognize them as married adults, not worthless kids dependent on their parents. Whereas classic images of hacienda paternalism depict the landlord as the primary source of material and psychological security for dependent hacienda residents (e.g., Wolf and Mintz [1957] 1977:43–44), the fiesta offered an alternative source of security in the divinity, the *fundador,* and perhaps other elders and adults in general.

The force of the pressures, incentives, and authority the elders could bring to bear on young couples and the meaning that young couples found in fiesta sponsorship are confirmed by developments in the fiesta system after the church took direct control of the hacienda and withdrew its support for the fiesta in the early 1960s. Even without priests' and landlords' support, villagers continued to celebrate the fiesta of Saint Rose under the direction of the *fundadores* in much the same way as they had before for over two decades, into the period when the laborers formed an autonomous community. On the other hand, the links between the fiesta and the hacienda are also recognized in contemporary local interpretations of the demise of the old fiesta system. Villagers sometimes talk about this collapse as being of a piece with the demise of the hacienda. This interpretation is promoted by the bearers of new forms of religiosity, both Catholic and Protestant, that promise liberation in one form or another. At the same time, this interpretation resonates with people's experience of the very real connections between fiesta authority and hacienda authority that we shall explore more deeply later.

The fiesta exemplified the deeply contradictory nature of indigenous culture under domination. It provided hacienda residents with a space to recreate Andean forms of reciprocity with deities and to experience reciprocity and redistribution as the basis of authority. As we shall see in the next chapter, these values provided the basis for a partial legitimation of the hacienda but also for a strong critique. At the same time, as we shall see in Chapter 7, the hacienda power structure made use of the authority generated through the fiesta. People participated in the fiesta and agreed to sponsor it not only because they accepted the cultural premises that underlay it but also because the combined power of indigenous elders and hacienda bosses could make them suffer if they did not sponsor.

CHAPTER 5

Reciprocity and Resistance

In Chapter 2 and the first sections of Chapter 3, we surveyed the history and administrative structure of Ecuadorian highland haciendas and hacienda Monjas Corral through the end of the last rental period in 1961. Then I turned the focus primarily to the resident community—residents' horizontal social ties; their assumptions and practices of reciprocity; and the relationship between authority, reciprocity, and redistribution associated with the fiesta. In this chapter, we return our focus to the relationship between the hacienda and the resident indigenous community. Our question now is how hacienda Runa perceived, experienced, and questioned this relationship, and, in particular, how their assumptions concerning reciprocity shaped their experience of the relationship.

Scholars seeking to understand the Latin American and, especially, the Andean hacienda as something more than a neofeudal European transplant have naturally been drawn to the concept of reciprocity. Murra (1962, 1978) and others have shown reciprocity to be a basic organizing principle both of Andean civilization prior to the European invasion and of contemporary Andean village life, so that placing the hacienda firmly in the Andean context requires examining it in the same terms. The hacienda used the "gift" as well as the "whip" in managing its labor force, allowing for some sense of mutual obligation between landlords and laborers. Influenced by James Scott's (1976) theory that peasants rebel in defense of a "moral economy" that guarantees subsistence, historians have given particular attention to peasant responses to the erosion of their traditional prerogatives in periods of market expansion and landlord aggressiveness. This perspective has helped them see how Andean hacienda laborers have actively shaped and responded to the hacienda system (e.g., Langer 1989; cf. Larson 1991).

My argument in this chapter lies broadly within the same approach but is not directly historical. That is, I am not trying to understand change and the reactions to change but to interpret the stable features and tensions of an entire period. In part, this is due to the paucity of the historical documentation available on Monjas Corral, which does not allow for a close tracking of changes in renters' economic strategies and laborers' reactions. It corresponds, at the same time, to my attempt to locate the sources of ideological resistance not in the memory of traditional rights increasingly under attack but in the enduring assumptions about reciprocity that were sustained in relationships among Runa and other peasants.

There is no doubt that, when hacienda landlords in the Andes tried to suppress popular festivals or increased their demands for labor, they were likely to arouse resistance. My argument is intended to complement that "moral economy" point. Some general and stable features of the hacienda as well as particular historical changes were persistent sources of friction; the relatively autonomous sphere of indigenous social relations as well as the past provided the moral basis of resistance. Some kinds of tension were recurrent, fluctuating, of course, with the aggressiveness of particular renters and stewards, but probably predating the political and economic changes of the late nineteenth century, the legal elimination of debt peonage, or the 1930s. An explicit memory of better conditions in the past does not seem to have been an important theme in indigenous expressions of resentment in Pangor. One may view the practices of labor exchange and other forms of reciprocity between indigenous people as constituting a kind of tacit, collective cultural memory, but the point is that resistance was not based on a historical narrative.

The period under consideration here is defined by the nature of the evidence. Three hacienda account books offer a glimpse of life on hacienda Monjas Corral in the 1880s and the 1890s, not long after its acquisition by the Diocese of Riobamba. Other than that, this chapter is essentially based on oral accounts that reach back to the early 1900s. Where published work on other Ecuadorian haciendas demonstrates the antiquity of some of the patterns I point out, I will also introduce that evidence into the discussion. The diocese took back direct administration of Monjas Corral from the last renter at the beginning of 1962, marking the end of the classic hacienda period on this estate.

The relationship between hacienda landlord and resident laborers did have some of the character of a pact of reciprocity. The hacienda provided plots for people to cultivate, pasturage for their animals, and other resources; labor was demanded in return. A part of hacienda products and profits was redistributed to the laborers. Ritual gifts and feasts on the hacienda re-affirmed the mutual goodwill and obligation that ideally characterized the relationship.

If there was a pact, however, it was a tense, conflict-ridden one. Some aspects of the hacienda system could not easily be reconciled with the morality of reciprocity. The relationship between hacienda bosses and resident laborers was characterized as much by mutual resentment as by mutual goodwill.

I open this chapter with general comments on how reciprocity shapes the structure of moral judgments of social relationships and systems. I then present an overview of the positive aspects of the landlord-laborer relationship—the ways that bosses could present it and residents experience it as one of reciprocity. This is followed by an examination of the tensions and conflicts in the relationship. My aim is to show how hacienda residents' moral understandings shaped their criticisms of the hacienda.

THE STRUCTURE OF MORAL JUDGMENTS

As voluntary contractual relationships became increasingly important in early-modern Western economies and societies, philosophers came to view voluntary contracts as the basis of legitimate relationships and even of society itself. In capitalist legal theory, as in Enlightenment social contract theory, persons begin as free individuals, and legitimacy derives from their free choices. Coercion automatically renders a contract invalid.

In the Andes, coercion can morally taint a relationship of reciprocity as well, if the form that coercion takes blatantly and irrevocably contradicts the ideal of mutual goodwill. Coercion certainly taints a relationship if it is used to exact contributions without any corresponding return.

On the other hand, in ongoing social relationships, gifts are rarely wholly voluntary anyway; they are an obligatory expression of goodwill, a voluntary recognition of social obligations (Mauss 1990; Parry 1986). People are born into obligations, and they have inescapable obligations to others throughout life. The obligatory character of a relationship and even the use of threats and sanctions do not automatically or absolutely render the relationship morally invalid. A parent, saint, or *fundador*, for example, can have goodwill and nonetheless threaten or use sanctions to remind a person of his or her obligations. The central moral issue is not the free or forced nature of the bond but the behavior of each party in an ongoing relationship—their responsiveness to each other's needs, the sacrifices demanded and accepted by each, and the display of goodwill both through generosity and through the observance of respectful etiquette (*respeto, delicadeza*).

This has broader implications for the structure of moral judgments. Western social scientists' discussions of hegemony sometimes focus on the question of whether people "merely" criticize individual landlords or rulers or "go beyond" that to question the legitimacy of the system or the social structure as such. But the Western idea of the social contract may have something to do with our assumption that personalistic and structural critiques are two distinct sorts of discourse. It is as though (in our eyes) personal criticism merely says that individuals are not living up to their contractual obligations, whereas a more profound critique denies the legitimacy of the contact itself. More broadly, contracts are instances of a general modern Western tendency to separate "scripts" from "enactments" conceptually and in practice; the same may be true of the distinction between structure and personal behavior (see Mitchell 1990).

I could not be a social scientist if I did not see some value in understanding structural or systemic patterns. But in interpreting the understandings of people who view persons and other beings in the world as inherently interdependent, it is not so easy to separate the abstract legitimacy of a relationship or a social structure from the personal morality of the parties. When hacienda Runa said that *amos* would suffer in the afterlife for mistreating their laborers, they were, in some sense, questioning the legitimacy of a system in which reciprocity was so often denied and perverted, as well as criticizing individuals—though they would not have been likely to put it in terms that distinguished between the two. Conversely, when hacienda Runa experienced the *amos* as generous exchange partners, as might have sometimes been the case, they probably experienced the system as legitimate, though, again, they would not have put it in those terms. I turn now to a consideration of the possibilities within the hacienda system for *amos* to present themselves and for Runa to experience them as engaged in a legitimate relationship of reciprocal exchange.

IMAGES OF RECIPROCITY
Land for Labor

The basic explanation that former laborers today give of the hacienda system is straightforward and closely follows the formal definition of *huasipungaje:* we lived on hacienda land, planted and pastured our animals on land belonging to the hacienda, and so we had to work for the hacienda. It is not always clear if they intend this sort of statement as a description of a fair exchange or a sad fact of life, but on some level, people recognize themselves as having exchanged their labor for access to the land. The local term for the usufruct plots provided by the hacienda, *ración allpa*, or "portion land," is indicative of the same sense of exchange. *Ración*, or "portion," is otherwise used by Quichua speakers to refer to compensation for labor in kind, usually a portion of the same product the laborer helped harvest or process. The term would be applied, in that sense, to an exchange among peasants. The phrase "*ración allpa*" construes the land (*allpa*) as a parallel sort of compensation for labor on the hacienda.

Beyond that, it is not easy to know how hacienda Runa viewed white people's monopoly of landownership and the hacienda's "gift" of access to the land. The main difficulties lie in the radical changes of the three or four decades after 1960: the agrarian reform has demonstrated that the hacienda system was not an eternal fact of life, while popular awareness of history has also been transformed. Indigenous people in Pangor have learned that at some point only indigenous people lived in Ecuador, that whites came from another country and took power and land by force. Older villagers testify almost unanimously that they and their elders did not know this before. The avenues by which this historical narrative has come into common circulation in the countryside are several: contact with agrarian reform agents, lawyers, and organizers in the 1960s and the 1970s; the church's campaign of "consciousness-raising" since the 1960s; the access of some young people to secondary education; and Quichua radio programs, especially during the years leading up to the quincentenary in 1992. The newly popularized narrative of invasion and dispossession is a central element in an emerging, reshaped indigenous identity. Its prominence obscures earlier visions of history, including the history of the land.

My tentative sense is that the legitimacy of white people's ownership of the land did not generally come up as an explicit question for most people in Pangor in the decades prior to 1960. Haciendas were simply a fact of life. Most villagers say that, before the changes of the last few decades, they and their parents did not know that there had ever been any other dominant form of land tenure. I was unable to learn about any "traditional" narratives or practices that implied any special association of indigenous people with autochthony, any identification with the pre-Conquest inhabitants of the land, or, indeed, any idea that the whites had their origin in a different place. The pre-Columbian notion of descent from local mountains was not preserved in Chimborazo province.

As elsewhere in the Andes (see Allen 1984; Bernand 1980), local oral traditions that clearly predate the new historical narrative portray time as a succession of stable eras, one divided from the next by a cataclysmic disruption in which basic features of the physical, social, moral, and cosmological orders were transformed. The Incas lived in the time of Dios Yaya, God the Father. Their age ended with the birth of Jesus, inaugurating the present age of Dios Churi, God the Son. Stories tell of Jesus as a "culture hero" in the common Andean mold, who decreed the incest taboo and marriage, taught men to plow, fixed the characteristics and uses of various animals and crops, maybe created the mountains. The origin of contemporary Runa and whites alike lies in this period; the accounts I collected did not suggest that either had any special connection to the Incas who came before. I never heard and was not able to elicit any explicit account of the origins of the vast disparities between the two "races" and the white people's monopoly of landownership—aside from accounts whose sources are clearly recent.[1]

Reinaldo Sisa's account of hacienda-era historical knowledge is typical:

> RS Since [my parents] didn't know, they didn't tell us about any of that [why only white people and not Runa owned land]. . . . They lived their lives thinking only that they had to serve the *amos*. . . . The *amos* own the land, who knows why. . . . We Runitos are here to serve the *amos*. . . . That's how they thought. . . .
>
> BL That is, the fact that at one time the land belonged to the Runa, or that it was taken away—
>
> RS They didn't say. No one said anything about that. . . .
>
> We've come to understand and know about that just these last years, through education, . . . newspapers, all that. (9/14/1992)

The absence in hacienda times of a commonly known local historical narrative explaining indigenous people's loss of the land and the formation of the hacienda may surprise those of us reared in Western literate traditions. In Chapter 2, I indicated some factors in regional and local history that may have shaped local historical consciousness. As we saw, haciendas did not take over indigenous lands in a single act following the Spanish invasion, but in a more complex and locally variable process. As colonial haciendas formed and expanded, Andean people escaping onerous tribute burdens often severed their local attachments, and mass internal migration dissolved old regional identities such as Puruhá. The Quichua language and the colonial category of "Indian" achieved their hegemonic status as basic symbols of identity in the same process. Puruhaes were dispossessed, and Indians were born as the heirs of that dispossession. The old oral traditions of cataclysmic change may reflect this historical discontinuity of identities.

To be sure, free landowning Runa communities in some areas did maintain an awareness of having possessed the land "from time immemorial," as their lawyers often put it in litigation (see Lyons 1994a). The central Colta valley, where many migrants to Pangor came from, however, seems to have been a zone of strong and early concentration of haciendas; landowning Runa communities were relatively rare. The pattern of migration from hacienda to hacienda must have also weakened any sense of ancestral rights to specific lands. In Pangor itself, the high *páramo* lands of the upper basin were probably not much used before the Spanish invasion. Finally, if many descendants of the Pangor natives who held communal lands up through the 1860s became mestizo, as surnames suggest, it would have been hard for Pangor immigrant hacienda residents to draw straightforward associations between indigenous ethnicity and ancestral land rights.

A complementary point is that origins may be ideologically less salient in a reciprocity perspective than they are in a liberal-individualist society whose foundational myth is the social contract. It seems that the more important question for Pangor hacienda laborers was not, "Did we (or our ancestors) really agree freely and fairly to this social arrangement?" but, rather, "Do they [the landlords] act as moral partners in reciprocity?" At any rate, no narrative explanation of the origins of racial inequality was apparently widely circulated. Jacob Sayay remembered laborers talking during work, wondering if God was angry at the Runa, why, and for how long His anger at them would endure. These were questions without easy answers.

In the specific case of Monjas Corral, some hacienda residents seem to have accepted the church's claim to owning the land as a delegate of God. José Pillajo spoke of Monjas Corral as God's hacienda and indicated that God blessed his hacienda with special fertility. He said none of the neighboring, privately owned haciendas were so fertile (7/21/1991). One implication might have been that Monjas Corral residents indeed owed gratitude to the church, and perhaps to the renters to whom the church delegated its rights, for allowing access to such blessed land.

The Generosity of Landlords

In addition to access to the land, laborers also received a portion of hacienda products and profits. Up to 1918, the debt constituted by a flow of goods and money to the laborer defined the hacienda-laborer relationship before the law. Such disbursements were legally defined as an advance on salary, but they could have been locally understood as an expression of generosity or as compliance with moral obligations in a "pact of reciprocity" (Guerrero 1991; Ramón 1987; cf. Keen 1985). Landlords and stewards recorded these disbursements, along with laborers' work, in account books.

These account books must be interpreted carefully: as I noted in the Introduction, José Pillajo reacted angrily to an old account book, saying it was full of lies designed to cheat laborers. On the other hand, it is hard to see why members of the church hierarchy—themselves members of the elite familiar with hacienda practices—would have been willing to reimburse renters for such disbursements if they were all fictitious. Renters may have been more "generous" before 1918 than they were in Tayta José's experience as an adult. At least some of the disbursements these account books record were probably real.

In the late nineteenth-century account books of Monjas Corral, as in other places, two forms of distribution appear. The *socorro general,* roughly translatable as "general help" or "general aid," refers to a sack or two of potatoes or grain given to each household at the harvest. For example, in 1887, the Monjas Corral *conciertos* each received two fanegas (large sacks of about 1.6 bushels) of barley after aiding the renter in the harvest on other haciendas and two sacks of potatoes from the Monjas Corral harvest (*Rayas 1887–1888; Figure 14).

The other type of distribution is the *suplimento* or *suplido,* "supplement." This refers to an item given to an individual laborer, usually at the latter's request. There was no fixed time of the year for disbursing supplements; a laborer could request one at any time. Grain or potatoes, money, an animal or part of an animal, and cheese all appear under this category in the account books.

The account books sometimes give a brief explanation that allows one to discern why laborers requested a supplement and the social context of the disbursement. We can classify the purpose of supplements into various categories:

1. Ritual expenses. The administrator who kept the accounts frequently mentions annual fiestas and, occasionally, life-cycle rituals such as a wedding or the death of a relative or neighbor. Some examples: the overseer of Monjas Corral received a peso in money "on the eve of Palm Sunday," a sheep for slaughter for Carnival, and another peso for the fiesta of Saint Rose. Segundo Manuel Sisa received a series of supplements in March and April of 1887, including two pesos "to go to propose marriage," four pesos for the priest's and assistants' fees for the wedding service, and a cow for the wedding celebration. Later the same year, he received two pesos and two rounds of cheese for the feast of Saint Rose.

2. Aid in special circumstances such as family illness or legal problems. Juan Sisa received a *tercio* of potatoes, having asked for it in connection with "the illness of his wife." In the account of José María Pillajo (my infor-

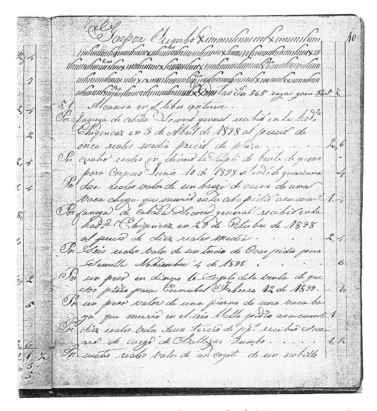

FIGURE 14. *Page from a Monjas Corral account book (*Rayas 1898–1902)*

mant's uncle or grandfather), the administrator notes "six reales in money, [which] I supplemented to him in Pangor, for him to pay the judge."

3. Potatoes for seed. Esteban Sisa, the Llalla cowhand, "asked for a *tercio* of potatoes, supplement, from the field of Caparina . . . he said for seed."

4. Money for clothing. "To buy a shirt," "to buy clothing," "to buy a poncho."

5. In a few cases, laborers with specific responsibilities over production received—or took—some of the product or the profits. The best example of this is the cheese maker, who took home a round of cheese every month or so. The account does not always specify the date or the circumstances, but there is a significant contrast with the cheese that other laborers occasionally received: whereas the administrator often notes that other laborers "asked for" the cheese, in the case of the cheese maker himself, it is ap-

parent that the administrator could not completely control disbursements. The charge in the account book, then, represents a tacit "legalization" after the fact of the cheese maker's having taken some cheese home—or the administrator's suspecting this.

6. Food items and money for day-to-day household consumption and expenses. Sometimes this is specified; for example, someone asked for a round of cheese, as the administrator notes, "for his consumption." Sometimes a cow or other animal died in an accident or from an illness without there being any particular ritual occasion, and people took a cut home. No doubt, many other charges whose purpose is not specifically noted by the administrator also fall into this general category. (*Rayas 1887–1888)

No one mentioned in the 1880s accounts is alive to dispute the administrator's version of events, so, again, conclusions can only be tentative. To the extent these supplements were really given, they represent distributions for various purposes associated with both routine needs and special circumstances. Although the administrator's lack of control over some disbursements introduces a discordant note that I shall elaborate on later, in general, the categories of supplements indicate that the hacienda responded flexibly to a variety of needs invoked by laborers in their requests. Compensation for labor thus took the form of aid in time of need rather than a contractual salary.

This interpretation is supported by statistical analyses of data from other haciendas. Two scholars have analyzed the evolution of disbursements to laborers over time on north Ecuadorian haciendas. Andrés Guerrero takes a twenty-five-year period at the beginning of the twentieth century and examines the relationship between total work performed and total distributions received by each laborer. He finds no correlation. In other words, while the hacienda administrators entered a theoretical daily wage into their calculation of laborers' debts, distributions to laborers were actually independent of each laborer's theoretical earnings (1991:255–260).

Galo Ramón, using a twenty-year series in the late eighteenth century, finds that levels of debt fluctuate systematically over the life cycle of the domestic unit. In the first fifteen years of married life, with each child and each year, the consumption needs of the household grow, but the children are not yet able to earn *rayas*. In this period, the debt grows: the laborer receives more in *socorros* and supplements than he pays off in work. Between fifteen and twenty years after marriage, as the children begin to pull their own weight, the debt stabilizes and may begin to decline. The debt, in other words, serves as a cushion during the most difficult period in the family's life cycle. Guerrero adds that even families at the height of their productive capacity sometimes needed supplements to tide them over a poor harvest or other misfortune (Ramón Valarezo 1987:251–254; Guerrero 1991:273–279).

The disbursement of *socorros* and supplements continued on Ecuadorian haciendas after the formal abolition of *concertaje*, and so can be approached through oral as well as documentary evidence. I shall discuss supplements on Monjas Corral in a more negative light later, as they appear (or fail to appear) in oral accounts. For now, let me note that in the mid-twentieth century, landowners and renters in Pangor and the Colta region did continue to give *socorros* at the harvest. As the *amos* distributed the *socorros*, they would say something like this, according to Andrés Yépez: "Now, for your work, take at least just this little bit to eat" (Q. Siquiera kayta mikuychic; or Kayllatapish mikuychic)(11/22/1992). This is the polite language that accompanies a gift made in recognition of a favor; it is standard form to downplay the value of the gift. It is difficult to know whether landowners and stewards in the 1940s and the 1950s actually spoke in this way in giving the *socorros*, or if Tayta Andrés was responding to my question by supplying the language as it "should have" been. At any rate, his answer indicates that he understood the *socorro* as an expression of thanks and repayment for labor.

While the old account book mentions seed potatoes as a supplement, a few informants mentioned that Monjas Corral residents who were short of seed often obtained it through sharecropping agreements—sometimes with fellow Runa, sometimes with the landlord. The sharecropper repaid the seed with half the harvest. While sharecropping arrangements can be quite conflictive, it is not impossible that sharecroppers experienced a landlord's provision of seed as a form of vital aid for which they owed gratitude. This aspect of the landlord-resident relationship may have been more important in hacienda times than would appear from the oral accounts I obtained.

The custom of gleaning—secondary harvesting after the formal harvest—can be considered another type of redistribution. In Pangor, women often went to the haciendas' potato fields on the days of the harvest and followed behind the harvesters, picking up what they had left. The hacienda owners, renters, and stewards accepted and allowed this. In various ways, then, hacienda residents may have experienced their bosses as sources of aid and subsistence security (Scott 1976).

Fiestas

Throughout highland Ecuador, hacienda landlords and residents engaged in ritual reciprocal exchange on the occasion of Catholic celebrations (Crespi 1981; Guerrero 1991:11–41). In Chimborazo, Carnival was the main such occasion.

Carola Lentz has provided a description of this aspect of the Carnival celebration on a hacienda in the central Colta area up to the 1960s:

> The Friday of the week prior to Carnival, families met at the call of the
> overseer on the path to the hacienda house, for the giving of the *kamari*
> [a gift, in a hierarchical context]. In the patio, they kept a respectful
> distance from the steps where the *patrón* was seated. . . . The overseer
> directed the collection of the *kamaris*, which generally consisted in
> four eggs on the part of the *ayudas* and, in addition, guinea pigs from
> the *huasipungueros*. Upon being named by the overseer . . . the head
> of the family had to step out of the line, kneel before the *patrón*, and
> put his *"obligación"* in the hands of the overseer, naming what he was
> giving. The gift was personal and public—not everyone gave the same
> thing . . . ; the hope was that the gift would guarantee favorable relations
> for the coming year. Then, the overseer presented the *kamaris* . . . to the
> steward, who . . . gave them to the *patrón*, thus following . . . the hier-
> archy of command. The hacendado, after receiving the *kamaris*, gave
> out cane alcohol and chicha, and, in addition, permitted, during this day
> alone, the free pasturing of animals in the hacienda pastures . . .
>
> On Ash Wednesday [five days later], the hacienda was again the stage
> of the fiesta. . . . The sponsors climbed the steps, and each one gave eggs
> and a cock to the *patrón*. He took the offering and served chicha and
> cane alcohol, drinking with the indigenous authorities and remaining
> by their side during the whole afternoon. He put on a cowhand's sheep-
> skin pants, a Mexican [large, broad-rimmed] hat, and a poncho that he
> took from one of those who had come up, and carried a drum and cow
> whip, likewise "stolen" from one of the sponsors. In other words: he
> dressed up . . . as an indigenous authority, and participated with them
> in the dancing, singing, and drinking spree. . . .
>
> On this day, the culmination of Carnival, the hacienda was practi-
> cally inundated by the indigenous world. . . . Through his change of
> dress and his active participation, the *patrón* was incorporated into
> the sphere of the [resident] community as one of its own authorities,
> thereby leveling the customary social distance and domination. In
> acting as an alcalde, the hacendado fell under the authority of the in-
> digenous *regidor*, and in accepting the gift-offerings of the alcaldes, he
> assumed the obligation . . . to contribute to . . . the fiesta. (1986:199–200)

Ritual exchanges between laborers and renters on Monjas Corral were
more limited. This is probably because renters' relationship to the hacienda
was more impersonal and transient than that of a lifelong individual land-

owner. In Monjas Corral, the renter did not generally receive the *kamari* in person on the hacienda. Instead, the steward would collect the *kamaris* on the hacienda, reading off the names of the laborers from a list. As Tayta Andrés remembers it, the laborers presented the *kamari* modestly, again in accordance with standard gift etiquette: "Even if it's just this little thing, take it, this little thing." An *acudero*, chosen from among the laborers, would bring the accumulated *kamaris* to the renter in town.

Tayta Andrés remembered that, in addition to the *kamari* for the land-owner or renter, it was the custom to give a *kamari* to the steward as well. "We would even give a *kamari* to the Runa overseer, if he was a good person." A little while later in the same interview, Tayta Andrés said that, even if the overseer was not a particularly good person, it was always the custom for everyone to bring him a *kamari* in Carnival. His vacillation on this point indicates that he conceived of the *kamari* as both an obligatory expression of subordination and a gift outwardly expressing esteem. The overseer would invite the other people of the hacienda community to his house: "Come, we'll have a little *aswa* [corn liquor], a little cane alcohol, come eat a few bites of food." The alcalde—that is, the sponsor of the Carnival festivities— led the way to the overseer's house; the rest of the community came as his accompanying party. Each family was expected to bring something along as a *kamari* (AY 11/22/1992).

In several ways, then, landlords could be viewed as participating in a rela-tionship of reciprocity with the resident laboring community. The land that people lived on and cultivated was a gift that they reciprocated with their labor. The hacienda redistributed a portion of the harvest and, at least in some periods, provided seed and aid in response to individual circumstances and the family's life cycle. The *amos* also participated in ritual exchanges with the laborers during Carnival, though, in the case of Monjas Corral, the renters' participation was less than that of private landowners in the central basin.

In spite of these elements of reciprocity, however, the hacienda was not a smoothly functioning system. We now turn to an examination of the sources of friction in the relationship between landlords, administrators, and resi-dent laborers.

RECIPROCITY DENIED

It would be wrong to think of the images and practices of reciprocity on the hacienda as simply a strategy adopted unilaterally by landlords in order to disguise exploitation. These "customs" were, instead, the outcome of a long history of negotiation, tension, and struggle that continued to shape and maintain them.

The basic benefits of land, *socorros,* and supplements, as we have seen, were established in the process by which *concertaje* replaced the mita as incentives for laborers to remain. While these laborers' bargaining position was weak, they did have the option of returning to their home communities, moving to towns, or leaving one hacienda for another. Labor continued to be a limiting factor in hacienda production, and laborers, as a last resort, continued to move from hacienda to hacienda until the 1960s. Landlords and stewards also had to contend with foot dragging and other forms of day-to-day resistance. Thus, landlords could not entirely ignore laborers' views.

Landlords themselves recognized their own displays of generosity as a response to the general recalcitrance of the labor force. Luis Alberto Borja, a Riobamba aristocrat, included this dialogue in his novel *Cabalgando sobre los Andes* (Riding over the Andes). Diego, the first speaker, is considering renting a hacienda in southern Chimborazo.

> "They say this is a difficult hacienda to manage, due to its distant location and the lazy and rebellious Indian work force. However, I think that these ideas are spread [by the current renter] with the intention of making [potential competitors for the rental contract] . . . afraid."
>
> "That is clear. The Indians around here are semisavage and reject the man of another race and other customs, but that's no reason that people like us, with determination, cannot dominate them, sometimes through showing strength, other times, magnanimity, the whip in one hand and in the other, bread, the gift, the cup of alcohol; that, Diego, is the key to the problem, and no one is afraid of such a small thing."
>
> "In reality, we are . . . conquerors of aggressive, resisting masses; subduers of colts and lassoers of wild bulls." (1953:299)

The renter's "magnanimity" appears here as a strategic response to the Indian laborers' basic hostility.

Insofar as there was an implicit pact of reciprocity, then, it was an inherently "conflictive pact," as Ramón puts it. Guerrero shows how the evolution of *conciertos'* debts responded to household needs, but he notes that the level of debt was also an index of the balance of power between landowner and laborers. Laborers continually pressured landowners and administrators to maintain or increase the level of redistribution (Guerrero 1991:304ff). Reciprocity was not simply a mask for exploitation but an outcome of ongoing struggle and an object of persistent tension (Scott 1985:308–309).

Ramón and Guerrero offer contrasting cases that illustrate what could happen if the moral and economic logic of each side, landlord or laborers, were followed without having to consider the response of the other side. Ramón's case concerns a large hacienda whose owner, Ramón de Borja, fell ill in 1802. Borja was bedridden for eight years and had no heirs or relatives he could trust to replace him in supervising the hacienda. He left his mestizo employees ("servants") in charge of the hacienda. They failed to look after his interests, however, as he wrote after his recovery and return to the hacienda in 1810: "The Indians, particularly those I call foremen [*capataces*], ran down the hacienda in such a way, and destroyed it so much, that I am not able to restore it easily . . . The servants, in cahoots with the Indians, all joined together, the better to usurp my domain and my legitimately acquired rights, and . . . didn't look upon [the hacienda] as someone else's property, but they all . . . treated it as goods without an owner." Ramón describes further what happened in Borja's absence and after his return:

> The servants and the Indians had significantly intensified their relations; many of them had become *compadres* in order to obtain many mutual benefits. The hurried pace of work had diminished, and redistribution from the hacienda to the Indians had increased considerably, while the servants made use of goods and labor for their own benefit. . . . The servants in charge of agricultural work . . . used the labor force on their own plots, while they allowed the plow oxen to work the Indians' *huasipungos* . . . So-called tolerated theft visibly increased, the idea flowered of the hacienda as a space for communal use from which one could take a bit of forage, agricultural products, firewood, and even a sheep now and then . . .
>
> Ramón de Borja . . . on his return fires all the servants . . . With words, whip, and imprisonment, he returns to the old relationship. . . . Borja argues: "If the bad Indians are not subdued . . . through the appropriate punishment . . . there will be no fruit, no progress, neither toward good moral order . . . , nor for the property owner's own benefit."
> (RAMÓN VALAREZO 1987: 255–257)

The situation during Borja's absence was not one of complete freedom for the laborers—the mestizo administrators retained positions of authority and privilege, based, ultimately, on their access to sources of power outside the hacienda. Nonetheless, the results of this period were sufficient for Borja to see an irreconcilable contradiction between the behavior of the "bad Indians," who had pushed their logic of reciprocity as far as they could, and his own interests as owner of the hacienda.

Guerrero presents an opposite case: the persons running the hacienda carry their search for profits to an extreme without worrying about the response of the laborers. This is something a landowner could never do, since the resident labor force was a significant part of the long-term value of a hacienda and, over time, the laborers' resistance or flight would affect profits. A renter, however, might well disregard the laborers' reactions for the sake of his or her own short-term profit, particularly toward the end of the rental period.

Around 1907, Sebastián Calisto rented three haciendas to two of his relatives, Nicolás and Guillermo Arteta. The Arteta brothers seem to have severely cut or stopped the distribution of *socorros* and supplements. When their lease expired, they "only returned eleven laborers, without their debts." They also suspended the local fiesta of Saint Peter, formerly an occasion for the distribution of money, food, and drink by the hacienda; instead, they occupied the laborers in the wheat and barley harvests. The result: within a few years, almost 80 percent of the resident labor force apparently abandoned the haciendas. Calisto, shocked on recovering his haciendas absent the labor force, called this a form of "damage that has no name." He resolved "that, if I cannot attend to them personally, I would prefer a thousand times to sell" rather than rent out the haciendas again.

As landowner, his own attitude toward redistribution had to take into account not only the immediate costs to him, but also the long-term importance of maintaining and reproducing the labor force on his haciendas. Put another way, redistribution was an unavoidable cost imposed on him by the resistance and danger of desertion of the labor force (Guerrero 1991:263, 288–293).

There was, then, an inherent conflict between the logic of the two sides; each, carried to an extreme, tended to a situation that would be intolerable for the other. This conflict can be expressed as a conflict between economic interests—the profit to the landlord of selling the products versus the interest of the laborers in capturing a greater portion for household consumption and other expenses. It can be expressed as a conflict between economic logics—the capitalist logic of profit and accumulation versus the logic of reciprocity.

As argued earlier, however, reciprocity is not simply an economic logic but also a moral system. The conflict has an emotive, moral expression; as Guerrero notes, one of its most commonplace expressions from the side of the *conciertos* is the idea that the *patrón* "*mezquina*," that is, stingily blocks or refuses access to goods that a normal, moral person would allow. In what follows, I wish to discuss in more depth the tensions between the two cultural, moral, and economic logics and the day-to-day expression of these tensions. My aim here is not to return to an old view of the hacienda system as based exclusively on coercion. A more complete view, however, requires an account of the ways that the hacienda incorporated principles of reciprocity—and the ways that indigenous residents did *not* view the hacienda as behaving like a partner in a pact of reciprocity. This second aspect represents the limits in the degree to which reciprocity could serve as a strategy of "disguise"; at the same time, it represents the limits in the degree to which indigenous people were able to impose their own vision of moral behavior on the hacienda. Their options and their bargaining strength, after all, were limited.

As Mauss argues (1990), assumptions associated with gift exchange continue to shape people's experience of social and economic life even in Western capitalist societies, so Western readers will not find what follows to be totally alien. At the same time, Ecuadorian villagers develop such assumptions in their own particular way, so that their critique of the hacienda will require some cultural translation. Moreover, reciprocity shapes their view of the world in a more pervasive and fundamental way than it does for most Westerners. Hence, their critique of the hacienda focuses more on landlords' failure to act as moral exchange partners than on the origins of the hacienda system as such. It stresses their own needs, sacrifices, and expectations of consideration more than impersonal rights or landlords' compliance with explicit agreements or with Ecuadorian law. Finally, it is cast more in terms of how landlords and bosses behaved than in abstract, structural language.

Labor as a Favor

An Ecuadorian villager requesting labor from a relative or neighbor will often refer to the labor as a *favor* (the Spanish word is spelled the same as in English; Quichua speakers in Pangor also use it). The notion of labor as a favor saturates the conventional forms of such transactions. Between households, between people who respect one another, labor is ceremoniously requested, not demanded. Even precolonial or early colonial chiefs—highly respected, powerful figures—"pleaded" or "begged" (rogaban) for their subjects' labor (Salomon 1986a:125, 131). Today, the act of calling on someone else's labor is referred to in similar terms: to "request," "plead," or "beg" the favor (*rogana* <Sp. *rogar*, *mañana*). The person whose labor is requested may plead inability: I can't on that particular day; I have a prior commitment; I am too far behind in my own work. Each side in a relationship of mutual goodwill is under the obligation to be considerate of the other side's circumstances and

needs. If someone is unable to perform a requested favor, both sides ask for the other's understanding and pardon: the person who refuses the favor for his or her inability to perform it; the person who requested it for having put the other one in the difficult position of having to refuse.

If the labor is performed, the beneficiary provides the laborer's meals (and sometimes alcoholic drinks). This is partly a matter of convenience, and in some circumstances, it may also be explicitly part of the payment for the labor. More fundamentally, though, food is a key symbol of gratitude for the aid the laborer is providing, an expression of respect, goodwill, and "consideration" for the laborer's own needs. Most broadly, the sharing of food underlines the social relationship in which other exchanges are embedded.

As for the pace and quality of the work, the beneficiary expects that the laborer will reciprocate a good meal with good work. If he is working alongside the laborer, as is typical, his ability to maintain a given pace sets a limit on demands on the laborer. He may exert pressure, but the need to maintain the personal relationship with the laborer keeps this pressure within the bounds of tact and good humor. Someone who exceeds the accepted limits of pressure will have trouble securing labor the next time.

The hacienda did not have to and did not operate on the same principles. Former laborers' accounts are unanimous in describing some features of the hacienda labor regime: *amos* made heavy, inflexible labor demands and enforced those demands through threats and whippings. The *amos'* basic stance toward laborers, their readiness to threaten and whip the laborers, was perhaps represented by another feature former laborers always mention: racial insults. Structural reasons can help explain this.

Under the *huasipungaje* system, the hacienda's labor costs were mostly fixed—the opportunity cost of granting usufruct of a plot and access to other resources. Monetary wages were quite low, payments in kind that were in direct relation to labor were limited to the harvest, and even food was provided to laborers only on special occasions. Once a laborer was on the rolls and occupying a plot, there was little marginal cost to the hacienda of demanding additional workdays. The hacienda had an incentive to squeeze as much labor out of its resident labor force as could be put to productive use. On a large hacienda with a small labor force and labor-intensive technology, this meant, essentially, as much labor as it could.

From the laborers' point of view, of course, the situation was exactly the converse. There was little marginal benefit to each workday on the hacienda; a nominal salary (if any) could not compete with the urgency of tending to their own family plots, which, together with their animals, were the basis of their subsistence.

There was, then, a built-in conflict between the hacienda's labor demands and the laborers' need to attend to their own plots. The compound family unit was a partial solution to this problem: adult sons or others living as *arrimados* evaded the full labor demands of the hacienda by delaying the reception of a plot in their own right. The *arrimados* could work the family plot while the *concierto* or *huasipunguero* head of the household fulfilled the hacienda's labor demands (Guerrero 1977:86–92). While the greatest labor demands were made of those whose names were attached to a usufruct plot, however, the hacienda did not refrain from demanding labor of anybody who lived on the hacienda or used hacienda resources. Even children contributed labor. Avelino Shagñay, for example, remembers that as a child he sometimes had to spend cold nights watching over pigs rooting in hacienda fields that had been plowed or hoed up, so that their manure would fertilize the field prior to planting. One of the things people today most frequently mention about the hacienda period is that they had no time to rest, barely time to sleep. The hacienda required four, five, or even six days of work per week of the *huasipungueros*, sometimes leaving only Sunday—the theoretical day of rest—for them to attend to their own agricultural labors.[2] Whatever the role of hacienda supplements in guaranteeing subsistence, then, the hacienda's own labor demands were one of the main threats to subsistence.

One way the hacienda squeezed labor from the resident community was to assign work by set tasks (*tareas*). A task was theoretically one day's work for one person and corresponded to one *raya*, but it was set at a very demanding standard. Sometimes two or more family members had to work together to complete the assigned task in a day. The tasks also often required the use of oxen or pack animals, which the hacienda did not necessarily supply. Task work was thus especially burdensome for those who did not have their own animals and for those without large families to help them.

The imposition of a uniform, inflexible standard through task work, with no consideration for differences in people's abilities to meet the standard, was especially resented as unjust. For example, José María Pillajo—who says he did own sufficient animals but who had a small family—comments on the situation of the five or six poorest *conciertos:*

> Those people didn't have anything . . . Nonetheless, on the hacienda, they received the same orders. . . . The same tasks, equal loads of potatoes to carry, or manure, whatever tasks had to be done. For hoeing tasks, fifteen *brazos*, you see? Fifteen *brazos* long, five wide. . . . One person alone, no way. . . . If there was no one to help, it would take two days, even three days, to do one task. . . .

The stewards, the overseers—well, the overseers were somewhat considerate. But on the other hand, the stewards were not at all considerate, no. That's how it was. (9/2/1992)

Rosa Condo recalled the help she received from others when she was a young woman fulfilling the labor requirement for her aged grandparents:

If there was no man who could help in the work on the day of the assignment, as a woman alone I had trouble loading up the animals. . . . I learned to ask relatives or neighbors for help. Some people were considerate. They saw that a poor woman alone can't be expected to work with the strength of a man, so they helped. So I learned to plead, "Please do me the favor of putting the load on the animal, please help me." I can't complain about my fellows: they did help me. (8/23/1992)

The ties of mutual aid among relatives and neighbors helped lighten her burden. This aid contrasted with what she described as the bosses' harsh and inconsiderate treatment. Reinaldo Sisa recalled hacienda life with less bitterness than any other former laborer. But he said the *amos* did not help in any way when a laborer was ill and required the laborer's wife to replace him in the fields. When a laborer asked for leave to attend to a wife in labor, he said, the bosses would tell the man to go and give birth and send his wife to work in his stead (RS 6/15/95).

In general, what stands out in accounts of the hacienda period is the constant tension between the hacienda's labor demands and people's household labor needs, the lack of consideration for the latter, the lack of allowance for negotiation and mutual accommodation. Again, José María Pillajo: "How it was on the hacienda! . . . We are doing some work for ourselves, . . . and at any moment the stewards pass by, shouting, giving orders to go someplace. Sending us somewhere, to Riobamba . . . , or for house service [*huasicamía*], or . . . for whatever. 'Now . . . it's your turn, now you have to go . . .' Now you have to go, you have to obey orders. That's how it was" (7/21/1991). The contrast with the etiquette of labor requests among indigenous people could not be sharper.

As for meals during work, labor on the hacienda was the opposite of labor exchange among peasant households: not only did the hacienda not normally feed the laborers, but stewards did not even allow them sufficient time to eat their own food. Some assignments, such as trips to town (*acude*) or house service in the hacienda, generally did come with meals, but the food was often skimpy and might be denied for the slightest offense. Let me cite comments from two interviews with Tayta José María:

The young girls had to go milk the cows at 4:00. The young boys had
to help in hacienda labors every week. There was no one to pasture a
sheep of our own, an animal, no one to look after anything. [We worked]
with food in our stomach or an empty stomach, without breakfast. The
women would have to follow later, bringing lunch to us where we were
working. We would be allowed to sit down for lunch at 12:00. Before
1:00, they would be telling us to get up. "Are you still eating? Do you
still have *mashka* [ground roasted barley]?" Already, the stewards would
be shouting. They made us get up without eating well. As I say, those
Laras were such bad people. (JMP 9/2/1992)

As for the *acude* . . . They would collect cheese and eggs . . . Come
Friday . . . someone had to go to Riobamba to leave the loads. Sometimes
we would get back on Saturday, sometimes on Sunday. . . .

If an egg broke, the *patrona* [the renter's wife] would be criticizing us,
insulting us something awful. We wouldn't get lunch. If we got lunch, it
was just a couple of reales [to buy lunch], that's all. (JMP 7/21/1991)

Along with their own food, laborers also had to use their own tools, animals, and gear to fulfill their work assignments. This is another frequent
point of criticism in my interviews. This practice on the hacienda contrasts
sharply with pre-Columbian norms; the Inca state demanded labor of its subjects but supplied the raw materials and tools. Just why this should be such
a sore point in modern times, when no one remembers the Inca practice, is
not explicit in my interviews. Again, though, it would seem to be a matter
of consideration. Laborers' tools and animals were indispensable for their
own subsistence. Just as consideration for the laborer's well-being and subsistence obligated the beneficiary to replenish through food the energy ex-
pended in labor, so the hacienda should have provided or replaced the tools
and gear and supplied the animals used in work for its benefit.

Another interview confirms that the criticism related to food, tools, and
animals is not simply a product of the changes of recent decades and retrospective comparison with current labor arrangements. The speaker here is
Carmelo Condo, a man in his seventies from the neighboring hacienda of
Ajospamba. Tayta Carmelo led his fellow laborers of Ajospamba through the
agrarian reform process; here he tells of giving testimony about labor arrangements in the agrarian reform office in Quito. Note the differences in
the way he speaks about food, animals, and gear and the way he talks about
vacations:

They asked about the gear used for the harvest: our own sack, straps,
and hooks [for tying sacks of harvested potatoes on the backs of horses],

our own animals. Because [on the hacienda] they didn't provide that, not even the animals, but they ordered us by force to work with our own animals, our gear, our food.

After that, they asked [about vacations]—the *amos*, it turned out, were supposed to have given us vacations something like two or three times a year. They didn't give us vacations either. (cc/vyu n.d.)

It is clear that Tayta Carmelo learned about the *amos'* obligation to give vacations from the agrarian reform agents. He uses the Quichua verbal suffix *-shka* in this context; this is used for secondhand knowledge or knowledge acquired only at the moment being narrated (i.e., Tayta Carmelo's encounter with the agrarian reform officers; I translate this as "it turned out"). In referring to the animals, gear, and food, in contrast, he comments indignantly that the hacienda used coercion to make the laborers work without providing these.

There is no reason to believe that resentment over food was associated with any memory of a period when the hacendados were more benevolent. From the beginnings of the hacienda system, even when it still depended on *mitayo* labor, there are records of protests against employers who did not feed their *mitayo* servants and laborers (Pérez Tamayo 1947; cf. Bonnet Vélez 1992:103–104, 120). This recurrent theme reflects, on the one hand, the constant attitudes of an elite that felt it had a right to Indian labor, not as a favor for which it owned respect and recompense, but as the tribute of a despised, conquered people; on the other hand, it reflects Runa peasants' continued practice of treating one another's labor with gratitude and respect.

It is quite possible that labor demands on Monjas Corral and other haciendas in Chimborazo were less intense prior to the market expansion associated with the late nineteenth-century cacao boom, the construction of the railroad, and twentieth-century population growth and urbanization. Oral history, however, offers no indication of any long period when hacienda labor demands were typically reasonable: informants born in the early and midtwentieth century seem to have learned from *their* elders that the hacienda experience was essentially the same from generation to generation. Different landowners, renters, and stewards would come and go, some of them a little better, others worse; at most, there is a sense of random fluctuation, not any long-term trend.

Whether this sense is a function of the limitations of oral memory, the nature of local history, or something else, the important point is that it was not *necessary* to preserve or construct any memory of a golden age in order to criticize and resent the hacienda's labor demands. Often, physical hunger, exhaustion, and worries about one's own crops and animals were sufficient grounds for resentment. In moral terms, it was enough to assume that the beneficiaries of one's labor should treat that labor as a favor, that they should be considerate of one's own needs and personal circumstances, that they should express recognition and gratitude for the favor, among other ways, by feeding the laborer. Hacienda Runa reproduced these assumptions not by recounting historical memories or utopian visions but, rather, in their own day-to-day labor exchanges and, more broadly, in all the domains of social behavior informed by the morality of gift exchange.

On a hacienda like Monjas Corral, belonging to an institution and rented by individuals, the renters faced a special problem in presenting a moral claim to the residents' labor. Renters viewed themselves as having paid for the use of the land and therefore the right to the labor of those using its resources during the rental period. For people who thought in terms of personal relations, however, claims on them could not so easily be bought and sold. The land belonged to the priests and nuns; the renters were strangers to whom they owed nothing. According to the late Pacho Pingos (a former *ayuda* laborer), this was one of the arguments Monjas Corral Runa sometimes used in conflicts over renters' labor demands or other issues: you do not own the land any more than we do; this land belongs to the priests and nuns (FP/JH 12/11/1990).

The case is familiar enough in everyday life in Ecuador. I may owe you a favor, and you may owe something to someone else who is a stranger to me. You might ask me to help you in some way to repay the stranger, but my obligation continues to be to you, not to the stranger. In the morality of gifts and favors, a debt cannot simply be transferred or sold to a third party—as contractual debt in a market economy can. I may do the service requested as a favor to you but will not feel under any particular obligation to the stranger. I might not work as hard or as well for him as I would for your benefit—unless that person gives me something in order to initiate our own personal relationship.

New renters could conceivably have reassigned usufruct plots as a way of demonstrating their power over the land and affirming their generosity. That does not seem to have been a general practice, however. Nor was I told of any special distributions on the part of new renters, any rituals by which they showed generosity as a basis for the relationship. In Reinaldo Sisa's depiction of the arrival of a new renter, only the laborers gave gifts to the renter, in the evident hope that this gesture might induce him to be moderate in his treatment of them. The renters based their claim to people's labor on the contracts signed in Riobamba and more directly on the notebooks containing the laborers' names, which Tayta Reinaldo compared to a list of prisoners. This dialogue is worth citing in full:

BL What happened when a new renter came? Would they gather together the people that day?

RS No. They would just arrange things among themselves, in Riobamba, I guess. When seven years was up, the old *amo* renters wouldn't come back. Then, the new *amo* renters would start to come around. So then people would say, "Now we have new *amos*. We have new *patrones*." They would just come and we'd see them, these other *amos* whom we didn't know.

"Now we have to serve them. Now they have rented the hacienda. The old renter has left, and won't come back now." . . .

Those *amos'* stewards would put us on a list, all of the laborers on this hacienda. We were fifteen or sixteen [full-time hacienda laborers], those years. . . . They would get all the names . . . written in their notebook, the names of husband and wife. Once they got the list, they would just keep that. Poor us, once we were entered on the list, like a prisoner or a debtor, once on the list, we worked. Yes, based on that, they would demand that we work.

If someone missed a Monday, they would be quick to strike him. If someone missed a Tuesday, if he didn't go join the others at work, they would be quick to strike him. That's how they treated people routinely in the old days, with beatings. They would refuse [literally, "take away"; Q. *kichuk*] the *raya*. They gave a *raya* for each day of work. The *raya* is what they called the mark in the notebook that showed who was absent, who missed work. They kept a record with the *rayas*. So if someone missed work, they would be quick to strike him. That's what people's lives—our lives—were like. . . .

BL So, when they came, . . . they would write your names in the notebook. And did they tell you their names?

RS Yes, the new *amos*, on Monday. That is, somehow—who knows exactly how—they would arrange things in Riobamba, in writing. I don't know, but sure, then, on a Monday they would come. We would all gather on the hacienda. I remember when I was little, a long time ago, and my parents went. Everyone went.

Afterwards, people said, "Now we've met the new *amo*. He's a good, old *amo*, he's a good, big old *amo*, a man of respect."

He said, "Now, I am your *patrón*. Now you will serve me. You will carry out orders." He wrote everything in the notebook.

"Husband and wife, husband and wife, husband and wife, he inscribes all of us in the notebook, poor us," people said. That's what people would be talking about.

When I was older, too, it was just the same. "The new *amo* is coming. The new owner of the hacienda is coming. Let's all go, let's all go to greet him, let's all go to receive him. A chicken, eggs, or cheese, we'll take that to give to the new *amo*."

So then, *patroncito*,	Shinashpaka, *patroncito*
so then, *patronita*,	Shinashpaka, *patronita*
You, our little bosses,	Shinashpaca, kan patrón wawakunatami
we are to serve.	ña servina kanchik.
You, our little bosses,	Kan patrón wawakunatami
we are to do what you tell us.	ña mandado rurana kanchik,
That's how people would plead.	nishpa, rogashpa.
We are the little laborers,	Nukanchikmi shina peón wawakuna kanchik,
the little laborers who work and live here.	peón wawakuna kaypi trabajash kawsanchik.
Now, you little bosses,	Kunanka kan patrón wawakunami
it turns out you are our *patrón*.	ñukanchik *patrón* kashkangi.

That's how the people would talk with the *patrón* and receive him. Likewise, the *patrón* would receive the people in turn. We and the *patrón* would continue to get to know each other. That's what our life was like.

BL And then, would you talk among yourselves, saying, this *amo* looks good, or looks bad?

RS Yes. That's what would be on our minds: Who knows what these *amos* will be like?

That other one was bad; perhaps this new one will be good.

The old *amos* hit people.	Ñawpa amokunaka makarka.
The old *amos* whipped people.	Ñawpa amokunaka acialarka.
The old *amos* clubbed people.	Ñawpa amokunaka garrotearka.

And now, this new *amo*, who knows what he will be like? That's what people would say.

And it just went from bad to worse. They all turned out the same. They beat people. . . . They called people *indio, rocoto, baboso*. That's how they treated us Runitos. "Baboso, indio, rocotos, verdugos [racial insults]." That's how the *amos* insulted us all the time. That's what we had to bear. (9/14/1992)

The renter established his claim to labor through the alien, coercive power of writing, not by demonstrating generosity and creating a personal debt on the part of the laborers. The laborers would nonetheless allow themselves some hope that the renter would behave like a "man of respect," only to be repeatedly disappointed.

Laborers often directed their resentment over the hacienda's labor demands toward those who were charged with enforcing these demands—the indigenous overseer and the mestizo steward. This put overseers, especially, in a dilemma. They found it difficult to balance fellow Runa's moral expectations of them with the bosses' demands. Several people told me of having refused the position despite the privileges it offered.

> JMP I said no. "Not me, *patroncito*, I won't be able to do it, no way, I won't do that."
> "Faggot, jerk, dammit! Why don't you want to serve as overseer?"
> "I won't be up to the job. I won't do that, I'm not going to do it."
> He didn't insist.
> BL Why didn't you want to do it?
> JMP I don't like anything about the overseers. The overseers would arbitrarily [*yanga*] give orders,[3] . . . and the people would easily get angry. They would get angry, hit him, insult him. That's why I said no. (JMP 9/2/1992)

Similarly, Reinaldo Sisa:

> Some people don't like the overseer. They're quick to insult him: "Lazy bum," they say. "He's just standing around. . . . He should take a hoe, too, or a machete. He should bend his back and work. He just goes around giving orders."
> That's how people would criticize the overseer. That's why I wouldn't listen [when asked to be overseer]. (9/14/1992)

The overseer's function, at least in the eyes of the laborers, was essentially coercive—to force them to work. Overseers are not described as having made any real contribution to the production process. At the same time, the overseer was subject to the pressure of social disapproval and even occasional counterviolence on the part of other laborers if he rigidly enforced his superiors' orders.

Gabriel Niamo's comments about his late father, who was a longtime overseer on Monjas Corral, provide a good sense of the importance of coercion on the hacienda, the difficulty of reconciling the hacienda's demands with Runa moral expectations, and the role of social pressure from below in moderating the overseer's behavior: "My father was named overseer . . . to make the people work. To make people from other haciendas come work [in *ayuda* labor]. They have animals on this hacienda, they gather firewood or straw on this hacienda. The *amos* would order him, 'Go and bring back *prendas*, be strict with them.'" A *prenda* was an item, such as an article of clothing or a tool, forcibly taken as a "security" and returned when the person worked. People would plead with the overseer to be flexible: "We don't have time; we'll come some other time":

But . . . the *amos* . . . demanded . . . "You be unyielding and bring back *prendas*. . . . Just make them work." . . .

My late father . . . wasn't like that. Just somewhat . . . he would give orders . . . tell people what to do. . . .

Sometimes people would be angry with him . . . "He doesn't have any consideration for us. The *amo* gives orders, and he carries them out," they would say . . .

But it wasn't his fault. When the *amos* gave orders, . . . sometimes, well, okay, he would obey. Sometimes, . . . he would just do a part of what they ordered and would pretend to do the rest. He wasn't altogether bad. . . .

The *amos* . . . would just order him to hit, to beat, to mistreat people. But my mother would say, "Don't be bad like that. You will become bad in people's eyes. People will become even angrier with you, they will behave like enemies. It's not good. It's easy for the *amos* to order you to do anything that occurs to them." . . . Mother taught him not to do what the *amos* ordered. (8/23/1992)

Tayta Gabriel appeared a bit equivocal, not entirely at ease in discussing this aspect of his father's life. Other people's judgments of his father might differ. What is clear is the inherent conflict the overseer faced between orders from above and pressures from the community, including his own wife.

As for the stewards, I have already cited José Pillajo: if the overseers were sometimes somewhat considerate, the stewards were not so at all. Lacking positive ties of reciprocity with laboring families, and having more access than overseers to external coercive support, stewards could be impervious to laborers' particular circumstances and needs (see also Brandi 1976:42).

A couple of other comments, however, suggest a situation that was a bit more complex. Tayta José did remark that there were some "good mayordomitos" (the diminutive of mayordomo), though his brief description was punctuated by the memory of the harshest stewards, Ignacio Lara and his associates: "Ignacio Lara, what a bad man! Then, other stewards would come. They were sometimes good *mayordomitos*, sociable with the people. If someone offered them lunch, they would eat it, be together with people, and give fair orders. The Laras, they were extremely mean" (JMP 7/21/1991). It was not impossible, then, that a steward could be thought of as "good"—and, by extension, that the hacienda's labor demands could be viewed as reasonable.

But the "bad" steward, Ignacio Lara, is the one people most talk about, most remember. In part, this is because he stands out as having been exceptionally cruel; yet, his name is often brought up as epitomizing stewards in general, the evils of the hacienda in general, the suffering that people had to endure on the hacienda.

Another reason that Lara is so remembered—and this is what is most telling—is that he was steward on repeated occasions over a long period of time:

Sometimes, . . . the *amos* say [the steward is] not doing a good job . . . of giving orders, and then they send that steward away. They bring someone else. . . .

[Ignacio Lara] came again and again. He would leave and then come back. He would say they had asked him to return: . . . "I'm walking around in Riobamba, and the *patrón* calls me. 'Ignacio, please return and serve me. The other employees [stewards] don't do anything. . . . You know when to plant, you know how to make the Indians work. Ignacio, come back and serve me.'" . . .

He wouldn't get along with us, and he would go away . . . to other haciendas, as steward. There, too, everywhere, since he was a bad man, people didn't want to see his face. (JMP 9/2/1992)[4]

This account suggests a pattern of alternation between more moderate stewards and the harsher steward. The more moderate stewards could even be brought into the net of reciprocity—they would accept food from people and be considerate in their demands; however, they could not satisfy the renters, who called in Lara to make people work harder. The harsher steward, on the other hand, eventually provoked too much dissatisfaction, resistance, and flight on the part of the labor force for him to stay indefinitely. A trio of Peace Corps volunteers who conducted interviews in Chimborazo in the late 1960s elicited comments suggesting a similar pattern: "Those are the ones who really screw you, the [stewards] and the [overseers]. When they're bad, the peons call them names like 'bastard' and 'ass-kisser.' . . . But if a [steward] or [overseer] is really bad, at the most he'll last two years, and not a year more. Of course, if the [steward is] good, he won't last more than three years anyway" (Brandi 1976:63). Beyond the individual qualities of particular stewards, then, there was evidently a structural difficulty in arriving at a "pact" mutually acceptable to landlords and laborers.

The Stinginess of Landlords

One of the attractions the Pangor area offered people from the crowded central basin was that landowners and renters were *not* "stingy" about land to cultivate and about the number of animals residents were allowed to keep on hacienda pastures. Land was relatively plentiful, while laborers were scarce.

On the other hand, former hacienda residents describe the renters as quite tightfisted in other respects. I have already noted the hacienda's "stinginess" with meals for laborers. *Socorros* seem to have been limited to one or two sacks of potatoes or grain a year. Let me return now to the question of supplements, which I discuss in some detail earlier on the basis of nineteenth-century account books and Guerrero's and Ramón's work on northern Ecuador.

I was never spontaneously told about supplements. Andrés Yépez insisted that the *amos* provided no aid in case of illness, fiesta sponsorship, or other necessity. He said that, in the event of crop failure, laborers had to sell animals in order to buy food. José María Pillajo confirmed all of this indignantly: "We would have to bear the costs [of illness]. . . . The *amos* wouldn't . . . look after the person, not at all. They were just interested in giving orders" (7/21/1991). Reinaldo Sisa likewise spoke of selling animals to get cash for various necessities. He pointed to aid between indigenous households as a way those whose harvest was poor were able to make up the shortfall. Households also sometimes sent some of their members to the maize region, where they worked in the harvest in exchange for grain.

A piece of indirect linguistic evidence supports these accounts. I asked Miguel Guailla, who was born on Monjas Corral in the late 1950s or the early to mid-1960s, how he understood the word *suplido*. I assume that Tayta Miguel's sense of the meaning of the word emerged from hearing his elders talk during his childhood and youth about the past and perhaps the transitional period on Monjas Corral. He explained that *suplido* referred to hunks of meat from animals that died in an accident or from disease on the hacienda. The meat was bought by laborers on credit (to be discounted from their wages). This was a type of supplement the hacienda could not avoid, since accidents or illness could not always be prevented. Selling the meat to the laborers was better than having it rot and losing an animal for nothing. This response suggests again that, at least toward the end of the hacienda period, supplements were indeed very restricted.

The same was true of other types of payment in kind. In labor exchange among households, it is common to give a payment in kind in lieu of a monetary payment, particularly when the labor involves harvesting or processing of food. This payment, termed a *ración*, generally consists of a portion of the same product the person was working with, as noted above. According to José Pillajo, however, the hacienda bosses "wouldn't give . . . any *ración*, nothing. On the grounds that they paid [money], they wouldn't give . . . any *ración*. Maybe we would take a couple [of potatoes] in our pocket. There would be some big potatoes. Sometimes, by the end of the afternoon, we would have four or five potatoes to take home. Nothing more. Do you think they would ever give a good *ración?*" (JMP 7/21/1991). Tayta José refers here to the customary right of laborers in a harvest to take home a limited quantity of especially big potatoes that they came across in the course of their work. Villagers who help to harvest one another's fields today continue to carry out this practice, called *wanllana*,[5] and the number of potatoes a harvester should take is similarly limited in that context. On the hacienda, however, where the laborers were not satisfied with the low or nonexistent money wage, the limited annual *socorro*, and the nonexistent *ración*, *wanllana* sometimes became an arena of conflict over the level of redistribution. Four or five potatoes could be pocketed openly, but the stewards would not allow more than that. People did sometimes take more, however. If the stewards noticed, they would take the potatoes away by force, Tayta José says—"with a beating, with a whipping. 'You people are taking too much'" (JMP 7/21/1991).

Postharvest gleaning could also lead to conflict. As a young man in Ajospamba, Avelino Shagñay was helping harvest potatoes for the hacienda. Women were following behind the line of harvesters, gleaning what they had missed. The steward accused Avelino of deliberately leaving potatoes in the ground for the gleaners and struck him with the whip. Avelino (by his account) stood up and swung back at the surprised steward with the handle of his hoe. For some time afterward, the steward swore he would kill Avelino.

One day, the steward ambushed him on a path and pistol-whipped him in front of some other Ajospambeños, who watched in fear.

Given the hacienda's stinginess in laborers' eyes, it is likely that a good part of the "redistribution" that took place on the hacienda actually consisted of covert appropriation—that is, theft, from the renters' and stewards' point of view. It is naturally hard to gauge the level of covert appropriation, but it was clearly significant on many haciendas—or could have been but for the stewards' vigilance. I mentioned above that the *concierto* responsible for making cheese in Monjas Corral in 1887–1888 was charged for about a cheese a month, on average. We cannot be sure, but these charges appear to have been based on the administrator's suspicions—perhaps on a count —rather than representing an open, mutually acceptable transfer or gift of cheese. The distinction may not have made any difference in the calculation of debt, but it must have made a difference in the cheese maker's experience of the hacienda. Instead of the administrator's generously giving him a cheese every so often in recognition of and gratitude for his labor and in consideration of his family's needs, the administrator attempted to prevent him from taking home any cheese and charged him a fine when he suspected he had done so.

One of the common forms of covert appropriation on the hacienda concerned the irrigated, specially planted hacienda pastures, officially reserved for hacienda animals. Hacienda laborers frequently pastured their own animals there at night. José María Pillajo was telling me about the Laras when I asked him if they impeded access to the hacienda pastures:

Yes, they impeded access, they impeded, they impeded. . . . Surreptitiously, we just . . . tied [horses] in the pastures . . . at night. Then, if they found out, . . . they would send the house servants [*huasicamas*] . . . "Go see, go bring the animals that are tied there back to the hacienda, to charge a fine."

Yes, they were really damnable. (9/2/1992)

Tayta José does not exactly spell out the moral basis of his indignation here; it has to be inferred from his language. I used the verb *mitsak* in my question to mean "impeded access." The word also suggests stinginess (or "stinged"), and it seems to take on this nuance in his response when he immediately repeats the word three times. The implication seems to be simply that a bit of nibbling by the animals at this desirable pasturage could and should have been tolerated, that the stewards had no need to charge a fine, that in doing so they confirmed their own stinginess and ill will.

Conflict over pilfering has been constant on Ecuadorian haciendas. Like elites elsewhere in similar positions (Scott 1990:188ff), the landowning elite came to attribute thievery to their subordinates' inherent racial makeup or cultural backwardness. A seventeenth-century bishop of Quito, Alonso de la Peña, devotes several pages of his guide for parish priests to elucidating the circumstances under which such theft is a justifiable response to tyrannical mistreatment or, to the contrary, a mortal sin calling for restitution. His answers are relatively favorable to the Indians, but he worries about the consequences if priests appear to excuse pilfering in confession. Thus, he instructs priests to rebuke penitents for even minor thefts more harshly than is theologically warranted in order to avoid giving any encouragement to the Indians, "who are truly inclined to theft" (Peña Montenegro [1668] 1985:166).

Landlords were forced to devise ways of minimizing such losses: "The property owner has to be constantly vigilant and alert, since, if he lets up his watch the slightest bit, the Indian . . . takes whatever object he can . . . In the harvests, it has become necessary to recur to a thousand stratagems to keep the Indians from reducing the yield by taking a part of it into their own hands" (cited in Espinosa 1984:167n68).

In Pangor as elsewhere, the *amos* attempted to maintain tight control over products and other goods by assigning responsibility for them to specific laborers and charging fines for any losses. Some of these fines went beyond charges for losses that might have been due to theft. The fines themselves became another source of resentment and conflict. Arbitrary fines are a prominent, emotionally laden theme in contemporary talk about the hacienda period, more so than, say, low monetary pay. They constituted a form of negative redistribution, as it were—the precise inverse of an appropriate recompense for labor.

Couples fulfilling their six-week turn of service in the hacienda house were charged a fine for any implements that were lost or even broken in the course of their work. In the potato harvest, someone was given the task of watching over piles of harvested potatoes through the night. Each pile was measured. Sometimes, as a result of faulty measuring, Alberto Yumbo said, a small amount might later appear to be missing. The *amos* then "would call us thieves" (7/16/1992).

One of the hardest jobs on the hacienda was that of cowhand. The cowhand had to watch over hundreds of cattle roaming over the cold, windy expanses of high *páramo*. He would be fined for a lost animal and sometimes even for an animal that died in an accident: "If an animal died, we would skin it, bring it down, and turn it over to them, with an explanation of how it died. Then, they wouldn't believe it and would get angry. 'Why did you kill it? What did you bring it here for? Take it away and do what you want with it,' they would say. We would plead to be able to leave the carcass hanging in the hacienda [yard]" (AYu 7/16/1992). If the steward refused the carcass, this meant he would charge the cowhand for the animal.

This practice of charging hacienda laborers for the death or loss of animals under their care is another old and recurring theme in criticism of the north Andean hacienda. Bishop de la Peña observed in 1668 that hacendados were imposing arbitrary fines to convert *mitayo* laborers into indebted *conciertos* (Peña Montenegro [1668] 1985:164–165; see also Juan and Ulloa [1747] 1990:297–298, 300–301). In his 1895 attack on *concertaje*, the liberal writer Abelardo Moncayo comments ironically, "[The *patrona*] is not immortal, but why shouldn't her horses be immortal?" ([1895] 1986:309). More than once, this practice led to open resistance: Pérez cites cases in 1679 and 1758 in which *mitayo* shepherds brought their protests before the judicial system (1947:101–109).

The practice was a precipitating factor in one of the rare instances of violence against the steward on Monjas Corral. José María Pillajo was cowhand when a cow died in an accident. The steward, Ignacio Lara, refused to accept the carcass, precipitating a bitter argument. Later, one night during the fiesta of Saint Rose, Tayta José and two companions got into a fight with Lara and his two assistants. As the laborers began to get the upper hand, Lara's assistants fled. Tayta José and his companions then took Lara to the icy river that ran near the hacienda house and forced him to "bathe" there. Forced immersion in a cold river was an old punishment traditionally applied by indigenous people to suspected animal rustlers. Perhaps its application in this case implied that Lara's behavior was an inversion of decent conduct analogous to stealing a laborer's animal.

Fines no doubt sometimes corresponded to something a laborer had in fact appropriated. In other cases, almost certainly laborers were charged for inevitable, normal, accidental losses and for mistakes in counting. In any case, covert appropriation, the imposition of fines, and laborers' resentment of fines all expressed a lack of consensus between landlords and laborers over redistribution. The relationship between hacienda and resident community was one of endemic conflict and mutual resentment as much as or more than one of institutionalized generosity and gratitude.

The deep suspicions that the people of Monjas Corral displayed toward the church's agrarian reform initiatives in the 1960s and the 1970s (to be explored in more depth later) are revealing of the nature of their previous experience. The church offered to sell tracts of land to the laborers on favorable terms. The people of Monjas Corral repeatedly refused the offers. Only after they saw several blocs of good land turned over to other groups of people and found themselves pushed up to the ridges on the western side of the hacienda did they finally agree to acquire titles. Still, some people left the hacienda rather than relocate within the hacienda and receive land. Later, when the community was in imminent danger of losing access to *páramo* grazing, it agreed to buy the *páramo* as communal land.

People today in the community lament what they see as their foolishness in the 1960s and the 1970s. "We didn't know," they say. Over the generations of hacienda life, the memory and sense of the possibility of any other system of land tenure had faded away. At a moment when the transfer of ownership to the laborers and the dissolution of the landlord-*huasipunguero* relationship was actually on the agenda throughout Ecuador, Monjas Corral residents could only see some sort of trick, not an opening for them to press for any utopian project of their own. As a result, they lost the chance to put more of their own stamp on the nature and terms of the transformation.

It is essential to stress that their response had nothing to do with any affection for landlords or sense of dependency. Instead, they were too cynical for their own good. The idea that the bishop had really felt something about their suffering under the hacienda and decided to be generous with them was totally implausible: "When are the *amos* ever going to just give us anything?" It could only be a scheme to exploit them, a way to entrap them more firmly in bondage. The *amos'* motives were, in fact, more complicated than compassion and generosity; but the Monjas Corral people's suspicions, well-founded in their own experience, prevented them from recognizing a novel situation and novel opportunities.

It seems, then, that in the 1950s and before, they saw themselves as condemned to live on haciendas and therefore to enter into a relationship of exchange with the *amos*. The hacienda and the *amos* were facts of life. As exchange partners, the landowners, renters, and stewards did at least allow access to the land and other vital resources—and fairly abundantly so on Monjas Corral, without too many restrictions. Hacienda account books suggest that renters were more willing to provide supplements to meet special needs in the late nineteenth century than people remember their being during the twentieth century.

Nonetheless, in many respects, the *amos* appear as morally perverse exchange partners. They did not treat labor as a favor but exacted it excessively and harshly, with little consideration for people's needs and circumstances. They were much quicker to give a whipping or an insult than a gift. They imposed fines for losses they should have tolerated, even losses incurred in the course of serving them. At least some of these points were long-standing features of the hacienda system or recurring tendencies, not twentieth-century innovations.

I do not claim here to have presented a unified, coherent image or evaluation of the hacienda, free of contradictions, that could be imputed to all indigenous people who ever lived on the hacienda. The range of possibilities is quite broad. In festive moments in the hacienda yard, drinking cane alcohol supplied by the renter, hacienda residents may well have felt that their *patrón* was generous. People like José Pillajo and Reinaldo Sisa, who lived most of their lives under the hacienda, sometimes mention "good" stewards or say proudly that their hard work, skill at particular tasks, or honesty earned them the "love" of an individual renter. At the other extreme, resentful over excessive labor demands and mistreatment, people sometimes denied that the renter had any legitimate claim over them at all. I do not think anyone ever talks about the hacienda today for more than a minute without some mention of harshness, cruelty, or miserliness.

Different hacienda residents could judge different renters and stewards differently at different moments. I do claim, nonetheless, that renters' and stewards' behavior, oriented by the goal of extracting a profit from poorly paid manual labor, tended continually to clash with Runa moral expectations. This clash generated the idea that the *amos* were morally perverse. To conclude this chapter, I now examine one important expression of this idea.

Landlords and the Devil

One of the largest indigenous rebellions of the colonial period occurred in the Cayambe-Otavalo region north of Quito in 1777. By that point, most of the indigenous people in Cayambe were living on haciendas as *conciertos*, and they were the main actors in the uprising (Ramón Valarezo 1987:200, 234). One incident provides an intriguing indication of their perceptions of landowners. The rebels sacked a hacienda-*obraje*, where they found a good bit of grain. They took some other goods but left the grain in the yard because they thought it was "bewitched" (*brujeado*), as one of them later testified (Moreno Yánez 1985:190).

What does this mean? In modern accounts, witchcraft is performed through the intervention of the devil or mountain spirits implicitly associated with the devil. Landowners are often said to be in league with the devil. It is tempting to read the "bewitched" grain in this light: the rebels viewed the landowner as the devil's client.

This may or may not be accurate; the notion of a supreme spirit of evil and of witches as his clients was originally a European import. The spread and development of this idea in the colonial Andes was a complex process (Salomon 1983; Silverblatt 1987; Taussig 1980). There is some evidence in contemporary oral tradition, however, that people in the Cayambe-Otavalo region viewed the formation of haciendas as the devil's handiwork (Crain 1991:75–76).

At any rate, the testimony is clear enough on one point: the bewitched grain was not fit for consumption. Food is a common vehicle of witchcraft today. A witch or someone employing a witch gives what appears to be good food to the victim, but the food contains invisible worms or some other agent of harm or control. Witchcraft thus cynically employs false generosity as a means to exert power. Whatever the nature of the supernatural power involved, the rebels evidently did not view the landowner as amassing grain for normal consumption or true generosity.

At a cosmological level, Pangor Runa's critique of the hacienda similarly rested on ideas about reciprocity and the ends of agricultural production. Indigenous planting rituals and the implicit theology of the fiesta suggested that God made crops grow and animals multiply so that people could satisfy their needs and share generously with others. Hacienda production, on the other hand, was oriented to extracting the maximum profit, beyond any normal consumption needs, and the hacienda was, accordingly, stingy with the products. This contradicted God's purposes.

I asked José María Pillajo who hacienda residents said ultimately made the *amos'* crops grow and gave them a good harvest:

> People in the old days said it was the devil who gave grain to the *amos*. "God does not give to those rich *amos*," the old people told us. . . . "Those tremendously rich *amos* . . . they are possessed by the devil," people would say. . . . "Why would God give to them?" . . .
>
> The *amos* harvested a tremendous amount of grain, a tremendous amount of potatoes. . . .
>
> God doesn't give to them; the devil gives to them. I heard the old people telling about that when I was a boy [at the beginning of the twentieth century]—my grandparents . . . would say that.
>
> They said the whites had a pact with the devil. . . . [When they die,] the devil takes them to hell. (9/2/1992)

The reward that the devil offered the rich was to make their crops produce in an abundance far beyond their needs. Superficially, if we assume that God is both more powerful and more benevolent than the devil, it might seem odd that people who depended on God received less than those who looked to the devil for aid. God (together with the Earth and saints), however, gives in accordance with people's needs and their moral behavior—including their generosity toward others, their fulfillment of ritual obligations, and their general respect for God and for others. The devil, by contrast, gives to his clients without regard to such limits and considerations, in accordance with the excessiveness of their greed.

People who receive the devil's aid can even cultivate without waiting for God to send rain (see Bourdieu 1977:62). Andrés Yépez told me that one of the last renters of Monjas Corral introduced the practice of planting potatoes in June and July, well before the normal onset of the rainy season. I asked if the plantings did not dry and whither. They were not irrigated, he said, but "these rich *amos'*" plantings did not dry out. Instead, they produced in marvelous abundance.

I wondered how this could be.

"I don't know," he answered. "They say the devil helps the rich. Who knows if it's true? Maybe the devil gives to them. The poor person, on the other hand, loses his crop if God's rain does not come."

Early in this chapter I noted the lack of a critique of private landownership based on any explicit or implicit vernacular history. Church ownership of Monjas Corral, specifically, was sanctified as God's ownership. Landownership and rental, however, did not entail unlimited rights to dispose of the land and exploit those who lived on it. Owners and renters who accumulated great wealth and did not act as moral exchange partners with laborers twisted the purposes for which God gave land and crops. They revealed themselves as dependent not on God but on the devil.

This critique, it should be noted, was not directed against conditions of proletarianization—hacienda laborers were not proletarians—nor was it directed against wealth per se. Rather, it was directed against the diversion of wealth from normal circuits of reciprocity and use to the end of irrational accumulation. The confrontation of two logics that Taussig found among recently proletarianized peasants in Colombia (1980) was a stable feature of hacienda life (see also Crain 1991; Edelman 1994).

A parallel critique is suggested by the belief that the souls of deceased people who left hidden stashes of money are condemned to suffer until someone finds the money. The souls sometimes appear in the dreams of the living to tell them where to find it. Money is associated with evil when it is taken as an end in itself. In general, to hoard irrationally, negating reciprocity and use, is an act "for the devil," one that aligns people with the devil.

Let me end this chapter by presenting a story and a song about a similarly condemned soul. In this case, the sin of the deceased was not simply to have hoarded money but to have denied reciprocity to the laborers on his hacienda in all the ways we have examined here.

Amo Castillo was the owner of the hacienda Guangopud until his death around 1950. After his death, his widow continued to run the hacienda. It is said that a man originally from a place called Gatazo was living and working on the hacienda. He pleaded with Castillo's widow to lend him a team of oxen. She did so but warned the Gatazeño to watch carefully over the oxen the night before he plowed to make sure they were not stolen.

The Gatazeño pastured the oxen at night right in front of his house while he sat awake in his doorway watching them. At midnight, however, he became sleepy and closed his eyes briefly. . . . When he opened them again, the oxen were gone.

Alarmed, he followed their trail, walking and walking for many hours, until, finally, he came to an opening in a rock. The opening was guarded by a pair of dogs, one black and the other red, but they were sleeping; the man quietly slipped by them and entered. He found himself inside the mountain abode of Mama Tungurahua (also known as "Grandma"), where the deceased go to receive punishment.

There, it is said, the Gatazeño saw *amo* Castillo mounted on his horse, both Castillo and the horse now covered with sores. Castillo said to the Gatazeño, "I brought my oxen here. They're not lost; I brought them." Castillo asked the man to tell his widow that he was there, suffering punishments, and to instruct her to give land to his godchildren on the hacienda and *huasipungo* plots to the laborers in general. The Gatazeño came back and delivered the message.

I will give the last word here to Avelino Shagñay. I suggested to him that the story would make a good basis for a song for a music festival, and he came up with these verses:[6]

Father Chimborazo, Mother Tungurahua	Tayta Chimborazo, Mama Tungurahua
live as husband and wife, it's said	Kusandik warmindik kawsakun ninmari
Thus have the ancestors told us	Ñawpa yayakuna chashnami parlashka
Thus have the ancestors taught.	Ñawpa yayakuna chashnami willashka.
Amo Castillo is roaming there	Amo Castillopish chaypimi purikun
amo Castillo is living there	amo Castillopish chaypimi kawsakun
for so much harshness to the Runa	runakunallata fiñak kashkamanta
for so many blows to the Runa.	runakunallata makak kashkamanta.

Other *amos* will go there, too
for making people work, and not
   paying.
They'll go to cook for Grandma
The fire will jump up toward their
   asses and their mouths.

You other *amos*, don't be cruel
treat the Runa with love
You might end up the same way
You might go burn there, too.

Shuktik amokuna chayllamantik ringa
mana pagashpalla, trabajachishpaka

Mama abuelapak cocinero ringa
sikiman shimiman nina jicharinga.

Kay shuk amokuna, ama millay kangi
runakunataka kuyangichikyari
Ñatik kankunapish chashna kangichikman
Ñatik kankunapish chaypi rupangiman.

PART THREE

Respect and Authority

CHAPTER 6

Disobedience and Respect: Two Accounts

In this chapter, I present two personal accounts of the hacienda period. I have selected these accounts for the particularly clear and rich way that they reflect attitudes toward domination and authority. At the end of the chapter, I will comment on the ways that each person talks about respect and rebelliousness. I will take up the same themes at a more general level in the next chapter.

JACOBA SAYAY: "YOUR LITTLE BLOWS WON'T KILL ME!"

Mama Jacoba was in her forties when I lived with her family during the first part of my fieldwork in the early 1990s. She grew up and lived on the hacienda Guangopud until she remarried and moved to Monjas Corral in the early 1970s, after the events related here. Before taping her account, I had already heard many of her stories about hacienda life while sitting on a stool on cold mornings by the fire in her kitchen, finishing my breakfast as she began to peel potatoes for lunch (Figure 15).

Mama Jacoba's father was from the hacienda Llinllín, on the other side of the mountain ridge to the east of Pangor. Llinllín is notorious in the region for the degree to which the sexual exploitation of resident indigenous women by the landowner was institutionalized. During the first half of the twentieth century, the hacienda was owned by a man who never married, a member of the provincial aristocracy. Mama Jacoba heard the stories from her father.

The old, old *amos* would just sit by their window and look out,[1] it's said. When the *amos* saw a girl of fifteen, or thirteen or fourteen, they had her parents summoned to the hacienda. They told the parents, "Send her to take care of the saddle, so the dog won't eat it. . . ."

The girls would go, thinking they were going to watch the saddle. A girl would spend the night there and come home the next day with a load of meat. The *amos* would send her back to her parents' home loaded down with things. That's what life was like on that hacienda . . .

If the girl refused, her parents got a terrible beating. The *amos* would have their dog bite them. That's what my dad said.

So, the girls would give birth to the *amos'* children. When they gave birth to a boy, the *amos* would not love the child. If it was a girl, the *amos* would be very happy. They would slaughter a cow and send meat for the mother to eat. Clothing for the child, soap, and bracelets, jewelry, bead necklaces for the mother. It was the same if a married woman gave birth to a girl.

They would tell the married men, too, "Send me your wife. I need her for something." The husbands would just send their wives, my dad said. The married women, too, would just go . . .

If the husband beat his wife, the *amos* would have him summoned to the hacienda. They would whip the husband, beat him, my dad said. "Why did you beat your wife?" The *amos* would have their dogs bite up the husband as a punishment before letting him go home.

If the husbands didn't object, they would give them a cow, a saddle, a horse. Even a poncho, a suit, if they just let their wives be with them. That's what my dad said.

When Mama Jacoba's parents married, they lived for a short time in Llinllín.

And then, the whites wanted to rape my mom. As my dad did not consent, the Llinllín *amos* beat my mom and beat my dad. So then my dad brought my mom back to Guangopud [where she was from], to live there.

My dad said, "Later on, the *amo* will want to rape my children. These evil people, these bad *amos*, they will do the same thing to my children. How can I live like this?" So he came to Guangopud.

Mama Jacoba's mother had grown up in Guangopud. At that time it was owned by *amo* Castillo, the same man who is now said to be paying for his sins inside Tungurahua.

FIGURE 15. *Jacoba Sayay (second from left) with family members*

My mother cried when she told me the story. When she was still single, still a girl, she was pasturing some animals. It was foggy and drizzling, and she was watching over a lot of sheep by herself.

Castillo went to make the rounds of his pastures. He appeared out of the fog, and said, "*Longa* [Indian woman], what are you doing?"

"I am pasturing the sheep," she said.

"Let's pasture together," he said.

Then he grabbed her and didn't let her go; he raped her, my mother told me.

"If you have a baby, I'll leave the baby the hacienda. I'll give him the hacienda," he said.

She was left with child. My mother had a baby before she was married—the landowner's child. My sister, the *amo*'s child, lives in Chillanes [in the lower Chimbo valley]. She is a real lady [*caballera*], with nice reddish hair. . . .

When the *amo* was dying, he tried to summon her [his daughter]: "Please call my child. She was my child." But her enemies did not convey the message. He must have wanted her called in order to leave her an inheritance. He didn't have another child.

When my sister was a child, he said, "Give me the child. She was my child." But my mother's parents said, "How could I give up the child?" They didn't give her to that *amo*.

She was pretty, my sister. A redhead, a real lady.

My mother's father, too, was white. My mother had curly hair. All of her hair was curly, and she had three pretty, curly locks that fell over her forehead. So my big sister, all the more so, she was born a lady. But she doesn't deny her family, may God repay her.

"How did your father treat her when she was a child?"

My dad loved her, he loved the child. "It's not my child's fault," he said, and he loved her. But my dad had a bad temper when he got drunk. He would hit my mother. He would think about that and really beat her up. He didn't hit her when he was sober, but when he was drunk.

"Great whore!" he would call her. "Mistress of the *amo!*" He hit her because she had already had a child when she married him.

So my poor sister, she says that she got married out of fear, from seeing how my dad hit my mom. My dad was mean when he was drunk.

By the time Jacoba was old enough to remember, Castillo had died and José Krueger, a gringo (from Europe or the United States), had acquired the hacienda. The gringo *amo* accused her father of stealing potatoes that he had been in charge of watching over and had him imprisoned for a time. After that, other laboring families, too, blamed her family for lost cattle or grain.

We spent our lives carrying out the *amos'* orders, with food in our stomachs or on an empty stomach, serving them. They didn't give even so much as a lousy cup of coffee in return!

The *amo* said to my father, "You're a smart-aleck. You act sharp." And he would hit him. The stewards beat him, and the *amo* beat him. My father was smart, and he didn't respect them. My father, too, hit back.

It was the same when he was in charge of the sheep. If a wolf ate a sheep or a sheep fell into some hole, he would be blamed. Likewise, if we were doing *huasicama* service in the hacienda house, the *amo* didn't appreciate our work. We made their breakfast, we attended to them, but they didn't take it into account; they would throw the pot of coffee at someone in anger. That's how we suffered terribly in the hacienda, in the old days.

"You told me once that when you were gathering firewood, the steward of this hacienda came to prevent you . . ."

That was when were doing *huasicama* service. My father, my brother, my sister, and I, [crossing over the boundary to Monjas Corral,] came to gather firewood. Up in Guangopud, there wasn't any wood, so when we did *huasicama* service we came to steal [*jillush*] firewood from this hacienda.

Ignacio Lara and Humberto Lara were stewards of Monjas Corral. Every day they made the rounds with their dogs, and when we were gathering firewood, they appeared.

They took everything away from us! They took our rope, machetes, shawls, ponchos, everything. What could we use to take the firewood back?

We twisted some *páramo* grass for twine and carried the firewood back using that. We had gone for wood at nine in the morning and got back at three or four o'clock.

The *amo* landowner was angry. "Dammit, look what time you get back! Did you spend the day lying on the grass?"

"*Amo niño*, how could we pass the day lying on the grass? We come with firewood from another hacienda. We worked without eating, getting firewood from another hacienda." We were angry when we got back. But we brought back the firewood. We told him how the stewards had taken away our things.

So the late *amo* . . . mounted his horse, took his rifle, and rode down with the overseer to Monjas Corral.

"So you took away my laborers' things. You dirty so-and-so, it's not your hacienda! If it were your own hacienda, you could take things away. This is the nuns' hacienda, the bishopric's hacienda. You're just a renter."

The late *amo* almost shot that steward. "Goddammit! House servants, bring me the ponchos, the ropes, give them back!"

The *huasicamas* kept their distance but reached out and gave him the rope, the ponchos.

"Let's hope from now on you people will be generous with those in need [*cariderolla*, < Sp. *caridad*, -*ero*]. It's not your hacienda. This is the bishopric's. These *amos*, too, are just renters, nothing but renters. You'll see, after a time, you'll go away and leave it all behind."

And that was true, Señor Barry. I was just a girl, and I thought maybe they owned the land.

That Ignacio Lara was a terrible brute, a vicious man. Poor us, he
would follow us, swinging his whip in the air. My sister and I would be
cutting and gathering firewood, and he would chase us on horseback.
We would run fast and cross over the boundary to our hacienda [a small
river]. There, on the other side, we would sit down and shout insults
at him. Once we were on the gringo's hacienda, we talked back to him
[kariyak].

"Mistresses, horny longas, I'll get you! [Wayna, longa arrechas, pero
japishami]," that Ignacio Lara would say.

"Cholo bandit!" we would shout back.[2]

Ignacio Lara, Humberto Lara, they were vicious, evil people, mean
for no reason.

When Jacoba was still a girl, her father died suddenly.

I don't know what illness it could have been that killed him. He died
very quickly, after four days or so. All of a sudden. I continued to live
after that with my mother. . . .

We were told that it might have been some evildoing [witchcraft]
that caused his death. There were enemies, because my dad was an
able, smart man. He was clever and good at everything. Because of that,
someone killed him with witchcraft, we were told; I don't know.

Fellow Runa killed him that way. . . .

When I was still a girl, . . . I did all the huasicama chores, cooking,
everything. Whether I knew how to do it or not, I had to do everything.
That's how we lived, suffering on the hacienda. Even if they didn't appreciate it [casui mana casui], we all—children, mother, and father—had
to carry out orders, day in and day out. We ourselves had to bring firewood. We ourselves had to cut fodder for the animals. We ourselves had
to do everything, as huasicamas! But they didn't appreciate anything,
not the steward, not the amo. At four in the morning, three in the
morning, we had to boil a tub of water with [medicinal plants] for washing the cows' udders and legs. We would be boiling that and washing the
cows when the sun came up.

The amo landowner wanted to rape me, poor me, when I was still
a girl, when I was serving in the hacienda house. He was a gringo; he
wasn't just any old white man, any old cholo. I said, "Amo niño, I am a
Runa woman. I'm not one of you."

He grabbed hold of my shawl. I got loose, leaving my shawl behind, and jumped through the window, landing in the yard. Then I got up and went to my mom's home.

That's how things were for me then. So out of my worry and distress, I decided to get married. I was afraid of the *amos*, so I went to my sister's house in Chillanes. She and my brother-in-law lived there.

They said, "What will you go back to Guangopud for? Get married here, and you'll have a life without trouble. Otherwise, who will support you? You don't have a father."

I was just a girl, and I listened to that bad advice, so I got married. I was afraid of those *amos*; the work on the hacienda was too much for me. On the hacienda, we had to do *everything!* We had to cut fodder for the animals . . . gather firewood . . . clean the stables . . . milk the cows. . . . I felt it was too much for me.

But it was the same bad story with my husband. . . . He beat me. He was jealous. And he didn't even buy me any clothing, nothing. He was lazy.

I accused my brother-in-law, "You told me to marry him. You got me to marry this lazy man." My husband was my brother-in-law's nephew.

I said, "He's a lazy bum. He doesn't want to work. How can I live like that? I grew up on a hacienda. I know how to do everything. I can do every kind of work."

"What did he think? Did he want you as his wife to support him?"

He said his parents would support us; he wanted to depend on them. He beat me. But I didn't heed him, not even a little, even though he might make me bleed, I didn't obey him, because he was lazy. I knocked him to the ground right in front of his father. Then his father told him to hit me in the legs with a stick: "Give it to her in the legs, then your wife will be afraid."

Seeing that I was far away from home, without my parents, his father told him to beat me. But I got so angry, I didn't care about anything. I knocked him down in front of his father. "What clothing have you given me? What are you doing to support me? What money have you given me?" I knocked him down.

Then his father came to stop me. . . . I almost raised my hand to hit my father-in-law, too. "What have you taught your son? Did you teach him to work? . . . He's a lazy bum, just like his father," I said, and I hit him.

Well, we just couldn't live together nicely, we were only fighting. So, after seven months of marriage, I left him. I came back to my mom's house. Back to suffer again on the hacienda.

Again, I had to do *huasicama* service and work in the hacienda fields. I worked right alongside the men. I gave two days a week of *ayuda* labor on the hacienda, for having animals.

And you see, because I lived honorably, I didn't have any children. Yes, I did have one child by my husband. After that, I didn't have any more.

Those stewards would say, "Let's be together, you and me. If you are with me, you won't have to work."

"Oh, yes," I said, "you're certainly a gallant suitor. What are you bothering me for? You'll be leaving tomorrow." I fought like that with the steward.

I spoke strongly to the steward's wife, too. "Yes, put your donkey, your whole burro, put in your tethering stake, your breaking thing, your skirt chaser [*waynandero*], your whole horse." That's how I insulted the steward's wife. "Yes"—well, I don't want to repeat bad words to you. I insulted the stewards' wives. I didn't submit.

When I got angry, when I got furious . . . I almost hit the steward with a stick.

I talked back to the overseer, too. So he told the *amo* landowner, "This Indian woman is disobedient."

The *amo* landowner said, "Why don't you obey the overseer? Why don't you obey the steward?" He wanted to whip me.

"Go ahead!" I said. "Give me a lashing, strike me!"

The *amo* landowner, too, said, "Here, take some money. Do you want money? Do you want a cow? Let's sleep together. No one will say anything."

I refused. "No. I'm a poor woman, and I'll die poor. I'm poor, and I'll stay poor. I don't want any money, I don't want any animal."

I just led my life without getting mixed up in anything. After I separated from my husband, I lived with my little brother, my other sister, and my brother-in-law, working alongside them. Thank God, my brother-in-law did not bother me. I just lived honorably, you see. When the *amos* said to do *huasicama* service, I did *huasicama*, too. When they said to work in the fields, I worked. But I haven't engaged in any, absolutely any, "playing," or any joking around. Now, you see, I'm an old woman. In my younger days, too, I didn't let anyone approach me with bad words. That's how I have led my life. Yes, I did have a baby from my first husband; the baby died.

My mother died, and I lived with my brother-in-law and my sister. Then, when I didn't want to get involved with the *amos*, they blamed my brother-in-law. "She must be sleeping with you, that's why she doesn't want to get involved with me," the *amo* landlord said.

That's what my poor life was like on the hacienda, after my parents died and left me. I thought that's how my life would always be. Now, thanks to the agrarian reform law, now we have some rest. Each of us rests in our own house.

On the hacienda, there was no rest. We had to milk the cows, make cheese, wash that gringo's socks and clothing. With all that washing, the skin on our poor hands would be split, our hands would hurt. He didn't pay a cent for it. He didn't even give us lunch. He didn't give us anything. Oh yes, he gave us work. We worked the same as the men.

The *amo*, the late José Krueger, was a widower for some time before he remarried. We cooked and fed him. We washed his clothes. Five children were left when his wife died. We cooked for and fed them, too. In Riobamba, they had cooks who fed them. Here, when the *amos*, the gringo, went to supervise the work, we followed with breakfast. We followed with lunch. We had to go far, carrying breakfast to give to the *amos*. We came back, and a little while later had to go with lunch. So we suffered: men, women, children, parents, everyone, not just one person.

He only wanted to do something to the really good-looking women. He didn't want others. Just those that his heart desired or something, I guess. He didn't say anything to the others. . . .

The *amo* landowner hit me here on my head with a stick. I don't know, I just didn't think about what I was doing, maybe because I was so angry: I stood up and said, "Hit me again!" Yes, in my fury, I stood up like that to the *amo* landowner, the gringo.

When we were working in the fields, he would be jealous of the other laborers. People would say, "He's jealous over you, he's jealous over you."

Then, when the *amo* came, we wouldn't even raise our heads. We wouldn't laugh, we wouldn't joke about anything. We would just be bent over working, very seriously, men and women together. Because we were afraid of the *amo* landowner. We thought he might get jealous and strike us.

Even so, he did beat us, all the people. He hit every single one of us on some pretext or other. And he didn't give us anything, nothing, not even a lousy little cup of coffee. . . .

When we were doing *huasicama* service, his dogs would bite us. . . . The *amo* would be lying down there, resting, and when his mean dogs saw one of us Runa, they would run out to bite us. The dogs were used to that. He wouldn't even call the dogs off . . .

The overseers, too, heeding what the *amo* told them, were mean. The stewards, too. When we were doing *huasicama* service on the hacienda, our little animals would sometimes enter the hacienda pastures. Immediately, they would be taken to the hacienda [to the administrative center], and we would be charged a fine. In those days, they fined us four hundred or five hundred sucres. Instead of paying, we would pay it off with four days or eight days of labor—depending.

Poor me, without a father, without a husband, that's how I have suffered. I suffered all of that, on the hacienda. The landowner didn't give absolutely anything. He didn't even give me a *huasipungo* plot [in the agrarian reform]. Nothing. Our life in the old days, it's the same as if we had been serving a dog.

The overseers would try to make us afraid of them by saying, "We are Krueger number two. We are *amo* number two."

We wouldn't be afraid.

"C'mon and work, you, too.
Bend your back, you, too.
You should carry a load, too.
Why are you giving us orders!"

But only those of us who were rebellious would say that. Those who weren't, no. I was rebellious. So they didn't want to see my face.

"You're insolent," they would say. "You talk back to the servants. You don't obey."

Nowadays, we just carry loads of a quintal [100 pounds]. In those days, we had to carry loads of a *barrica*, more than a quintal. We had to bring loads of potatoes from the fields far away down to the hacienda, bearing loads of a *barrica* on our backs. We would arrive in the hacienda yard bearing the loads, just like the men. We all suffered that way, carrying out orders. That's what our life was like. The stewards, the overseers, oh yes, they were up there looking clever.

"And what about the people who weren't so 'smart,' who didn't rebel?"

The people who weren't so smart, who didn't rebel, just suffered. They would do whatever they were told, like fools. They weren't rebellious, and the stewards would strike them, the overseers would strike them; they bore it.

"Because they were afraid, or why?"

Because they were afraid. For example, in the potato harvest, all of a sudden the overseer or steward would just strike out with the whip. "Do a good job of picking up the potatoes, look carefully for the potatoes in the ground, do a good job of digging them up," they would say, and just let out with the whip.

"In a fiesta, for example, when people were drunk, didn't they ever hit the overseers, or . . ."

No. They didn't say anything to the overseers. It's only nowadays that people are getting smart, it's like people are waking up. The young people nowadays are becoming smart. In the old days, it wasn't like that. People just endured it, through life, like fools. It's only now that people have been waking up, both men and women. That's how our poor lives were, Señor Barry.

"Were the *fundadores* of Guangopud . . . only *fundadores*, or were they overseers as well?"

They themselves were overseers. They themselves went through life giving orders, as *fundadores* and as overseers as well.

"Did people respect them more because they were *fundadores*?"

Yes, yes. We respected, and they respected.[3] Because they were *fundador*, they were big bosses. We called them *fundador*. That's how it was. If someone didn't give food and drink to them, they would say, "This person is no good" and be a bit ill-disposed and angry. . . . If you gave them drink and food and set off fireworks when they came down, then they were greatly pleased.

"And did people respect them in work, too, because they were *fundador*?"

Yes. As *fundador*, they were big, important people.

"And carry out their orders?"

Yes. Because people carried out their orders and were serving them, they were indeed big, important people. We thought—I thought, with my girl's head—that maybe one shouldn't talk back to the *fundador*. I thought that the Virgin would punish that. [Mama Jacoba chuckled at herself here] . . .

It was just my own idea. That if one talked back to the overseers, then—no, I mean the *fundador*—if one talked back to the *fundador*, the sponsors, the *fundadores*, then the Virgin would punish that. That's what I thought, in my childish way of thinking.

"And did you think the same way about talking back to the *amo*?"

No. What I was afraid of, in my heart, was that if I hit back or rebelled against the *amos*, they might expel us from the hacienda, or beat my father. That's what I thought, in my heart. But even at the risk of being expelled, or hit, I didn't obey them. I didn't heed them at all—certainly not the overseers and stewards. I don't know what happened to me, maybe I lost my head, maybe it was from being so angry, but when the *amo* steward struck me, I stood up and said, "Give me another one!" He stopped hitting me and stood up, and I stood up, too.

A wolf ate a big sheep [when my little brother was in charge of watching over the sheep]. My brother Pablo was still just a boy. Being just a boy, he was afraid. He didn't have a father or a mother; he was orphaned when he was still a boy. He thought, "They'll hit me," so after taking the remains of the sheep down to the hacienda, he just ran to hide when the *amos* came. I stood up for him.

The *amo* yelled, "Dammit, you didn't hear anything! [i.e., you didn't hear the wolf and chase it away.] Now, take it and stuff your bellies with it!" It's a bad, rude word, "stuff your bellies" [*saksaychik*]. And he threw the sheep carcass to the ground.

I said, "I'm not going to eat your sheep; I'm not a dog." And right in front of him, I took the carcass and flung it over to the dog.

The *amo* wanted to hit me.

"Go ahead, hit me," I said. "Did I eat your sheep? Go on, hit me," I said, standing up.

He just gave me one blow.

"Your little blows won't kill me," I said. That's what I said. I didn't submit [*casuk*].

Whenever a wolf ate an animal, or a lamb died, my little brother was afraid and would hide, as if we had done something. He was afraid of a conflict with the *amos*, and he would just go. But I wasn't afraid.

"When he got older, did he rebel, too?"

Yes. As he grew older, he got to be another one, too. He learned to rebel, too. He would stand right up to the stewards, the overseers.

That's why they would call us bad people [*millay*].

"You are bad people.
You don't obey [casuna].
You say bad words.
Bad people, wicked people."

The people and the stewards would talk like that about us, the men and women of my family.

"Other Runa, your peers, too, heard what the *amos* said and thought in the same way?"

They thought and talked the same way about us. "Yes, you people, men and women alike, you don't heed." To this day, Señor Barry, they call us bad spoken, bad people, foulmouthed. "Men and women alike, you have a nasty tongue, a bad tongue."

To this day, when I feel anger, when I feel fury, I don't pay any heed, not even now.

"Did your father teach you to rebel?"

No, he didn't teach me. He didn't teach me, "Rebel in this way," or "Talk back like this." When someone insults me or whatever, it just makes me feel a tremendous rage. It's out of our own hearts, our own thinking, that, once we've learned to rebel, we don't heed. We didn't heed the steward, or the overseer, or the people, or the *amo* landlord. When I'm overcome with anger, it wouldn't matter if they threatened me with a bullet or a knife; I don't feel fear. Not that moment when I'm facing somebody; maybe later on, when I'm not talking back, when I've gone away, and the rage passes.

REINALDO SISA: "THE *AMOS* CALLED ME BY NAME, MAY GOD REPAY THEM"

The Sisa family group was one of the most important on the hacienda Monjas Corral up to the mid-twentieth century, when many of the residents moved away to escape harsh treatment by Ignacio Lara. Reinaldo Sisa, born around 1919, is one of the few who remained (aside from a short stint in Guango-pud). He does not live among the other former *huasipungueros* in Tepeyac Bajo but in another portion of the former hacienda, among people from else-where in the province who resettled there and were granted lands in the 1960s (Figure 16).

I had not met him prior to visiting his house together with my wife late in my fieldwork to request an interview. He knew about me, however. As described in Chapter 3, he knew that I had married a woman from a family he had ties to in the maize country, and he received us very warmly. I said I would like to learn about his life, especially in "the old days," and we agreed on a time when he would be able to spend a whole morning talking with me. When I returned, after he served me breakfast, he took me into another room for the interview. He had mentally prepared and organized his account and simply began to talk, without any need for questions.[4]

'Not Once Did They Hit Me"

Our life in the old days was to be under the *amos'* orders. We didn't own land, so we went through life doing what they said.

The *amos*, the *patrones*, the owners of the land—they were like our parents. Whatever they ordered, we did it. When they said, "Come and do *huasicama* service," . . . we had to go serve them. . . .

We men served the [male] *amos*. We took care of the *amos'* horses, their cows, milking the cows, making cheese, making money for the *amos*. The women, like my wife, in turn, served the [female] *patrona amas*, as cooks. What they called *huasicama* was to take a turn serving for a month and two weeks. Each laborer took a turn.

FIGURE 16.   *Reinaldo Sisa (right), with granddaughter and the author*

After that, we went back to agricultural work. We worked from Monday to Thursday, four days a week. Everyone had to be gathered for work by 7:00, wherever it was that we were working. If someone did not make it by 7:00, the *amo* [white] employees were really quick to strike them with the whip. They would be cracking the whip, cracking the whip, cracking the whip, at the poor laborers who didn't get there good and early.

So, in that respect, our lives were hard. The stewards, the employees, would hit people with the stick handle of the whip. They hit people on their heads, giving them head wounds. Sometimes, they hit people on their arm . . . [or] on their back . . . [or] on the leg. . . .

Well, as for me, for my part, in my long life—I'm seventy-three years old now—the *amos* did not hit me. I was a good worker, and quick. Wherever they sent me, I went fast and came back fast. Thanks to that, the little *amos* didn't hit me. I won't lie to you and say, "The *amo* hit me, too," or "The *amo* struck me with the whip." No, they didn't hit me. Those who were slow, those who were heavy, those who spoke bad— that is, who talked back—they were the ones who got the beatings. Their lives were sad: to be hit, whipped, not given food. Not me.

"Not even once?"

No, not once did they hit me. They loved me. And wherever they went, they took me along—those big, rich *amos* from Riobamba who rented this hacienda Monjas.

"Reinaldo, c'mon with me. You accompany me as my page, my boy servant."

When I went along with them as a boy servant, it was good. I won't say to you without reason, "They hit me, too, they didn't give me any food to eat, either, they had me go hungry and tired, too." No, I can't complain. I was fine.

"How did you feel, when you went along with those *amos?*"

I felt, "They love me. The *amos* take me along with them wherever they go. Maybe I have a "good back," maybe I'm of "light blood," maybe that's why they love me." That's how I understood it. . . .

Here, we say "light blood"; it means someone is a good person [*alli runa*], who does not speak bad words, ugly words. Someone who has respect. That's what they call "light blooded." . . .

A "good back" is just the same. Let's see, how can I explain? "This person has a good heart. . . . That's why nobody gets angry with him, none of us speak badly of him. This is a good person." That's how people talk.

That's how I have led my life, *compañero* Braulito [Barry].

As for agricultural work, they would put me in charge of four- or five-year-old horses—grown, wild horses—and say, "Tame it for me, domesticate it for me." I tamed the horses for them by putting a saddle on, mounting the horse, and having another horse lead—the "godmother." The horse that is already tame is like a godmother. The other horse bucks, it throws your behind up in the air, it stands straight up. But I was able to ride it out; I didn't fall to the ground.

Once I tamed the horse, I gave it back to the *amos.* That's why they loved me:

"This boy, he's smart.
This boy, he's quick.
This boy, he tames these wild horses."

For plowing, they had oxen . . . When they said to teach the untamed ox to plow, I did that. We hitch one tame ox that already knows how to plow together with one wild one that doesn't know how to plow. The tame ox keeps to the line as you plow and holds still; we call that the "godmother." The other ox zigzags up and down, but the "godmother" ox holds the other one to the line, just like a Christian [a person]. So, I would plow, keeping to the line, and plow a *lot* in a day. . . . After four or five times plowing, the ox is tame. It keeps still, it pulls the plow nicely, in a straight line, not twisting up and down.

That's how we lived, serving the *amos*, doing all that they ordered.

They had six or seven hundred sheep. They said, "You take charge of the sheep; everyone has to take a turn." So I tended the sheep—many, many sheep, an entire flock. I was in charge of the sheep for three months. . . .

The stewards, or the *amos* when they came to the hacienda from Riobamba, said, "Are all the sheep there?"

"The flock seems to be complete. I don't know, I can't count all these animals, but I ward off danger, I tend them. No wolf has eaten them, nor have any died. They're all here."

"Let's count," they would say.

All of the laborers would be gathered to help in the sheep counting. The sheep would jump around and make it difficult to count. The little *amo* stewards would count . . . They would make a mistake and come up short. Then, the Runito overseers would count, and they would make a mistake. Either they came up with too many or too few. "Some sheep are missing," they would say. Or, "It comes out to too many." They just couldn't get the number of sheep to come out right.

Then they would say to me, "Reinaldo, you count. It seems we counted wrong. You count."

"Okay. Maybe Tayta Amito Dios will help this poor man."

Then with all the people standing around the sheep, the sheep would file out from the middle, one by one, just following each other in a line. So I would count them as they filed out: one, two, three, four, five . . . and come up with the seven hundred sheep, or whatever number it was.

Then the employee *amo*s would look in their notebooks and say, "This is how many sheep you were charged with. That's how many sheep there should be," they would say.

When I counted, Yayito Dios, God in Heaven, on the first try I got it right. They had it written down in their notebook just how many animals there should be, and that's exactly what I came up with. "This is how many I count. It's complete by my count."

They would count once again. But they just couldn't get it right. They would count wrong.

I would count again, and however many I had counted on the first count, it would turn out exactly the same on my second count.

"Oh, we have to hand it to this boy: he is better than us," they would say. "We know how to read and write, and we can't add up the sheep. We're no good at counting. And you who don't know anything . . ."—I don't know how to read and write or anything.

"I don't know those things, sir. My father and mother didn't put me in school. But in my good little head, my good little heart, I do understand everything." So, they would praise me.

And all my life, I have been honest. I don't know any trickery: my good God is my witness, I never stole from anyone.

The *amo* renters would come from Riobamba, and in the hacienda house down there, the nice house, in their nice rooms with a table, they would drink nicely their morning coffee with rolls and cheese. And they would call me, too, "Here, take this," and give me a cup of coffee with a roll or whatever. I would say, "May God repay you" and take it and drink it. . . . And there, on their dining table, would be left a little cheese, a few rolls, some money.

Then they would go out to work, taking me along. "Let's go, Reinaldo, come with me. We'll come back later."

Then, at the place where people were working that day, far from the hacienda house: "Reinaldo, go back and bring me such-and-such from my room." They would hand me the key and send me on the errand.

I came back to the hacienda house from the fields in the mountains. The stewardesses said, "What did he send you for?"

"He told me to come back and get something for him. 'It's in my room. Go look for it and bring it back,' he said. That's what I've come for."

The stewardess *amas* said, "Did he give you the key?"

"Yes, I have it here."

"Give it to me, give it to me. You can't enter the room. We'll go in. Whatever it is, we'll find it and send you off with it."

I said, "He didn't tell me to give it to you. He told me to enter the room. He didn't say to give the key to the *amitas*."

"Why didn't he tell you to give me the key? You can't enter. It's not appropriate for you to go into the *amo* gentlemen's room. Whatever it is, I'll find it and give it to you. Give me the key."

"I won't give it to you," I said, and I didn't. I myself opened the door, and went in. There was the table, with money lying on the table—coins. There was the cheese. There were the rolls.

I never, ever took anything to eat or took money. *Diosito,* I wasn't like that. I had a clean hand and a clean heart. Thanks to that, the *amos* loved me. . . . They took me along with them wherever they went; they trusted me and loved me.

On the other hand, they would get angry at the other little laborers. "Those ones are not good. They have long fingernails." That's what they call someone who steals: "long fingernails." "They just take what they can, they put it in their pockets, or they hide it."

So, during the time I was growing up, I was loved. That's what I can tell you about that aspect of my life.

In turn, as for the holy earth [*santo suelo*], agriculture: one had to work. You turn up the earth with a hoe, first turning over the hard earth, then hoe it again, and break up the clumps of earth, make it soft. That's how you plant nicely, dedicating yourself to the earth. We planted six or seven quintals of seed potatoes—some years, with the aid of other laborers, up to ten quintals. And for each quintal of seed, we would get ten quintals in the harvest. We would pile up the potatoes . . . Yayito Dios would give us food.

Thanks be to God, I always had enough to eat, a normal amount, as God commands. When God gave it, I ate meat, eggs, milk, cheese, good food. When God didn't give that, we always had at least some *nabito* [wild greens], some barley. We lived with what God gave us to eat.

We sold a portion of the potatoes in town. We put aside another part for seed. Another part, we traded for barley and maize, with little men from the maize country whom we made friends with.

We planted *ukas* [an Andean tuber], potatoes, fava beans, and scallions. We kept hens. Sometimes we sold the eggs; sometimes we ate them.

In the old days, my parents had ninety, ninety-five, one hundred sheep. When we wanted to eat meat, we slaughtered a sheep and ate it. Every three months or so we slaughtered a sheep. And we had cheese and milk almost every day, when there was a cow with a calf. . . .

My father had 40 head of cattle. My father was a cowhand on the hacienda. He watched over 370 head of cattle for the *amos.* Every day he herded them and gathered them together so they wouldn't be rustled, or die somewhere, or get lost.

So, since this was a big hacienda, with lots of *páramo*, my father had our own, separate herd, and just let them multiply. My father let them multiply up to forty. So, we weren't lacking for a milk cow; there were always one or two. We always had cheese and milk.

But only some people had enough. Other people didn't have enough to eat, because they didn't work. They didn't do a good job of cultivating the earth, they didn't break up the clumps nicely; they would lose the crop. Yayito Dios wouldn't give to them. Or maybe they were a little lazy, and they didn't plant a lot. They harvested less than others. They didn't have all the food they might need. There were always differences among us.

So, well, I always like to be generous; one wants to give them something to eat. "Here, take this, and go cook a sweet gruel," I would say. "Take this and go boil it." Or I would tell my little wife, "Look, see how that little woman is roaming around, in a sad state," or "See that man. Give them a tray of potatoes," or "Give them some *ukas*. Poor them, they don't have a lot of crops planted, they don't have a lot to eat, it seems. Give them a tray of potatoes, *ukas*, or *mashwa* [another tuber], before they go on their way." And she would give it to them; that's how she is. That's how we live. We get along well with everyone. Everyone has always spoken well of me.

And people are thankful. "This Runito, Reinaldo, is beautiful. He's a generous person, a person who gives people food to eat. May God give him more." The little people pray to God for me in that way.

And, in turn, there are the *virgencitas*, the *tayta amitos*, in images, like a photo. We adored those. "Tayta Amito," we would say, taking off our hats, putting our hands together in supplication, kneeling. "Give me, please, a little cow. Give me, please, some little crops." We just praised those little photos and forgot altogether about our God up in heaven.

Down in Pangor, in the church, they would tell me, "Reinaldo, next year, you sponsor the fiesta." . . . There were *fundadores* for the saints. "This saint is marvelously miraculous, and will give you money, crops, whatever. . . ."

I said, "Okay, yes." So that was our worry and preoccupation for the next year: to gather money and food to attend to the people and feed them. August 30 was the date to give food to people. Maybe you've seen the image of Saint Rose—I served Saint Rose.

When the date was approaching, I went to [a town in the Chimbo valley] to buy maize and brown sugar blocks for *aswa.* Maize to boil, to feed people. And I slaughtered a cow, to give people. . . .

We call all the people, invite them: "Everybody come, we'll all drink together, we'll all eat together." The drinking was Friday and Saturday. And Sunday, we "earned" Mass; we paid the priest to come from Cajabamba. We brought him, and had him say Mass, and drank and ate, and went around in the procession, carrying the *virgen,* to earn our honor. . . .

"This Runa has earned the Mass; now he has gained honor," people say. "Now he has made himself look good." That's what people call "honor," when they say someone looks good.[5]

So I have gathered the people together and fed them. I've . . . made *aswa,* given cane alcohol, set off fireworks the day of the Mass; I have served the people. I brought a lot of cane alcohol, distributed it by the bottle, got people drunk, got them singing, got them fighting among themselves. They would fight among themselves when they were drunk—women with other women, and men with other men . . . They would just swear at each other . . . And I couldn't listen to it. "I didn't serve you alcohol for that. I didn't give you food for that. . . . I didn't invite you here for you to fight. I called you here for you to eat and drink nicely. And I got the people together to earn the Mass, and to adore this *virgen mamita.*" That's what I would say.

Tayta Reinaldo converted to Protestantism in about 1974. This gives him a particularly critical stance toward the Catholic religiosity of the hacienda period. His comments on the lack of recognition of God in hacienda times should be understood in this light. His Protestantism strongly emphasizes the absolute centrality of God and Jesus and rejects the cult of the saints and the Virgin. Still, the picture he sketches of hacienda religion in the following passages is otherwise not very different in its main features from the accounts provided by Catholics: the veneration for priests, nuns, and even, to some extent, hacienda renters; the power of priests' and nuns' blessings;[6] and, at the same time, the contradiction posed by priests' sexual exploitation of indigenous brides.

In my way of thinking, it was as if I did not have God. Not the God who gives us life. I said, "Where do plants, crops, our breath, our health, our life, where do they come from? How do we have these things?" I didn't remember God, I really didn't. "Who knows how we appeared here?

Who knows why we're here speaking, walking on our two feet?" That's how I thought. I didn't know about the existence of God. No one told me about that.

The *amo* renters, the nuns, the priests would arrive. I would call *them* "God [Tayta Amito]," and worship them with a kiss, on my knees. I called the bishop, the priests "Tayta Amito," and wherever I met them, I took off my hat, kneeled, and kissed their knees [their robes, around the knees]. I called them "Father God [Tayta Dios]"—the priests, the bishops. I didn't remember our God.

"It was as if they were gods."

They were like God. It was the same as if they were gods. That's how it seemed. That's what I thought. I didn't think there was a God in heaven, nor did anybody talk about that.

"And the *amo* renters, they, too, were called Tayta Amito?"

I called the renters "Niñito" [Little Child]. We took off our hats and addressed them as "Niñito Caballerito [little gentleman-child]." In the old days, we didn't say, "Good afternoon" or "Good morning." The greetings were different: "Alabado Jesucristo Niñito [Praised be Jesus Christ, Little Child]." For the women *amas*, "Alabado Jesucristo Niñita [Praised Be Jesus Christ, Little Girl]." We took off our hats to them. That's how we respected and obeyed them.

"Why were they called *niñito, niño, niña?*"

Who knows why it was that people addressed them like that. That's what people called them. Our parents did it, and we followed the same custom and just said the same thing.

"But was it as if they were like a Christ child?"

That's how it turns out. We didn't know. It turns out that's what it was like. It was only later that we Runa peasants were able to raise our heads and our eyes, because of Dr. José María Velasco Ibarra [Ecuador's president during several terms in the mid-twentieth century] and Leonidas Proaño. The two of them, in effect, opened our eyes. Now new laws have come, and with the new laws, the children go to school and learn to read and write.

It turns out it wasn't good to call those images "God." Those were just human fabrications, made by human hands. That's how we feel and think now.

"And the old-time priests, how would they sermonize?"

Well, in church, in Mass, they , , , went up to the main altar, to the pulpit, standing high up there. Then . . . "Little father priest is sending out his sermon," we would say. From there, high up, father priest would give the blessing with his hand, again and again and again: that's how he would sermonize. "Father priest is sermonizing," we would say, and all of us, everyone inside the church, would bow our heads.

Then the priests would take the Host, and their drink, and nicely season it in the goblet, praying to God, and showing it to God, and they would drink it.

Then we would think, "Why is he drinking that? Why does he hold it up toward the sky, showing it, before drinking it?"

Then the sacristan made the bell ring, "*chilín chilín chilín*," and we would all bow our heads, looking at the ground. We didn't look at the priests. But I did look up, like this [out of the corner of the eye, head down], to see those wondrous things, how they held up the little dish and then drank. I have seen that. . . .

"Did they talk to you?"

To all the people, maybe they said we must pray to God; I don't know what it was they said. We didn't understand. Who knows what it was the priest said in the sermon.[7] But then they would give a blessing and have us get up and go out. So then we would leave the church and go outside.

"And at that time, what did you think about that? What was that blessing for?"

"As long as we receive that blessing," we thought, "our lives will be *happy*. No illness, no pain will befall us. The animals will multiply. We'll have animals, we'll have crops to harvest, potatoes to dig up, with his blessing."

And so, we didn't think about our God. We thought about the priests. The priest, he must be the one who helps, the one who saves, we thought. . . . It's only in these last years that we don't call the priests God. . . . Tayta Amito, it turns out, is someone else, in Heaven. . . .

We called the nuns "Mother Virgin." "Mother Virgen Little Mothers." We worshipped them, too . . . They would have us kiss the cross on their rosary. . . . We thought we would have good health, our bodies were made well and healthy, through kissing that cross or receiving Tayta Amito's blessing.

When the priest gave his blessing, we would open our hands and our arms to hold the blessing. "Ay, Tayta Amito!" we would say . . .

"What about confession, how was that?"

During Holy Week, we all went to the town of Pangor. . . . We would all go one afternoon to confess. Tayta Amito would put up something like a tent. We kneeled on one side and put our two hands together in prayer.

"All right, now, you all tell your sins here."

So we would begin to tell him, one by one.

"What sin do you wish to confess?"

We didn't understand. "Tayta Amito, please ask."

So, then, "Have you stolen?"

"No," we would say.

"Have you committed adultery?"

"No," we would say.

"Have you felt envy?"

"No," we would say.

"Have you talked back to your parents?"

"No," we would say. Sometimes people said, "Yes, we talked back."

Then, "Have you been ill spoken, have you sworn?"

Sometimes people said "No." Sometimes, they said, "Yes, we have, when we were overcome by anger."

Then, in turn, the priests gave good moral counsel—they did give good instruction.

"Don't drink. Don't get drunk. Don't commit adultery. Don't speak badly of others. Don't criticize others. Don't envy. All of those will be sins for you. Lead a good life, get along with others, give food and greetings to this one and that one. It's not good to drink, to get drunk. It's not good to steal. Don't envy or desire something that someone else has. Live like that." That's what they said.

They spoke well, the little priests did. Those were good words.

We heard and understood that and got up and went off to the side. Other people would be waiting behind . . .

Sometimes, a thief, come time to confess, would say, "We don't steal." They find themselves in a lie. Sometimes, someone who is involved with other women says, "No, I don't have anything to do with other women." They don't confess the truth. It was a real shame the way we lived. . . .

The priests said, "Don't lie. Whatever it is, tell the truth. If you lie, it will remain as your own sin. Confess to me, and you will be forgiven, and your souls will be saved."

"In my wife's village, they say that if someone doesn't make a good confession, he drops the Host. Do they say the same thing here . . . ?"

Oh, yes, yes. We all kneeled in a line with our tongues stuck out to receive the Host. . . . Sometimes it would stay on our tongues and quickly become moist. That was when we hadn't lied, people said. But when someone lied, they said, it wouldn't stick to his tongue, but just fall to the ground. . . .

"And what did people say the Host was?"

Who knows? Well, the priests said—and we thought as they said— that "this is like having Tayta Dios on your tongues. Now, after this, don't drink cane alcohol. Don't smoke. It's as if you have God on your tongues." That's what they said; that's how we understood it.

Sometimes, once Mass was over, we filed out past Tayta Dios, each one kissing his knee before stepping outside. . . . We didn't remember God, but we thought that the priest does everything.

"But people said he was a human being, with a father and mother, or . . ."

Yes. We thought he was a person with a father and mother. But he was well educated and became holy. He was set apart, chosen, we thought, to be called Tayta Amo. We didn't remember God in heaven, but called the priests "God."

"Some people say that the priests often abused brides. Even despite that, you considered them like God?"

About that, my parents did say, "How could the priests be like God? They are the first ones to do what they want with the brides, taking the place of the groom. And they say, 'We are holy, we are the holy, sacred priests.' How can the priests be holy?"

Before performing a wedding, the priests would say, "Can you say your prayers, the Our Father and the Hail Mary?"

When the brides weren't able to repeat the prayers, the priests would say, "Come here, come."

They had the bride come into a room and said, "You don't know how to pray. Well, I will forgive that. You come here and be with me."

Some of the brides would just do what the priests wanted, there inside a room. . . . On the other hand, some brides didn't agree to be with the priest. So the priests would charge them money for not knowing the prayers. They would charge 200, 100, or 150 sucres, in those days when everything was cheap. . . . On the other hand, if the bride agreed to lie down with the priest on a bed there in the room, then the priests didn't charge her. They just performed the wedding ceremony.

That's why the people who really knew would say, "Dirty priests. Dirty priest, how can he be Tayta Amo?"

"So they didn't believe in the priests."

That's right. Then they didn't believe so much in the priests. That's how it was.

"I Respected the Amo Bosses"

My father said that when he was a young man, *amo* Leandro Barba rented this hacienda. He also rented another hacienda, Llanos, down below Pallatanga. There was a sugar mill there. The *amo* would send my father with two mules to bring up [contraband] cane alcohol in big animal-skin saddlebags. . . .

My father said, "I would load up the mules and leave that hacienda at 7:00 or 8:00 at night, travel all night with the cane alcohol, and arrive at this hacienda at daybreak. I evaded the police for a time by traveling only at night."

But one night, the police finally caught up with him. They wanted to catch him and imprison him, but he said he ran and got away. The policemen took the mules with the cane alcohol. He said, "I ran into the brush, just tripping and rolling, with nothing but the shirt on my back. I stayed all night in the brush, and came home the next day. Who knows where they took the mules and the alcohol. . . . If they had jailed me, I don't know how many years it would have been before they set me free.

"Since then, I don't bring cane alcohol up. 'Vicente Sisa, I order you to be cowhand,' the *amo* said. 'You tend our cattle, see to it that they multiply. . . . That will be your task.' I became cowhand, and my life was filled with agricultural labors and watching the cattle, under the *amos'* orders."

That's all my father told us. He was a cowhand for a long time, from the time he was young until he died as an old man.

My mother, in turn, served my father—her husband. She gave him breakfast, washed his clothes, tilled a little bit of land around our house for us to eat. That was my mother's life. . . .

My father left the house to tend the cattle at six in the morning. Sometimes, he ate breakfast first; sometimes, he left without eating. It was sad how my father suffered. I remember that. He would get up and just leave without eating, by himself, to gather the cattle in the mountains, tend to them, spend all day up there, and come back at the end of the day. Sometimes my mother went up to the mountain to give him some food to eat, for breakfast. Sometimes, he ate breakfast at home, and took a bit of roasted corn with him. . . .

Once I was old enough, I would go with my father. If my father didn't eat, I didn't eat, either. We just got out of bed and went to spend our day up on the mountain with the cattle. We got back home at six or seven at night. Then we ate breakfast. We spent the day without eating. . . .

We left the cattle gathered in a group and came home. We didn't put them in a corral. But for fear of them crossing over into some other *amos'* hacienda, or being rustled or getting lost, we had to tend them and count them every day. If one got lost, the *amos* would charge us Runa cowhands. Yes, they charged us. Even if a cow died, they charged us. If a cow fell into a gully and died, as they do once in a while, we took it and skinned it, and told the stewards. "A cow has died. It fell into that hole," or "that gully," or "rolled down that hill."

"It's not my concern," they would say. "That's your problem. You do what you want with it. We'll take one of your cows and brand it, that's all."

We would plead, "It's not our fault. We didn't send it rolling down the hill. We gathered them in the afternoon and came home. And the next day, we found it dead."

They wouldn't listen. They would charge us by taking one of our live cows and branding it. And at the same time they would take the meat from the dead cow to the hacienda and sell it themselves. They were bad. . . .

That's how in the old days, sometimes we suffered sadly. Now that has all ended, because another law has come. The young people, women and men, know how to read and write. Now, these last years, our life is good. In the old days, our life was sad, very sad.

"What sort of moral instruction [*consejos*] did your father and mother give to you as children?"

Yes, as for that, they said,

You must work.
You must show respect to the amos, *to those who own the land.*
You must pray to God.
You must not steal. If you ask God, God himself will provide.
Don't neglect to work. Get up in the morning, take your hoe, break up
    the earth, turn over the earth, till it, plant—this must be your
    custom.
You must not envy what someone else has, or want it and go steal it . . .
    Don't bring criticism on us someday by stealing someone's animal.
    . . . We eat and live by our own sweat, by bending our backs and
    working.
That way, everyone will love us.
People will say we are good men and women.

That's how they taught us. Those are the "histories" [*historias*, impor- tant, durable words] our parents left us.

Don't envy someone else for having more grain, more animals, or more
    money. It will only lead God to give you even less. . . .
Don't lie. Don't speak ill of other people.
That was their moral instruction [consejos].

Also, "Don't take another woman." That was the instruction for the men. To the women, "Don't take another man. God commands us to have only one. One man, one woman. Marry and live according to God's commands. Don't cheat and take another. That's why they beat their wives. Or the wives, too, leave their husbands and go away. Don't live like that. You must love each other. Once the husband's and wife's names are entered on paper in the registry, you must live as a married couple. Once you have entered the church and gotten married, you leave the church as a married couple. In the same way, husband and wife will be separated in the church when one of you dies and is given over for burial; the husband or wife will then go back home—that's when you'll be separated."

That's how they give moral instruction when people marry, they give that good advice.

My wife, when she was a girl living with her parents up in Guangopud, her parents were in charge of the hacienda's sheep. So my wife, as a young woman, roamed in the mountains herding sheep—many, many sheep. I was cowhand here in Monjas, and she was sheepherder up in Guangopud. We would meet up in the mountains and we agreed to get married. She was a shepherd, I was a cowherd.

We would meet during the day. "Segunda Clariiita!" I would call. "I don't see the cows! Where could they be?"

And she would answer, "Here they are. The cows are here, back in here." . . .

There's a place up there called Yagüil, where she was herding the sheep one day. A rainbow appeared. Drizzle and fog surrounded her. She had two white dogs, she says, that did not leave her. She was there herding the sheep, carrying her distaff with a big ball of wool. When it began to rain and the fog surrounded her, the dogs began to howl, she says. "Dogs, what's wrong?" she said.

Then the rainbow appeared. And someone shouted. She was there alone with the dogs, herding the sheep. And someone let out a long yell, "Ahaaaa!"

"Then I got afraid," she says. "Who could it be?"

When the voice shouted, the fog opened up and all disappeared. The rain, too, dried up after the shout.

She prayed to God, and the dogs barked. All the sheep crowded together, baaing loudly. They put her in the middle, she says. The sheep took care of her. Maybe God did not consent to her getting involved with the *chuzalungu* [in oral tradition, a boylike being with a monstrous phallus, linked to mountains and wildness; see Lyons 2002b].

That man shouted for a long while, she says, "*Tuuuc* hahaaa! Sshhhh!" The dogs barked. The sheep were afraid. She says she didn't see anything, but her body was filled with fear.

Then, after the dogs barked and the sheep cried, her spirit began to get calm. Then the sheep began to go off to graze. The dogs stopped barking.

She told all that to the old people, and they said, "It must have been the *chuzalungu*, that man of the mountain. He shouts like that. It's a little, little man, with a *puzu* [interspersed black-and-white] poncho." So the old, old people told her about the *chuzalungu*.

As a young woman, she was a pretty woman, with reddish hair, a reddish face, nice clothes. The *chuzalungu* wanted to get involved with her, as a good-looking young woman.

My wife said, "The *chuzalungu*, that mountain, almost 'tempted' poor me. If the mountain had 'tempted' me, maybe I would have been given over to the devils."

She says, "Because of that fright, that worry, I married you. The mountain man, the *chuzalungu*, began to pursue me. What could I have done if he had made me fall? Maybe the mountain *chuzalungu* would have killed me."

When my father could no longer be cowhand, they gave the job to me. "Your father is old now; he can't do it anymore. Now you receive the cattle as cowhand, as an inheritance."

Since I lived on the *amos'* land, I accepted it. That was after I came back from military service and I was married.

We were two cowhands, who watched over 360 or 370 head of cattle. Alonso Guevara was the renter of this hacienda. That's the same *amo* Alonso Guevara who loved me, who took me with him wherever he went.

Well, when Alonso Guevara was finishing up his seven years as renter and was about to turn this hacienda over to someone else and leave, he said,

"I paid for all of this as renter.
I have been paying a lot of money.
And you all live without a worry,
you just plant without a worry,
you increase your herds of sheep and cattle, without a worry.
We poor renters, we indebt ourselves terribly to pay the rent to the
*   bishop.*
We spend all our money, our last dime.
Now, I'm turning over the hacienda. I'm going to rent another hacienda.

*I will take my animals—all those horses and cattle that you have
been tending—to that other hacienda."*

He told the steward, "I've borne the costs for this whole hacienda. I'm
going to take all of the laborers' animals with me to that other hacienda.
Why should I leave anything? I'll take away the Runa's horses, their
cattle, everything, and leave them with nothing."

Along with his own animals, he said he would take our animals, too.

That was allowed, it seemed—to take all the Runa's animals to another hacienda.

The steward himself told us, "Runitos, this is what the *patrón* is saying: 'I'll leave them with their arms crossed, empty-handed. Why should
they remain with their increased herds on the hacienda that I rented?'
That's what he's saying. Defend yourselves, get a lawyer."

At that time, my father had thirty-five or thirty-six head of cattle. . . .
I myself had just seven of my own. I don't remember how many years it
was after I got married.

The steward told everybody what the boss was saying, but they
were all afraid to defend themselves. So my brother and I went to Riobamba on behalf of all the people. They didn't give us anything for our
expenses, but they all agreed we should go. "Please go on our behalf.
Please find out what you can and come back. . . ." The women were
crying; the men were sad.

Following the steward's advice, in Riobamba we consulted with a
lawyer. He told us what to do. "Go to Quito and appeal to the doctor
[Velasco Ibarra]. Take this paper, this memorandum." Dr. Velasco Ibarra
was president at that time.[8] So we went right off to Quito—my brother
and I—to obtain an order in our defense.

We arrived at the presidential palace in Quito. We gave that piece of
paper, that letter, to the palace doorkeeper. The doorkeeper passed the
paper on inside to the government. I suppose the government read it;
then another piece of paper came back out. We took that piece of paper
with us back to Riobamba.

When we got back to Riobamba and gave the piece of paper from
Quito to the lawyer, he said, "You've done well. He won't take the
animals away. It's not allowed now for him to take away all the little
animals from the Runitos." So, my brother and I just came back here,
from Riobamba.

By the time we got back, the employees had been talking to the
people, scolding them: "Troublemakers, people who go to lawyers!"

All of the people's hearts had turned, and they had said, "We didn't have anything to do with it. Those two, Reinaldo Sisa and Esteban Sisa, just rushed off to Quito."

"They thought they were clever, and they rushed off to Quito. All of you were together in this. You must have given them something for them to go."

"No, we don't know anything about it. They didn't tell us anything." They all denied it, our fellow laborers, the agricultural laborers.

Poor us, then, when we arrived back here, again we were called to Riobamba [to the renter's house]. The steward and overseer said, "You two have to go to Riobamba."

My brother did not go; he went into hiding. I went by myself.

There, *amo* Guevara said to me, "You bandit, you troublemaker-bandit, going to Quito, I'll put you away now." He spoke on the telephone, and right away a van came with policemen. Poor me, the police bound me, put me in the van, and took me to the station. There, they left me in prison, in what they call the dungeon.

It was a room with tall walls, and very dark. They made me go inside. "This is the dungeon, for you, for being sneaky, a bandit, going to Quito, getting a lawyer."

They put me in the dungeon on Friday; they took me out on Monday afternoon. I went hungry until then.

That lawyer, may God repay him, spoke and got me out of there.

Then, the *amo* had said to the people here, "You clever ones. You got together and sent these two poor guys. So now, I'm not going to take all your animals away, as I was going to. They rushed off to Quito to make a written appeal, on paper. From Quito, the order came. You should thank those two for that. Otherwise, I was going to take all of your animals, every last one, to another hacienda. I was going to leave you all empty-handed."

The people did thank us. "May God repay you, thanks to you, the *amo* will not take away our horses and cows, all the animals we have. Otherwise, he was going to take them away to another hacienda he is renting and leave us with nothing. But because of you, he's not going to take them away, he told us."

Maybe God gave us some intelligence; we were smart, and we got that piece of paper. Once we submitted that paper, the boss didn't take the animals away. But poor me, they put me in the dungeon, from Friday to Monday.

The steward said, "You two have rushed off to Quito. Yes, I did tell you about it. Well, good, you went and you had good luck. If it were left to these other dummies, he would have taken away every last cow, each person's four or five head of cattle. . . . Now, you all be thankful to Reinaldo Sisa and his brother; because of them, the boss is not taking your animals away."

My father was a cowhand all his life. I helped my father from the time I was seven up to when I was thirty. Then my father died, and my mother died. They [the *amos*] didn't have me continue as cowhand any longer, so I worked as an agricultural laborer for the *amos*. . . .

That's how I have lived. Plowing, taming the oxen. Mounting the wild horses and taming them. Breaking up the clods of earth to plant the crops, to have something to eat. And carrying out the little *amos'* orders with all goodwill, doing and fulfilling whatever they ordered. That's what life was like for all of us.

As I say, the little *amos* loved me. They didn't speak harshly to me at all. They didn't whip me at all, they didn't club me. I'm a person who lived my life nicely. I'm not ever a bad person, I don't ever deny anyone anything. I give food to everyone.

Those people who were a little lazy, those who didn't obey, they bore punishments. The *amos* made them suffer. When they didn't carry out the orders, the *amos* took their whips and whipped them, they *clubbed* them.

"After being whipped, did they get angrier?"

No. Then they showed some respect and just walked off, cringing. If someone got angry, it was much worse for him. They just clubbed him on the head, made his blood run down his face. They sometimes gave people two or three blows on the back. That's what some poor people's lives were like.

Only I didn't suffer that. "Go run an errand," they said; I went quickly and came back quickly. . . . That's why they loved me. . . .

[Many people] left this hacienda. The *amos*, the employees treated them with anger, beat them, so they left and went to live in other places.

"And why were they beaten like that?"

It was because they didn't want to carry out any orders. When they were sent on an errand, they didn't like to come back quickly. They were a little lazy. We also have another word, *rudos* ["dull," "thick-headed" in

Ecuadorian Spanish]. People who are lazy, who don't want to carry out any task, they call *rudos.*[9] That's why they were hit. "You don't quickly carry out what was ordered, you don't like to do what you were ordered to do. You're disobedient." And they would be hit.

But I'm not that way. I respected the *amo* bosses. I carried out the orders with respect; that's how I led my life. I've stayed right here. . . .

Since they didn't mistreat me, they didn't beat me, I didn't go anywhere. I did go to the hacienda up there, but they called me right back. "You were a good Runa. No one said anything to you. Come back," they said. The *amos* brought me back here, and I stayed here. I didn't leave again. Now I'm an old man. That's what our life was like.

"I Want to Leave That Hacienda"

Now, no amo *gives any orders anymore,*
nor is there any overseer giving orders.
There is no patrón *giving orders.*
Now, thanks to the agrarian reform, we each have our own parcel of
    land.

Now, as I say, for some years, no one mistreats us.
No one beats us.
No one calls us "indio."
That way of treating people is finished —
calling them indio,
calling them rocoto,
calling them verdugo,
no one speaks like that now.
We live a peaceful life, these last couple of years.
They would call us verdugos, babosos, rocotos.
That's how we Runitos were mistreated,
yelled at like a dog.

From the time I remember, our only role in life was to serve the *amo* renters, with fear, obeying and respecting them. To respect the *amos,* to obey, and to work. We never lacked for work. Sometimes we had five days a week of hacienda work, from Monday to Friday. That's why our life was sad. We didn't have time to work to feed our wives and children. That's why people lacked food — they lacked, and so did we. That's what our life was like.

I left and went up to Guangopud. The *amo* employees here gave me too much work; they brought me along wherever they went. I didn't have time for my own work. We almost had to suffer hunger, we almost didn't have food to cook, because all we did, my wife and I, was to serve the *amos* all the time, both of us. So, we couldn't bear it. "What will we eat? What clothes will we wear? Let's leave."

"When you went to Guangopud, how did the *amos* there receive you?"

I asked the amo *first,*
"Patroncito, give me some little place.
Give me a ración *of land to live on.*
I want to leave this other hacienda.
These amo *employees are so terribly bad, so vicious, so nasty.*
They just hit people, club people, whip people.
*They don't leave us any time to work the holy earth [*santo suelo*],*
to plant potatoes,
to plant ukas *or any other crop.*
So my wife and children are a little hungry.
Those amos *take me along with them wherever they go,*
almost like a personal servant.
That's why I want to leave that hacienda."

"Come up here, son," he said. "Come, you can work here, no problem. We are in need of laborers. Come."
So we left the bishop's hacienda and went to Guangopud, putting ourselves under this other *amo*.

"And did the *amos* of this hacienda just let people leave, or did people go in secret?"

They wouldn't let people leave. I went at night, in secret. I put our things in sacks and loaded them on horses. I was here at nightfall; the next morning, I was up in Guangopud, and our house here was empty.
It's only now, after the agrarian reform, that people build cement-block houses. In the old days, we just dug a big hole in the ground and put straw thatching on for a roof.
Early the next morning, the *amo* employees came following us. "Why did you leave and come here?"

"We left because we couldn't live there. We didn't have food. Every day there are orders to work, but we lack food. We have to eat in order to work. That's why we left."

"C'mon, let's go, come on back."

They wanted to bring us back here, to the same place we had been living. We didn't listen. "No."

"Did they say they wouldn't order you to do so much anymore?"

No, they didn't say that. "C'mon back with us. We always need laborers. How could you leave? Why should you leave? C'mon."

The stewards kept insisting, and later I did come back, after some time.

"Reinaldo," they said, "what's with you? C'mon, come back.

You carried out orders quickly.
You were respected/respectful [respetado].
None of us will say anything to you [i.e., we won't speak harshly or
*   hold it against you].*
Yes, it's true, we do whip and club these other ones who are lazy,
these other ones who don't do what they're told,
who don't carry out orders.
But none of us has been saying anything to you.
We've always treated you with love. And even so, you've come here. You
*   have to come back."*

So I did come back.

It's true, the stewards did love me. They showed me goodwill. So when they called me back—may God repay—after I went back,

they didn't hit me,
they didn't say anything bad to me.
They didn't call me indio.
They didn't call me rocoto.
They didn't call me runa.
They called me by name: "Reinaldo."
Whatever they wanted to tell me to do,
whatever errand they wanted to send me on,
they called me "Reinaldo!"
The amos *called me by name, may God repay them.*

That's what our life was like, *compañero* Braulito. I wasn't very mistreated or anything. I lived contentedly. Some other people went through life a bit mistreated. Poor people, it was really sad to see: beaten, whipped, clubbed. With tears in their eyes, lamenting their sufferings. But I didn't suffer. I carried out the work they assigned me quickly, and so I didn't suffer. I just lived happily.

"Didn't those other people ever say, 'Let's rise up, all together?'"

No, no. People couldn't rebel in those days. If someone rebelled, the employees, the *amos*, wouldn't hesitate to kill him, for sure. "Impudent, insolent," they would say. "You are impudent. You are rebellious. These other people are not like that." If someone talked back a little, if someone said, "Let's rebel," oh, boy, they would take a club and give it to him on his poor back, the back of his neck, beating him to the ground. So we could not rebel. We didn't think about rising up. We just bore it in silence, that's all.

As I say, the lazy people suffered. They lacked for food, for something to put in their cooking pots. On the other hand, for those of us who were quick, who just carried out what we were told to do smoothly, Tayta Dios, there was food, there was something to cook. Our life was all right. It depended; our lives were not all the same. Some people's lives were sad; other people had enough to eat.

COMMENTS

Students of oral history and life histories have stressed that memory is in continual dialogue with the present. Oral accounts reconstruct the past as the subject addresses a particular interviewer and, more broadly, the dilemmas, ideological currents, voices, and projects of the present. Before asking what Mama Jacoba's and Tayta Reinaldo's accounts tell us about the past, then, let us first examine this implicit dialogue with the present.

Remembering the Hacienda Today

Jacoba Sayay mentions that the Guangopud landowner did not give her a *huasipungo* in the agrarian reform, despite all her suffering on the hacienda, and goes on to say that it was as if hacienda laborers had been serving a dog—an obvious symbol for the landowner's failure to conform to normal expectations of reciprocity.

The agrarian reform process often portrayed itself as the fulfillment of a long-delayed reciprocity, and that image clearly influences Mama Jacoba's perspective here. During the agrarian reform, government agents would formally tally hacienda residents' contribution to the hacienda in the form of labor, animals, and tools used in hacienda tasks; they likewise calculated the hacienda's liability for unfulfilled legal obligations to the workers, including unpaid wages. The distribution of *huasipungo* plots was then conceived as payment for the resulting debt; if the value of the land exceeded the value of the debt, laborers sometimes had to make up the difference. Pastureland and other land that was transferred to collective ownership were likewise figured into the same calculations.

Even in cases such as Monjas Corral, where land distribution was not calculated exactly in this way, it took the same broad form. Plots were allotted to those who had been full-time laborers on the hacienda (with *arrimado* and *ayuda* laborers at a disadvantage compared with *huasipungueros*), and the land distribution was portrayed as a settling of accounts, a compensation for their contribution to the hacienda in sweat and suffering over the years.

This whole conception of agrarian reform obviously rested on a judgment that laborers' contribution to the hacienda was not fairly compensated under the hacienda system itself. I argue in Chapter 5 that such a judgment was common prior to the agrarian reform—while also arguing that indigenous expectations of reciprocity were far more complex than a ledger sheet, involving matters of personal consideration, flexibility, and respectful treatment along with material contributions and returns. The agrarian reform itself did not create the bitter memories of unfair fines, excessive and rigid work demands, insults and violence, or the notion that rich *amos* had made a pact with the devil.

I also recognize in the last chapter that such a judgment was not laborers' only perspective toward the hacienda, or even necessarily always the dominant perspective. The agrarian reform, however, took this judgment and attached to it the notion of individual landownership (together with collective pastureland) as fair compensation for the years of hacienda labor. This move was not always immediately accepted. On Monjas Corral, as we shall see, laborers refused for some years to accept the breaking up of the hacienda. Ultimately, however, they were forced to accept it, as were laborers on other haciendas.

Older villagers today speak of having earned their rights to land through their suffering on the hacienda. This notion plays a role in contemporary intergenerational tensions between the initial recipients of individual and communal land rights and younger villagers, who do not yet have full access to land in their own right. The image of the hacienda period as a time of un-requited suffering, thus, has a political use today.

Another contemporary use of the image of hacienda suffering is as part of a general historical narrative of movement from backwardness to moder-nity, oppression to liberation, ignorance to knowledge, and darkness to light, which has become popular in the decades since the agrarian reform. Several ideological currents and projects of social transformation have participated in the elaboration and diffusion of this narrative in different forms: develop-mentalism, liberation theology, the indigenous evangelical movement, and the organized ethnic political movement, among others. Jacoba Sayay's hus-band, a local political leader, has appealed to this historical narrative in call-ing on other villagers to participate in electrification and communal animal-raising projects.

Even those who resist participation in contemporary projects of social change often speak of the hacienda period in ways consonant with the his-torical narrative of progress, awakening, and liberation. They may balance their criticism of the harsh labor regime with nostalgia for certain aspects of hacienda life: they were free to plant and keep animals in an extensive area. They may even say, resentfully, that no one made exactly the same kind of demands that community and church leaders now make on their time, pocketbooks, energy, and cooperative spirit—putting aside the quite heavy demands that the hacienda and religious authorities did make on them. De-spite this nostalgic countercurrent, though, it may be that the agrarian re-form and subsequent developments have tended to highlight in oral mem-ory the negative aspects of hacienda life and to obscure the extent to which some people could have conceived of the *amos* as moral exchange-partners.

On the other hand, Reinaldo Sisa's remarkable lack of bitterness in speak-ing about hacienda life can also be related to posthacienda developments. Al-most alone among the former Monjas Corral laborers, he converted to evan-gelical Protestantism in the 1970s. This movement calls for patience and moderation in dealing with conflict, frowns on overt expressions of anger, and tended, up to the early 1990s, to oppose the radical ethnic political move-ment and its promotion of a strong sense of historical grievance. Protestant-ism also seems to cultivate a self-confident attitude that, if one behaves up-rightly, one has nothing to fear from other people, be they *amos*, gringos, or fellow Runa. Tayta Reinaldo insists that mistreatment and hunger on the hacienda was a consequence of laborers' own behavior—their laziness, slow-ness, disobedience, and dishonesty. Might it be that he is reinterpreting ha-cienda life in line with contemporary Protestant ideology?

Our suspicions to this effect might be intensified when we note that an-

other, contradictory, strand also runs through his account, one more harmonious with other people's bitter memories than with his emphasis on individual blame for suffering. He tells of his father's hard life as a mule driver
for the renter and later as a cowhand, the unjust confiscation of family cows
to replace dead hacienda cattle, Alonso Guevara's plan to confiscate all of
the laborers' animals, and his own imprisonment for impeding this plan. He
ends up admitting that his family, too, suffered hunger (if not violence) on the
hacienda. While many of his relatively favorable comments about his experience under the hacienda were part of the overview with which he opened the
interview, many of the unfavorable incidents and comments only emerged
in response to my questions. It is tempting, then, to suppose that his favorable comments correspond to a contemporary ideological wish, and that the
unfavorable strand corresponds more closely to the reality of the past.

Turning now from Jacoba Sayay's and Reinaldo Sisa's general judgments
about the hacienda to their portrayal of their own and other people's stances
toward hacienda authority, we can draw the same sort of connections to
the present. For Jacoba Sayay, one aspect of the dark ignorance of the hacienda period was most people's foolish submissiveness, their meekness.
The Catholic-indigenous ethnic movement and especially liberation theology often portray the past in a similar way—a "centuries-long slumber," as
Leonidas Proaño put it (1989:87); the liberation theology church takes some
credit for "awakening" indigenous people politically. Mama Jacoba endorses
this picture of the past while at the same time she exempts herself and her
family, depicting them as already "smart" and rebellious under the hacienda.

Reinaldo Sisa shares Mama Jacoba's image of an awakening, but his is
not an awakening from meekness to rebelliousness. For him, the darkness
and ignorance of the past refer, above all, to the religious sanction given to
racial and ecclesiastical hierarchy—the special religious greetings used to address *amos* and the worship of images and priests. In his dramatic account
of his conversion to Protestantism (not included here), he tells of repeatedly
addressing a mestizo missionary as *patrón*, to the missionary's dismay. The
missionary insists that he should be called "brother"; the only *patrón* is God
up in heaven. Tayta Reinaldo eventually converts and learns to address the
missionaries as "brother" and "sister."

This religious egalitarianism, however, does not imply approval of rebellion. Instead, Protestantism calls for strict compliance with an exalted personal ethics, including honesty, hard work, and respect for authority. It en-
courages a confident self-assertion, but not belligerence.

Tayta Reinaldo's account, again, clearly reflects these values. He depicts
himself as having been deluded in religious terms but as having, nonethe-

less, abided by the sort of ethical code that Protestantism now espouses—and as having been rewarded adequately by God and the *amos* for his uprightness. His description of fiesta sponsorship is largely similar to other people's accounts but differs significantly in his stress on his own role in controlling unruly behavior associated with drunkenness. One of the most culturally salient features of Protestantism in Chimborazo is its ban on alcohol.

In juxtaposing here Reinaldo Sisa's and Jacoba Sayay's different versions of the past, then, am I simply reproducing as history a very contemporary debate—that between indigenous Protestantism, with its stress on moderation and opposition to radical politics, on the one hand, and liberation theology Catholicism and ethnic protest, on the other?

I would respond that there are two ways we can deny a connection between past and present in these accounts, and both are wrong. One would be to take them as disinterested, objective data about the past and to ignore altogether the ways they are influenced by contemporary concerns. This would clearly be a mistake.

It would be equally mistaken, however, to deny that these accounts speak to any true past at all—to imagine that the past is reinvented wholesale to fit current desires. The implication is that the real past left no durable impact—that old dispositions, ideologies, and memories are reshaped but have no real power to shape present perceptions. This is, in fact, an unspoken implication of many of the popular conceptions, self-portrayals, and journalistic celebrations or condemnations of both liberation theology and the Protestant movement. Both liberation theology and Protestantism portray themselves as shining a new light to dispel the darkness of the past, but both actually have a much more complex relationship to that past. The opponents of each polemically depict indigenous people's experience of these movements as something akin to brainwashing, or "invasion" by an alien mentality. In the first case, ignorant Indians are seen as easily manipulated by red clerics (see, e.g., Arellano Gallegos 1985); in the second, North American missionaries buy souls, destroying indigenous culture to replace it with capitalist values made in the United States (see, e.g., Albán and Muñoz 1987). Indigenous people's experience of contemporary religious movements, however, is deeply and complexly rooted in the past—in the assumptions, ideologies, and practices of hacienda life and the dilemmas bequeathed to them by their recent history. Positioning themselves comfortably in relation to that past is, indeed, one of the main challenges for indigenous people today. If the past is a powerful symbol in contemporary debate, it is precisely because it left a durable impact that demands to be reckoned with.

These accounts of the past, then, do reflect a contemporary debate, but it is not an entirely new debate. In the hacienda period, different people had different attitudes about "respecting" or "disrespecting" authority. Indigenous adherents of liberation theology and Protestantism each take up different strands of these old attitudes, focus and develop their critiques of old forms of authority in partly different ways, attempt to reformulate "respect" and authority in different ways. Mama Jacoba's involvement with liberation theology through her husband and Tayta Reinaldo's conversion to Protestantism may indeed be reflections and developments of their prior dispositions.

The reinterpretation of the past that occurs in accounts such as those I have presented, I think it is safe to say, is a matter of what people choose to tell, what they emphasize, the way they tell it, the explicit and implicit links they make to the present—but not generally a matter of outright invention or denial of basic patterns. For example, those who define the past as a time of ignorant submissiveness do not deny that people engaged in covert appropriation, foot dragging, and flight; they simply do not emphasize these responses or define them as forms of resistance. Thus, we are not forced here to choose between mutually incompatible accounts. Reinaldo Sisa, Jacoba Sayay, and others all acknowledge that people responded to the hacienda in a variety of ways, besides those they each describe as their own. By juxtaposing and comparing accounts from different perspectives, by attending to the internal inconsistencies of each as well as the agreements and disagreements between them, by paying close attention to the details of language that reflect old cultural or ideological configurations, we can still reasonably hope to learn something about the patterns of experience during the hacienda period.

To Be Smart and to Be Good

Jacoba Sayay emphasizes her rebelliousness toward the hacienda, Reinaldo Sisa, his respect for hacienda authority. Each recognizes costs as well as benefits associated with their respective attitudes but each argues that those who behaved in the opposed manner suffered even worse. We can use their descriptions of these costs and benefits to analyze each type of response as a strategy.

Reinaldo Sisa says that, through honesty and good work, he gained the *amos'* appreciation, praise, and benevolent treatment—they even fed him well when he accompanied them as a personal servant. More than positive benefits, however, he repeatedly stresses that, through his respectful behavior, he avoided the insults and violence that other laborers suffered.

His personal morality and respectfulness even allowed him certain victories in relation to his social superiors, as he tells it, by winning him the benevolence of those even higher up. The renters' trust gained him entry into their private room, in an evident humiliation for the female stewards to whom he refused to hand over the key. God helped him face the challenge of the sheep counting, so that he counted correctly when the stewards and overseers could not.

In his demeanor, his tone, his general lack of bitterness, Tayta Reinaldo conveys a sense of equanimity and self-confidence that seems to be reflected in his perception of his relationship with both *amos* and peers. The same qualities can be seen in his response when conflict with the renter was inevitable. He was willing to challenge the renter legally in defense of his and his peers' animals. He stresses, at the same time, that the steward himself suggested the idea and that the other laborers "all agreed we should go." He presents himself as someone who simply carried out his duty well, sometimes his duty to *amos* and, in this case, his duty to peers, but did not look for conflict. At no point in his account of the incident does he apply to the renter or steward any of the critical epithets that are common in other people's talk about the *amos*, such as "cruel" or "morally ugly" (*millay*); he simply recounts what he did and what happened to him.

Yet, despite his general equanimity, Tayta Reinaldo admits that at one point he, too, like so many others, found his situation on the hacienda intolerable. Like others, he complains that the renters did not allow his family time to work their own usufruct plot—though, ironically, in his case, this appears as the result of the renters' "love" for him and his wife as personal servants. This points out how foot dragging, covert appropriation, and general recalcitrance in the face of orders could be tactics against excessive labor demands; Tayta Reinaldo was "loved" and called on for personal service because he refrained from such tactics. His characterization of other laborers as "lazy" and dishonest suggests that he must have had to give an extra measure of hard work and personal sacrifice in order to gain the *amos'* goodwill. Still, he insists that his situation was preferable to that of other laborers who were harshly mistreated.

Jacoba Sayay, on the other hand, characterizes as "fools" those who did not talk back to the *amos*, those who just did whatever the *amos* ordered. She describes being the target of hacienda violence but says that this was the common lot of "every single one of us." It seems clear that sometimes she might have been targeted as a response to her insubordination. She also suggests, however, that her displays of defiance, her willingness to talk back or hit back, might sometimes have given pause to the *amos*, thus allowing her a little more room for noncompliance with their demands. Those who were meeker obeyed orders but were nonetheless hit, it seems, because the stewards and overseers knew they could do it without risk.

José María Pillajo—like Jacoba Sayay, a Catholic, but about forty years older than she and much less involved with liberation theology—confirms that it was sometimes possible under the hacienda regime for someone to gain a relative immunity from violence by displaying a readiness to fight back. After he "bathed" Ignacio Lara in the river, Lara threatened vengeance but backed down in the face of Tayta José's defiant challenge. In contrast, he says, Lara clubbed and whipped at will those who were afraid to stand up to him. Tayta José's open defiance thus won him relatively tolerable conditions through the years of abusive stewards, which allowed him to stay while others saw no option but to leave.

Reinaldo Sisa and José Pillajo are both exceptions—Monjas Corral old-timers, born on the hacienda in the first decades of the twentieth century, who were still there at the end of the century. There were a few others whom I simply did not get there in time to meet. But most of the long-term laborers, as Tayta Reinaldo says, left. If I had been able to track down the survivors, I would probably have more to say about a third type of response to the hacienda, somewhere between the extremes represented by Reinaldo Sisa and José Pillajo. From the accounts of these two, one gathers that many others were unwilling or unable to devote as much energy to satisfying the *amos'* demands and gaining their appreciation as Reinaldo Sisa did, but neither were they willing to accept the risks associated with open defiance. A combination of overt respect with some covert noncompliance and foot dragging was probably a very common strategy. Also, individuals probably sometimes shifted between different strategies, depending on the nature of their relationship with specific stewards and overseers, the kinds of demands being made on them, and other circumstances.

Despite the possibility of different strategies, we should not exaggerate the room for maneuvering that people were allowed under the hacienda. All these strategies were aimed at securing improvements in day-to-day conditions—avoiding physical punishments, fines, and sexual abuse, for example. No strategy could always be successful even at that level, as long as the basic structures of land, labor, and power remained the same. Jacoba Sayay, Reinaldo Sisa, and José María Pillajo all speak of excessive labor under the *amos'* orders as an inescapable fact of hacienda life. This is not to minimize the importance in people's lives of issues of day-to-day treatment, or to deny that daily resistance over such issues can have long-run structural consequences (Scott 1985). It is simply to recognize the constraints within which people made their strategic choices. Jacoba Sayay mentions the risk of expulsion from the hacienda; Reinaldo Sisa points to the vicious clubbings and even the possibility of being killed as the ultimate constraint preventing rebellion.

Along with these general constraints on everyone, particular structural positions also certainly influenced people's strategic choices. Jacoba Sayay married with the idea of escaping from the harsh labor regime and the threat of sexual abuse on the hacienda, but she found that she had simply traded one form of suffering for another. She evidently saw little alternative beyond submitting to her husband and father-in-law or going back to the hacienda and decided on the latter. There, as a woman separated from her husband and without a father or older brother, she was probably particularly vulnerable to abuse, sexual or otherwise. Her displays of anger and defiance were no doubt in part a shield against the possibility of rape. Defiance in Quichua is associated with "maleness," as we shall see; Mama Jacoba may have seen herself as forced by her own lack of male protection to be more self-assertive. At the same time, generally accepted gender definitions probably restrained hacienda authorities from inflicting on her the sort of vicious clubbing that Reinaldo Sisa remembers being inflicted on defiant men. A woman's challenge would not be seen as so threatening, and thus requiring such harsh punishment, as a man's.

Thus, her attitude reflected in part her particular position. Again, this does not negate choice. She partly chose her position in separating from her husband and then remaining single. She could have remarried earlier than she did. She could have chosen a different mix of defiance and acquiescence in negotiating her treatment on the hacienda. She could have accepted the deal that the landowner and stewards offered her of gifts and labor exemptions for sex—as some women (and some women's husbands) did. Obviously, each of these choices would have entailed its own costs, risks, and benefits.

The structural elements associated with José María Pillajo's defiance of the Laras are of a somewhat different nature. His defiance was not simply a solitary decision but was supported by alliances of friendship and kinship. His associates in challenging the Laras included members of two large family groups, one of which he was tied to by kinship and by a shared grievance against the Laras.[10] In addition, he was on very friendly terms with two overseers—one of them his wife's brother. This helps explain his ability to challenge the Laras and continue to live on Monjas Corral. Preexisting demographic and kinship structures, strategic formation of alliances, and personal dispositions were all involved in his response to the Laras.

Thus, we can draw a picture of different responses to the hacienda as strategies with discernable costs, risks, and benefits. This picture, however, is incomplete. Jacoba Sayay, Reinaldo Sisa, and José María Pillajo all describe their own pattern of behavior as a strategy, but not only that. Their attitudes are partly pragmatic but also involve judgments of the moral worth, abilities, and savvy associated with each type of response. Let us now turn to the value judgments that are bound up with these choices.

The moral dimension is strongest in the case of Reinaldo Sisa. He associates his positive relationship with the *amos* with having a "good back" and "light blood." "Good back" is commonly used to refer to someone who has "good luck" and brings good luck to others, "light blood" to someone who is easily likeable. But in explaining the terms, Tayta Reinaldo links them to moral qualities associated with respect. He says they both refer to a "good person," well spoken, respectful, of a "good heart," and generally well liked. He speaks of refraining from covert appropriation as having "a clean hand and a clean heart." At some points, he seems to imply that a generous attitude of sharing food with peers and a positive, respectful relationship with the *amos* were two sides of the same coin, both part of being a good person. Those who took a different approach to the hacienda, on the other hand, he describes as lazy, slow, "heavy," and ill spoken. He expresses sympathy with them as victims of insults and violence but at the same time implies that they brought their sufferings on themselves.

For Jacoba Sayay, the contrast between those who rebelled and those who did not is not exactly moral. It is, rather, a matter of "smarts"—of a clear-eyed awareness as opposed to foolish meekness. It is also a question of fearlessness and of a disposition toward strong, overwhelming anger.

José María Pillajo shares Jacoba Sayay's indignation over hacienda abuses, but his terms for contrasting types of responses are different. For him, it is a matter of masculinity versus cowardice: "Some of us were real *males* —we, too, dammit! Some little people were a bit weak [*medio flojo*], cowardly . . . ; they were clubbed, beaten up, hit all the time" (JMP 7/21/1991). Note his expression "we, too [*ñukanchikpish*]," implying that the forceful, violent domination he was reacting to was itself a markedly male practice. Domination was masculine, and so was the ability to stand up to it in forceful resistance. In recounting his resistance, he describes a strategy but also affirms an identity.

Reinaldo Sisa, Jacoba Sayay, and José Pillajo, then, do not present themselves simply as having made strategic choices. The value of a choice, as they describe it, was partly a function of its success—but it was more than that. They do not talk of their own or other people's choices as coolly calculated decisions but as determined in part by personal characteristics of morality, intellectual ability, and masculinity.

To Act Like a Man

The values Reinaldo Sisa, Jacoba Sayay, and José Pillajo each invoke are part of a collective field of representations that is and was culturally and socially structured. We shall examine this field and its structuring with a broader social focus in the next chapter. To close this chapter, let me briefly show how some of the themes emphasized in one or another of the accounts I have discussed are shared among them. First, I would like to point out how local gender images influence Jacoba Sayay's and Reinaldo Sisa's accounts as well as that of José Pillajo. I then return to the notion of respect that Reinaldo Sisa expresses most clearly and note how this notion is reflected in Jacoba Sayay's account as well.

Reinaldo Sisa and Jacoba Sayay both use the common Quichua verb *kariyana* to refer to insubordination. This word is built on the root *kari*, "male." The suffix *-ya* means "to become" or "to get." Literally, then, *kariyana* means "to get male." *Kariyana*, as in "to defy, to rebel," thus implies that insubordination is a typically "male" act, and to use the word is implicitly to reproduce the association (see Lyons 2002b).

The interplay between domination and gender is very evident throughout Jacoba Sayay's account. The stewards and landowner tried to convert their power into sexual access, offering her exemption from work or material rewards. Her mother and other women likewise suffered sexual abuse on Guangopud and Llinllín. Moreover, not only did powerful men try to convert power into a sexual relationship, they also seem to have viewed sex as sealing a relationship of power and submission. As Mama Jacoba tells it, the landowner's threats of a whipping for disobedience to the steward alternated with his sexual advances, as if he viewed her sexual acquiescence as solving the problem of her insubordination by fixing her in a submissive position.

This relationship between power and sex could also have reverberations within the domestic unit. Jacoba Sayay's father evidently viewed her mother's first child—the offspring of rape by the *amo* when she was single—as his own humiliation. Blaming her for it, perhaps suspecting her of consenting to sexual relations with the *amo*, he enacted his own masculine role by beating her when he was drunk.

The same equation of domination and sex takes on a more metaphorical cast in other incidents. One is Mama Jacoba's description of the exchange of insults she and Ignacio Lara shouted at each other across the river over firewood. She and her sister's own shouting of insults she terms *kariyak*— again, insubordination or aggressive self-assertion implicitly associated with taking on a "male" quality. Ignacio Lara's response was to underline in a sexual idiom their femininity and his own masculinity: "Mistresses, horny *longas* [Indian girls], I'll get you!" He accuses them of an illegitimate, excessive sexuality; this may allude to the possibility of using areas with brush where firewood is gathered for a surreptitious rendezvous. In terms of the virgin/whore dichotomy, their participation in such activities would make them legitimate targets for sexual aggression on his part. He swears to "get" or "catch" them—on the face of it, a threat simply to catch and punish them, but also interpretable in sexual terms. They respond, "*cholo* bandit [*bandido*]"; this is an attack on his own sexuality as illegitimately unrestrained. *Cholo* also throws back at him the ethnic accusation in his insults: he implies that uncontrolled female sexuality is a particularly Indian characteristic; they reply that mestizo men are the sexual offenders. Thus, an argument between a man and two girls about firewood, hacienda boundaries, and authority takes the form of sexual accusations and counteraccusations.

Jacoba Sayay also tells of an argument with the female Guangopud steward whose husband had been making sexual advances toward her. She does not give much detail about the cause of the argument but focuses on her own insults, which refer to the steward, his phallus, and the female steward's involvement with the latter: the steward is a skirt chaser (*waynandero*), his phallus, a tethering stake. Here, Mama Jacoba's defiance of a female authority takes the form of scornfully pointing out the latter's own sexually determined submission to a man to whom she herself refuses to submit sexually.

Domination, then, was metaphorically associated with sexuality for both mestizos and, sometimes, indigenous people as well, with the male role being that of dominator. Mestizos and indigenous people of both genders also associated insubordination with masculinity. At the same time, a woman like Mama Jacoba can speak of acting with "manly" defiance (*kariyana*) in defense of her sexual honor or in response to various abuses. In indigenous gender ideology, strength and self-assertion, while marked as particularly "male" qualities, are also encouraged and admired in females. While Mama Jacoba says that other people criticized her for her defiant attitude toward hacienda authority, I have no indication that she or any other woman was criticized specifically as a woman for this; Mama Jacoba's father and brother suffered the same criticism.

Finally, let us note that Reinaldo Sisa, while he may represent an extreme end of the spectrum, is not alone in attaching a positive value to respect and hierarchy. Jacoba Sayay acknowledges that she and her brother have incurred the disapproval of their peers as well as their social superiors for their rebellious attitude. Moreover, she herself, at some level, seems to accept the racial superiority of whites over Runa; this is clear in her way of talking about her half sister, the landowner's daughter.

Why would indigenous laborers have disapproved of one of their fellows' standing up to the bosses? How could someone even as sharply critical of the *amos* as Jacoba Sayay accept values associated with racial hierarchy?

If domination was symbolically male, did indigenous people view and experience obedience as necessarily "feminine" or emasculating? How is it that Reinaldo Sisa, as a man, can describe his respectful behavior toward the *amos* with pride? Was there another metaphor through which the relationship of domination and submission could be understood and accepted and that continues to shape Tayta Reinaldo's feelings today?

To begin to answer these questions, we must explore in greater depth the notion of "respect." That is the agenda for the next chapter.

CHAPTER 7

Respect, Authority, and Discipline

INTRODUCTION
Two Runa Meet Jesus Christ

At one time, it is said, God wandered this earth—God the Son, Jesus Christ
—as an old white man. His enemies, the devils, were pursuing him. In his
flight, God encountered a Runa who was planting a field. He asked the Runa,
"Look, Runito, what are you planting?"

"White thief [Tsala shua]! I could be planting stones! I could be planting
thorn bushes! You're a white thief; why do you want to know?"

"Well, then, Runa, tomorrow come and see. Tomorrow come and see."

God continued on his way and came upon another Runa planting a field.
He asked again, "Runito, what are you planting?"

"Amito, little father, I am putting the potatoes, the *uka*, the fava beans,
the corn, the quinua that God has given, all the crops that Father God created, into Father God's hands."

"Well, then, early tomorrow morning come and look. Some evil ones will
come by then, following me."

The next day, the first Runa's field was full of stones, thorn bushes, and
lizards.The second Runa, on the other hand, came to find his field full of
crops ready to be harvested in marvelous abundance.

The evil ones passed by and asked him, "Look, Runa, when did a *cholo*
pass by here?"

"The day I planted these crops he passed by."

"Who knows when that could have been?!!" The evil ones concluded that
the trail was cold.[1]

This widely told story forms one episode in a larger cycle in which Jesus Christ takes on various guises—a person, a burro, a rooster—as he flees his enemies and blesses or curses people, plants, and animals according to how they treat him. In other stories, Jesus disguises himself as a beggar asking for charity. The stories do not suggest that every white man is God any more than they imply that every beggar or rooster is God. Yet, villagers do tell these stories to convey moral lessons: be hospitable and charitable, for example, because a beggar calling at your house might really be God. Rural mestizo parents and grandparents in Bolívar province tell the story of the two Runa farmers to teach children that they must respect their elders. As told in the past by hacienda Runa in Chimborazo, the story of the two farmers hints at some of the hacienda-era connections I shall be exploring here between respect for elders, respect for *amos,* and divinity.[2]

A Lesson in Respect

Lessons in respect sometimes took the form of a story, and sometimes they took a more directly forceful form. Alberto Yumbo described how he learned to greet stewards, overseers, and religious authorities properly as a youth (Figure 17):

> We had to greet them formally from afar, saying, "Blessed and praised, Sir alcalde, Sir *regidor,* Sir *fundador"* . . .
> If we didn't greet them well, they said, "Insolent one, who taught you like that?" and they struck with the whip. They pulled on our ears, they admonished us. . . .
> Sometimes we cried. Sometimes we walked away laughing. If we laughed, they said, "He is not heeding," and *again* they struck us.

HEGEMONY AND DISCIPLINE
Discipline and the Arts of Domination

In this chapter I develop an interpretation of concepts such as coercion, persuasion, discipline, and hegemony for understanding the type of interaction Tayta Alberto described as well as broader relations of authority and resistance. I critique James Scott's analysis of domination (1985, 1990) as a way of examining some common assumptions that I consider problematic. What I seek to add to the debates on Scott's work (see, e.g., Gal 1995; Howe 1998; Levi 1999; Mitchell 1990; Ortner 1995; Tilly 1991; Woost 1993) is a different way of looking at coercion and its relationship to persuasion.

FIGURE 17. *Alberto Yumbo*

In an influential book, *Domination and the Arts of Resistance* (1990), Scott treats domination as a kind of performance. Through economic compulsion and physical coercion, he observes, rulers force subordinates to behave and speak in ways that present an image of society drawn according to the rulers' wishes. Scott calls this performance a "public transcript." However, this coerced compliance "virtually inoculates the complier against willing compliance" and induces a psychological need to express dissent (1990:109). When subordinates are safely "offstage," among peers, they develop a "hidden transcript" that expresses their rejection of the public transcript. Such hidden transcripts sustain ubiquitous practices of covert practical resistance to domination. In Scott's view, the existence of covert resistance and oppositional transcripts shows that domination rests on compulsion and coercion and not, in any significant way, on ideological hegemony. He interprets Gramsci's notion of hegemony as asserting that subordinates accept ideas that reinforce their own subordination—a claim that Scott rejects (1985, 1990).

At first sight, the interaction Tayta Alberto described seems like a straightforward example of Scott's model. Religious authorities and hacienda bosses imposed a public transcript of deferential greetings and whipped subordinates who failed to follow the script. Young Runa were expected to make at least a show of accepting the lesson. If they displayed bravado or mockery by laughing, their superiors punished them again to force this oppositional transcript off the public stage. Youths thus learned from such experiences that they could express irreverence only when they were among their peers.

Yet, Tayta Alberto's account, like many others I gathered from former hacienda residents, diverges from Scott's model in two crucial respects. The first concerns the relationship between coercion and consent. When we talked in 1992, there were no hacienda bosses coercing his deference. He had the opportunity to express a resentment that he might have hidden in the past. Instead, after describing his lessons in deference, his narrative took a rather surprising turn. Far from saying these coercive lessons "inoculate[d]" him "against willing compliance," Tayta Alberto testified to the positive, deep, and enduring effects they had on his subjectivity: "That life was a marvelous life, because of the admonishments, the words of instruction. . . . That's how the elders taught us greetings. 'You are greeting Father God, not us,' they said. . . . If someone who was not too much of a troublemaker listened to what they said and responded, 'May God repay you,' Father God then remained in our memory and in our little heart."

Second, Scott divides society into two classes, dominant and subordinate, with subordinates switching between a public transcript they do not believe in and a hidden transcript of dissent and resistance that more truly expresses their feelings (also see Gal 1995; Ortner 1995). Tayta Alberto was speaking of a considerably more complex system of social relations. On the one hand, the authorities who enforced deferential greetings were linked to the landlord elite. On the other, some of them (especially alcaldes) were also ordinary hacienda laborers, subject to the same oppressive conditions as other Runa. More broadly, Tayta Alberto's use of the category "elders" alludes to the fact that similar practices, expectations, and discourses permeated and organized elder-junior relationships among Runa and were not restricted to specific authorities and their subordinates. As a laborer in the fields, an individual could easily find himself or herself at the receiving end of a lesson in deference; but as a parent or godparent, the same person imparted similar lessons to others.

Still more broadly, these relationships between authorities, elders, and juniors regulated other relationships: a Runa embroiled in conflict with a spouse or neighbor knew that they could call on the same authorities and elders for help. Hacienda residents themselves sometimes solicited ritualized lessons in respect. This is part of the reason why Tayta Alberto and his peers, now elders themselves, look back with such nostalgia to the ways hacienda-era authorities inculcated respect. While Scott would call *respeto* a public transcript, in this case, the public transcript was not mere dissimulation (see Gal 1995).

Material, Social, and Cultural–Ideological Hegemony

These two issues—the relationship between coercion and consent and the complexity of social relations and subject positions—yield different approaches to the concept of hegemony. Scott exemplifies a tendency among some scholars to interpret hegemony as referring exclusively to consent in the realm of ideas and consciousness. He does recognize that alliances and cleavages that complicate the opposition between dominant and subordinate classes, such as kinship ties across class divisions or ethnic–religious "communalism" among subordinates, make it difficult for subordinates to unite. However, he takes such ties and divisions as given features of the social landscape and not as expressions of "consciousness" that might themselves contribute to, or result from, any sort of hegemony. Thus, his concept of hegemony divorces consciousness from material social relationships. By identifying hegemony only with consciousness, he forgoes an inquiry into how such alliances and divisions are constructed, maintained, and expressed (Scott 1985; see Mitchell's critique, 1990).

In contrast to Scott's interpretation, I understand hegemony to refer to practices and relationships that are at once material, social, and cultural and that establish or maintain domination on a broader basis than simple coercion while also not precluding it. Some scholars, in accord with this view, have focused on the ways ruling groups can gain the support or acquiescence of other groups through economic inducements and concessions. For example, Steve Stern (1982) has shown how "Indian Hispanism" in colonial Peru helped consolidate Spanish rule by linking the native elite materially and subjectively to Spanish culture. Native lords adopted Christianity and other aspects of Spanish culture as part of a new social identity while privatizing land and pursuing other opportunities for wealth and status under colonialism. Stern is not implying that their cultural conversion was merely superficial or cynical. On the contrary, Spanish cultural categories were fundamental to the lords' reconceptualization and reconstruction of their social identities and their relationships to subjects and land. Thus, rather than taking social identities and alliances as a given and then inquiring into the ideological response of a particular category of subordinates, a more fruitful approach to hegemony examines how these categories and relationships are produced and reproduced in the first place.

Coercion or force can play a more complex role in shaping identities than is often recognized. Coercion and consent are generally viewed as two distinct sorts of relationship or strategy, mutually complementary at best, with coercion coming to the fore in moments of crisis and otherwise staying in the background while more complex strategies of cultivating consent do their work.[3] Such a view certainly captures some truths, especially about the political histories of Western capitalist societies and their (apparently) self-regulating markets, the cases most central to Gramsci's own concerns. Yet, this image of coercion and persuasion as essentially separate strategies is too limiting, especially for the case that concerns me here.[4]

One way to broaden our understanding of the role of coercion is to note how it parallels material inducements in shaping patterns of alliance and cleavage through which identities and subjectivities are produced. Neither rewards nor punishments fall uniformly on a homogeneous population of subordinates. As with rewards, punishments can be addressed to differentiated interests among subordinates and used by elites to heighten such differentiation. Both punishments and rewards, therefore, can generate loyalty and legitimacy as well as resentment. Coercion can be a tool of moral regulation, allowing those who wield it to appear as the representatives of a morality that stands above particular interests. This kind of "moral and intellectual leadership" (one of Gramsci's definitions of hegemony) is a cultural achievement rooted in material and social practices. On Ecuadorian haciendas, Gramsci's "intellectuals" sometimes held a whip.

This focus on moral regulation and its connections to social identities echoes the work of Philip Corrigan and Derek Sayer on English state formation (1985). Drawing on Marx, Gramsci, and Durkheim, they describe how the English state used law and other forms of moral regulation to construct a hegemonic sense of social reality, including differentiated classifications such as gender, age, and class as well as an overarching English identity. Understandings of Englishness and proper English conduct legitimated the state and capitalism even as hegemonic notions of Englishness were always open to contestation.

Similarly, I argue that moral regulation on Ecuadorian haciendas constructed identities and relationships of gender, age, and class that were fused with a moral language of respect (*respeto*). Notions of respect both legitimated hierarchy and provided, in Roseberry's phrase, a "language of contention" (1994). I shall refer to these notions of respect and the related system of elder–junior hierarchies as the "respect complex." This was not simply a set of ideas but a domain of mutually constituting meanings and relationships embedded in linguistic, disciplinary, and religious practices.

Discipline, Coercion, and Persuasion

Having proposed that coercion can be examined together with consent or persuasion as an integral part of hegemony, I shift now from the term *consent* to *persuasion* to focus on elites' strategies to persuade rather than simply on consent as an outcome. Timothy Mitchell has pointed out that the distinction between persuasion and coercion is rooted in the mind-body dichotomy that pervades modern Western thought. Given this dichotomy, it seems self-evident that "power may operate at the level of ideas, persuading the mind of its legitimacy, or it may work as a material force directly coercing the body" (1990:545). This logic has shaped the sort of question scholars have typically posed about acts such as a whipping or a sermon. A conventional approach would be to assign the whipping to the category of coercion and the sermon to that of persuasion and then to determine the role of each in maintaining the social order. Thus, Scott takes as his central issue "the relative weight of consciousness, on the one hand, and repression (in fact, memory, or potential) on the other, in restraining acts of resistance" (1985:40). Even Bourdieu, whose concept of "symbolic violence" is part of a broader project of transcending the mind–body opposition, seems to reinstate it when he opposes "symbolic violence" to "overt violence." He says these are two "interchangeable ways of performing the same function," with one or the other chosen according to social conditions and strategic considerations (1977:191–192; cf. Mitchell's commentary on Bourdieu, 1990:550–551).

Mitchell suggests that we abandon the distinction between persuasion and coercion altogether because of its problematic opposition between mind and body. My solution is less radical. I argue that we can preserve this distinction while recognizing that thoughts, emotions, and the body are implicated in both persuasion and coercion. The difference between them lies in the distinction between meanings and consequences. I define persuasion as symbolic action (including verbal communication, ritual expression, and other transactions in meanings) that (when successful) brings the dispositions and subjectivities of others into a closer alignment with the desires or interests of the persuader. Coercion, on the other hand, is the threat or imposition of undesirable consequences for undesired behavior.[5]

Although these concepts make an analytic distinction between different aspects of strategies and social practices, they are not mutually exclusive. One aspect may be more salient, but both can be present simultaneously. At least some minimal transaction in meanings is involved in coercion: threats may be verbally conveyed, links may be specified between behaviors and consequences, and pain may be used as a sign of more pain to come if behavior is not altered. Where meanings and effects on subjectivity are restricted to threat, pain, fear, and a recognition of the power to coerce, I would call this a "thin" form of persuasion (loosely echoing Scott's notion of "thin hegemony," 1990:70ff). However, the relationship between coercion and persuasion is sometimes much more complex. Coercion can be a vehicle of rich meanings in deeper forms of persuasion for the individual who is being coerced as well as for others. If this is so, we should not view persuasion and coercion as two functionally interchangeable tools for achieving the same result (compliance) or assume that more of one necessarily implies less of the other.

Hence, my approach is not to assess the relative weight of coercion and persuasion on Ecuadorian haciendas but to address a different sort of question: How were they interrelated in the practice of discipline? What forces and consequences did the sermon invoke, for example, and what words, symbolic gestures, and understandings accompanied a whipping? This line of inquiry reveals that discipline consisted of more than simple acts of force. It took culturally specific forms shaped by local history, possessed complex cultural meanings, and had multiple social functions.

I use the term *discipline* to encompass coercion and persuasion and thereby address the problem of reifying and opposing the two. The connotations of discipline extend across the spectrum from purely verbal moral instruction or admonishment to physical punishment. Discipline refers here to the entire gamut of ways superordinates attempted explicitly to shape and regulate the dispositions and behavior of their subordinates. The term eliminates any need to categorize practices as either coercion or persuasion, thereby allowing us to examine both aspects together without prejudging hacienda residents' views. Calling a practice a form of discipline implies neither legitimacy nor illegitimacy in the eyes of those disciplined, those otherwise involved, or those recalling it today.

My definition of *discipline* is broader than the way Foucault uses the term. In Foucault's work (1995), it refers to a specifically modern set of techniques, methodically calculated, for administering, controlling, and training persons and bodies. My use of the term corresponds more to the broad range of meanings the word has in everyday language, as in current Anglo American discourses about parenting (e.g., Leach 1990:456–467). No other word seems to encompass as well a range of practices from physical punishment to verbal admonishment.[6]

As we would expect, some of my informants were more critical than others of the way notions of respect supported both hacienda-era religion and mestizo domination. They nonetheless converged in one point: hacienda landlords and stewards, in conjunction with indigenous authorities, administered discipline in ways that went beyond simply enforcing an oppressive labor regime. This certainly constituted one aspect of discipline, but discipline was also complexly articulated with internal indigenous community politics and with Runa notions of morality and respect.

To be sure, the nostalgia permeating some of these accounts reflects the present as well as the past. Alberto Yumbo, for example, contrasted the respect that reigned in his youth with the failure of young people in the 1990s to politely greet others and more generally to lead a proper, "educated" life. Current intergenerational tensions and other discontents inflect the older generation's discussions of the hacienda period.

Yet these accounts also reflect the past. Elders in the 1990s saw clearly that hacienda-era disciplinary practices allowed their own elders to demand respect with more persuasive force than they were able to leverage in the present.

During my fieldwork in Pangor, informants' accounts of *pascuanchina*, a form of ritual discipline observed during Holy Week, were what first made me aware of the cultural complexity of discipline. *Pascuanchina* was the most elaborate hacienda-era disciplinary ritual and had clear and deep historical roots. In the discussion below, I sketch those historical roots and then use *pascuanchina* as an entrée into the cultural meanings of ritual discipline. *Pascuanchina* expressed an understanding of God, the nature of evil, the afterlife, and the presence of the divine in society and ritual practice, and it intertwined these cosmological understandings with power relations. This analysis leads into an examination of how hacienda authorities dealt with conflict and regulated social relations, especially gender relations, within the resident community. Next, I point to some ways that the authority of *amos* mirrored the authority of parents and indigenous elders. I then turn to the contradictory and contested role of discipline in supporting the hacienda labor regime. Hacienda bosses adopted the forms and arguments of ritual discipline to legitimate their violence, a strategy with mixed success. In closing, I elaborate on some of the theoretical implications of this case for our understanding of coercion, consent, and hegemony.

RITUAL DISCIPLINE AND THE RESPECT COMPLEX
Pascuanchina: *Discipline as a Sacrament*

Rituals of confession, moral instruction, and purification, including whipping with religious overtones, have a long genealogy in the Andes. Confession to native Andean priests was practiced before the Spanish invasion. Andean priests were viewed as "enlightened elder brothers and sisters" (S. MacCormack 1991:421). A penitent would ceremonially bathe and then receive a whipping with nettles (Cobo [1653] 1990:124). Inca youth also underwent an initiation during which they received moral instruction and ritual whipping (Zuidema 1989:263–264; idem 1997).

Confession was also a Catholic practice, of course, and *pascuanchina* was associated with Holy Week, when confession, absolution, and Communion were incumbent on all Catholics (the word *pascuanchina* is based on the Spanish *pascua*, Easter, with Quichua suffixes). The Spaniards also brought to the Americas the custom of penitential processions during Holy Week, sometimes involving self-flagellation (Foster 1960:181). By the early seventeenth century, native Andeans were participating in this practice while following Andean ritual traditions that treated sin as a substance that could be extracted by the whip and even transferred from one person to another. A Spanish missionary friar observed that, after the procession, "they hang up their whips on crosses . . . saying that anyone who takes the whips down from there will take their sins with him" (S. MacCormack 1991:202–203).

Self-flagellation was one manifestation of a broader European and Spanish colonial tradition that incorporated physical pain, self-inflicted or otherwise, into forms of religious devotion. Monasteries had been important bearers of this tradition since medieval times. Talal Asad makes a crucial point about the role of pain and force in what he calls "a monastic technology of the self" (1993:110), a point that could also be applied to *pascuanchina:* "The Christian monk who learns to will obedience is not merely someone who submits to another's will . . . by the threat of force . . . [O]bedience is *his* virtue . . . a Christian virtue developed through discipline. . . . [F]orce is a crucial element in a particular transformation of dispositions, not merely in the keeping of order among inmates" (1993:125–126; original emphasis). Religious orders played a prominent role as evangelizers and landowners in the colonial period, a fact that may help explain some of the parallels between monastic penance and ritual discipline in the Andes (Ramos in Juan and Ulloa [1747] 1990:316n).

As a product of this complex history, ritual whipping takes varied forms in the Andean region today. In the middle Chimbo valley, rural mestizos whip fruit-bearing vines and trees during Holy Week while exhorting the plant, "Don't be lazy! Bear fruit!" Scattered through modern Andeanist ethnographies are numerous references to the mythological or ritual use of whips to transform nature or expel hunger, evil, or the spirits of the deceased (e.g., Botero 1992:189, 191–192, 201–202; Isbell 1978:128–132; Poole 1990).[7]

Pascuanchina took place at various points during Holy Week throughout Chimborazo province, as well as in other parts of highland Ecuador.[8] In the Pangor area, the rite was typically conducted at the initiative of each indigenous family together with its network of kin and *compadres.* Those desiring *pascuanchina* for themselves or their children brought gifts of food and drink to the home of a respected indigenous elder or of a sibling or *compadre* who had agreed to invite an elder to administer *pascuanchina.* I choose the word *penitent* to refer to the person receiving *pascuanchina* both to underline the links between it and Catholic penance and because repentance of one's bad deeds was an appropriate motivation for undergoing *pascuanchina.* Although both males and females could take the role of penitent, and, although in some contexts females as well as males might impart moral instruction, in *pascuanchina* the elder seems always to have been male.

Pascuanchina typically occurred at night. The penitent knelt before the elder to signal a request to receive it. He or she then confessed to bad behavior and asked for forgiveness. The elder admonished the penitent for these misdeeds and also for bad behavior that the elder had observed or had heard of from others and then instructed the penitent in proper moral behavior. These admonishments seem generally to have focused on disruptive behavior such as swearing, quarrelling, sexual misconduct, or showing disrespect to elders. Here is how Gabriel Niamo recited such instruction (Figure 18):

> Don't be like that. With one's wife, with one's children, one must live together nicely, not get angry at each other. . . . Whether it's with some neighbor or with some relative, one should not get into quarrels . . .
>
> God will punish you if you don't respect, if you don't believe. Don't be insolent to the old people. Don't do anything bad to anyone at all.
>
> You should live with respect toward your family, toward any other relatives. Get along nicely with them, with a nice respect.

Following these admonishments, the elder served the penitent a drink of alcohol and then had him or her lie face down. The elder prefaced the lashing with further admonishments, of which two of my informants provided vivid samples:

FIGURE 18. *Group of villagers. José Amancha is second from left, Gabriel Niamo, second from right.*

Ah! Now it's time. . . . Now you're in my hands: Now let's see you run to do these things, run to do those things. . . . Let's see if this doesn't hurt you. Take this!

This is so you do not challenge your mother, your father, your older brother [male addressee], your older sister [male addressee]. This is respect.

The elder gave the penitent three lashes in, respectively, "the name of the Father, the Son, and the Holy Ghost" with a whip, belt, or piece of twisted leather rope. After receiving the lashing, the penitent knelt and recited Catholic prayers. The elder then served the penitent another shot of alcohol, asking the penitent's indulgence for the whipping and criticism and thereby concluding the moral instruction. Finally, the elder blessed the penitent by making the sign of the cross while invoking the Trinity or "Our Father" and "Our Lord Jesus Christ Resurrected" (on Easter Sunday). The penitent kissed the elder's hand, thanked him, and rose.

On one level, we can understand *pascuanchina* and other disciplinary rituals as forms of coercion. Children and youths, rather than voluntarily kneeling, were sometimes held down by others to receive admonishments and a lashing without having made any confession. Ritual whipping aimed to modify behavior through imposing physical pain as a consequence of undesirable acts; the accompanying verbal admonishments specified the reforms demanded in order to avoid future punishment. "For having had fault," Tayta Gabriel said even of voluntary *pascuanchina*, "well, they had to bear it, even being hit, with pain." It would be a mistake to ignore this, portraying ritual punishment as all ritual and no punishment—or, much worse, to ignore the pain and fear associated with hacienda violence more generally.

At the same time, to describe *pascuanchina* merely as punishment is clearly inadequate; punishment was not the only or even the most important aspect of the practice. A fuller understanding of *pascuanchina* requires an examination of the internal process of moral reform it was thought to effect, its connections to other practices such as confession, and the ways it invoked a whole cosmological system and located both the person receiving and the person administering it within that system. My aim is not to substitute cosmology for power but to explore their interrelation. *Pascuanchina* can be read as an elaborate argument, forcefully impressed on the penitent, about the relationship between power and cosmology—between moral reform, elder-junior relationships, social hierarchy, and God. The ways *pascuanchina* was understood to work confounds any neat body–mind dichotomy and any assumption that coercion and persuasion are opposites.

Pascuanchina combined the notion of punishment as affecting the calculations of a rational and sovereign will with the Christian notion of the body and soul as the stage of a battle between forces of good and evil. The will and soul were both protagonist and prize in this battle; they required external aid to strengthen themselves on the side of good. *Pascuanchina* was infused with an explicit religious symbolism—the Trinity, prayers, and the gesture and words of the blessing—that invoked God's aid in warding off or expelling evil. In effect, the elder administered a sacrament: he mediated between the penitent and God so that God would bring about changes in the penitent's soul. In this sense, *pascuanchina* complemented the obligatory confession and Communion during Holy Week. It paralleled confession in addressing itself to the evil inside the penitent; it shared with absolution the aim of reconciling the penitent with God and securing his forgiveness.

The culmination of *pascuanchina* and the most explicit symbol of this sacramental quality was the blessing. Blessings are always given "in the name of" God. Aside from *pascuanchina*, the blessing was (and, to some extent, remains) one of the rituals of everyday life, given by priests, nuns, parents, grandparents, and godparents. When two adults who have fought agree to reconcile, each kneels before the other and receives a blessing. The blessing conveys both material benefits (health and prosperity) and forgiveness, although one or the other may be emphasized in particular contexts. People refer to the gesture of the sign of the cross and the accompanying words in *pascuanchina* as a "blessing" and as "forgiveness" (*perdón*).

The blessing received in this life helps the soul obtain forgiveness in the next. Agustín Paca said that in the afterlife people repeat the act of blessing and forgiveness with the same people as in this life. God sends a person to grant forgiveness to a newly arriving soul, but it must be someone whose blessing the new arrival asked for in this life. If the newly deceased seriously wronged someone and did not obtain forgiveness, neither God nor the person wronged can grant forgiveness in the next life.

According to one of my informants who was from an area where *pascuanchina* continued to be practiced more recently than in Pangor, the whipping itself had a strongly sacramental nature: "The theological belief of the person who receives the whipping . . . is that it is not the man who whipped me, but, rather, it is God who whips me, and that's why my way of thinking is changing, is going to be transformed." Again, the elder was the minister of a sacrament, in the sense that Catholic theology gives to that term—a sign that points to the divine and serves as an effective channel for God's grace. More broadly, to request and submit to *pascuanchina* was "to respect" the elder —and through him, God. The ritual put the previously wayward, insolent person into a position of physical subordination. He knelt and lay down to receive the elder's admonishments, punishment, and blessing, thereby returning to a proper relationship with elders and God.

Within this ritual context, there was also an implicit mechanics that is reminiscent of the pre-Columbian ritual treatment of evil as a substance that could be physically expelled. The same informant I have just cited compared ritual whipping to shaking the dust out of a handkerchief: "A handkerchief . . . put on the ground . . . gets dusty, right? And you have to shake out that dust. So then, to shake it out, you have to move it with your hand, right? So then, it's the same thing: that—that thing, that, that—evil that is inside, when they give a whipping, then with that it goes, like it leaves. So, that's it. And with that, he's left something like—purified . . . changed." Ritual whipping thus appears as a technique for shaking loose the evil and making it leave the person. It is parallel in this respect to the widespread healing technique termed "sweeping" or "cleaning" (*pichana*, "to sweep," Q.; *limpiar*, "to clean," Sp.), that involves vigorously rubbing and striking the patient with a bundle of plants, a young guinea pig, a belt, or some other object, in order to expel "evil air" (Sp. *malaire*) from the body.[9]

The transmission of positive qualities from the elder to the penitent was another aspect of *pascuanchina*. Parents asked elders known not only for generally upright behavior but also for hard work and agricultural wealth (livestock and good harvests) to discipline their children. Ritual whipping at the elder's hand would help the children be similarly well behaved, hard working, and successful.[10]

Beyond its effects on the penitent's moral disposition and success, *pascuanchina* may be understood as a theatrical representation of the general authority structure of the hacienda community as a hierarchy of respect and moral discipline. The elder who administered *pascuanchina* was not simply an old man but a "man of respect." *Fundadores* and *regidores* were particularly likely to take this role; they were the paramount elders.

The authority of elders was intertwined with hacienda power. Landlords in the Pangor area commonly selected the *fundador* or *regidor* as overseer; an overseer who was not already *fundador* or *regidor* would often attain at least one of these positions eventually. Landlords thus employed a man who could command respect based on his religious position as a key link in the formal chain of command. Religious service could help neutralize the animosity that other laborers often directed toward the overseer while the overseer's salary helped finance religious service. Thus, joining both hacienda and religious authority in the same individual served the interests of both landlord and overseer (cf. Lentz 1986:194–195; Mangin 1954:v–79).

On some haciendas, mestizo and indigenous authorities administered a collective *pascuanchina*. Andrés Yépez, who grew up on a hacienda in central Chimborazo, recalled that the steward, overseers, or landowner would give "everyone," including men, women, and even small children, three lashes in the hacienda yard on Easter Sunday or Monday. The adults drank chicha, and then the alcaldes led people to the overseer's house. The drinking and ritual whipping continued there into the early morning. The alcaldes received whippings and moral instruction from the overseers and in turn administered *pascuanchina* to younger people. Tayta Andrés remembered accompanying an uncle who was an alcalde and listening to the moral instruction that the overseer gave his uncle. "That's why I, too, speak to my grandchildren here, telling them not to be insolent, not to fight with anybody." Moral instruction thus flowed down through a multitiered hierarchy —from the hacienda owners and supervisors to the whole resident community, from overseers to alcaldes, from alcaldes to their juniors, and from adults who had received or heard instruction in these contexts to their own descendants.

Pascuanchina dramatically wove together force, pain, and punishment with an elaborate cultural argument to form a complex ritual with a deep cultural history. Many scholars, from Gramsci to Scott, have certainly been aware that physical or other sanctions commonly back up attempts at persuasion. Yet, it is all too easy to assume that force steps in only where persuasion fails—to see the two as functional substitutes for one another and therefore present in inverse proportion. In *pascuanchina*, the whipping itself was an integral part of the argument, a vehicle of meaning, a religious act, as well as a technique of punishment. It was not applied because persuasion had failed but, rather, as the climax of the attempt to persuade, purify, and transform the penitent.

Earlier in my research, I thought I might be able to draw a clear line between ritual discipline administered by indigenous elders, which Runa accepted as legitimate, and the illegitimate and arbitrary violence hacienda bosses used to enforce their orders. However, I came to see that legitimate ritual and illegitimate violence were not totally separate phenomena but the opposite poles of a single complex field. Moreover, hacienda society could not be neatly divided between bosses and a homogeneous group of indigenous subordinates. On which side of the line would one place a Runa *fundador* or *regidor* who was also an overseer? In some areas, mestizo hacienda bosses as well as indigenous elders administered *pascuanchina*. In Pangor, hacienda bosses participated in another form of ritual discipline I consider below. As for the legitimacy of ritual discipline, a young man who had been forcibly subjected to *pascuanchina* might well be unrepentant and resentful. Therefore, highly ritualized forms of discipline were not the domain of Runa authorities alone, nor were they automatically legitimate for all concerned. Conversely, even more casual forms of discipline employed by bosses in the fields sometimes echoed the same cultural argument developed so elaborately in *pascuanchina*. Moving now from *pascuanchina* to more everyday forms of ritual discipline and then to more casual, work-related discipline, we shall listen for those echoes and see how hacienda Runa could differ among themselves in distinguishing between legitimate and illegitimate discipline.

The Doctrina: *Maintaining Moral Order*

The most frequent forum for ritual discipline was the *doctrina*, an obligatory weekly meeting for religious instruction and prayer. The *doctrina* was a legacy of colonial Christianization strategies. In the 1860s and the 1870s, town governments and the conservative Catholic regime of Gabriel García Moreno revitalized the institution, partly in reaction to a brief period of popular liberalism in the national government that had threatened to undermine landlord control over laborers (Williams 2003). In the middle decades of the twentieth century, Chimborazo hacienda residents congregated for prayer in the hacienda chapel one day a week in the early morning. Prayers were led by an indigenous man called the *rezachidor* (Q.; Sp., *doctrinero*) who knew the prayers by heart. The *rezachidor* recited the prayers and others repeated or responded in chorus.

Coercion was used to ensure that all members of the resident hacienda community attended the *doctrina:*

> When someone didn't want to go, they asked, "Why hasn't your kid come?"
> "He didn't want to come. He didn't listen; he was disobedient and stayed home."
> Upon hearing that . . . the overseer, the stewards would go to the house to bring the kid. Whip in hand. . . .

In addition to prayers, the *doctrina* was an occasion for religious elders and hacienda authorities to impart moral instruction, reinforce moral order in the community, resolve conflicts, and discipline malefactors. "Morality" here refers to the code of *respeto.* This includes respect for parents and other elders; the obligation of young lovers to marry; mutual fidelity, fulfillment of material obligations, and general harmony between husband and wife; and respectful greetings, gentle speech, and peaceable behavior toward one's neighbors in general. José Amancha described this aspect of the *doctrina:*

> The elders talked about how to work . . . how to live. About how we should live between wife and husband. . . .
> If a wife and husband were quarreling or fighting, or children didn't obey their parents, . . . the elders told the stewards and overseers in the *doctrina* . . . The stewards and overseers would set an example. In the yard in front of the people, they whipped them so that they would not be insolent . . . ; they corrected them.
> That's how we lived. Due to that, we were *very "obedient" people, very much people who greeted others.*[11] Even men, even old people, and even children, that's how we went through life.

Whippings administered by stewards and overseers in the *doctrina* took much the same form as in *pascuanchina:* three lashes in the name of the Trinity, accompanied by moral instruction, and followed by prayers and thanks on the part of the kneeling person being punished.

Through moral correction in the *doctrina*, hacienda and religious authorities attempted to resolve quarrels or other problems between neighbors, spouses, or others:

> If there was a quarrel, or some problem, . . . the stewards, the *regidores*, the *fundadores*, would call them together and ask what happened, have them each give their side in each other's presence, and see who was to blame . . . They whipped those who were at fault. Invoking the Holy Ghost, they gave them three lashes, such that, well, they gave it to them good. . . .
>
> The overseers, the *regidores*, the *fundadores*, . . . they were the elders [*más mayores*]. They made people understand. They . . . explained by way of a moral example. "Don't live like that, don't be like that. Leave those quarrels behind . . . ," they would say. (JA 9/2/1992)

Likewise, according to Andrés Yépez, if a boy was talking back very insolently to his parents, the parents might ask the steward or overseer to whip him in the *doctrina*. He said this sometimes "straightened out" [*derecharin*] the youth (8/22/1992).

Enforced attendance and whippings in the *doctrina* no doubt generated individual resentment at times. Without firsthand observation or multiple and detailed accounts of particular quarrels, it is very hard to reconstruct how the parties to a conflict and others in the community may have felt about this process of conflict resolution. There may not have been any simple consensus. On the other hand, the fact that quarrels seem to have been regularly brought before the elders and stewards for resolution does suggest that at least *some* adult hacienda residents in *some* contexts considered this process necessary and legitimate.

The participation of mestizo landlords and stewards in ritual discipline can be seen as an extension of the way respect relationships operated among Runa. When a child or youth did not heed his parents' admonishment, they might ask someone else to admonish or punish the youth—an older uncle or aunt, a godparent, the *fundador*—on the premise that greater social distance and status as an elder would lead the youth to respect the latter. The racial and class difference between landlords or stewards and indigenous people was but one more increment in a series of steps on the social ladder extending from elder siblings and parents up to the *amos*.

"What Did You Get Married For?"

Guaman Poma wrote that, since pre-Inca times, weddings had been occasions for "great sessions of moral instruction and sermons and good lessons, [in the] service of God," aimed at helping the newlyweds "live well as a married couple" ([1616] 1988:54). In hacienda times (and still in the 1990s) in Pangor, the bride and groom knelt before their elders, who admonished them concerning their mutual obligations and blessed them. This practice linked *respeto* between spouses to respect for elders. Marital harmony was also one of the chief concerns of the *doctrina*.

María Maji, an elderly woman from Guangopud, told me the landowner intervened when her husband beat her. As a result, she said, "I wasn't too mistreated at all, may God repay." She continued: "Husbands and wives lived nicely together, sometimes. There wasn't too much quarreling, too much jealousy . . . May God repay them, the stewards, the *amos* did not allow husband and wife to fight for no reason . . . That's how they watched over things . . . They gave moral instruction" (MM 11/6/1992). In defending women against marital violence, the hacienda authorities were not thereby allying themselves with subordinate women against subordinate men in a way that might arouse generalized male resentment. They admonished both husband and wife to fulfill their reciprocal, complementary obligations. Men as well as women described these admonishments with approval. Agustín Paca offered a richly detailed account, tinged with nostalgia:

The older people . . . would tell the lords . . . that someone had beaten his wife . . .

The lords, or the stewards, listened to what the overseer told them, and they said, "Go, bring them. . . . I want to know why that happened. Why is he doing things like that? Why is he behaving like that?" . . .

The lords . . . had them each give their side, face to face, and punished both sides . . . So then . . . there was good respect, in the old days. . . .

If a man had beaten his wife: "Why did you beat your wife?" . . . If there was blame on the wife's part, they punished both of them. . . . They settled things, better than a public authority, before letting them go.

"Now, go. From now on, in the future," they instructed the wife, "cook. Grind flour. Wash the clothes. . . . Go to where he's working and give him lunch. What did you get married for?" . . .

In the same way, to the husband, they said, "What did you get married for? If you didn't want to support her, if you didn't want to clothe her, if you didn't want to buy salt and lard, you should have just rested and kept your mouth shut." . . .

They made them lie down in the middle of the people, the laborers, and whipped them. They admonished both of them, husband and wife. If one of them was more to blame, they punished that one harder.

Although mestizo and Runa gender ideologies differed,[12] the lords' emphasis on men's obligation to work hard and provide and women's complementary obligation to cook and feed was hardly alien to long-standing and widespread indigenous assumptions about gender (Allen 1988). Moreover, when the lords intervened to reinforce a man's economic ties to his family or to punish him for philandering and beating his wife, the intervention could benefit male as well as female children and kin. These considerations make it seem likely that some men, women, and children viewed the hacienda authorities' disciplinary role in marital conflicts as a good thing.

Hacienda landlords and supervisors thus participated in important ways in the internal social and political relations of the resident community. They supported the authority of *fundadores* and, with it, the fiesta system and the authority of elders generally. They cooperated with *fundadores* and other elders in regulating gender relations and dealing with marital conflicts. In the *doctrina*, bosses and elders espoused ideals of *respeto* and they judged and punished all manner of violations.

It would be difficult to think one's way out of the coercion/persuasion dichotomy if one were only able to see masters exploiting and oppressing subordinates. How could subordinates ever perceive discipline as legitimate if its only social use were to keep them oppressed and exploited? On the other hand, once we recognize not simply subordinates but, among them, men and women, juniors and seniors, people with their own internal politics, individuals with personal quarrels, the matter changes (see Ortner 1995). Abu-Lughod has noted that "resisting at one level may catch people up at other levels" (1990:53). On Chimborazo haciendas, resistance at one level could be linked to discipline at another, as when women resisted domestic abuse by appealing to their overlords to discipline their husbands. Conflicts to which we would not necessarily apply the concept of resistance, such as disputes between neighbors, could likewise "catch people up" in discipline at the hands of hacienda authorities.

This situation allowed hacienda discipline sometimes to take on positive moral connotations in indigenous eyes—discipline maintained respect. The term *respeto* sums up a model of how society should function as a moral order. Although sometimes colored by nostalgia, these accounts still provide some insight into the social and ideological workings of discipline. What nostalgia is most likely to obscure is the fact that ritual discipline sometimes surely failed to resolve tensions and could even have added new resentments to existing conflicts. On the other hand, it would be surprising if hacienda residents—some of them, some of the time—did *not* attach moral connotations to a power that they called on to help regulate such fundamental social relations as those between parents and children, elders and juniors, husband and wife, or neighbor and neighbor.

"THE *AMOS* WERE LIKE OUR PARENTS"

The obedience and law that they had is to obey the old person and not the youth. . . . Oh, what a good law of God in the world! And thus they feared the honorable old person like their father, like their mother. . . .
—GUAMAN POMA DE AYALA ([1616] 1988:415)

I have shown that mestizo bosses and indigenous authorities worked closely together in dealing with conflicts and imparting ritual discipline, and I noted that hacienda administrative authority and religious authority often coincided in the same person. Elders administered discipline to juniors, and one of the main purposes of this discipline was to instill respect for elders. That is, different sorts of authority—that of hacienda bosses, religious elders, and elders generally—supported one another in a practical manner; they were functionally interwoven. I now consider the relationship between different sorts of authority from another angle, asking in what ways hacienda residents might have viewed *amos* metaphorically as elders or parents. In other words, in addition to being functionally interconnected, did these different sorts of authority also mirror each other symbolically?

Amos *as Elders*

We have seen that stewards, renters, and landowners as well as respected indigenous people took an active role in imparting moral instruction and correction. Indigenous people themselves sometimes called on *amos* to take this role. Was there anything about *amos* that made them plausible "elders," appropriate delegates of God? In examining economic relations on the hacienda from the standpoint of reciprocity, I described a view of *amos* as stingy, cruel, and possibly in league with the devil. Could such a view coexist with a view of *amos* as elders?

We must remember that what we are trying to understand here is not the philosophical system of an individual, constructed according to self-conscious criteria of coherence and consistency, but a collective field of possibilities and constraints. This field was socially constructed and reproduced in multiple and changing relationships of tension and conflict. Furthermore, it was not present as a stable whole to any individual independent of context; it looked different in any given context.

For example, a young woman who was insulted or subjected to sexual pressures by a landlord during service in the hacienda house might recall her grandmother's words about the *amos* being accursed and allied with the devil. The same woman a few years later, faced with a husband's mistreatment, might be grateful to the steward for admonishing her husband to mend his ways. Her brother might find himself applauding the steward's intervention on behalf of his sister one day and cursing the steward for whipping him in the fields the next. If there was a contradiction, it was not necessarily recognized as such.

At the same time, throughout this book I have been examining the relationship between different practices or domains—the fiesta system and views of landlords, for example—on the assumption that, while cultures are not totally coherent and consistent, neither are they bundles of elements utterly lacking in logical connections. Cultures gain some partial, provisional, logical coherence because participants sometimes take the understandings, expectations, and conclusions they draw from their experience in one domain and apply them to another domain. Thus, we may ask what sorts of experience and understandings could support a view of *amos* as elders.

First, villagers discussing discipline commonly suggest that a certain degree of fear is useful to reinforce respect. To call on the *amos* to instill respect was thus to press their power, even their propensity to inflict harsh punishments, into a positive social purpose. In any particular situation, the choice of recurring to the *amos* was probably most immediately a pragmatic accommodation to the existing realities of power. Someone who had refused to heed the admonishments of family and indigenous elders had to take more seriously the *amos'* warnings and punishment. The hacienda elite, at the same time, seems to have realized that things would go more smoothly on the hacienda and its own authority would be enhanced if it took an active role in resolving conflicts and imparting moral instruction. For the elite itself, this role fit well into its self-understanding as heirs of the Spaniards' Christianizing and civilizing mission.

Second, hacienda residents could understand respect for landlords as a concomitant of reciprocity on the hacienda. Avelino Shagñay remembers learning as a child on Ajospamba to greet the landowner with the *alabado* prayer, after which the landowner would toss him a coin. I have noted the difficulty of gaining access to how Runa in the past viewed the *amos'* owner-

ship of the land and their own usufruct rights. It is possible that they understood their access to land as a gift from the *amos* and that, despite mistreatment, they viewed themselves as obliged to respect *amos* in recognition of
that gift. That would be one way to interpret the moral instruction Reinaldo
Sisa remembers receiving from his parents: "You must show respect toward
the *amos*, to those who own the land."

Third, interracial etiquette and everyday racism in the Andes have long
portrayed *amos* as belonging to a superior order of humanity closer to God.
While all greetings to other people were simultaneously greetings to God,
the obligation to greet *amos* with a prayer constructed the latter as the representatives of God par excellence. I have heard the word *niño* ("child" in
Spanish), the customary and obligatory form of address for landowners and
renters, used in Quichua in only two other contexts: to refer to the Christ
child, and the form that saints might take when they appear in dreams.

It is difficult to assess to what degree hacienda residents accepted racist
assumptions about *amos'* inherent superiority. Even today, though, everyday
aesthetic evaluations of physical features associated with race indicate some
internalized racism. Indigenous villagers routinely speak of light or curly
hair, light skin, and green or blue eyes as good or beautiful and darker features as ugly. These judgments seem to be taken for granted, as though they
were simple, obvious facts. Recall Jacoba Sayay's praise of her half-sister's
"pretty," "lady"-like features, the result of the landlord's rape of her mother.
No doubt, such comments partly reflect pragmatic assessments of a person's
prospects in a racist society, but language binds pragmatic assessments with
deeper judgments of value when people speak of "good" and "bad" features,
"beautiful" and "ugly."

I once asked a meeting of people from Pangor villages what color they
thought Jesus' skin, eyes, and hair were. One of the leading catechists—a
middle-aged man of self-identified indigenous ethnicity and fairly dark features himself[13]—answered that Jesus must have been white, as he could not
have had any of the "defects" or "ugliness" that "we" have. This was in 1992,
two years after a massive indigenous uprising that shook the whole country,
at the culmination of a campaign of several years to "revalue" indigenous
culture and identity, and the speaker was one of the most active local participants in the liberation theology movement and its project of forming an
"indigenous church." It points up the depth of these aesthetic perceptions
that this answer could be given and generally received as reasonable in those
circumstances.

Color points to moral-cosmological qualities as well, with white being
associated with God, black with the devil. People say that it is good to keep

white dogs, cats, and chickens and important to treat them well, because they will help the soul on the journey to "God's land" (Diospak llakta) in the afterlife. A pair of black dogs, conversely, guards the entrance to Mount Tungurahua (purgatory/hell). Agustín Choca told me that people who engage in witchcraft find their bodies beginning to turn black; this is a sign that they already belong to the devil before death. I never heard these color associations explicitly extended to "white" people and Runa as races, but the possibility was at least implicitly available as support for the notion that "whites" were closer to God.

A final consideration in understanding the "respectability" of *amos* is the association between race and knowledge, which paralleled the association between age and knowledge. Moral instruction carries weight when it is imparted by someone who "knows." The Quichua term for "elder," *yuyak*, carries the double connotation of chronological or physical age and mental capacity. It is the agentive form of the verb *yuyana*, usually translated as "to think." Indigenous elders "thought" and "knew" because of their *experiencia*—a Spanish word borrowed into Quichua to refer to life experience in general, but especially to the morally significant experiences of marriage, rearing children, supporting a family, and fulfilling ritual obligations. Penitents in *pascuanchina* might thank the elder for his moral instruction in these terms: "An old person speaks from experience and knows what he is talking about [Shuk yuyak genteka, experienciawanmi rimak, yachashpami rimak]" (GN 8/23/1992).

The category of *amo* also implied a special, superior access to knowledge—in this case, knowledge associated with schooling and literacy. Let me cite here José Amancha's account of literacy as an ethnic marker in hacienda times, one that reinforced the linguistic opposition between Spanish and Quichua and, at the same time, the obligation to greet whites with special respect. He began by talking about priests' collaboration in maintaining whites' monopoly over powerful knowledge.

> JA They [priests] didn't tell us things, not anything at all. It's only now, these times, that priests are . . . as if declaring things to us.
>
> Before, whatever it was, they knew it only among themselves, as whites . . .
>
> Before, . . . they didn't allow us to say something in Spanish. People went through life speaking only Quichua. If someone said something in Spanish, . . . the stewards, or some other whites, said, "Look at this piece of paper. . . . Do you know how to look at paper?"
>
> So, they didn't allow it. Not like now, in these times, for example,

to good white people,[14] too, we say "Good day" or "Good afternoon" [in Spanish]—no, they said. They didn't allow it. . . .

BL "When someone couldn't read what was written on the paper, what did they say?"

JA . . . "If you don't know how to look at anything on paper, well, then, why do you speak in that way, 'Good day' or 'Good afternoon,' speaking in Spanish? How do you know?" they said. (JA 9/2/1992)

"Good day" or "Good afternoon" (Buenos días, Buenas tardes) are casual, everyday greetings among peers. The prayer formulas with which Runa were expected to greet whites were, in fact, in Spanish, too. The point here, though, is that whites constructed literacy as an essential distinction between themselves and Runa, one closely tied to knowledge of Spanish and the right to speak it.

Literacy and Spanish were not simply arbitrary markers of difference. Runa were constrained to accept, as Tayta José does here, that white people's knowledge was real and powerful. Writing and Spanish were (as they still are) the tools and language of power. Moreover, when they observed priests reading from the missal in Mass or recording a baptism or wedding in the registry, indigenous people also experienced a link between writing, sacred knowledge, and sacramental practices (see also Wogan 1998).[15]

Much as it appears to contradict the notion that rich *amos* had a compact with the devil, then, several clusters of ideas, practices, and social facts could have made it seem appropriate for *amos* to mediate between God and indigenous people in maintaining and instilling respect. *Amos* had the power to make a troublemaker or penitent take their words seriously; they provided access to land and, occasionally, to other goods; according to racial etiquette and ideology, they belonged to a "better" class of people, closer to God; and they possessed special, powerful, even sacred knowledge that indigenous people lacked. In the role of imparting moral correction, *amos* presented themselves to indigenous eyes as elders, thereby reproducing the old colonial relationship of "elder" to "minor."

Amos *as Parents*

If *amos* could be like elders, could they be like parents, specifically? In suggesting parallels between parental authority and hacienda bosses' authority, I follow in the footsteps of many scholars who have analyzed "paternalistic" forms of authority. I depart from that tradition in two important ways, however. First, models of paternalism have often taken for granted what paternal authority is all about: paternal figures display benevolence and expect loyalty and obedience in return. Some scholars, such as Anrup in his study of Cuzco-area haciendas (1990), have applied universalistic psychoanalytic theories in an attempt to add psychological depth to this model. Such analyses may be fruitful as far as they go, but they ignore cultural variation in parenting practices and understandings of child rearing. Examining such practices and understandings ethnographically adds another dimension to the analysis.

Second, "paternalism" has generally been understood as a theory of how authority becomes legitimate in subordinates' eyes, that is, as a theory of persuasion. In Chimborazo, persuasion was combined with coercion in both parental and hacienda discipline. Parental discipline probably did prepare hacienda residents to accept hacienda discipline, but children's resentment of parents' discipline may also have fed into their resistance as adults to hacienda practices. Thus, while parallels between parental and hacienda discipline were a component of hacienda hegemony, this was not an "ideological hegemony" of pure persuasion.

In some ways, *respeto* as a key moral value was (and is) rooted in rural Ecuadorian understandings of child rearing. Ecuadorian villagers are not generally Rousseauians: parents' main responsibilities are not to allow and encourage children to develop their natural goodness and individual creativity. Instead, they view parents and other adults as having a very strong, active role in shaping children, to an extent that is striking from a Western individualistic perspective. In Chimborazo, midwives literally physically shape newborn infants by arranging the limbs in a straight position and attempting to mold the facial features to avoid an unattractively protruding nose or ears. My mother-in-law, from Bolívar province, gently pressed a bean into my infant son's cheeks to give him dimples (it worked on one side!). Indigenous mothers and midwives in Chimborazo also move a piece of straw back and forth across the infant's mouth each day for the first month, symbolically sewing the mouth shut so that later the child will not be ill spoken toward other people and will not talk back defiantly to parents. Children are thus seen as highly malleable, and their behavior reflects directly on their parents' guidance.[16]

At the same time, children have some inherent tendencies to be unsocial, insolent, and lazy, so parents must provide strong, stern guidance. Unbaptized children are termed *auca*, or "savage," and are sometimes said to have a tail; baptism "cuts the tail" and makes them *cristiano*, a word commonly used to mean "human being." According to some local interpretations of the orthodox Catholic doctrine that babies who die without baptism go to purgatory, the babies are punished for their disrespectful kicking inside the womb or pulling on their mother's hair. Parents' sentiments toward their babies' behavior are, of course, complex. A mother who calls her baby *malcriado* (insolent) may do so with laughter, love, and pleasure in the child's development, much as English-speaking parents sometimes lovingly call their children "rascals." Children are sometimes referred to as "these lazy kids" or "insolent kids" with a combination of affection, irony, and criticism, almost as if "kids" automatically implies "lazy" or "insolent." Male children, especially, are expected to be by nature at least somewhat insolent, and the overt disapproval expressed in the phrase may be tinged with pride in their masculinity. Still, boys as much as girls (if not more) must be tamed and educated to be respectful and hard working.

Parents use corporal punishment not only to teach children to respect and obey them but also to ensure that children take their tasks seriously and do them well. Children learn to hide or flee to a neighbor's or relative's house when they damage or lose something and to wait for their parents' anger to pass. Many adults describe their parents as having been "fierce" and disposed to inflict strong physical punishments. Rosa Condo refers here to her grandparents, who reared her:

> RC They were good. They were very fierce [*bravísimos*], but they were good.
>
> MG Why [were they fierce]? Did they punish you, too?
>
> RC *Juu*, for everything! You see, sometimes, well, I couldn't bear it, and I talked back. So then, they punished me. [She laughs in a half-amused, half-embarrassed manner.] Yes. [I was a] child; I didn't think right, then. Uh-huh.
>
> MG And how did they hit you? With a stick?
>
> RC With a whip . . . [or] a switch . . . or a bath in [cold] water. [Laughs.] (8/23/1992)

Mama Rosa's account is more or less typical, though some people's descriptions are more explicitly ambivalent about the fairness of the punishments.

Let me recall now some of Reinaldo Sisa's opening words in describing life on the hacienda:

> Our life in the old days was to be under the *amos'* orders. . . . The *amos*, the *patrones*, the owners of the land—they were like our parents. Whatever they ordered, we did it. When they said, "Come and do *huasicama* service, come and serve us," we had to go serve. . . .

> We men served the [male] *amos*. . . . The women, like my wife, in
> turn, served the [female] *patrona amas*, as a cook.

Tayta Reinaldo uses the analogy of parental authority to describe hacienda labor, emphasizing, however, not benevolent care but the obligation
to obey orders and serve in whatever form was demanded. Service in the hacienda house appears as a particularly salient example of the *amos'* parental authority. In that context, that authority was not specifically paternal
but dual, as in the family. Children generally accompany and learn gender-
specific tasks from the same-sex parent. Similarly, male hacienda laborers
served the *amo* while women served the *ama*.

Rosa Condo, telling my wife, Mercedes, about her experiences on hacienda Ajospamba as a girl in the interview cited above, linked discipline on
the hacienda to discipline within the family in a way that seems to assume
an analogy between bosses and parents. As is often the case when people
speak of the hacienda—or their parents—her words were not lacking in ambivalence. First, she spoke very critically of the landowners' and stewards'
cruelty. She nonetheless used the verb *corregir*, "to correct" (in the sense
of moral correction or discipline)—"That's how they corrected us." A little
later, she suggested that the discipline she received as a girl on the hacienda
served her, as a parent, as a model for imparting discipline to her children:

> The bosses made the women serve them in the hacienda, apart, cook-
> ing. We cooked, and then went after them to where the people were
> working, bringing them [the bosses] their lunch. In turn, if we didn't do
> that quickly, . . . we had to take a whipping. That's how it was.
> So then, we have to take a lesson from that, and likewise admonish
> and correct our children, too. (8/23/1993)

I would not argue that parents mechanically reenacted the labor discipline of the hacienda with their own children, let alone that the parent-child
and the hacienda-laborer relationship were simple reflections of each other.
Yet, hacienda residents could sometimes apply a common framework of expectations of authority to both relationships.

Even one of the most conflictive practices on the hacienda—charging
laborers for the accidental death or loss of animals—had a close parallel
within the family. José María Pillajo, who as an adult fought with the steward
over this issue, mentioned his parents' analogous reaction as an example of
their sternness. He attributed his parents' severity to the priests' teachings,
not directly to the hacienda itself:

BL Did your father and mother rear you with strictness, or . . .

JMP With strictness, yes, with strictness. Our parents reared us children with fierceness [*braavo*].

The *tayta amito* little father priests, in their explanations in church, said [switches from Quichua to Spanish]:

You have to reprimand your children, make them understand.
They should not be insolent,
they should not be hot-tempered . . .
It depends on you, on the father and mother.
You must reprimand them.
You must teach them . . .

That's how they talked, yes, in Spanish.

Since they said that, our parents were fierce; they whipped us.

If we were tending the sheep and, by chance, a wolf ate a little sheep, or . . . a sheep got lost somewhere, we would go hide, because they would beat us.

. . . Sometimes, I went to my granddad's house. But my granddad wouldn't keep me in his house. "They'll be talking now, wondering who will tend the sheep . . . Let's go, I'll take you home now. Mama, hurry up, give breakfast to the kids; I'll have to take the kids back home."

BL But then, when he took you home, would he say, "Don't punish him"?

JMP Yes, yes. "Don't mistreat the children so much. Don't . . . don't hit them, don't beat them," he said. My granddad counseled them and left. (9/2/1992)

In Tayta José's case, it does not seem that his childhood experiences prepared him to accept similar treatment on the hacienda. Instead, this account adds another dimension to our understanding of his rebellion against the steward over this issue. As a child, he took refuge with his grandparents, and they admonished his parents to be more moderate in their treatment. As an adult, he said, he complained about the steward to the renter, who actually encouraged him to fight back.

Many Runa children growing up on the hacienda seem to have learned that any person with authority, including parents, could sometimes be expected to apply severe punishments. Parental authority rested on and reproduced some of the same general assumptions as other forms of authority. The family was not, in any simple sense, a refuge from the stern discipline of the hacienda. Instead, it helped prepare children for that discipline—prepare them to expect it, sometimes to resent it, perhaps to resist it by recurring to a higher authority, and to understand it as characteristic of authority. Parents and hacienda bosses alike sometimes meted out harsh punishments in anger and sometimes imparted discipline as part of a project of shaping respectful subjects.

A conventional analysis of the role of hacienda discipline might begin and end with an examination of how the hacienda bosses exerted coercion to enforce their orders and maintain the hacienda system itself. Instead, I have looked first at some of the other forms, functions, and meanings of discipline on the hacienda. With this context in place, we are now prepared to analyze discipline concerned more narrowly with bosses' authority and control over labor. This is not to suggest that all forms of discipline had the same degree of legitimacy. If notions of respect joined indigenous authority and hacienda authority in a hierarchy of moral discipline, they also shaped the language of ideological struggle over the appropriate forms and limits of discipline.

WHIPPING THE LABORERS
Thanks for the Whipping?

The hacienda system involved a built-in tension between the hacienda's demand for labor and the resident laborers' need for time to attend to their own usufruct plots and animals. Hacienda authorities frequently whipped laborers to back up their demands. The whip was thus at once an instrument of purification and moral correction and an instrument for enforcing the labor regime.

By the late colonial period, if not before, hacienda authorities attempted to combine these two functions of the whip by using ritual discipline as a general template for violent punishments. Jorge Juan and Antonio de Ulloa, Spaniards who traveled around the Quito region in the 1740s, observed the following:

> [U]pon any mistake or carelessness, [hacienda stewards and their mestizo assistants] order [Indian laborers] to lie down on the ground, face down, and . . . [whip them]. Afterward, they get up, and they have taught them to go kneel in front of the person who punished them and, kissing his hand, to say, "May God repay you," and thank him for having punished him. This . . . is a general practice with all the Indians on the haciendas and in the curates, and anybody may do it with the Indian . . .

[who] does not fulfill so punctually what they have ordered him to do.
(JUAN AND ULLOA [1747] 1990:316)

The obligation to kneel and give thanks for the whipping suggests a connection to ritual penance, as does the observation that priests or their assistants in the curates administered the same form of punishment.[17] Yet, this punishment was applied for any fault or lack of punctuality in carrying out orders.

In twentieth-century Chimborazo, a laborer who had defied the overseer or steward would receive the ritual three lashes in the *doctrina*, just like quarrelsome neighbors or spouses, accompanied by admonishments: "Don't be insolent like that. Respect your elders." As in other types of ritual discipline, the person punished was expected to show repentance and gratitude for the correction (AYe 11/22/92). Even violence outside of the *doctrina*, such as in a work context, could be portrayed or reinterpreted later as moral correction. Here Alberto Yumbo describes how overseers in Pangor administered violence and attempted to control its interpretation:

> The overseers gave orders, carrying around whips. . . .
> [They were] cruel [*millay*]. Striking, with whips, but with two knots, three knots. With those they struck.
> With that . . . , our poor flesh hurt as they struck, and we had to bear it.
> Then, after that, . . . "Was it good?" they said.
> "May God repay you," [you] said.
> And wherever [i.e., in an encounter later], offering a shot [of cane alcohol] or whatever, "I struck you. I taught you," they said. . . . "This is how you were, that is how you were, boys," they said.
> When you thanked them for that . . . "This boy is respectful," they said, and they were happy. (7/16/1992)

The overseers demanded thanks for whippings used to back up their orders and—in a gesture reminiscent of *pascuanchina*—offered the victim a shot of alcohol, thereby constructing the punishment as moral education in an elder-junior relationship.

That was the overseers' point of view, however, not necessarily that of the laborers. To what extent did this representation structure laborers' own interpretations? In Tayta Alberto's description, the overseers' attitude appears rather cynical. The word I translate as "cruel," *millay*, might also be translated as "morally ugly." It is wholly disapproving and would not be used to refer to severity that could be justified as necessary to a legitimate end. As we have seen, overseers were, in fact, subject to strong pressures and disapproval from below. Rosa Condo offered another image of how some laborers reacted to punishments during work:

> RC Out of fear of punishment . . . we didn't talk back at all. We would take punishment, and , , , in the end, it was left to God [*Diosito*], that he see.
> "They will do what they will do, but let God see," we said. . . . "They are accursed people." . . .
> MG You didn't plead with God to punish the bosses?
> RC Yes, some people , , , spoke like that, [after they were] whipped. . . .

> *If something happened [to them], or*
> *[God] punished [them] . . .*
> *It would be* beauuutiful!
> Beautiful *God,*
> *oh yes, then we would be happy,*
> *[they] said. [She laughs.] . . .*

> When we were big, we, too, said that. . . . But as a child, no, no. . . .
> MG And . . . has God punished the bosses?
> RC Yes , , , yes . . . Don't you see, due to the [laments of] "My God" [spoken] . . . by the indigenous people, something happened to the *patrón* [name]. The bus turned over, and he, too, was injured. . . . Now . . . he has been given a lesson [*tiene experiencia*]. Then he didn't mistreat, after that. (8/23/1992)

The image is almost biblical. Mistreated laborers cry out to God in anger and distress. God hears their laments and punishes their oppressor, in this case, by means of a bus accident.

Still, the strategy was not a wholesale failure. Recall Reinaldo Sisa's account of how his parents counseled him to respect landlords. Tayta Reinaldo was not alone in expressing pride in the praise his bosses gave him for his good work. While expressing compassion for the victims of excessive hacienda violence, he also suggested that they brought such violence on themselves through disrespect or laziness. Guerrero, analyzing paternalism on northern Ecuadorian haciendas, draws on oral histories to argue that hacienda violence was partly successful in creating a "division between good and bad 'children' (*hijitos,* as landlords addressed 'their Indians'), analogous to the situation of affective preferences of the domestic *pater* within the family; . . . a situation experienced as a relationship of personal preferences, of feelings and affinities, of hatreds individually defined between lord and *huasipungueros*" (1991:202–203).

Fear worked as the hacienda authorities' ally in this respect. In a few instances, laborers openly confronted abusive stewards, renters, or landowners. Recalling such incidents, the protagonists sometimes fault their peers for distancing themselves from the conflict or taking the authorities' side. When a steward or overseer punished someone harshly for allegedly shoddy or slow work, it seems that bystanders' reactions were likewise generally passive. Victims' and others' accounts hint that, in village gossip, the bystanders would justify their lack of solidarity by appealing to common notions of respect for authority, even endorsing the authorities' characterization of the victim as insolent. Thus, even (or especially) in the most arbitrary, unregulated, and unritualized forms of violence, fear helped the authorities impose their interpretation of that violence as punishment for disrespect.

What people might have said out of fear and self-justification, of course, is not necessarily what they believed at every level. I do not mean to suggest that the rhetoric of respect created a coherent, seamless, and all-encompassing understanding of hacienda violence within the consciousness of individuals, let alone one shared by laborers as a whole or between laborers and bosses. It would be a mistake to expect to find just one commonly shared interpretation; what we should expect in general in such cases are tensions and competing interpretations. Respect was a language of contention among laborers and between laborers and authorities, as well as of consensus. How those who lived and labored on haciendas viewed and responded to hacienda discipline is an empirical question. We cannot know their judgments a priori —contrary to what a reified opposition between coercion and consent would seem to imply.

Respect and Resistance

The analysis thus far undermines any romantic notion that laborers were essentially united in a stance of constant resistance. Instead, their relationship to hacienda discipline varied with their individual perspectives as men and women, elders and juniors, engaged in complex and sometimes contentious relations with each other as well as with their overlords. Yet, none of this negates the fundamental inequality and conflict of interests between mestizo bosses and indigenous peasant laborers. Despite their internal differentiation, hacienda laborers shared a sense of collective identity linked to their common ethnic, racial, and class position as hacienda Runa, and they resented and resisted their overlords in various ways, as we saw in previous chapters. What, then, was the relationship between respect and resistance?

Scott points out that dominant ideologies necessarily idealize social reality and thereby provide the basis for a critique of society insofar as reality falls short of the ideal (1985:335–340). Thus, Runa resented hacienda bosses for violating norms of conduct implied by the respect complex. Some of my informants' accounts imply a conceptual opposition between appropriately ritualized or relatively moderate punishments designed to instill respect, on the one hand, and the excessively harsh punishments hacienda bosses also inflicted. José Pillajo's account of confession during Holy Week points to a similar contradiction. Tayta José began by presenting an idealized image of a hierarchical society united in common submission to God:

> All the ladies and gentlemen, everyone
> white, Runa, all will confess.
> Everyone, in turn.
> Each day, they are called to the Confessor,
> each hacienda was called to the Confessor.

Yet when I asked him if the stewards confessed, too, his tone changed abruptly:

> The stewards, garbage—
> These Laras never went to confess.
> Such drinkers as they were,
> such—rude people,
> weren't about to go confess. (JMP 9/2/1992)

According to their ideal role, the stewards should have been paragons of respect. Instead, the Laras exemplified the clash between ideals and bosses' behavior.

A similar tension arose in relation to hacienda authorities' ideal role in regulating sexuality and marital relations. Landlords, stewards, and indigenous overseers sometimes used their position to seduce or rape indigenous women, doling out rewards and punishments to obtain the acquiescence of parents and jealous husbands. On those haciendas where sexual abuse was institutionalized, *amos* intervened in marital conflicts to secure their own monopoly of male violence against women and their sexual access to wives.

Several informants' parents or grandparents fled from Llinllín to Pangor-area haciendas to avoid such abuse. Men and women today tell of such cases with an emphasis on the lords' cruelty and sexual perversity. While in some contexts villagers may speak of the hacienda period as a time of respect, in recalling sexual abuse, rude insults, and arbitrary violence, they may say there was no respect at all.

However, there is more to be said about the way the respect complex shaped and constrained the meanings of resistance under the hacienda. I showed in Chapter 5 that long-standing indigenous practices of reciprocity underpinned a critique of the hacienda. Yet, it does not seem that Pangor Runa subjectively understood their own acts as carrying on a venerable indigenous cultural tradition of resistance. At issue here is how discourses shaped by the respect complex constructed resistance as an expression (or not) of collective or individual agency, identity, and tradition.

Respect, we know, was treated as a norm that elders must explicitly teach and inculcate in their juniors. Conversely, oral accounts tend to portray defiance of hacienda authority as an initiative that emerged spontaneously from rebellious selves. Thus, Luis Amancha, one of a group of brothers who sued the steward and landlord over physical abuse and lack of payment for their labor in 1961, contrasted "the people in the old days [who] took it" and "just kept quiet" to "we people of a later generation," who decided "we couldn't take that anymore." When I asked him if he and his group had in mind any case from the past that helped give them courage, he insisted strongly on their own authorship of their ideas and courage:

> No, we [didn't take from] anybody not their courage
> or their ideas, no.
> We, we ourselves thought
> To defy.
> No longer to take the lords' beatings,
> to be called "son of a whore," sworn at.
> "We won't hear it anymore," we said.
> Because I don't know,
> the late old people from before,
> if they ever sued somewhere, or didn't sue, or who knows how they
>   lived.
> Thus, they were treated like a—like an animal,
>   whipped
>   under the lash
>   beaten

they must have just gone through life [like that].
We, later, in our agreement, just out of our thinking, we were [defiant].
(8/2/1992)

Jacoba Sayay told me proudly of her and her father's defiance of abusive hacienda bosses, but when I asked her if her father had taught her to be rebellious, she answered in similar fashion: "No, he didn't teach me. . . . It's out of our own hearts, our own thinking, that once we've learned to rebel, we don't heed." Parents and other elders did, in fact, teach their children a critical understanding of landlords' behavior, including stories of landlords in league with the devil, and they probably sometimes initiated youths into practices of covert resistance such as pilfering from hacienda fields or surreptitiously grazing their animals on restricted pastures. What the testimonies of Lucho Amancha, Jacoba Sayay, and others seem to indicate, however, is that there was little self-conscious sense of a collective tradition of resistance that Runa maintained and passed on as an ethnic inheritance.

I have not found any words in Chimborazo Quichua that correspond very closely to "resistance" as this word is used in academic social science. The closest Quichua word is *kariyana,* which I translate as "to defy" or "to challenge" authority or "to rebel." The same word can refer to defiance of parents or of abusive bosses. Built on the root *kari* (male), the word implies that defiance is a masculine act, perhaps one expected of males at some stage of their development, although grammatically conceivable for female subjects as well. Yet, *kariyana* is morally ambiguous; it is not associated with mature masculinity but, rather, with an asocial, wild strength and willfulness. In *pascuanchina,* mature men used their strength to tame wildness and instill respect, and *kariyana* was precisely one thing they admonished their juniors not to do. *Respeto* and its verb form *respetana* were semantically opposed to *kariyana,* as society and culture were to the wild (see Lyons 2002b).

In some parts of the Andes, indigenous people conceive of indigenous identity as rooted in pre-Christian autochthony and wildness (Allen 1983; Platt 2001; Salomon 1981; cf. O. Harris 1980). One might imagine that a notion of defiance as wild could have linked up with such a notion of collective identity and with a project of resistance envisioned in ethnic terms, that is, as a recovery or enactment of a wild indigenousness opposed to the Christian social order of respect and mestizo domination. Among Pangor Runa, however, I found no evidence of such associations in hacienda-era practices or narratives. On the contrary, older informants said their elders told them that Runa and mestizo alike were created when Jesus Christ came to the world, and they did not link either group to pre-Christian peoples or wildness. Even in the 1990s, a group of young Runa from around the province found it shocking and insulting when their instructor in a history course told them that their pre-Columbian ancestors were not Christian. This lack of an ethnic identification with pre-Christian autochthony may in itself be a sign of the historical power of haciendas and the respect complex in Chimborazo.

On Pangor haciendas, the respect complex shaped Runa understandings of resistance in ways that undercut its potential force by coding it as wild rather than social. This can be seen in the case of the Amancha brothers' suit. It seems reasonable to suppose that the Amancha brothers might have received at least covert support from their peers. In fact, only one other laborer joined them in their suit, and they felt undermined by others, including the *fundador*, who criticized their actions as antisocial and insolent. These criticisms reflected both the meanings carried by words such as *respetana* and *kariyana* and the social patterns associated with those meanings—the stakes that elders and other adults had in the respect complex and the coercive power that supported it.

There were, indeed, various acts, notions, and traditions (often covert) that we might see as a kind of counterpoint to *respeto*—the defiant smile surreptitiously flashed toward a peer by the victim of a whipping, the stories about landowners who were in league with the devil, even the concept of *kariyana* (however ambivalent). Yet all that does not make respect just a front. The ways that training in respect was incorporated into indigenous child-rearing and ritual, the criticism that Luis Amancha and Jacoba Sayay received from fellow laborers for their lack of respect, the stakes in the respect complex held by indigenous elders and others, and even the nostalgia for respect today, all testify that respect was much more than a façade.

HEGEMONY?

I have tried to develop some new questions and insights by suspending the analytic opposition between persuasion and coercion. On Chimborazo haciendas, domestic quarrels, challenges to generational authority, and feuds between neighbors provided an occasion for landlords and hacienda administrators to employ violence and give instruction in ways that legitimated their authority. They commonly exercised this discipline in ritualized forms that drew on, contributed to, and mirrored practices of indigenous authority. Hacienda landlords, stewards, and overseers, together with religious authorities, acted as elders to enforce moral order.

Discipline on Chimborazo haciendas was associated with a rich domain of symbolic representations. The term *respect* is a key to this domain. Discipline and respect were not only an aspect of hacienda power and mestizo ideology but also part of the culture and the social relations of indigenous laborers. Respect was what young people gained when they became full social persons on sponsoring a fiesta, and what they continued to give to their elders. It shaped cosmology and child rearing, annual rituals and everyday greetings. Respect was at once an aspect of mestizo domination and a theme in indigenous culture; a code of behavior instilled and enforced by hacienda lords and indigenous elders; the language of coercion and a symbol of morality. It did not keep laborers from bitterly resenting the hacienda bosses' use of arbitrary and excessive violence, their stinginess, and their inflexible labor demands, or from resisting in a variety of ways. The respect complex did, however, set the terms of contention between laborers and bosses, as well as among laborers themselves, over obedience and violence. It also constructed acts of resistance as wild by tending to limit the degree to which resistance could be explicitly conceptualized as a collective project.

Was this hegemony? If we mean by hegemony that persuasion replaced coercion in masters' day-to-day ability to secure compliance, then the answer is no. Landlords had to contend with laborers' chronic resentment over labor demands, levels of redistribution, and other issues. The use or threat of force was never far in the background in deciding such issues, and former laborers today unambiguously name both fear and their lack of economic alternatives as reasons they had to obey. Their acts of surreptitious and occasionally open resistance also testify to the failure of pure persuasion. Yet by juxtaposing coercion against persuasion, fear against consent, we cannot fully grasp how these elements sustain a social order. It is not enough simply to identify one of them as central or pervasive. On Chimborazo haciendas, coercion and persuasion did not appear only as pure elements but together as a complex alloy. Instead of weighing each separately, therefore, we must understand their interrelation.

This approach reveals aspects of the landlord-laborer relationship that have been virtually invisible in the scholarship on haciendas. Landlords were not able to persuade laborers to comply with their economic demands without coercion, but they did secure a social role and cultural meanings for their power that went beyond the purely economic. Landlords and stewards enforced racial and cultural distinctions between themselves and indigenous laborers, but they also joined with indigenous elders in administering culturally hybrid forms of discipline. The respect complex did not eliminate resistance, but it shaped how laborers understood resistance.

This case shows what can be lost when we identify "hegemony" with "false consciousness." I have treated hegemony, instead, as a social phenomenon associated with patterns of authority, alliances, loyalties, and cleavages. These patterns are not purely ideological but, rather, take shape simultaneously in social practices and in the ways people understand these practices. Forms of discipline that blend persuasion and coercion can contribute to vertical loyalties and horizontal disunity, thereby complicating the lines between oppressors and oppressed and constraining resistance. The respect complex was hegemonic in this sense.

In Gramsci's terms, we might speak of a "hegemonic bloc" comprising landlords, hacienda authorities, and indigenous elders. The respect complex linked elders to bosses while giving them authority over juniors. During the period of open agrarian conflict in Pangor after 1960, some *fundadores* and regidores supported landlords against other laborers' demands, as the notion of a hegemonic bloc would predict.

At the same time, the image of a structurally defined bloc obscures the fluidity of relations among landlords, elders, and juniors. Even older hacienda residents could resent landlords' demands. Conversely, young laborers might demand respect from even younger siblings, and they might look forward to receiving greater respect as they matured. As Scott notes, the fact that juniors eventually become elders helps explain the stability of age-graded systems of domination. Scott, apparently assuming that the development of large-scale agrarian societies erased age seniority as a significant basis of domination, considers this phenomenon irrelevant to "large-scale forms of domination" (1990:82–85). However, other types of domination often build symbolically and structurally on the authority of seniors over juniors, as in the Andes.[18]

Loyalties and resentments based on gender were equally complex and fluid. In long-term historical perspective, the hacienda system may have reinforced indigenous men's authority over women. Erin O'Connor has argued that landlords and male laborers formed a "patriarchal pact" (1997:249–277), and male Runa sometimes recycled the harsh treatment they received in the fields into domestic violence. Within the confines of the prevailing gender norms in hacienda communities, however, landlords were not categorically allied with either gender when they dealt with marital discord. Those norms prescribed mutual obligations and rights for wives as well as husbands. Women probably called on hacienda authorities to enforce the norms as much as men did, if not more so, and feelings of loyalty, gratitude, or resentment toward the authorities on the part of men and women were contingent on the situation rather than structurally predetermined in any simple sense. The same is true for other sorts of internal conflict, such as quarrels between neighbors. The hacienda authorities' quasi-judicial role thus bears comparison with the role of the state and the law under capitalism, as an ostensibly neutral arbiter that appears necessary for sustaining harmony and social order.

The hacienda was a social order in which coercion was pervasive but often wrapped in varied ideological garments with deep cultural roots. Hacienda Runa sometimes administered discipline, they sometimes benefited from it, and they were sometimes its target; at times, they endorsed the accompanying argument, and at other times, they rejected it. They certainly defied authority on occasion, but when they did, the respect complex contributed to their understanding of such defiance as spontaneous wildness rather than as rooted in traditions of legitimate resistance.

Lest the argument be misunderstood, it is important to note once again that, for hacienda laborers, *respeto* did not justify the hacienda bosses' extremes of cruelty. As I come to the end of my examination of the hacienda period, I recall one of the images with which I began, that of Manuel Yépez pushing up his pants leg to show me where the steward struck him with the whip, his anguish and indignation still fresh after four decades. And then Jacoba Sayay speaking with pride at having stood up to the landowner, telling him that his little blows would not kill her—not because they did not hurt, but because her own rage at being exploited and mistreated was stronger than fear and pain. I remember, too, the tone of moral indignation in José Pillajo's voice, speaking of defying the stewards—"and why should we just take it?" In the account of every former resident, life on the hacienda was a life of insults and beatings, and for that it is a good thing that the old-time *amos* have disappeared forever. When the Ecuadorian president proposed modifying the agrarian reform laws in 1994 in ways that seemed to allow for the return of the old hacienda system, massive numbers in Pangor and throughout the highlands blocked roads and marched in demonstrations to make sure that would not happen. And it will not.

PART FOUR

The Legacy of the Hacienda

CHAPTER 8

The Demise of the Hacienda

DEMANDING AN ACCOUNTING:
THE AMANCHA BROTHERS REBEL

One April morning in 1961, the last year of Carlos Arturo León's rental period, a young *ayuda* laborer named Manuel Amancha went to the corral by the hacienda house to milk the cows in lieu of his sister, who was ill.[1] Then he joined other laborers in a field where they were harvesting potatoes. There, he got into trouble with Ignacio Lara, the steward, and his nephews. By his account, one of the Laras had sexual designs on his sister and had evidently hoped to pursue those designs when she came to milk the cows; Lara was angry at Manuel for having come in her stead. The steward took his tardiness in arriving for the harvest labor as an excuse to strike him. Manuel fought back, whereupon the steward clubbed him on the head with the whip handle.

This sort of mistreatment was not novel, but this incident occurred in a changing context. Manuel had five older brothers, and they had been talking among themselves and with others about their growing impatience with the stewards' abuses. Manuel's brother Luis (Lucho) suggests that the clubbing of Manuel may have been meant as retaliation for this talk. He recalls:

> *There was a lot of mistreatment by the stewards.*
> *Without restraint they called [us] "sons of whores," swearing*
> *whipping with the whips, beating [us].*
> *One couldn't talk back [kariyana] to them at all.*
> *Whatever they said, we had to keep quiet and work, with our backs*
> *bent.*

So then we couldn't take that anymore.
Sure, the people in the old days took it.
They suffered.
If one was killed or one was beaten, they wouldn't say anything.
They just kept quiet.
But we people of a later generation began not to accept the stewards'
    mistreatment. . . .
[Talking] among a group of us, [we said:]
    "We won't tolerate it. . . .
    We'll take them and bathe them!
    We'll pay them back very well!"
    We were saying among ourselves.

But . . . to this day there are . . . bad people, bad neighbors.
    They heard and just told the stewards:
    "So-and-so and so-and-so are saying this."
So then, . . . when my brother said something and defied [the steward],
[the steward] just broke his head [i.e., made his head bleed]. (LA
    8/2/1992)

When the steward struck Manuel, his brothers decided to go immediately to Riobamba to file a legal complaint. They sought the advice of the previous renter, Guillermo Novillo, with whom they as a family had had a good relationship free of corporal punishment. This man told them that the law now required hacienda laborers to be paid. That was not, in fact, totally new, although a decree had been issued the previous September setting a minimum wage. León had apparently never paid the Monjas Corral laborers. Novillo introduced them to his lawyer and encouraged them to sue León for pay as well as an end to physical mistreatment.

It was a risky move for the Amanchas to complain about the steward to judicial authorities and sue the renter. They say the Laras threatened to beat them, to burn their houses and expel them from the hacienda, and even to kill them. Novillo and the lawyer, on the other hand, reassured them that the stewards were bluffing and that the state would not necessarily support the stewards in the current political context. "When we learned a bit about . . . the law, then we weren't afraid." Their numbers as six brothers also helped give them courage: "'Well, if one of us dies, we won't all die,' we said" (LA 8/2/1992).

Among the other laborers, however, only Andrés Yépez and perhaps a few others joined them in this suit. Joaquina Niamo told me openly that the *amos* gave her first husband, who was *fundador* and *doctrinero*, a horse and five large sacks of potatoes in order to secure his noninvolvement. Mama Joaquina's account was generally sympathetic to the Amanchas, but as she introduced the story, she started to say that the Amanchas "got insolent (*malcri[arirka]*)," then edited herself and switched to the more neutral verb, "rose up (*alzarirka*)." The Amanchas and Tayta Andrés say others were afraid to join them. But a number of other hacienda residents went beyond neutrality and actually "took the *patrón's* side," they say. These people criticized the Amanchas and Tayta Andrés as troublemakers and *malcriados*, "insolent ones."

For about two months, the Amanchas continued with their suit. When Carlos Arturo León's local political influence seemed to be blocking a favorable resolution, Lucho Amancha and Andrés Yépez traveled to Quito, where Tayta Andrés had been before as a *huasicama* house servant for a central valley landowner. "God helped us," Tayta Lucho says. The period was one of increasing indigenous political mobilization in the northern and central highlands and growing pressures from other sectors as well for agrarian reform. This trip resulted quickly in a settlement.

The minister of social affairs and labor ordered local officials in Riobamba to visit the hacienda and oversee a settling of accounts. In a meeting on the estate in early June, lawyers for the two sides argued over how many years' back pay the laborers could claim and how the accounts could be settled, given that the hacienda bosses had not been keeping any records of laborers' work or of supplements and other disbursements. In the end, they agreed that the renter would pay one year's wages. Four full-time laborers joined the Amancha brothers in receiving back pay, while a number of other full-time and resident *ayuda* laborers, perhaps about ten, still stayed out of the fray. For one year's labor, the renter had to pay 504 sucres ($34.00 at the 1961 exchange rate) to each full-time laborer, an additional 198 sucres ($13.00) to those who had served with their wives in *huasicamía*, and 126 sucres ($8.40) for *ayuda* labor to Manuel Amancha, whose conflict with the steward had started it all. The total came to 4,950 sucres ($330.00), about three weeks' rent or less (*Liquidaciones 1961:6/2, 6/6).

Oral accounts also tell of a judicial order that restrained the steward from further physical punishments. Still, even at the very end of the rental period, in December 1961, Ignacio Lara was apparently taking vengeance on the Amancha family and Andrés Yépez. According to a complaint they filed, Lara had tried to persuade Pedro Amancha's wife to leave him, confiscated some of his animals, and accused Andrés Yépez of stealing hacienda cattle (*Actas 1961:n.d.[Dec.], and Dec. 16).

By 1961, Leonidas Proaño had been bishop of Riobamba for seven years. As a priest in his native Imbabura (in northern Ecuador), Proaño had been active in the Catholic workers' movement, part of the church's response to the secular Left. Social unrest in Chimborazo probably influenced the church hierarchy to designate him as bishop of Riobamba in 1954 in the hope he would win back adherents among workers and indigenous peasants.

The son of a humble couple who wove straw hats and cultivated a small plot, Proaño felt a connection to peasants and indigenous people unusual for a bishop, and he was shocked by the poverty he saw as he traveled around his diocese. At the same time, the growing competition from leftist organizations and Protestant missionaries added to his sense of urgency about the need to broaden the church's approach from its traditional emphasis on the catechism and sacraments.[2] He decided to devote his attentions above all to the indigenous peasantry and began to take steps oriented toward material as well as spiritual improvements (Ayala Mora 1989:151–154; Gavilanes del Castillo 1992:85–131; Proaño 1989:17–22, 70–85).

Joaquina Niamo told me that when Bishop Proaño learned of the Amanchas' suit, he "took our side" and decided to cease renting out the hacienda (JN-MY 6/29/1992). Proaño had, in fact, been contemplating, since at least 1956, taking charge of church haciendas and giving some land to indigenous peasants as a way of "incorporating the Indian into civilized life" (Gavilanes del Castillo 1992:126–127). Still, it is possible that the suit helped clinch his decision and that it contributed, along with many other incidents, to his deepening awareness of the landed elite's oppression of indigenous people. In the 1960s and the 1970s, his aim turned from "civilizing" to "liberating" Indians and the poor, and he became a firm ally of indigenous peasants struggling for land throughout the province.

To tell the story in this way, with feared or actual indigenous political activities and protests contributing to Proaño's designation as bishop, his early initiatives, and his later radicalization, is to reverse a common narrative in which priests and nuns guided by liberation theology awaken hitherto quiescent Indians and other peasants (see, e.g., Argueta 1983; Lernoux 1982). The relationship between the church and indigenous Catholics is best characterized as one of reciprocal interaction and mutual influence. Thus, I do not mean to suggest that Proaño simply followed his indigenous flock's lead any more than the other way around. Proaño was very much his own man. He participated actively in the Latin American Council of Bishops and the Second Vatican Council in the early 1960s, experiences that reshaped his outlook. His personal transformation was part of a much broader transformation in the Catholic Church in Latin America and the world under Pope John XXIII's leadership (Gavilanes del Castillo 1992:89–170; Proaño 1989). No simple narrative will suffice. Yet, it is necessary to underline the points that are left out of accounts shaped by the trope of "awakening": indigenous peasants were resisting oppressive conditions on haciendas *before* liberation theology, and their actions may have influenced the evolution of the diocese and its bishop. It does not diminish Proaño's stature to suggest that, before being the bishop who proclaimed a message of liberation, he was a man whose ears and heart were open to his indigenous parishioners' grievances, and that what he learned from them contributed to his own political "awakening."

"NOW WE ARE FORGETTING THE *AMOS*": FROM HACIENDA TO COMMUNITY

The renaming of Monjas Corral exemplifies the ways the church and indigenous peasants have influenced each other and sometimes misunderstood each other in the 1960s and since. On taking direct control of the estate, Proaño renamed it Tepeyac, after the site where the brown-skinned Virgin of Guadalupe appeared to Juan Diego, a humble indigenous man in early colonial Mexico. On one level, this apparition symbolizes the Christianization of Indians on the heels of the Spanish conquest. At the same time, the apparition can symbolize indigenous people's ability to make Christianity their own and to insist on their own vision of the faith. Tepeyac was already the site of an important Aztec shrine where pilgrims venerated a female deity. According to the story, Juan Diego had to repeatedly visit the local bishop and bring him proof of the apparition before the bishop would believe him and heed the Virgin's wishes for a shrine in Tepeyac. In this sense, the story presents the Indian Juan Diego as evangelizing the bishop, rather than the other way around.

Monjas Corral residents, however, knew nothing of this story—I do not think many of them knew the story even in the 1990s. For old-time residents, only the name Monjas Corral resonated with their own history, their sufferings on the hacienda. During my fieldwork, they still sometimes spoke scornfully of the new name, which was "empty" of such associations. People in the area use both names, and the community assembly asked me to identify the community with both names.

Given Monjas Corral residents' dissatisfaction and their successful protest in 1961, one might imagine that they would leap at the chances that Bishop Proaño offered them in subsequent years to gain individual and communal ownership of hacienda lands. The story of the transformation and division of the hacienda, however, is more complex and ambiguous than that. It involves disparate agendas, tensions, misunderstandings, and losses as well as mutual influences and beneficial results.

In 1963, the diocese proposed that Monjas Corral residents form a cooperative and offered them land. They refused, whereupon three hundred hectares were granted to indigenous peasants recruited into the cooperative from another part of the province (CEAS 1971:2). The senior leader of this group, an elderly man when I met him in the early 1990s, told me that people in their community of origin had joined Eloy Alfaro's revolutionary armies. This history seems to have prepared them to understand that the church's invitation to form a cooperative and receive land represented a real possibility of change in their situation. Later, while remaining grateful to Proaño for the land, this group asserted its independence of mestizo clerical control by converting to an evangelical Protestant sect.

Hacienda residents evidently kept their distance from these newcomers, were suspicious of the mestizos and foreigners who worked with them, and were not much influenced by their example. Local landowners and others apparently spread rumors about communists who were plotting to steal villagers' children, thereby deepening Monjas Corral residents' distrust. Until the mid-1960s, the long-term residents continued to work for the hacienda, now under the direction of administrators appointed by the diocese. Their working conditions were considerably better than ever before. The administrators paid them a daily wage and were prohibited from using physical violence. They recall with particular appreciation and affection one Armando Guerrero, who managed the estate in 1965–1966: he was a good man, they say, who shared food generously with the *huasicamas* and ate with the laborers in the fields.

Guerrero's period was a critical time in the history of the community and in Ecuadorian agrarian history generally. The military junta then in power had decreed an agrarian reform law in 1964 that called for resident full-time laborers (*huasipungueros*) to be granted title to the family *huasipungo* plot. Anticipating and following the decree, many highland landowners, taking advantage of provisions of the law that allowed them to keep the most productive and valuable valley lands, moved *huasipungueros* to small plots on the more marginal, erosion-prone hillsides. Other landowners evaded the law by selling off land to third parties; some resisted the law by beating or expelling hacienda residents who demanded its application or by tying up the process in the courts. Even some bishops, many of whom came from elite

THE DEMISE OF THE HACIENDA 265

landowning families themselves, evaded the law by selling off church lands at market prices or selling the land at favorable prices to their cronies (Ayala Mora 1989:154; *Jordán to Muñoz Vega 1970).

Leonidas Proaño was willing to give up practically the whole of Monjas Corral to the resident laborers, Guerrero told me. Others around the bishop, however—including members of the council officially charged with overseeing the diocese's assets—resisted giving more than one or two hectares to each family. Perhaps they considered it their duty to defend and conserve the church's property, and they may have worried about losing revenues that helped support priests' education. They may have also shared the opinion of the Riobamba elite that the church would be setting a dangerous example if it simply gave up its haciendas. At this stage, Proaño was apparently unable or unwilling to overrule them.

The fact that Monjas Corral residents lived in a dispersed pattern, most on the eastern side and a few in the hills on the west, also presented a difficulty. Proaño and his advisors seem to have agreed that it would be impractical for the diocese to grant titles to the dispersed plots the residents occupied, leaving the church with a Swiss cheese pattern of landholdings. Instead, the residents had to be granted land in one contiguous bloc. The bishop's advisors—following the pattern on other haciendas around Ecuador—were especially opposed to giving up the relatively flat and fertile lands on the eastern side of the estate, where most of the resident laborers lived. Guerrero proposed giving twenty hectares on the western side to each family. By his account, Proaño's advisors objected to giving that much even on the western side, but after an influential national political figure intervened at his request, it was agreed to grant each family ten hectares (Figure 19).[3] In the same area as these family plots, they would also be granted a plot for communal use, a standard feature of agrarian reform settlements in the period.

Guerrero felt he had secured a victory for the laborers, but they refused to accept the land. Alberto Yumbo told me that he and Andrés Yépez went to the headquarters of the government agrarian reform institute in Quito to request that they be assigned land where they lived. Those who lived on the eastern side did not want to give up their houses and the fertile plots they had been working in order to relocate in the more frost-prone, rocky, and sloping land on the west, where they would have to break up the tough *páramo* grass and start anew. Guerrero also attributed their refusal to some interpersonal animosities between those who lived on the two sides (2/2/1992).

Bishop Proaño himself visited the hacienda more than once to try to persuade the residents to accept land titles. Reinaldo Sisa recalled these at-

FIGURE 19.   *Foreground: Caparina, part of the area villagers were relocated to in the 1960s*

tempts along with some of the other reasons that the Monjas Corral residents persistently refused:

> We didn't know. Leonidas Proaño begged us. "Runitos, take the land. This agrarian reform is coming. You take it because you have worked. . . . Instead of paying you, the renter *amos* gave you beatings. . . . So now, the agrarian reform is coming and you should accept the land. . . ."
>
> Some of the people didn't believe it. . . . "When are they going to give it to us? They're going to give us land? Who can believe it? Why should we accept it? They're not going to give it for nothing. They won't give us anything just to give it." . . .
>
> "If we take that *huasipungo* plot, how will we live just on ten hectares? On the same plot, [how will we find room] for pigs, for sheep, for cattle, and to plant? How will we live on that little bit of land? . . ." (9/14/1992)

In other words, Monjas Corral residents both distrusted the church's intentions and disliked the idea of being confined to limited individual plots; they worried that this would mean losing access to pastureland and other resources. Mariano Niamo, the old *regidor, fundador,* and overseer, and his family seem to have been particularly influential in persuading others not to accept the arrangement. They argued that those who accepted land would be stealing it from the bishopric:

> They said not to accept it. "How can it be appropriated? That can't be. This is the bishopric's hacienda, all of it. There can't be any law like that. . . . Don't take it. This hacienda, the bishopric's hacienda, how can it be divided? How can it be sold?" . . .
> They criticized [people who were considering accepting the land], saying, "[They are] stealing lands, robbing. They will bring misfortune . . ." They insulted with bad words. . . . The late Mariano walked around looking fierce, carrying his club. (AYU 6/13/1995)

This account suggests division among hacienda residents as to how to respond, a division seemingly exacerbated by uncertainty about the political and legal situation and perhaps by the contradictory interests and ideological commitments of the *regidor-fundador*-overseer.

In the face of the residents' refusal, Guerrero felt he had to pressure them more forcefully to relocate:

> It was even necessary to trick them . . . [by telling them] that "the law doesn't permit it . . . you have to be together in just one group." That "it's impossible to transfer [land] there . . . if you don't accept it, maybe the army is going to come and expel you from here . . . with tanks . . ."
> It was necessary to . . . make them afraid . . . so that they would leave, in the end. (5/5/1992)

Some families apparently left the hacienda rather than be forced to relocate to the western hills. But finally, one by one, most of the resident families relocated. Guerrero said the overseer was among the first to assent, and he helped persuade the others. Still, the residents showed little interest as their plots were measured and marked. They built their houses and began to farm roughly in the area that Guerrero indicated for each one, but only several years later did they begin to ask him exactly where the boundaries of each plot ran. They continued to pasture their animals in the *páramo.*

By the late 1960s, Proaño was apparently ready to go further and sell most of the remaining hacienda land on very favorable terms to indigenous peasants. Armando Guerrero returned in 1968 to oversee the process. He first tried to persuade the people of Monjas Corral to buy land. They had the opportunity now to recover fertile lands on the eastern side that they had been forced to leave just a few years earlier. Again, they repeatedly refused the church's offers. As they told Guerrero later, they had been robbed too often by others. They thought Guerrero was planning simply to pocket their down payments himself, and whatever land they ostensibly bought would later be taken away. In the early to mid-1970s, some finally did supplement their *huasipungo* plots by buying additional land in the same area. Other residents who had not been full-time laborers and had not received a *huasipungo* plot in the 1960s now also bought plots.

Monjas Corral residents might have been able to acquire substantially more. Instead, after they refused, the church sold a large chunk of the lands residents had until recently occupied to an association of peasants from the central basin. A group of impoverished Pangor mestizos acquired another chunk of land in the southeastern corner.

At some point in the 1970s, as land struggles intensified throughout the province (Charvet 1986:154), the fact began to sink in among former Monjas Corral laborers that the division of the hacienda into privately and communally owned lands was real, not just some trick, and that it was going to shape their lives for years to come. In 1976, they agreed to buy over one thousand hectares in the western páramo that they had been using as communal pastureland. In the mid-1970s and again the mid-1980s, they also submitted a series of proposals to buy various tracts in the valley, including, at one point, all the land still owned by the diocese. They contemplated invading the core area that the diocese had retained and demanding more land. Armando Guerrero recalled berating them:

> "Yes, now you want it, don't you? . . . Now you want to invade. Why didn't you want it before?"
>
> They said, "You're right, we are fools. Why didn't you *beat* us," they said then. "Why didn't you make us understand by force? . . . The thing is, we thought that that down payment that we were going to give, you were going to steal it from us. And that you were tricking us into thinking you were giving us land, and after a few years you would take away the land, and you wouldn't give us the money back. That's what we thought. Because everyone, *everyone*, has robbed us." (5/5/1992)

Their pressures on the diocese did help the former laborers gain a small tract of choice, flat valley land in 1984. At some point, the church also granted the community a small plot in the core area on which to build a school and a community meeting house. They use some nearby buildings

FIGURE 20. *Part of core area retained by the Diocese of Riobamba, with Tepeyac Bajo school at center-right*

and land for other communal purposes: a cooperative store, a chapel, a tree nursery, and areas for playing sports or celebrating fiestas. The diocese also sold additional valley land to a group of people who had taken jobs as wage laborers in the core area, some of them landless junior members of longtime resident families. For most of the former hacienda residents, however, it was too late to return to the valley. Church officials and advisors argued that they had already been given ample land, that any additional land transfers should benefit others who had no land, and that the diocese should keep some land to serve larger goals.[4]

Of the three thousand–hectare estate, the diocese retained about seventy hectares around the historical central administrative area, an area of prime land in the southeast (Figure 20). In the early 1960s, it had established an institute there that for some years trained peasants from around the province and the country as community-development workers. Monjas Corral residents do not seem to have participated much in the institute's activities except as laborers, although some may have taken adult literacy classes there. In subsequent years, the diocese has vested control over much of this area in other church-affiliated organizations. During my fieldwork in the 1990s, it was managed by the Movimiento Indígena de Chimborazo (Indigenous

Movement of Chimborazo), a largely Catholic indigenous organization that Proaño had helped establish in the 1980s (Proaño 1989:88–90, 215–224).

I have perhaps labored too hard in the last several pages to fashion a coherent narrative out of disparate strands. In one strand, present in both Guerrero's account and those of former hacienda laborers, the laborers had very good reasons for resisting relocation and even sent delegates to Quito to press for an alternative arrangement, but the church and Guerrero pressured and tricked them into accepting land on the west. In another strand, the laborers could have gained virtually the entire hacienda but they let opportunities slip away until the last moment, when they finally salvaged something. Maybe these strands are not exactly contradictory—each refers primarily to a different stage of the process. The sense that the former laborers acted in puzzlingly contradictory ways may also come from the fact that I have mostly written of them as responding as a group. If I had more detailed information, I might be able to write a more complexly differentiated narrative of individual laborers' responses and the tensions among them. Yet, it is the second strand that tends to dominate accounts today, those of former laborers as well as Guerrero's. Villagers lament what they see as lost opportunities and blame their own foolishness or lack of knowledge.

Their actions in the land reform period do suggest something of what their own alternative vision might have been, had they fully understood that the old hacienda labor regime was coming to an end. They appreciated some aspects of the hacienda land tenure system: their flexible access to land not being used by someone else, with some ability to choose their plots and disperse themselves on a large estate, as opposed to having plots permanently fixed and limited by individual ownership; and their common access to ample pastureland in the *páramo*, firewood, and other resources. Their resistance to the transformation was partly animated by attachment to these benefits (and certainly not to the hacienda labor regime). They did, in the end, maintain access to communal pastureland. They might have been able to retain a larger portion of the estate in undivided ownership, including much of the land on the eastern side, had they better understood the opportunities in the 1960s.

When some of them told me in the 1990s that they did not know anything before—they sometimes said this about the past generally, not only about the agrarian reform period—I was at first inclined to see this as a reflection of currently popular narratives of enlightenment that oppose modern knowledge to traditional ignorance. I worried that internalized racism, colored by the stereotype of the *indio bruto* (brutish Indian), made it too easy for them to accept such narratives. I preferred to view them as having been wily, effective resisters—an image popular in much of the scholarship on peasants and other subordinate people since the 1980s. As an anthropological researcher, learning day after day from my informants about their world, I came to respect their knowledge: they are the authorities on their situation. All this, along with a generalized, probably too simplistic, sense of cultural relativism, made it difficult for me to accept the idea that their own cultural knowledge could have been inadequate for dealing with the situation they faced in the agrarian reform period.

I still worry about internalized racism and modernist ideological dismissals of older generations' knowledge. In judging themselves as having been ignorant and foolish, villagers might forget that they had solid reasons for their refusal to relocate and for their distrust. They might forget that they had what amounted to an alternative vision of agrarian reform (though they did not necessarily articulate it as such). At the same time, though, their assessment that they "didn't know" represents an appreciation of the importance of knowledge and its connection to power in the sense of the ability to act effectively. Their resistance had ironic results, particularly in the late 1960s and the 1970s, because it was literally misguided—by limited knowledge of changes in the national and provincial political structures and of agrarian reform struggles on other haciendas, and hence by a mistaken assessment of what was going on around them, of the opportunities and risks they faced. This experience has contributed to their interest and participation in forms of learning that were not available to them in the hacienda period—schooling for their children, adult education classes sponsored by a variety of nongovernmental organizations, radio programs in Quichua, and Bible study meetings, to name a few of the most important. I shall explore the ambivalence associated with such activities in the next chapter, but villagers do sometimes use metaphors of a change from blindness to sight to talk of them with a sense that they are now being let in on powerful knowledge that mestizos and priests used to keep to themselves.

Despite the difficulties and losses they suffered in the agrarian reform, villagers today express gratitude to Bishop Proaño for ending the hacienda labor regime and facilitating the transfer of landownership. "Now," José María Pillajo said, "we live pretty much in peace. . . . Now that I have my little *huasipungo*, I have . . . a rest" (7/21/1991). Similarly, Alberto Yumbo drew a contrast between the past and the present:

> In those days, there was no such thing as schooling. . . . All of our life was serving the *amos*, just on the hacienda, from the time of our parents, our grandparents. . . .

But now, . . . we have gotten our plots. Father God [Yayito Dios] helped us, because we prayed to him. So now we are forgetting the *amos*. Now, who knows where they are dying? Now they've gone away. . . . They've sold all the land, and we've bought it, and now we have our little plots.

So now we work in our *comuna*. We have animals in our *comuna*. We talk with each other in the *comuna*, we have classes, we reflect and make decisions. (7/16/92)

What has replaced the hacienda as an administrative structure is the *co-muna*, a form of village organization. Following Ecuadorian law, villagers annually elect a president and other officers to represent the community. They occasionally compare these positions to fiesta sponsorship, and they similarly tend to rotate them among the members of the community. The community assembles weekly for a formal meeting, and one day a week, occasionally two, villagers work together in tasks for collective benefit—cleaning or repairing irrigation ditches, maintaining paths, cultivating potatoes on communal land, fixing up the village meetinghouse, planting trees on communal land, and so on. As in the hacienda period, labor obligations are linked to land rights: only those with access to communal pastures and a share in other communal land in their own right are full members of the community (*socios*), with the full obligation to join in communal labor. Others who make use of communal resources such as firewood or pasture have the obligation to provide occasional labor; as in the hacienda period, they are called *ayudas*. Membership is carefully regulated: at least as of the early 1990s, each member could pass on membership only to one heir. The official name of the community comprising the former laborers of Monjas Corral is Tepeyac Bajo or, more formally, the Association of Former Huasipungueros of Tepeyac Bajo.

A NEW CATHOLICISM: FROM SAINTS' FEASTS TO BIBLE STUDY

Changes in the social, economic, and political structures of the village have facilitated radical changes in local religious life as well since the 1960s. The old system of fiesta sponsorship collapsed, the patron saint's feast took on a new structure and significance as an expression of community solidarity, and Bible study displaced feasting and *doctrina* as the basis for religious authority and, to some degree, as the central communal religious activity.

Several factors conspired to make villagers increasingly reluctant to sponsor fiestas. One goal of old liberal and indigenist projects of "incorporating the Indian into civilization" was to turn indigenous peasants into consumers —to draw them more fully into the market economy. In this respect, land reform, the improvement of road networks, and other associated developments succeeded, increasing villagers' reliance on cash. In the hacienda period, Pangor Runa built their huts out of earth and straw; wove their clothes out of wool from their own sheep; fertilized their plots only with animal manure; and ate little that they did not grow themselves or barter for. In recent decades, they have begun to build cement block houses with corrugated metal roofs, to buy synthetic fabrics in town, to use chemical fertilizers and pesticides in their fields, and to supplement their home-grown food and replace barter with market purchases. Moreover, even with the favorable terms they were given on Monjas Corral, villagers needed to save money to pay for the land they purchased in the late 1960s and the 1970s. A few families then sought to complement their highland plots by acquiring land in the Pallatanga area and at lower altitudes. All these new ways of spending money competed with the expenses of fiesta sponsorship as demands on limited household income.

At the same time, while land reform unquestionably left the beneficiaries better off in terms of working conditions and personal liberty, the effects on the size of their herds and the volume of their harvests are not so clear. They have gained more time to devote to their own animals and fields, but they are restricted to the less-fertile lands on the western side. Meanwhile, at least in the 1980s, the market value of highland agricultural products declined (Rosero 1990:55–60).

Fiesta sponsorship was always a burden for young or relatively poor couples, and some resisted even under the hacienda. The division of the hacienda into communally and privately owned sections introduced new difficulties for young couples in gaining access to land in their own right. In the hacienda period, they were pressured to take up their place as a new *concierto* household farming hacienda land. Today, parents may assign them land to work and harvest, but they remain in a somewhat more dependent relationship with the parental couple until they have title to the land—which may not happen until after the parents' death. Many young couples instead leave the village periodically or permanently to work as laborers in Quito or the lowlands. In some cases, young men work outside the village while their wives stay and tend to the children, a few animals, and a small plot. Fiesta sponsorship formerly would have signaled and effected their achievement of a recognized position as adults within the community. It does not have the same meaning for young couples, whose position in the village is relatively precarious, and especially for migrants who have less stake in their seniors' approval. At the same time, land reform eliminated the coercive structures of the hacienda that formerly helped *fundadores* and *regidores* pressure reluctant potential sponsors.

Religious influences from outside the village operated in tandem with these factors. North American evangelical Protestant missionaries established a center on the shores of Lake Colta in the early twentieth century. Evangelical Protestantism grew explosively beginning in the 1960s, initially in historically autonomous (landowning) indigenous villages, then in communities newly autonomous following land reform (Muratorio 1980; Santana 1990; Tolen 1995). The community formed by former Monjas Corral laborers has remained Catholic, but they have heard Protestant critiques of Catholic practices: "These Evangelicals say, 'These saints' images are just made of earth,' or 'They're just old papers. . . . They don't speak, nor do they hear,' they say; 'they're just there getting covered in dust. And besides, in doing fiestas, we have spent ourselves out and become poor . . . That hasn't helped us in any way.' So [Catholics hear that and now they] . . . don't want to take on any fiesta obligation" (JA 9/2/1992). There have probably always been some skeptics, but Protestant attacks on saints' images as idolatrous have helped spread skepticism.

Catholic theologians, priests, and nuns developed and promoted a complementary critique. Beginning in the 1960s, many came to view much of popular religion—including the saints' feasts—as alienating and oppressive as well as superstitious. Like priests before them, they focused their criticism in part on alcohol consumption and on mestizo shopkeepers in parish centers who sold alcohol for feasts. What was newer was their extension of this criticism to all of the other expenses associated with fiestas and their willingness to do away with *regidores*, *fundadores*, and the whole system of sponsorship: "It used to take a lot of money to buy fireworks. The priests said, 'God won't give thanks for that. Don't spend money to bring bands . . . Spend the money on a house or land or something for the children'" (AS 9/4/1992). Vatican II called on pastoral agents to promote an explicit, discursive understanding of the doctrines underlying Catholic rituals and to recenter the laity's attention on Jesus and the Bible in place of the saints and festivals. This call gave a new impetus to pastoral agents' rejection of much of the fiesta system.

The people of Monjas Corral came into particularly close contact with pastoral agents espousing such ideas during the 1960s. A group of nuns worked with the peasant training institute on Tepeyac in the early 1960s, and the parish priest resided in one of the institute's buildings for a period in the mid-sixties. Monjas Corral Runa did not simply accept these pastoral agents' ideas and the changes in their pastoral practice without resistance. Some apparently spoke disparagingly of the "evangelical [i.e., Protestant] priest" and "big-tail nuns" (referring to the habits worn by the nuns)—I imagine it was religious elders especially who were unhappy. But the church's pressure on the old fiesta system continued over the following decades and, combined with Protestant influences and internal dissatisfaction with the system, had its effects.

The positions of *regidor* and alcalde were the first to go. Before the last *regidor-fundador* died (I believe, in the 1960s), others agreed to take over the role of *fundador*, but after him there was no one to continue as *regidor*. It is easy to see why the position of *regidor* was more vulnerable than that of *fundador* to the withdrawal of clerical and hacienda support. The *regidor* was officially named by the priest and had acted as an intermediary between the priest and the community. With the priest no longer supportive, that function was obsolete. Economically, this position was probably more burdensome than that of *fundador*, as it entailed responsibility for two annual fiestas rather than one. Finally, these fiestas, Carnival and Corpus Christi, were more closely bound up with hacienda authority and less with local agricultural fertility and identity than that of the patron saint.

The *fundadores* continued to select sponsors for the feast of Saint Rose, but they encountered increasing difficulties in finding candidates who would accept. They sometimes had to pay for Mass and bear other expenses themselves, but they, too, began to find this too much of a burden. Finally, they turned over responsibility for the fiesta to the community around 1986, following the parish priest's suggestion and the agreement of the community assembly. The former *fundadores* and their family continue to contribute a little bit extra to the fiesta expenses. Acting like sponsors, they might treat worshippers in the chapel to hot cinnamon tea infused with alcohol on the night before Mass; they will also carry the image at the head of a short procession around the chapel and the village meetinghouse. Essentially, however, the fiesta is now the community's affair, not theirs. The same transformation has occurred in other indigenous villages in Pangor and, indeed, much of the province.

The community finances the fiesta out of communal resources—potatoes from the communal field might be cooked to feed celebrants on the day of the Mass, for example—and by collecting a modest, fixed quota from each member household. I was told that the community put on a lavish celebration the first year it took charge of the fiesta, but by the early 1990s, the fiesta was reduced to its indispensable elements: a Mass, food, and drink. As before, individual celebrants, on their own account, often bring a bottle of alcohol or, occasionally, a pack of cigarettes to distribute during the festivities.

These individual contributions aside, the fiesta of Saint Rose has changed in its basic structure from one type of redistribution to another, very different, type. The redistribution that *fundadores* and their designated sponsors carried out was an "organization of reciprocities," in Sahlins's phrase (1972) —a flow of gifts into the hands of *fundadores* and sponsors, between them, and out to other celebrants, with each transaction an expression of personal ties and debts. Now, the community treasurer and president collect contributions, as rule-bound officers of the community. The amount is explicitly fixed beforehand by common agreement and is the same for every member. When the president distributes liquor and food, the act does not express his personal generosity or devotion to the saint but his status as a representative of the community. As such, he is treated with great respect, but members are quite conscious of their equal rights to receive, and they sometimes remind him of this if he overlooks them. This form of redistribution expresses a sense of equality among members, their identification with the community, and the generosity of the community as such vis-à-vis members, their households, and any guests from neighboring communities who may have come to the celebration.

In other ways, the fiesta today also represents communal autonomy and indigenous solidarity. The saint's image used to be carried in procession to the parish center for Mass, thereby expressing indigenous villagers' ethnic subordination to the mestizo town. Now priests come to community chapels such as that in Tepeyac Bajo to say Mass, and the procession is limited to the communal spaces around the chapel. In some parts of Chimborazo, villages hosting fiestas invite neighboring indigenous villages to send groups to play in Quichua music festivals or sports matches, and they award prizes to the best performers or winning teams. In the early 1990s, some in Tepeyac Bajo were discussing hosting such competitions for the fiesta of Saint Rose as a way of enhancing their ties with neighboring communities.

There was also some talk in 1992 of reviving individual fiesta sponsorship in modified form. The initiative seems to have come from a group of young men who wanted a way to gain their elders' respect and to improve relations with the community association, which had become strained over a land conflict. They recruited a respected community leader to join and lead them as *priostes*. They planned to contribute a bit more than the standard quota—if each member household was assessed 10,000 sucres (about $3.00), each *prioste* might give 15,000 sucres. The would-be *priostes* discussed using their contributions to hire a band, make improvements to the village chapel, or award prizes in music and sports competitions. As it turned out, the community was preoccupied that August with the vigilante-style detention of an alleged cattle rustler. The priest objected to some of the community's actions and refused to come and say Mass. Thus, there was not much of a fiesta at all that year. Nonetheless, in recent years, some young as well as older villagers in Tepeyac Bajo seem to have come to view individual fiesta sponsorship as an aspect of "indigenous culture" that should not be lost. By my last visit in mid-2003, they were anticipating a good upcoming fiesta that year because of the contributions of three *priostes*, two of them emigrants resident in Quito. Still, individual sponsors are not expected to bear the full burden, only to supplement the contributions of the community at large, which retains control of the fiesta.

As for the weekly *doctrina*, obligatory attendance and ritual whippings must have ceased in the 1960s. The last *doctrina* prayer leader (*rezachidor*) in Tepeyac died in 1968. Bible study has replaced the weekly rote recitation of prayers. Some villagers still think of and use Bible study meetings as a sort of *doctrina*, as I shall discuss in the next chapter.

In place of the old religious authorities, the church has encouraged villages to name catechists, who receive church training and are charged with leading Bible study and preparing villagers for the sacraments. As catechists must be able to read the Bible, the oldest villagers are excluded from this role. In Pangor in the early 1990s, the oldest indigenous catechists were men in their forties, while many others were in their twenties or thirties. Catechists are often the sons or grandsons of *regidores*, *fundadores*, or *doctrina* prayer leaders. Unlike the *regidor* or *fundador*, who was often overseer as well and whose authority in resolving disputes was supported by the hacienda, the catechist's authority is primarily spiritual. It is supported, to some extent, by the prestige attached to literacy and the catechist's role as gatekeeper to the sacraments. Catechists may enhance their authority by helping their community obtain material resources from the diocese or other institutions for projects such as a new chapel or communal livestock production.

Other developments in the diocese have also affected local religious life. Since the 1980s, the theological concept of "inculturation" has joined that of "liberation" at the center of the Chimborazo church's definition of its long-term project: true liberation is seen to depend on the incarnation of the Gospel and the church in indigenous forms, within indigenous culture. God, according to this theology, planted the "seeds" of Christianity within every culture, so that each culture has its own integrity, which missionary work must respect. In the mid-1980s, responding to the desire of some indigenous catechists and lay missionaries for more intensive, formal training and to the local hierarchy's dream of forming an indigenous clergy, the Diocese of Riobamba established what is sometimes referred to as the "indigenous seminary," the Centro de Formación Indígena (CFI), Center for Indigenous Study and Training. This is a centerpiece of the project of constructing an "indigenous church," faithful to the universal Catholic Church but with its own liturgy, theology, and social role based on indigenous culture, and with indigenous people in leadership positions. Given that CFI study is easiest for those with some formal education and a degree of freedom from family responsibilities, CFI students and graduates tend to be fairly young—from their teens to around forty—and are mostly male. One young man from Tepeyac Bajo (a grandson of the last *fundadora*) studied in the CFI for three years. More important, local catechists frequently interact with CFI students and graduates from around the province in diocese-level meetings, and CFI graduates have come to Pangor for local meetings and celebrations. Through these contacts and other routes, Pangor Runa have participated in the development of new Catholic discourses and a revitalized sense of indigenous ethnicity and culture.

Changes in both land tenure and local religious life in what used to be Monjas Corral have thus been shaped by a complex interaction between indigenous villagers and the institutional church. Local historical experience has shaped villagers' perceptions of the ongoing relationship, even as new developments have reshaped villagers' understanding of their history. The next chapter takes up the role of *respeto* in contemporary Catholic practice and ethnic politics, exploring the ways old ideas and practices both inform the present and are reinterpreted and redeployed in new circumstances.

CHAPTER 9

Liberation Theology and Ethnic Resurgence

BRINGING RESPECT INTO LIBERATION THEOLOGY

The spirit of liberation theology pervaded the Good Friday ceremonies in Pangor in March 1991. Runa from various Catholic villages in the parish, mestizos from the parish center, and the Bolivian nun who lived in the town all gathered that morning in Guangopud, now, like Tepeyac Bajo, an autonomous community. After a ceremony inside the chapel, the celebrants walked outside in a procession reenacting the Stations of the Cross. At each Station, a man read aloud a commentary—provided by the nun—that connected the persecution of Jesus to historical and contemporary issues: the Spanish Conquest; human rights; the bleeding of Ecuador's economy through its foreign debt; recent attacks on the diocese for its commitment to the poor; and the struggles of indigenous peoples for land.

My only glimpse that day of how Holy Week was celebrated before Vatican II, liberation theology, and land reform was through an offhand joke. After the Stations of the Cross, the celebrants sat in clusters on the grass, waiting for lunch to be served by the host community. Sitting by me, Avelino Shagñay, the senior catechist of Tepeyac Bajo, pointed up to a man standing nearby and said with a smile that he would whip me for my sins. He went on to explain *pascuanchina*, the ritual whipping that instilled respect in hacienda times (Figure 21).

This chapter examines religious change, authority relations, and ethnic resurgence in Chimborazo through an analysis of the meanings of respect in recent years. Despite the abandonment or modification of some of the old rituals of respect, notions of respect continue to figure prominently in local talk about religion, ethnicity, authority, and change. In Chapter 8, I empha-

FIGURE 21.   *Avelino Shagñay*

sized how villagers responded to Catholic Church initiatives in the 1960s and later in complex ways shaped by their own agendas, views, and historical memories. Similarly, in this chapter I show how liberation theology has been reshaped in local interactions among pastoral agents and villagers. Although the Good Friday ceremonies in 1991 gave the impression of a radical disjunction between the old and the new ways of celebrating Holy Week, in fact, old notions of respect have been brought right into the fora created by liberation theology. In the process, Runa notions of respect and pastoral agents' practice of liberation theology have been transformed.

Beyond markedly religious contexts, the practices and meanings associated with *respeto* have also played an important role in indigenous ethnic politics, changing definitions of indigenous identity, and indigenous communities' political self-assertion. The relationship between Runa and nonindigenous institutions revolves in part around competing visions of "modernity." The changing meanings of respect will provide us with a good window on the ways modernity is locally promoted, resisted, and redefined.

REMEMBERING THE ELDERS, REDEFINING RESPECT

Avelino Shagñay's joking allusion to *pascuanchina* on Good Friday in 1991 expressed an ironic attitude toward the old respect complex rooted in his personal history, but it also revealed some of the issues that indigenous people confront as they recall the past and ponder the meanings of respect today. Despite Avelino's father's heavy investment in fiesta sponsorship, his mother died when he was a child, an event Tayta Avelino views as contradicting the idea that saints bestowed blessings on fiesta sponsors. His father migrated to the lowlands, leaving the boy to be reared by his grandparents on a Pangor hacienda. Redemptorist missionary priests seem to have recognized his quick intelligence and took him along on some of their visits to various haciendas. Looking back, and with some disdain for the elders and for their efforts to enforce respect, he compares his childhood religious knowledge to that of prominent elders:

> Those priests loved me, and I went around with them. . . . I learned quickly. . . . Those big elders, those . . . so-called overseer-wives, those grand bigmouths . . . they were just good for talking [criticizing others]. . . . When we didn't greet them quickly . . . they would greet us first, beating us to the punch, . . . and call us "insolent." But when they were asked about God, they didn't know where God lives, nothing. So during that old-style missionary visit, those priests . . . would come. All the Runa would kiss their hands and call them "God" [Tayta Amito]. (8/21/1991)

For Tayta Avelino, respect was based on illusion and was bound up with the Runa's ignorance and their humiliation by mestizos. He analyzed the authority structure in the hacienda era as a way that priests and landlords co-opted the brightest and most self-assertive indigenous people by placing them at the top of an ultimately vacuous prestige scale. In turn, these authorities taught other Runa to respect them and their overlords. In his retrospective account, at least, Tayta Avelino's religious knowledge allowed him to see through the elders' pompous façade.

This learning was the beginning of a lifelong thirst for religious under-standing. As an adult, Tayta Avelino learned to read and began to study the Bible, first with a Protestant missionary. Later, he associated himself with Catholic liberation theology, becoming one of the leading local catechists as well as a political leader in the 1980s and the 1990s. He continues to associate religious learning with challenging the social hierarchy: only when indigenous people understand God, the Bible, and Catholic doctrine and symbols will they be able to gain equality alongside nonindigenous people within the church and in the world at large. For Tayta Avelino, knowledge—especially of books and the Good Book—is power.

Avelino Shagñay sometimes acknowledges the importance of respect for elders, even while pointing out its limitations as a guiding central value. Most indigenous people in Pangor are less overtly critical of respect as a value than he is, although the term often arouses mixed feelings. Some even refer to the respect of the hacienda period with nostalgia. I now want to ex-plore the sources and uses of this nostalgia, the complex ways that contem-porary projects deploy memories of the past and rework notions of respect.

"WHO ARE OUR ELDERS?": CULTURAL IDENTITY AND CATHOLIC ACTIVISM

As a single young woman in 1990, Amelia Morocho was accustomed to wear-ing mestiza-style shawls and skirts, rather than the indigenous *bayeta* and *anaku* worn by her mother and most of the women of Tepeyac Bajo.[1] Her mother told me, as if it were the most natural connection, that Amelia had stopped wearing the *anaku* because she had learned to read. Yet, after Amelia married a young man in Tepeyac Bajo that same year and went to live with him in his parents' house, she went back to the *anaku*. Her in-laws might have otherwise interpreted her mestiza dress as a disrespectful assertion of superiority over her *anaku*-wearing mother-in-law.

Amelia's case illustrates the possibilities (and the temptations and pres-sures) for indigenous youth now to take on the symbols of mestizo identity. The situation also exemplifies one way that notions of respect for elders constrain young people to maintain an indigenous identity. Indigenous chil-dren in Pangor today attend primary school, something that was the exclu-sive prerogative of mestizos just a few decades ago. Adolescents and young married adults often work in the cities, sometimes for several years. As they perfect their Spanish in the cities, they are continuously exposed to a scale of values in which everything urban, mestizo, and "modern" is preferred over anything rural, "Indian," or "old-fashioned." They may encounter discrimination for the traces of their rural and indigenous background that they continue to display. When these migrants return to their villages to visit or live, they sometimes favor Spanish over Quichua and wear jackets and sunglasses instead of ponchos and hats, or skirts or slacks instead of *anakus*. Some young men and women have their hair curled. All of these choices are understood and often meant as a claim to having crossed over from an indigenous to a mestizo identity, or at least to having become less Indian and more modern and urban. As a display of preference that accords with the prevailing ethnic hierarchy, such a claim also implies superiority to villagers who continue to display the markers of indigenous identity. One of the most common complaints of indigenous villagers is that returned migrants fail to greet peers, and especially elders, respectfully, as if their ethnic self-transformation has canceled out the obligations of respect and deference they would have as indigenous youth.

In response to this phenomenon, indigenous villagers are engaged in a contemporary version of what Steve Stern calls a "struggle for solidarity" in colonial Peru (1983). They pressure each other, and especially those who might be wavering, to maintain their indigenous identity, to share in the common lot. In contrast to Stern's Hispanicized indigenous elite, who were tempted to convert a privileged position in the native hierarchy into greater power and wealth on Spanish colonial terms, today's primary school graduates and young migrants are not a particularly privileged group. Their peers and elders are asking them to accept a position of relatively low status and power within the village. Yet, it would be too simple to view the concern over youths' self-presentation and ethnic identification as merely an assertion of elders' power over their juniors. At stake, ultimately, is whether Runa, young and old, will be able to respect themselves and each other as Runa or only by becoming mestizos (Figures 22 and 23). At stake also is whether indigenous people can continue to use their identity as the basis for vigorous political self-assertion, as they did in the 1990s and are doing in the first years of the twenty-first century.

The defense of this historically stigmatized identity is often charged with ambivalence. Sometimes it takes the form of cutting down someone's pretensions while accepting or playing on a racist scale of prestige. Consider the case of a young woman, María Lema, who went to Quito as a teenager and returned to Tepeyac Bajo some eight or ten years later, in the late 1980s. In one of her first jobs in Quito as a servant, she said, her mistress obliged her to switch to "decent" mestiza dress. She got used to wearing skirts and continued to do so after her return to Tepeyac Bajo. Back in the village, however, she was criticized as foolish for displaying her dark Runa legs. These com-

FIGURE 22.   *Tepeyac Bajo youth*

ments did not cease until she went back to wearing the *anaku* (which covers more of the legs than the shorter mestiza skirts). This ridicule was based on the assumption that dark skin was ugly, and it did not keep her from recalling later, with a tinge of pride, that she had dressed like a mestiza during one period in her life. The criticism nonetheless succeeded in forcing her to re-identify herself through her dress as an indigenous woman.

In this context of ambivalent struggles over identity and respect, Catholic activist discussions have generated a rhetoric aimed at persuading people to continue displaying markers of indigenous identity. This rhetoric explicitly associates ethnic markers with respect for elders, building on the implicit everyday association exemplified by the case of Amelia Morocho. Catechists and other activists argue that respect for one's parents and grandparents demands maintaining the dress, language, and identity that they have passed down.

Beyond the defense of markers of ethnic identity, indigenous Catholic activists have helped diffuse a narrative that affirms the continuity of that identity over time and roots it in the pre-Columbian period. The participants in a 1994 diocese-level meeting asked themselves, "Who are our elders?" Their answers encompassed not only "our grandparents" but also the pre-Columbian peoples of Ecuador, such as the Puruhaes of Chimborazo. Even

under Spanish domination and the hacienda system, they affirm in their report, "We indigenous people preserved in hiding our culture, our religion,
our [way of] life" (*CFI 1994). In Pangor, at least, this explicit recognition of
descent from pre-Columbian peoples is something new.[2]

This narrative recodes much of the everyday culture of older generations
as a sign of ethnic identity and resistance. It posits a continuous history of
"five hundred years of indigenous resistance," to quote from a slogan popularized in the early 1960s, and thereby suggests that elders' beliefs and practices can inform contemporary struggles. Avelino Shagñay's song about Amo
Castillo, quoted at the end of Chapter 5, illustrates this. The song begins by
invoking the ancestors as the source of Runa knowledge about mountain

FIGURE 23. *Young couple, Tepeyac Bajo*

FIGURE 24.   *Village music group, the Ovejeros de Tepeyac Bajo (Shepherds of Tepeyac Bajo), in Pangor for a performance*

spirits and describes how cruel landowners pay for their sins. Written a year after the 1990 uprising while negotiations between indigenous leaders and the government dragged on, the song concludes by calling on contemporary *amos* to "treat the Runa with love" lest they suffer the same fate in the afterlife as the old landowners (Figure 24).

At the same time, this view of ancestral indigenous culture and identity allows Catholic activists to argue for maintaining certain indigenous customs and beliefs without endorsing wholesale a frozen vision of their culture exactly as practiced by their parents or grandparents, and even while arguing for changes. The concept of an indigenous culture maintained "in hiding" under domination implies the need to distinguish among what is authentically indigenous and should be conserved, what ancestral practices might need to be revived, and what is alien and historically imposed. For example, pastoral agents and indigenous activists often portray indigenous tradition as economically "communitarian." They urge communities to maintain communal land tenure where it exists, to continue or revive communal labor practices, and to initiate communal productive projects. Some indigenous activists have been collecting accounts of local "sacred places," recognizing that, although these places have often been Christianized through apparition stories, they also fit into a long-standing Andean religious topography.

On the other hand, activists in the early 1990s commonly dismissed patron saint images and fiesta sponsorship as having been imposed by priests,
mestizo townspeople, and landowners. This interpretation has been recon-
sidered in the course of the 1990s and the early 2000s, with activists increasingly recognizing that, despite the exploitative and imposed aspects of
fiestas, festive reciprocity and redistribution are old Andean practices. Still,
where elders and juniors remain at odds over fiesta sponsorship, the narrative of domination and clandestine cultural resistance allows activists to remain true to "our elders" while rejecting the means by which their parents
or grandparents gained respect and showed respect for their elders.

This situation puts the current generation of elders in a highly ambiguous
position. On the one hand, the Catholic activist discourse construes these
elders as links to an authentic indigenous past whose experience, knowledge, and guidance should be valued. On the other hand, this discourse conditions the elders' authority on the cultural authenticity of their beliefs and
practices, as assessed by the Catholic activists, their juniors. Elders' status,
traditionally based on their service to the saints, is thereby demoted implicitly in favor of ancient Puruhá ancestors. Of course, elders do not uniformly accept this. As a result, "respect" has become a term of contention,
a value that people appeal to equally to protest or to defend recent changes.[3]

Older religious traditionalists can take some comfort in the fact that both
pastoral agents and indigenous Catholic activists also construe respect for
indigenous elders as entailing loyalty to Catholicism. Given that Catholicism was imposed on indigenous Andeans, this view may seem paradoxi-
cal. Such an interpretation of respect must be understood in the context
of intense competition between Catholicism and evangelical Protestantism.
While redefining and reinforcing indigenous identity in its own way, evangelical Protestantism demands a sharp break with the past as a time of ignorance, idolatry, drunkenness, and degradation. It also rejects a broad range of
popular beliefs and practices from folk medicine to the customary burning
of household sweepings and old grains at Pentecost. Father Carlos, the mestizo priest in charge of Pangor and of programming for indigenous people (the
Pastoral Indígena) in the diocese, made the counterargument at a course for
Pangor catechists in 1992. It is true, he conceded, that the elders had some
faults, but that does not justify rejecting them and their cultural inheritance
wholesale: "They taught a very beautiful respect; they were good workers;
they taught beautiful customs. . . . Nonetheless, we cast blame, saying that
they were drunks . . . [and] did bad things. . . . But not for one or two sins
should we forget them. We have to remember our fathers and mothers, we
have to love them, we have to learn about them."[4]

Father Carlos said that "the forefathers and indigenous culture" were the first foundation stone of the Pastoral Indígena. In other contexts, especially Holy Week celebrations, he sometimes invites villagers to ask for instruction and blessings from their elders and leads the way by kneeling before an elderly indigenous man or woman. He thus uses ritual language adapted from *pascuanchina* to endorse indigenous respect for elders and to display his own (and, by implication, the Catholic Church's) respect for indigenous culture.

Priests such as Father Carlos and indigenous Catholic activists have also revived a classic missionary and Andean Catholic view that Catholicism parallels precolonial Andean religious traditions in important ways. The modern theology of inculturation leads them to expect such parallels. For example, Inca names of deities are interpreted to correspond to the Catholic Trinity. Father Carlos construes Andean mountain spirits as intermediaries between indigenous believers and God, much like saints in orthodox Catholicism. Thus, instead of opposing each other, Catholicism and the culture of indigenous ancestors can validate each other (see Klaiber 1992; S. MacCormack 1985).

Villagers' conceptions of elders show continuities as well as changes. In the hacienda period, indigenous elders were part of a hierarchy of respect that extended up the ethnic-racial ladder, and, in the context of ritual discipline, mestizos could also be viewed as elders. Villagers today still sometimes kneel before a mestizo priest or bishop to request his blessing and seem to view it as especially efficacious—a hierarchy of respect spanning the ethnic boundary is not altogether gone. It is a source of frustration to indigenous catechists and lay ministers that many villagers still consider their religious authority secondary and minor compared to that of the mestizo priests. In contrast and in response to such attitudes, current Catholic activist rhetoric at once extends the conception of "the elders" back in time to pre-Columbian ancestors and ethnically circumscribes it: the sources of wisdom, of moral examples to be emulated, are "our" indigenous elders, "our ancestors." The next section examines how, along with this changing notion of respect for indigenous elders, contemporary indigenous political rhetoric is reworking the notion of respect between indigenous people and mestizos into a demand for reciprocal respect.

REBUILDING COMMUNAL AUTHORITY: INDIGENOUS LAW

Indigenous political structures throughout highland Latin America have historically been shaped through interaction with the state, and much of what is now seen as indigenous tradition is partly a product of colonial or republican legislation. The formal community structures of contemporary Ecuador derive from legislation such as the 1937 Ley de Comunas and are subject to government oversight. Yet, indigenous people have used these community structures as well as parish and higher-level federations built on them to press for their own goals. Communes and cooperatives have served as important tools in indigenous land struggles in Ecuador. Tanya Korovkin (1993) has argued that contemporary indigenous ethnic politics in Chimborazo can be interpreted as a movement by communities and federations to gain control over local development policies in order to challenge capitalist models. Community and federation assemblies and leaders were instrumental in mobilizing the mass protests of June 1990, dubbed the Levantamiento Nacional Indígena (National Indigenous Uprising), which signaled the emergence of indigenous people collectively as a strong political force (Zamosc 1994). The communities have mobilized again in similar protests several times since 1990. Indigenous communities have thus been the building blocks of the contemporary indigenous political movement.

Communities and community federations have been seeking to strengthen their role in resolving conflicts and punishing offenses to the point of contesting the monopoly of law enforcement by the state (or by other organs of the state not under indigenous control). This effort encompasses two aspects of conflict resolution. The first concerns conflicts within the community: like hacienda authorities, community assemblies and leaders sometimes take a role in handling domestic quarrels, disputes between neighbors, alleged theft, accusations of witchcraft, and other kinds of disorder. The second aspect concerns offenses committed by outsiders within community boundaries against community members. Animal rustling is a particularly volatile issue. At least since the late 1980s, one hears and reads in Ecuadorian newspapers of highland indigenous communities or parish-level federations detaining, investigating, and punishing alleged rustlers. This practice, too, has precedents in the hacienda period, when landowners sometimes acted as a law unto themselves in conflicts with outsiders that involved their property or resident laborers.

The communal pastures, periodic communal labor, suspicion of outsiders, and occasional communal justice that characterize many indigenous communities all contribute to a perception among mestizo peasants and others that indigenous communities are united and strong. Yet indigenous villagers in communities like Tepeyac Bajo frequently lament their divisions and their own lack of respect for the authority of the community assembly or president. They compare their contemporary internal politics less with mestizo peasant communities or urban neighborhoods than with the authority of the hacienda. By that comparison, contemporary communal authorities are indeed handicapped in maintaining order and enforcing their decisions.

Individual landownership and a worsening ratio of residents to land have created sometimes bitter conflicts over boundaries and inheritances. Analogous conflicts over usufruct plots sometimes occurred on the hacienda, but the local landlord was the ultimate authority for resolving them. In contrast, legal authority for resolving conflicts over private property today is located outside community boundaries. More fundamentally, with the land subdivided under private ownership, no one is beholden to the community for his or her livelihood. Community presidents are not also supervisors of everyday work, as most of the hacienda elders were. They have no special religious authority, either, as did *fundadores* and *regidores.*

Nor do indigenous community authorities wield the strong influence over the state that the landlords could use to support their authority. The landlords could "demand" that the parties to a conflict respect the resolutions devised on the hacienda, as Agustín Paca recalled in his comments (cited below). Community presidents, in contrast, can do little to prevent a dissatisfied party from taking his or her case to the government-appointed *teniente político* (the civil parish authority) in Pangor or other authorities in town. A community leader who tried to interfere with this process would risk legal troubles of his own. The risks are even greater when communities attempt to impose a settlement or punishment on outsiders, such as suspected rustlers. Thus, while the community has occupied part of the local political and legal space vacated by the hacienda, the state has also expanded into that space and strengthened its role in rural areas.

One of the consequences is increased litigiousness and litigation costs. Yet, few Ecuadorians of modest means, indigenous or mestizo, believe that the legal system is impartial. Judges are said to be swayed by personal connections and bribery. Lawyers for opposing sides are rumored to conspire with each other and with judges, dragging out cases to extract more in fees and bribes. Almost everyone seems to know of instances of criminals who were caught in the act but quickly bought their way out of prison. Cultural and ethnic factors add another twist to the alienation of indigenous people, who generally have little or no formal education but must deal with an urban legal system based on written documents in Spanish and run by mestizos.

In this context, the memory of moral discipline administered by hacienda bosses and indigenous elders offers a model for strengthening the contemporary indigenous community and its disciplinary authority. A conversation I had with Agustín Paca illustrates this point. Born in the 1940s, Tayta Agustín grew up on one of the neighboring Pangor haciendas and married a woman from Monjas Corral. He was telling me about the arbitrary violence associated with the hacienda and commented, "It's good that we're free now of the *amos*." He elaborated on the various forms of violence the *amos* employed. "On the other hand," though, now "there is a need for those lords to give a good moral example like in the old life, to instill respect." Within the community, he said, "there is a bit of disrespect"; villagers "don't heed each other."

In recent years, Tayta Agustín has been embroiled in a conflict over land with his wife's half brothers. He believes one of them hired a shaman to make him ill. Although these problems were presented at various points to the community assembly and the authorities in Pangor, the matter dragged on without resolution for several years.

"If the old-time lords were around," Tayta Agustín said, "there would be some settlement. . . . There wouldn't be legal battles." Villagers would not have to recur to public authorities in town to resolve disputes. He recalled how the *amos* handled quarrels between spouses or neighbors. If community authorities today were to follow the same model, he said, they would give wrongdoers a lashing and "lock them up in the community house" for twenty-four hours. That would serve to maintain "good respect" in the village, because "everybody would have some fear." Unfortunately, though, community presidents "don't have that authority. . . . With these community presidents it's just verbal, just talk . . . , and they don't pay attention now. . . . They don't even have just a little bit of respect. . . . That's why those lords are a bit missed now." Tayta Agustín's recollection of the past is typical of the older generation's in its ambivalence, at once sharply critical of the hacienda's excessive violence yet nostalgic for its moral order.

While community authorities do not routinely apply physical punishment, as Tayta Agustín laments, the memory of hacienda discipline and the desire for enhanced community authority constitute a powerful social force. Several of the communities around Tepeyac Bajo joined to physically punish the man Tayta Agustín thought had had him bewitched after several others also implicated this man in witchcraft and animal theft. Some of the punishments applied in such cases—whipping or forced immersion in cold water— recall common hacienda punishments.

At the same time, the memory of arbitrary and excessive violence on the hacienda creates fertile ground for a "human rights" discourse drawing on the Ecuadorian Constitution. Lawyers and others who worked with villagers during the agrarian struggles, radio stations, the Catholic Church, and various other organizations have all helped diffuse this discourse in the countryside. Villagers and others sometimes invoke human rights to argue that punishments should be regulated and moderate.

While Agustín Paca's comments centered on the memory of hacienda discipline and the lash, he also suggested that wrongdoers should be locked up. This form of punishment was not used by haciendas in the Pangor area, to my knowledge, but is employed by the *teniente político* in Pangor. Monetary fines may be the most frequent and broadly accepted form of internal discipline in indigenous communities. Community authorities sometimes inscribe dispute settlements in the official record of community resolutions (Libros de Actas), in which each party commits to paying a large fine if found to have repeated the offense or renewed the quarrel. This practice, too, is probably borrowed from the *tenencia política*, whose archive contains similar documents from the 1950s. The use of fines to replace the lash evidences increased unease with physical punishment. Young and middle-aged parents likewise report using less physical punishment in child rearing.[5]

Another significant development is that punishments are apparently becoming increasingly divorced from their former religious significance. While villagers do sometimes call on catechists to help resolve domestic quarrels and give moral instruction, catechists do not apply physical punishments. They learn in church courses that they represent a loving, liberating God who addresses his Word directly to the individual conscience (*conciencia*) and respects human liberty—not the God of the hacienda era, who routinely used punishment to remind people of their obligations. Moreover, catechists are not usually viewed as elders who might give a lashing as God's deputies. Villagers say, "There are no elders anymore," meaning that there are no *regidores* or *fundadores*, no one with the authority to administer punishment as sacrament. Fines for wrongdoing and even imprisonment avoid subjecting the offender personally to another individual, thereby reflecting an increasingly democratic, secular view of communal authority. These choices also show that the community models its judicial practices after those of secular civil authority as well as the hacienda. Further investigation is needed to determine the extent to which the lash, when used, continues to be infused with religious symbolism.

While the memory of the hacienda and the model of local civil authority both influence community practices, in Catholic activist and ethnic-political ideology, the indigenous community is a prime expression of indigenous culture and identity. The last section showed how the new narrative of identity and a historically expanded, ethnically circumscribed notion of "our elders" provide a charter for redefining and authenticating aspects of the remembered past as "indigenous" culture. Admonishments and punishments by elders or communal authorities fit into this narrative as "indigenous law." At the 1994 meeting of indigenous Catholic activists, participants were first asked to discuss in groups the social organization, laws, economy, religion, politics, and culture of "our elders." The report documents these responses:

> Before the conquest, our peoples had their own form of organization. . . .
> They admonished the young people and helped in marriage . . .
>
> They had a general governor, *regidor*, alcalde, *rezachidores*. They
> were the authority in our communities. . . . They had their own laws
> to obey, so that things were controlled . . . , and so there was respect
> among all. . . . The elders admonished and punished for one's own
> good. . . .

Under the heading, "Ourselves and Our Children," the report cites these comments:

> The mestizos have filled our heads with ideas that are not our own. We
> do not have our own laws, made with our own ideas and thoughts.
>
> Yes, we do have laws; the problem is that we are not taking them
> into account.
>
> What are our laws?
>
> When they catch a thief, they punish him, putting him in jail, they
> make him "bathe," and they whip him and strike him with nettles so
> that he doesn't do it again. . . .
>
> If a married couple in the community is not getting along, they give
> them a lashing. They also make a written resolution, and they punish
> them with a fine.
>
> Our law is oral, but it is obeyed. The elders don't let the young people
> learn bad habits, for example, they don't like them to get drunk. . . .
>
> To punish, the community gets organized; they bring a tank of water,
> nettles . . . to punish them severely, and the elders admonish them. (*CFI
> 1994:7–9)

Again, participants contrasted mestizo ideas and indigenous law. Elders play a prominent role in indigenous law. In discussing the future, the participants similarly called for "taking into account our elders, continuing to value the laws, the admonishments; this way we will be able to live . . . the way they lived" (*CFI 1994:16).

The detention of a suspected animal rustler in the Pangor area in 1992 provides a dramatic example of the role of indigenous law in local practice. A moderately wealthy mestizo who had become notorious in other parts of the province for allegedly stealing cattle and mistreating his indigenous neighbors had bought some land at the top of the Pangor basin. Following a series of animal thefts in various local communities, most of the communities in the area united to detain him. They seemed to have strong evidence implicating him in the rustling. As the condition for his release, the indigenous leaders demanded that he agree to leave the area, that his land (allegedly used for embarking stolen cattle) be turned over to the communities, and that the cattle found on his land be used to compensate those whose cattle had been stolen. Several weeks of fruitless negotiations with the man's family and government officials followed. One Pangor leader was captured in town and charged with kidnapping. Under the threat of army intervention, the Pangor villagers finally turned the suspected rustler over to the government authorities. From their point of view, their distrust of mestizo justice was confirmed when the man was released after a brief detention while their own leader was imprisoned for two years.

It is clearly difficult for indigenous communities to assert extralegal authority over powerful outsiders. Parish-level federations in some areas in Chimborazo, however, have reportedly been successful in eliminating animal rustling by imposing their own punishments.[6]

I cannot assess this case from a legal standpoint here or explore the difficult practical and moral dilemmas that those involved found themselves caught in. What is relevant is the prominence of "indigenous law" in local discussions of the conflict. Just as Runa have had to respect *mishus* and their law (that of the state), so, too, villagers argue, the *mishus* must respect indigenous law in this issue vital to local indigenous livelihood. A broad and politically complex coalition of indigenous communities and leaders—some Catholic, some Protestant, some affiliated with leftist political parties, some associated with rival community federations, and from different parts of the Pangor valley and even beyond the parish boundaries—could all unite under this banner, at least temporarily.

To argue that contemporary notions of indigenous law are a recent construction is not to suggest that they are inauthentic. Catholic activists and ethnic militants are by no means mistaken in seeing continuities with old, even precolonial, Andean traditions. If their public discourse tends to obscure the role of nonindigenous others in reshaping "indigenous law," that is no more selective than most public historical memory. If indigenous people choose to define certain practices they have long participated in as "indigenous," then those practices become indigenous (Jackson 1995:19–20).

At the same time, the sort of historical analysis engaged in here can serve a useful critical function. Some journalists and people associated with the official legal system view cases like the detention of the suspected rustler in

Pangor as the expression of an atavistic mentality of primitives who simply do not understand that a modern state requires citizens to give up private justice and subject themselves to the universal rule of law. Yet, most of those involved in the Pangor case would like nothing better than for the state to live up to its claim of representing the rule of law. They will no doubt continue to see a legitimate role for local community authority in conflict resolution, and their perspective on the operation of the official law will continue to be shaped by the particulars of their historical experience and culture. But had they had a reasonable degree of confidence that their accusation against the suspected rustler would be processed efficiently and impartially through the official legal system, with appropriate punishment if sustained, they probably would never have undertaken the burdens and risks of detaining the man themselves. The concept of indigenous law expresses long-standing Andean sensibilities, but it also arises from an ongoing relationship with nonindigenous others and is therefore responsive to changes in that relationship. It is not simply a fixed or mindless tradition.

INTERPRETING THE BIBLE:
THE MIXED BLESSINGS OF LITERACY

I turn now to the continuing significance of respect within the contemporary religious arena and specifically in relation to the Bible. The Catholic Church since Vatican II has encouraged lay Catholics to read the Bible. Among Catholics in Chimborazo, the liberation theology movement has promoted a new religious activity called Reflexión de la Palabra de Dios (Reflection on the Word of God). It begins with someone reading aloud a Bible passage, either the passage of the day according to the Catholic liturgical calendar or one selected by the pastoral agent or person leading the meeting. Usually the passage is read first in Spanish. If someone has a Bible in Quichua (as is increasingly common), it is then read in Quichua as well. Generally, the reader is a catechist or other literate male villager who takes off his hat (as do the listeners) and stands while reading. He concludes with the phrase, "That is the Word of God." The leader then invites other participants to reflect on the passage and apply it to reality—to interpret it and draw out the lessons it suggests for their lives and the broader society. At the end, the leader often summarizes and expands on others' comments.

It has become standard practice to include reflection as a part of the Mass, at the opening of meetings of Catholic religious activists, and at the beginning of meetings of organizations such as the Directiva Central in Pangor, a parish-wide federation of communities formed under church guidance.

Catholic pastoral agents also encourage (and sometimes pressure) indigenous communities to engage regularly in reflection during their community assemblies or lunch breaks from communal labor. Reflection is likewise a central part of *misiones,* in which pastoral agents and lay activists (mestizo and indigenous) go as individuals or in small teams to communities for several days to visit families, participate in communal activities, and hold daily religious meetings.

Liberation theology views the Bible as a message of liberation addressed, above all, to the poor and oppressed, who therefore possess special interpretive authority. The Word of God is an active force that helps the oppressed understand oppression as a consequence of sinful social structures and moves them to act as historical subjects to transform the world in accordance with God's plan. As an expression of this vision, Reflection on the Word of God parallels similar activities practiced in the ecclesial base communities that the liberation theology movement has created elsewhere in Latin America.

The commentaries that indigenous participants make during reflection often express ideas that liberation theology anywhere in Latin America would recognize as its own. For example, in the Corpus Christi Mass in Pangor in 1992, the reflection was based on I Corinthians 11:23–26, in which Jesus instructs his disciples to eat the Eucharistic bread and drink wine "in memory of me." Asked by the pastoral agent leading the reflection for what purpose Jesus wants to remain with us through the Eucharist, one catechist responded: "[So that we continue] searching for justice, for love, . . . as brothers, indigenous people and mestizos, as Jesus taught us . . . demanding justice and equality." Exposure to the Bible and the guidance of liberation theology–oriented pastoral agents in interpreting it certainly helped shape the political consciousness of many indigenous Catholics who have asserted their demands for justice and equality since the 1970s.

Yet, indigenous interpretations of the Bible are more complex and varied than simply an expression of liberation theology. Contemporary theologians and pastoral agents themselves speak of the need for the Gospel, the Catholic Church, and pastoral agents to be inculturated—to assume the specific culture of each group being evangelized, even as the Son of God took on a particular cultural identity in incarnating himself as a Jew. They expect God's Word to express itself differently in each culture, without compromising the essential truths. In practice, tensions naturally arise among mestizo pastoral agents and indigenous Catholic activists over different understandings of inculturation. But some pastoral agents encourage indigenous people to value at least some of their elders' customs. Pastoral agents sometimes guide reflection toward this message. Therefore, it is not surprising that traditional notions of respect inherited from the hacienda period inform contemporary indigenous views and interpretations of the Bible.

Older villagers often refer to reflection as the *doctrina*. The fundamental purpose and effect of the *doctrina*, as older people remember it today, was to inculcate respect. To call reflection *doctrina* is to imply that it has (or should have) the same purpose and effect. If asked to assess either one, older people are likely to say, "It's for our own good," just as they say about other forms of instruction and discipline by which people learn proper behavior. From this perspective, what has happened in the shift from *doctrina* on the hacienda to reflection is that, while ritual punishments have disappeared, the Bible has replaced them as a means of reinforcing respect.

For a week in December 1989, villagers met each day in the Tepeyac Bajo chapel for a *misión* led by a longtime lay missionary, an indigenous man from another part of the province. The theme for one day was, "How should we educate our children?" The missionary divided the participants into groups of five or so and had each group read and comment on Luke 2:41–52. In this passage, twelve-year-old Jesus, having accompanied his parents to Jerusalem for the Passover festivities, stays behind without their knowledge. When his parents find him three days later in the temple, he asks, "Why did you look for me? Don't you know that I must be with my Father?"

A semiofficial Catholic interpretation of this passage is found at the foot of the page in the Spanish-language Bible distributed through the Catholic Church in Ecuador and used in meetings such as this one. This edition was translated in Chile in 1972, and the commentary was written in the post–Vatican II spirit with strong echoes of liberation theology. According to the commentators, this incident was "Jesus' first demonstration of independence," a radical declaration of liberty for which he "did not feel guilty":

> After this, he would continue obeying [his human parents], but he
> had shown them that he knew very well who he was, and that he was
> capable of any . . . breach in order to serve his Father in the manner that
> seemed good to him. In reading this text, it is appropriate to reflect on
> the respect that parents must have for their children's path [*vocación*,
> or calling] and the effort that parents must make to understand them
> when they begin to be independent. Instead of speaking of the lost child,
> it would be more accurate to say that the adolescent Jesus has found
> himself. (RICCIARDI AND HURAULT 1989:NEW TESTAMENT 100–101n)

In this analysis, Jesus' behavior is not simply an indication of his exceptional, divine nature but a model for the adolescent search for self and need for independence. Like Jesus, every adolescent has received some sort of calling from God. Parents must therefore respect their children's attempts to discover and follow their own calling.

In contrast to this individualistic and antiauthoritarian interpretation, villagers' comments in the meeting in Tepeyac Bajo stressed the importance of parental guidance and punishment in shaping children into good people:

> "Why have you done this?" Jesus' mother said—these things that you should not have done. He was a bit disobedient to his mother.
>
> When a child goes to a fiesta he has to go home with his parents, not stay behind playing. We have to instruct them not to do that, not to misbehave and do whatever they want.
>
> When a child is insolent, we must punish him, and when he is big, we must . . . teach [him] the Word of God, put him in school, and teach him not to be insolent.

According to this view, not even Jesus—whatever his sense of his divine mission—was exempt from the duty of obedience to and respect for his parents. Parents' task is to instill respect. The last comment implies that "the Word of God" can help in teaching children "not to be insolent." The Word of God is coupled with "school," suggesting that the speaker sees not only the Bible but also education in the written word more generally as reinforcing respect.

Yet even while indigenous people call the Bible into the service of reinforcing respect, the relationship between the written word and the traditional respect complex is profoundly ambivalent. Priests were among those who traditionally imparted moral instruction, purification, and discipline. Their authority was associated with their command of esoteric sacred knowledge, knowledge now symbolized by the Bible. Indigenous Catholics sometimes say of their new access to the Bible that priests have begun to let them in on knowledge that they formerly kept to themselves. In this sense, Bible reflection represents a democratization of moral authority in relation to ethnic and ecclesiastic hierarchies, as liberation theologians envision. In reading a message of respect from the Bible, indigenous interpreters are assuming a role formerly reserved for priests. Still, for many or most indigenous people, obstacles of language and illiteracy make it difficult to gain a sense of mastery of the Bible. For this reason, the demand that they interpret the Bible seems to leave some feeling more intimidated than empowered (see also Burdick 1993:75–80).[7]

From another angle, it is instructive to compare the authority associated with the Bible with the authority of religious elders. Elders instilled respect in their juniors through interpersonal transactions, as in *pascuanchina,* and their authority was tied to personal histories. It was based on their accumulated personal experience, their comportment, their service as *funda-dores*, *regidores*, or *priostes* to saints, God, and the community, their success in agriculture, and their kinship or godparent relationships with specific juniors.

The Bible, like the written word generally, offers a very different kind of authority. Like other modern forms of authority, command of the written word is formally independent of personal histories and relationships. Even schooling is not a necessary part of literate catechists' personal histories; some older catechists have learned to read through other means. What matters is that they possess the skill, not the social relations through which they acquired it.

Catechists are not elders but experts. Their authority is based on knowledge accessible, in principle, to all, cultivated through institutional training (church courses and meetings), rather than on personal relationships, life experience, or signs of divine grace. In the hacienda era, only the weak authority of the *rezachidores*, based on memorizing standard prayer formulas, was somewhat similar. Shamanic healers (*yachakkuna*, or "knowers") deal in specialized knowledge but are not experts in the same sense. A person is selected for a shamanic career by God, saints, or mountain spirits, who initially appear to him during a grave illness, after striking him with lightning, or in a dream. What training the shaman receives is through personal apprenticeship to another shaman, and he will continue to rely on personal relationships with mountain spirits or saints in healing.[8]

A career of religious service in the old fiesta system depended on, intensified, and displayed *fundadores'* and sponsors' engagement in local webs of reciprocity. The subjects of such a career were a couple, wife as well as husband, who both called on their social networks for aid and gained prestige from their religious service. The career of a catechist, in contrast, takes the catechist outside the community, and sometimes the parish, for church courses and meetings with other catechists and pastoral agents. The catechist's authority rests in part on the knowledge he brings back from this training. The catechist is an individual rather than a couple, and indigenous catechists are usually male and sometimes unmarried (males are more likely to be literate, enjoy more freedom of movement outside the house and the community, and wield a stronger voice in community meetings). If a spouse is said to "support" the catechist, it is in the limited sense that she does not complain about his travels or the time and money required. Similarly, the community may support the catechist by granting him leave from communal labor obligations and perhaps contributing toward his travel expenses. Little else is required of the catechist's local social network.

The subversive nature of the authority of the written word vis-à-vis intergenerational hierarchy can be appreciated on noting that primary schools only began to be built on former haciendas in the 1960s, and most of those born before the middle to late 1950s cannot read. It is, above all, those born since the 1960s who are potentially empowered by access to the Bible. Use of the Bible to reinforce respect is thus fraught with ambivalence and contradiction. Although Bible passages can be interpreted as lessons in the need for respect, reliance on the Bible is possible only because youths now have access to forms of knowledge denied their elders, and youths' knowledge can undermine their respect for their elders' wisdom.

In a broader sense, Bible reflection can be seen as part of the postconciliar church's project of constructing a new kind of religious subject, one strongly guided by *conciencia* (conscience or consciousness), where faith, respect, and ritual participation used to be sufficient. The requirement that people wishing to receive one of the life-cycle sacraments for themselves or their children first take a preparatory course with a catechist represents a demand that lay Catholics gain an explicit understanding of the doctrine and symbolism involved in the sacrament. According to orthodox views that older Pangor Runa seem to have largely accepted, sacraments effectively brought God's grace and blessings down upon those who received them, cleansing the baptized baby of original sin and turning him or her into a Christian or helping the married couple live a healthy and harmonious life together. When catechists and priests explain the sacraments now, they do not give much emphasis to their automatic efficacy. Instead, they stress that the sacrament expresses a commitment to a code of behavior. For example, parents should rear the baptized baby as a good Catholic and teach the child through example to act according to the baptismal formula as "priest, prophet, and king"—with a special accent on the prophetic struggle for justice. The preparatory course aims to ensure such a conscious commitment. In diocese meetings, pastoral agents and catechists lament the prevalence of "social" motivations for undertaking the sacraments: family obligations; village social pressures; shame; or the desire for *compadrazgo*. They contrast these motivations with what they consider more authentic religious motivations such as "mature faith" and conscious commitment.

As a replacement for *doctrina*, Bible reflection is relatively individualistic in a similar way. Whereas attendance at *doctrina* was obligatory, attendance at reflection meetings depends on each person's *conciencia*. Older villagers sometimes remark on this contrast uneasily as another factor in the decline of respect. A central part of *doctrina* was the collective rote recitation of prayers, a form of respect for God that helped secure his blessings, whereas reflection calls on each participant to struggle for an intellectual understanding of the message contained in God's Word. In *doctrina*, elders instilled respect through moral instruction and ritual punishment, but reflection was designed in part as a tool of *concientización* (consciousness-raising). *Conciencia* cannot, in principle, be transmitted from elder to junior, as respect can.

Both the use of the Bible and the associated ambivalence could be seen in another *misión* in Tepeyac Bajo led by two nuns in August 1991. In the opening meeting, villagers expressed their hope that the *misión* would address what they referred to as the lack of respect today. They cited the need to bolster the authority and unity of the community and, more broadly, the need for "education" (*educación*) among community members, meaning moral instruction and respectful behavior. One speaker assessed the state of the "organization," that is, the community as a formal entity with political and economic functions: "In our organization we are disunited. . . . We don't heed anything, as if we were deaf. . . . Because we don't have respect among ourselves, we do not move forward."[9]

In response to these concerns, the nuns chose for the first reflection session I Corinthians 12:12–21, 27, in which the Christian community is described as the body of Christ, all of whose members must work together for the body to function. A middle-aged catechist from a neighboring community alluded to a recent quarrel between two Tepeyac Bajo men in his comment: "Each person is important and merits respect and consideration; so let's not speak those [swear] words. The community is a body. . . . When such words are spoken, and . . . there is drinking, it leads to fights. Even when the parents do not know how to read and write, the children know, and they must take the Word of God and correct their parents." This literate catechist's image of children admonishing their quarrelsome, illiterate parents, Bible in hand, illustrates the perceived power of the Bible to teach respectful behavior and, at the same time, to subvert the generational hierarchy traditionally associated with respect.

A comment made in a later reflection on Ephesians 6:1–4 during the same *misión* provides an interesting contrast. The passage calls on children to obey their parents and on parents to "educate [your children] using the admonitions and warnings that the Lord may inspire" (Ricciardi and Hurault 1989:New Testament 372): "From the time our children are little, we have to teach them . . . to greet, to be educated [well-behaved]. Not just hand them the Bible and say, 'Read it yourself.' . . . We must teach them." This speaker chose to underscore the insufficiency of the Bible in inculcating good behavior independently of parental guidance.

Other comments on the same passage linked respect for parents to the preservation of indigenous customs and ethnic markers. Tayta Avelino, for example, argued that rejecting traditional practices like weaving and grinding grain by hand with stones "is a way of not heeding what our parents have taught us." He criticized youth who change from indigenous dress to mestizo styles and curl their hair and lamented the failure of modern education to teach *educación* in the traditional sense of "proper behavior": "In the old days, they gave a good whipping, they punished people. Now, we put our trust in the school, that it will educate the children, but that is not true; it only teaches letters, but not education." This ironic play on the ambiguity of the word *educación* is commonplace among the older generation. Probably no one would openly, explicitly place the written Word of God in the same category as "letters" and contrast it to moral "education"—certainly not Tayta Avelino, a catechist who leans on the Bible for support in preparing villagers for marriage or their children's baptisms. But Tayta Avelino is selective in his defense of the elders' "customs." In other contexts, he appealed to the Bible in rejecting some aspects of saints' feasts, for example. The Bible occupies an ambiguous category of its own, more broadly assumed to bear a message of respect than are secular "letters" yet also potentially subversive of respect.

One option for indigenous communities and elders faced with this contradiction is to accede formally or opportunistically to pastoral agents' pressures to engage in reflection while devaluing it and the authority associated with it. Communities tend periodically to revive the practice of holding weekly reflections, either in the genuine enthusiasm sometimes generated by a *misión* or when a community has a special interest in gaining pastoral agents' goodwill—only to let it lapse after some weeks or months. When a church-sponsored meeting is held in a community, it seems to be common for nonattendees—especially among the older generation—to comment dismissively, "They're not going to give anything to eat."[10] On one level, this could be interpreted simply as a statement that one's time is better spent attending to one's crops and animals. The comment might also be interpreted as pointing to a contrast with the fiesta, its associations with feasting and agricultural fertility, and the edifice of authority built on it. It is as though nonattendees refuse to contemplate that religious authority could be generated outside of the sort of exchange cycles associated with the fiesta.

In reality, the authority of catechists is often rather weak. They persistently complain that other villagers do not respect and support them. Couples wishing to marry or baptize a child find ways to circumvent the catechists' authority as gatekeepers to the sacraments. Community presidents do not allow time for reflection in community assemblies. Communities refuse to grant catechists leave to attend church courses and meetings on communal workdays. Again, these patterns can be interpreted as resistance to the growth within the community of religious authority based on mastery of the written Word.[11]

Some participants in reflection subvert the power of the written Word in more subtle, perhaps unconscious, ways. Alberto Yumbo, the son of a *regidor* and *fundador* of Guangopud, married into Monjas Corral, sponsored the fiesta of Saint Rose, and acceded to the requests of other laborers to serve as godfather for their children's baptisms. His son and son-in-law are both catechists in other Pangor villages. Tayta Alberto is a pious man who speaks of priests and nuns with great respect. Earlier, I cited his comments about the respect that reigned when he was a young man and his dismay at the lack of respect among youth today.

Tayta Alberto regularly attends church-sponsored meetings, and he speaks up in the reflections. His contributions are consistent, regardless of the content of the passage being discussed. He may draw a tenuous connection to the specific passage at the outset, but he often leaves it far behind. He reiterates the importance of respect for God and among people, the need to devote oneself to agriculture with faith that God will provide, the need for people to greet each other properly, to avoid ugly speech and quarrels, and to cooperate with each other in the community.

Tayta Alberto's rhetoric in reflection does not simply duplicate what the elders might have said in *doctrina* on the hacienda. Its nuances reflect his own current preoccupations and current issues in the community. Yet, the similarity to *doctrina* goes beyond the message of respect. In *doctrina*, the oral recitation of formulaic prayers lent a sacred frame to moral instruction, itself understood as the expression of the elders' life experience, not as exegesis of the prayers. Tayta Alberto seems to use the oral reading of Bible passages similarly as a frame for moral instruction, without letting the passage determine or restrict his message. Like others, he ends by saying, "That is what I have understood," indicating his recognition that reflection is ostensibly interpretation of the Bible and invoking the authority of the passage. But the substance of his reflections constructs that authority as one of sacred frame, not as the fount of wisdom. Given that reflection, in any event, calls on participants to draw both on the reading and on personal experience in formulating their comments, Tayta Alberto's comments might be taken as a limiting case in which convictions associated with a lifetime of experience almost completely overshadow the particulars of the reading.

That these ways of responding to the Bible speak to current conflicts within the community—albeit usually in a generalized, somewhat oblique manner—is confirmed by the tensions that occasionally become manifest. In one *misión*, some young men finally expressed resentment at the repeated comments by their elders on the younger generation's lack of respect. The young men had also had to listen to criticism directed at some of their peers who played volleyball outside rather than sitting in the *misión* session. The players later agreed to suspend their playing during the rest of the *misión* sessions, and in the last session, the younger people were able to point to a favorable comparison between their attendance and that of the older generation.

Together with tensions over fiesta sponsorship and ethnic loyalties, another underlying source of such conflicts is the desire of young people, especially married couples, for access to land in their own right. The division of hacienda lands into individual plots owned by their elders made it harder for young couples to establish separate households without working outside the village. In 1991–1992, a group of young men formed a Young People's Organization (Organización de los Jóvenes) separate from the older Tepeyac Bajo community structure, the Association of Former Huasipungueros. The new organization as a group asked the bishop for permission to use land on a section of the former hacienda still belonging to the diocese, despite the objections of older Tepeyac Bajo leaders.[12] It helped the new organization that two or three of the young men were already catechists, and others began to attend parish-level church meetings and courses in neighboring communities. They impressed the local pastoral agent with their espousal of a vision of working collectively under the guidance of the Word of God, their ongoing practice of reflection in their own meetings, and their attendance at church meetings. She supported their request, and the bishop granted it. Here reflection can be seen functioning as a kind of counter-*doctrina*, a means by which a group of young people have reinforced their challenge of the older generation and claimed religious sanction for that challenge.

Since 1990, some of these intergenerational tensions have eased. Men and women who came of age under the hacienda, participated in their families' struggles to make a living in the face of the *amos'* harsh demands and punishments, and experienced the transformation from hacienda to autonomous community in the 1960s and the 1970s still dominated the community in the early 1990s. Since then, most of them have passed on their land and membership rights in the Association of Former Huasipungueros to their children, born as the hacienda system was dying. Meanwhile, a new community organization has been formed to encompass all the residents of Tepeyac Bajo, including members of the association, the Young People's Organization, and others; its president during my last visit in 2003 was the son of the president of the Association of Former-Huasipungueros. Young villagers also showed that they had not entirely abandoned their elders' religious practices: the Young People's Organization had adopted its own patron saint with a fiesta in January, and three people agreed to sponsor the fiesta of Saint Rose that year. Still, with the proliferation of formal organizations and the inevitable differences in perspectives among villagers, factional tensions will probably always be a part of village life.

CONCLUSION: HISTORY AND MODERNITY

A historical perspective is vital for understanding the contemporary inter-actions among indigenous people, Catholic pastoral agents, and the state. Although liberation theology has reshaped indigenous religious conscious-ness and practice in Chimborazo, an active historical memory continues to influence contemporary religious thinking, and part of that reshaping neces-sarily takes the form of reinterpreting the past. Thus, local expressions of lib-erationist Catholicism are creative and distinctive. Mestizo pastoral agents, drawing on an old ritual language to make a novel argument for indigenous loyalty to a changing church, kneel before indigenous elders. Indigenous Catholic activists join pastoral agents to develop a new narrative of con-quest, resistance, and religious and cultural continuity with pre-Columbian peoples, and they condition elders' authority on cultural authenticity. Vil-lagers look to the Bible for support for communal harmony and youthful re-spect for elders. This is all much too complex to be explained either by top-down models of liberation theology as a finished product of pastoral agents or by bottom-up models of liberation theology as a spontaneous popular cre-ation. Instead, these expressions are the product of interaction between vari-ous actors: pastoral agents; indigenous Catholic activists; and other indige-nous people of different generations and stances toward the Catholic church, favorable and otherwise.

Out of the interactions among indigenous people and the church, the state, and a changing social and economic environment, a discourse and a politics of indigenous ethnic resurgence have also emerged. In Chimborazo, as in many parts of Latin America, as indigenous people mobilize on the basis of ethnicity, a notion of "indigenous culture" has moved to the center of their self-definition and political vision. Thus, they have been led to at-tempt to define this indigenous culture more explicitly than they needed to before. In this context, rituals and notions of respect for elders have become salient yet problematic memories.

In rituals of respect, elders explicitly espoused rules of behavior, making these rituals a logical template for current explicit reflections on indigenous culture. At the same time, the old respect complex is problematic because of its historical links to racial and class inequality and also because the same changes associated with ethnic resurgence tend to undermine current elders' authority. The system of fiesta sponsorship and the associated positions of religious authority broke down in the wake of agrarian reform. Members of the younger generation today seek social and economic advancement in ways that sometimes put them at odds with their elders. Catholic and political activists have reworked the notion of respect and associated definitions of the elders to integrate them into a discourse of ethnic pride, mobilization, and resistance. Even so, some indigenous youth find the pressures and temptations strong to opt out of an indigenous identity.

One theme running through the last two chapters has been the various ways that projects of modernity have been ambivalently promoted, accepted, resisted, and reshaped in the interactions among indigenous people, the Catholic Church, and the state. Liberation theology–oriented pastoral agents can be seen as advancing a Catholic version of modernity, in some ways, consciously and wholeheartedly, and, in other ways, almost in spite of themselves. Their sympathy with the Enlightenment is fairly straightforward in their egalitarian belief in social-political "liberation," their encouragement of community efforts to improve material living conditions, their human rights discourse, their view of religion as a voluntary ethical commitment, their deemphasis of the automatic efficacy of ritual, and their faith in the transformative powers of explicit discursive knowledge. Pastoral agents may be less conscious of or more ambivalent about the individualizing effects of their pastoral methods, their endorsement of the power of writing and forms of authority that depend on literacy, and their withdrawal of support for personalistic forms of mediation and cycles of reciprocity between humans and the divine associated with the saints and their feasts.

While advancing the liberation theology project, Catholic pastoral agents must contend not only with previous versions of official and popular Catholicism but also with a competing project of ethnic redefinition and adaptation to modernity, represented by the indigenous evangelical movement. Catholic liberation theology differs from classic and mestizo nationalist visions of modernity in attempting to reconcile a universalistic religious faith with the celebration of cultural diversity and in viewing communitarian folk traditions as an alternative to capitalism. These features of liberation theology recall the Romantic response to the Enlightenment and contribute to pastoral agents' interest in cultural anthropology as a tool for understanding indigenous culture.

The Ecuadorian state over the last several decades has enthusiastically es-

poused its own vision of progress and modernity. Yet, the state has had difficulties, along with some successes, in implementing this vision. The spread
of formal education in rural areas has been a notable development, with
complex ramifications for intergenerational relations. The agrarian reform
dissolved servile forms of land tenure and labor on haciendas. Former hacienda peons were reorganized into legally recognized communities under
state oversight that are capable of interacting directly with state administrative and development agencies. The agrarian reform also extended the reach
of civil authority and the law into areas formerly under landlords' personal
authority. Yet, state agents have not seemed capable of vigorously implementing the universal rule of law or of convincing indigenous peasants that
they represent the rule of law. The state has also been forced by the indigenous ethnic movement to shift its discourse of modernity from one that demanded the integration of indigenous groups into a mestizo nation to one
that accepts Ecuador's multiethnic future.

While no one in Tepeyac Bajo misses the oppression of the hacienda
era, their contemporary situation as indigenous peasants in a mestizo-
dominated, capitalist society occasions new forms of ambivalence. Indigenous people are free not to be "Indians" anymore, but they must choose
among living with a stigmatized identity, attempting to redefine that identity as a source of pride, or abandoning it and becoming mestizo. As they try
to redefine their identity, difficult questions arise. Can forms of knowledge
and authority historically identified with mestizos be used to strengthen indigenous culture? How can one create a positive identity out of a history
of oppression? As the young use their new access to literacy and the Bible
to strive for equality with mestizos, do they necessarily leave behind their
elders, respect, and even indigenous identity? These are not just abstract
philosophical questions. They are the stuff of everyday decisions about how
one dresses, what language one speaks, how one greets others, and what cultural guidelines one follows in everyday life. For young people migrating
back and forth between the village and the city, faced with the contradictory
pressures of the two milieus, the questions may be particularly pressing, but
their peers and parents in the village must also negotiate conflicting notions
of prestige and respect.

Likewise, as villagers deal with domestic quarrels, disputes with neighbors, or animal rustling, they are forced to confront another series of questions. Does the landlords' disciplinary authority, gone forever, have to be replaced with a more distant, culturally alien, and frequently corrupt set of
representatives of the official legal system—or with moral anarchy? Or can
the indigenous community reestablish effective mechanisms for dealing

with conflict that can be reconciled with contemporary attitudes toward punishment and human rights, and that the state will respect?

Interacting with pastoral agents and the state, villagers addressing these challenges have developed a new set of discourses and practices that appear quite modern in contrast with the respect complex of the hacienda period. Community organizations, rather than attempting sacramental purification to transform those who misbehave, employ secular punishments such as fines, on the premise that rational people will thereby be deterred. Moral instruction, severed from punishment and ritual purification, attempts to persuade the conscience through appeals to the impersonal universal authority of the written Word of God. Saints' images have partly been replaced by the Bible; cycles of reciprocity and redistribution surrounding fiesta sponsorship, by more democratic and bureaucratic modes of financing fiestas; elders' admonishments and rote recitation of prayers, by collective reflection on the Word of God; and the fiesta, landlords, and elders' experience as sources of authority, by community offices and mastery of the written Word. Yet many villagers use the Bible to support what continues to be an anti-individualistic message, one meant to reinforce the authority of parents and other elders. Catechists find that mastery of God's Word gives them only weak authority in the eyes of fellow villagers. Meanwhile, the memory of respect on the hacienda and the desire for respect from mestizos fuel the self-assertion of the indigenous community as an important political and judicial entity—one created and regulated by the state in a sense, but one that challenges that state on various fronts. A strong indigenous movement, based on a redefined ethnic identity, insists that, if Ecuador is to be a modern state, it must recognize the distinct culture and political organization of its indigenous peoples (Zamosc 1994).

The fundamental social changes since 1960 have thus led indigenous people to rework and combine hacienda-era practices with newer ones in response to new challenges. The interplay of different positions and perspectives has carried this creative process forward. As during the hacienda period itself, poverty and racism sometimes exacerbate internal divisions. As during the hacienda period, village social life is not a purely local, Runa creation but a product of continual interactions with mestizo pastoral agents, the state, and others. Nonetheless, if we compare today's village life with that of four or five decades ago, we have to credit Pangor Runa with some impressive achievements. They have developed a strong local democracy, embodied in community and parish-level organizations whose members meet regularly to discuss their common concerns and work to improve their lives. They have overcome some of the stigma associated with indigenous identity by developing a historical narrative that allows for both pride in the past and flexibility in the future. They have linked their local organizations to a national-level movement and joined in that movement's struggles to shape national government policies. The indigenous movement has made significant political gains since the 1990 uprising, winning posts in local and national governments and recognition as a legitimate and important political force. The former peons of hacienda Monjas Corral and their counterparts around the country have a right, I think, to feel proud of what they have created during this period.

These achievements, nonetheless, are incomplete and will always have to be defended and renewed. Indigenous farmers are facing worsening economic conditions, partly the result of neoliberal government policies and growing competition from cheap agricultural imports. The proposed free trade area of the Americas threatens to intensify these pressures to the point of making their livelihood untenable. Increasingly, the issues that confront Runa in communities like Tepeyac Bajo and the issues that confront readers in the United States are the same issues. The people of Tepeyac Bajo approach these issues with an acute distrust of the powerful and a commitment to political discussion and collective action that might serve all of us well.

NOTES

CHAPTER I

1. Quichua is the Ecuadorian spelling; elsewhere in the Andes the spelling is Quechua.

2. Readers may find more extensive comparative and historical discussions of haciendas in Duncan and Rutledge 1977; Langer 1989; and Larson 1998.

3. The literature on the issues sketched in an extremely condensed way in the last two paragraphs is vast, but a few influential theoretical statements and useful reviews are Bourdieu 1977; Brumann 1999; Ortner 1984; Rodseth 1998; and Wolf 1981.

4. In an otherwise useful review, Thurner suggests a bit unfairly that such authors believed peasants could build the base of the triangle only *after* land reform and with outside help (1993:44). Whyte and Alberti (1976) and Tullis (1970) both emphasize peasants' own initiatives in organizing before land reform.

5. A pseudonym.

6. It also encompasses embodied and sometimes inarticulate sensations, desires, and dispositions shaped by power relations as well as more readily verbalized understandings. Writing about the hacienda period, for which I necessarily depend on oral accounts, I do not give much explicit attention to embodiment, aside from the aesthetic experience of racial inequality. Weismantel (1988, 2001) offers some sensitive discussions of embodied experiences, hegemony, and resistance in Zumbagua, an area very similar to Pangor.

CHAPTER 2

1. Readers who travel in the Andes should not assume that they can wander uninvited into indigenous villages and necessarily receive such a warm welcome.

2. Cantos's report provides only brief summaries, and it may postdate the local application of the colonial policy of *reducción*, when dispersed populations were forced to resettle in central towns and local social organization was disrupted. Obviously, it also postdates Inca transformations. These limitations make any inferences about precolonial and pre-Inca Pangor necessarily tentative.

3. This conclusion is supported by a comparison of the names of colonial *parcialidades* with modern place names.

4. A document from a few decades earlier names a Diego Pasto as a cacique of Pallatanga (and his subjects have other surnames; *Camino 1668, 5v, 6v, 7).

5. Around 1992, some indigenous activists and Quichua radio hosts began to revive the term as a designation for the people of Chimborazo province.

6. It could refer to Manuela de Alvear y Orosco, a widow with no surviving children, who owned Guangopud at her death in 1792. She willed her possessions to be auctioned off to pay for Masses for her soul (*Testamento 1792).

7. The documentation in the Riobamba bishopric's archive on this episode is voluminous; see, for example, *Acta 1918; *Estado 1918; *Pérez 1918; *Venta 1918.

8. The bishop of Riobamba counseled indigenous people to "be very devoted to our Mother the Virgin Mary, above all, now, when some wolves in sheep's clothing, called socialists, try to deceive certain ignorant little Indians. Don't worry, because our Mother will save you" (*Ordóñez 1936).

9. The García Moreno regime promoted the *doctrina cristiana*, something like a recitation of the catechism, in parish centers, perhaps giving impetus to the *doctrina* on haciendas as well. García Moreno also encouraged the creation of the Diocese of Riobamba and of the Redemptorist mission in Riobamba, both of which probably helped spread the practice of the *doctrina* on Chimborazo's haciendas.

10. This pastoral letter, published in Spanish and an ungrammatical Quichua, contains other interesting recommendations for the bishop's indigenous flock: "Love, revere, and obey your parish priest, responsible for looking after your souls. . . . If you have a master, fulfill all the work he may order without laziness, and never take what is not yours. . . . So that you and your children do not go ill clothed, buy new clothes" (*Ordóñez 1936).

CHAPTER 3

1. According to the nineteenth-century account books and Joaquina Niamo (8/22/92) talking about her late husband, Segundo Ángel Guailla, in the early 1960s. This is disputed by others, however.

2. Hacienda residents who lacked seed also sometimes entered into such sharecropping arrangements with the hacienda and with each other.

3. I present a fuller theoretical and ethnographic argument that an adequate account of strategy demands attention to sentiment and moral expectations in Lyons 1994b:Chap. 2.

4. Mangin similarly observes, "Fiestas in Vicos . . . strengthen intercommunity bonds. . . . Vicosino participation in the fiestas of [neighboring communities and towns] . . . is characterized by an attitude of good will . . . generalized to the whole community" (1954:v–88).

5. *Ay* and *caramba* are interjections, perhaps translatable as "Oh, boy!" or "Yes indeed/No indeed!"

6. In some areas, the word has taken on strong negative associations even for indigenous people speaking in Quichua (Weismantel 2001:xxvi), but I did not find this in Chimborazo in the 1990s.

7. I learned Ecuadorian rural Spanish and heard *runa* as a pejorative before I learned to speak Quichua and to use *runa* in its Chimborazo Quichua sense. Only with indigenous people's cultural self-affirmation since the early 1990s have I begun to feel comfortable using "Runa" in English as an ethnic name.

CHAPTER 4

1. Some villagers attribute the contemporary decline in local agricultural fertility to the decline of the fiesta of Saint Rose and other fiestas. A priest still comes every year to say Mass in honor of Saint Rose, and the village holds a small fiesta, but this is apparently not sufficient to gain her full favor. The association between the fiesta of Saint Rose and the renewal of agricultural fertility is widespread in the Andes, and Skar suggests that it echoes the precolonial festival of the moon (1981:202n10).

2. This echoes the pan-Andean notion of *pachakuti*, or epochal world-turning, but it may also allude to the burial of the old town of Pangor in an earthquake and mud slide, probably in the nineteenth century.

3. An 1881 inventory of the hacienda confirms that there was a statue of Saint Rose. By 1898, the old house that had housed the chapel with the statue had burned down (*Legajo 2 bis 1881–1909).

4. It is hard to know whether these metaphors predate the last several decades of post–Vatican II "purifying" efforts and local Protestant-Catholic controversy over whether the cult of the saints is idolatrous.

5. Aychi is also said to aid travelers in their trips and to have aided hacienda cowhands in guarding hacienda cattle from harm or loss.

6. Oral tradition associates Carnival with a pair of quasi-saints called Tayta Carlos and Mama Eva, who repaid sponsors and celebrants in the same ways as other saints did.

7. My informants did not say explicitly that, in fiestas, they made offerings to the divine through other people, but their accounts strongly indicated that they understood all of sponsors' fiesta expenditures as constituting their service to the saint. I have also witnessed discussions among village catechists and others in which they explicitly called the provision of food and drink and other fiesta expenditures a "sacrifice" while contrasting this with current church teachings about the sort of "sacrifice" God wants (behavior guided by a self-conscious ethic of social justice).

8. Dry corn, with the "skin" of the kernels removed by soaking in water with lime or ashes, and boiled.

9. He refers to male saints in his dreams as *wawa niñitokuna* and female saints as *wawa señoritakuna*. Both of these phrases carry connotations of white social status; *wawa niñitokuna* implies aristocratic landholding status.

CHAPTER 5

1. There is one possible exception: see Lyons 1994b:Chap. 4.I.(1); see also Chap. 9n2; and, similarly, Abercrombie 1998:117–118.

2. The oral testimony is not entirely clear and consistent as to the number of workdays required per week on Monjas Corral; perhaps it varied through time.

3. *Yanga* has the sense of something lacking in reason or worth. In addition to arbitrariness, here it suggests an activity that makes no real contribution to anything.

4. I have condensed and slightly rearranged this text.

5. The same word is used to refer to bringing home-cooked food from someone else's house, as during a fiesta. This is the verb form of *wanlla*, defined by Weismantel as food "that is not part of a meal" and food given as a gift among peers or to express social superiority (1988:110–113, 139–141). I am not sure whether Weismantel's discussion applies exactly to Pangor, but I do agree that *wanllana* connotes gifting; for harvesters, the potatoes are a sort of countergift that the owner of the field gives in recognition of the gift of labor.

6. I was Tayta Avelino's scribe for several songs he composed as the leader of a village music group. It was my honor to be the lead singer of this song in a festival sponsored by a Riobamba radio station in 1991. The composition earned second prize, and the song was replayed frequently on the early-morning Quichua broadcast. The song was requested of me at meetings of Quichua speakers wherever I went. Thus does anthropology offer unexpected opportunities for fame (if not fortune). See Lyons 1999, 2002a, 2004.

CHAPTER 6

1. I am not sure why she uses the plural throughout this account.

2. I have inserted this line from my notes on a previous telling of the same encounters (Notes, 8/4/1991).

3. "Respetak karkanchik, y respetak karka." The subject of the second clause is not given, and it could be interpreted as "they [other people, too] respected [the *fundadores*]," or as "they [the *fundadores*] respected [us, the people in general]."

4. Despite some rearranging, the first section below, "Not Once Did They Hit Me," corresponds roughly to his "opening statement." The account of Mass and confession was prompted by my questions (the account of fiesta sponsorship was not).

5. Tayta Reinaldo's way of putting this as a matter of "looking good" may sound ironic to North Americans, who view image management as an insincere and inauthentic concern. I do not think any irony is intended in a

context in which it is morally expected that people should care how others view them.

6. The sacred aura around priests was not simply a spontaneous projection of peasant naïveté. As late as 1958, on the eve of Vatican II, the bishop of Riobamba invited young people to take up the priesthood in these terms: "Through the priesthood, Jesus perpetuates his presence in the world . . . The priest is another Christ" (*Proaño 1958b).

7. Tayta Reinaldo may be referring here more to the prayers and rites in Latin.

8. Velasco Ibarra was in power from 1944 to August 1947, near the end of the Guevara family's last rental period.

9. The different meanings of this word, *rudo*, hint at hacienda workers' use of a mask of incomprehension or incompetence as a tactic for evading orders or not carrying them out quite as intended. The word probably entered into the local lexicon via the reprimands of mestizo stewards and landowners, for whom it would have meant "dull" or "thick-headed." Tayta Reinaldo, however, uses it to refer to simple laziness or unwillingness to carry out orders. The notion that Andean natives had less mental capacity than Spaniards is a colonial idea still reproduced in common racial epithets such as *"indio bruto,"* "brutish/stupid Indian." The mask of incomprehension made use of this idea.

10. His sister Martina was Marcos Sisa's wife. After the couple left Monjas Corral for another hacienda, the Laras fatally stabbed Marcos Sisa in an encounter on the way to Cajabamba. Another Sisa joined Tayta José in "bathing" Ignacio Lara.

CHAPTER 7

1. I base this summary closely on Andrés Yépez's narration (8/22/1992).

2. A story told in Pindilig, an indigenous town in southern Ecuador, draws similar connections. Adam had two sons, one of them respectful and one disrespectful toward their father. God said to the respectful son, "You will give orders and you will be white" while condemning the disrespectful son to be an Indian and serve his brother (Muñoz-Bernand 1986:191).

3. This indeed appears to be how Gramsci conceived of the relationship in some contexts; in others, the distinction is even sharper, with political forces coercing "antagonistic groups" and cultivating the consent of "kindred and allied groups" (1971:57–58, a passage Kurtz [1996] stresses). While Kurtz (1996) argues that Gramsci's conception of hegemony is clear and consistent, other studies reveal ambiguities and shifts in his usage (e.g., Anderson 1976–1977). Without minimizing the insights to be gained from close engagement with Gramsci's writings, the present argument is less concerned with demonstrating a correct interpretation of Gramsci than with interpreting and using his concepts in a way that proves fruitful through engagement with an ethnographic case.

4. Another way of locating my argument is to say that I join with anthropologists and others writing largely outside a Gramscian framework in

showing that violence is deeply shaped by cultural assumptions and categories of identity and is not simply instrumental, while bringing this insight to bear on Gramscian categories. Anthropologists have been relatively slow to subject coercion to cultural analysis. They most commonly write about violence in extreme forms, such as intercommunal conflict, where the question of hegemony does not seem to arise. Those who have addressed more regulated or "normal" violence have been inspired more by Foucault (1995) than by Gramsci.

5. This definition makes it easy to see that coercion and positive inducements (desirable consequences for desired behavior) are two sides of the same coin; in fact, refraining from or withholding one can be a form of the other.

6. Corrigan and Sayer (1985) use the term *discipline* (together with *moral regulation*) in a broadly similar way (following Durkheim's usage).

7. Another example is Pentecost in some parts of Chimborazo, where the holiday is termed *warmi*, or "female," *pascua* and serves as a ritual preparation for bringing the new harvest into the house. Villagers strike the ground with a whip while saying, "Leave here, hungry one!" The ritual is very similar to the Inca feast of Citua, which Guaman Poma describes as the "fiesta and *pascua* of the [female] moon" (Botero 1992:191; Guaman Poma de Ayala [1616] 1988:253). Holy Week is sometimes termed *kari*, or "male," *pascua*, by contrast with *warmi pascua*. This might refer to *pascuanchina*'s "male" concern with hierarchy, as opposed to *warmi pascua*'s "female" concern with the household food supply, though Botero also provides accounts of something very much like *pascuanchina* in *warmi pascua* (1992:191; cf. Allen 1988:78–85).

8. Further research is required to determine the geographic extension of this practice and of the broader patterns of authority and discipline described below. Similar practices of ritual whipping have been noted in widely scattered areas of Latin America: among the Ñähñu in Mexico (Bernard and Salinas Pedraza 1989:434); southeastern Colombia (Taussig 1987:41–43); northern Ecuador (Oswaldo Sinchico, pers. comm. 1994; Yánez del Pozo 1988: 137–138, 224–226, 230–232); and southern Peru (Anrup 1990:83, 216; Bruce Mannheim, pers. comm. 1993–1994). More broadly, north and central Peruvian haciendas seem to have had a structure of authority and language of respect similar to what I describe below (Deere 1990:94; Doughty 1965; Vásquez 1963). The respect complex can be considered a variant of the widespread ideologies that Laura Nader has termed "coercive harmony" (1990).

9. I develop a comparison between ritual whipping and sweeping in much greater depth in Lyons (1994b:Chap. 6.III.2). In a film on ethnomedicine in highland Ecuador, a healer explains that a child afflicted with evil air can be cured by striking the child over the whole body with the child's father's belt and then leaving the belt outside through the night (McKee 1985).

10. Again, there are parallels outside of ritual discipline. The first person to hold a newborn infant can similarly transmit personal qualities to the child, as can a godparent holding a child for baptism.

11. The word *obediente* and its antonym, *rebelde* ("rebellious"), are generally used in rural highland Spanish—and here, as part of a Spanish phrase inserted into Quichua—to refer to obedience or disobedience to rules of morality, especially in the sense of interpersonal *respeto*. Someone who does not greet his or her neighbors may be called *rebelde*. This usage, perhaps odd to most North Americans, expresses the entanglement of personal morality and authority that I am getting at in this discussion. The use of "obedient" here also echoes Talal Asad's discussion of medieval Christian monasticism (1993; original emphasis).

12. See Harrison (1989) for a discussion of their differences in Chimborazo and elsewhere; O'Connor (1997, 2002) on slightly earlier encounters among what she calls "dueling patriarchies"; Lyons (1994b:Chap. 6.II.4) for a comparison between rural mestizo and indigenous gender ideologies and practices in the late twentieth century; and idem (2002b) for a fuller treatment than I can offer here of Runa gender ideology in the hacienda period and the 1990s.

13. Some biographical particulars make his ethnic status unusually ambiguous.

14. When he speaks of "good white people" (alli blancostapish), I don't think Tayta José means "good whites" as opposed to "bad whites." Instead, he means "good white people" as opposed to ordinary, not-so-special Runa, different human types who in the past received different greetings. This pairing of "good" with "white" is an everyday linguistic convention that Tayta José reproduces unconsciously even in this critical reflection.

15. Mestizo peasants in Bolívar similarly extend to the representatives of literacy and formal schooling the same respect that they otherwise reserve mainly for elders. My wife, Mercedes, recalls the case of a primary school classmate who had struck an adult. His parents brought him to the teacher for a lashing, after which they told him to kneel before the teacher and ask forgiveness.

16. Mary Weismantel has similarly observed that, in rural Andean thinking, "[b]ody and identity . . . originate in the intimate physical relationship between persons and their social milieu," not in inherited genetic endowments (2001:191–192).

17. The Catholic Church accepted force as a necessary instrument for Christianizing indigenous Andeans (MacCormack 1985), a policy that perhaps contributed to the spread of forms of discipline that in Europe were more restricted to voluntary devotees. Parish priests in the colonial Diocese of Quito commonly applied the lash to their indigenous parishioners for raising a hand to parents when drunk, living openly "in sin," or other offenses against the church (López de Solís [1594] 1978; Peña Montenegro [1668] 1985).

18. The view that parental authority is irrelevant as a model for the authority of rulers only began to enter Western common sense during the Enlightenment; its classical expression was Locke's ([1690] 1993) critique of royal absolutism. Without this "commonsensical" divorce between parenting and politics, it would be harder to assume that coercion and persuasion

are separate things. After all, adults commonly teach children what is "good" by punishing "bad" behavior.

CHAPTER 8

1. In Lyons n.d, I elaborate on the broader historical context for land reform on Monjas Corral, draw on Gramsci's (1971) ideas about intellectuals to develop the argument sketched here about the indigenous "awakening," and consider more generally the role of the church in indigenous agrarian struggles and ethnic mobilization.

2. Monjas Corral residents did not have any contacts with leftist organizations or Protestant missionaries in the 1950s so far as I learned, but residents of some neighboring haciendas and communities did in the 1960s and the 1970s (or before). In a 1957 letter to the parish priest of Pallatanga, Proaño said, "The 'indigenous *comunas*' . . . are not exactly bad organizations, but they do carry the danger of falling into the hands of left-leaning leaders. . . . [W]atch them closely . . ." (*Proaño to Castro 1957; see also *Acción Subversiva 1959). Proaño, evidently aware that the church's association with the elite handicapped it in competing for adherents, also lamented the "apathy of wealthy Catholics, who are moved neither by the poverty of those around them nor by the progress . . . of the heretics [Protestants]" (*Proaño 1958a).

3. José María Pillajo (7/1991) recalled that the laborers were also given the option of taking five hectares each on the eastern side, again in one contiguous bloc. I did not locate much of the relevant documentation from the 1960s and the early 1970s, so my account is based largely on interviews. The record of the adjudication of *huasipungo* plots in 1965 confirms the church's wish to maintain a contiguous bloc of land as the motivation for the relocation of resident laborers (*IERAC 1965).

4. In addition to interviews, my account of the mid-1970s–1980s period is based on *Cons. Gub. 1969–1985; various letters from Tepeyac Bajo officials, church advisors, and others found together with that book in the same archive; and *Diócesis-Tepeyac 1976 and a few other documents found in *Tepeyac/CESA 1969–1977.

CHAPTER 9

1. The *bayeta* is a solid-color cloth embroidered around the edges and worn as a shawl; the *anaku* is a dark cloth with embroidery along the bottom edge and worn as a wraparound skirt.

2. When an instructor told CFI students that their ancestors were not "Christian," some felt quite disturbed and insulted; *cristiano* is commonly used as a synonym for "human being." I was told that other students pointed to me as an example that one could be a normal human being without being *cristiano* (I am Jewish).

3. The most recent revival of modest individual fiesta sponsorship as a complement to communal sponsorship in Tepeyac Bajo suggests the fluidity of this situation and the flexibility of notions of "indigenous culture."

4. The first-person plural here, in which the speaker rhetorically includes himself with his audience, is a common feature of local Quichua and Spanish oratory.

5. The belief that physical punishment can disable children's minds for formal education, parents' fear that teenaged children might run away to the cities, and the demise of the hacienda with its routine violence might all contribute to this decline.

6. In the mestizo parish of San Ramón in Bolívar, no strong community organizations apart from the official civil parish structures existed until a nighttime patrol was created in the late 1990s. Bands of criminals had virtually a free hand in nighttime rustling, robberies, and assaults. By light of day, fear of reprisals and the lack of confidence in the legal system kept anyone from taking action against the criminals, despite general knowledge of their identity. Thus, peasants have reason to see their choice not as one of private justice or the rule of law but as communal justice or none at all.

7. In my experience, pastoral agents in Chimborazo are generally a thoughtful lot, and they do reflect on the consequences of their pastoral methods. They could point out that some indigenous people have gained a sense of familiarity and self-confidence in interpreting the Bible and that, as catechists, they translate their understanding into terms accessible to others. Arguably, this is an empowering process in the long run. Also, in the late 1990s, a committee including several CFI graduates was working on a new Quichua translation of the Bible that may be easier for villagers to understand, although it seems that conflicts over interpretive authority plagued and perhaps stalled this project.

8. My notion of "experts" here is related to classic sociological themes such as functional specialization and differentiation, bureaucratization, and rationalization, and differs from definitions that focus on the authority that modern experts' discourse grants to science rather than to morality or God (e.g., Rose 1995:218–219). A concept of religious experts that might allow us to compare and connect religious modernity to the modern rise of experts in other domains requires a definition focused not so much on the content of discourse as on the credentials involved.

9. Blindness is a common metaphor for illiteracy, deafness for disrespect: moral instruction is oral. Reading requires only an individual's ability to "see" the printed word; respect comes from a person's "hearing" another person's spoken word.

10. The host community generally serves lunch.

11. Catechists sometimes ruefully compare their position with the much greater authority that they feel evangelical Protestant communities grant their pastors. A comparative study would be illuminating.

12. The older Tepeyac Bajo leaders argued that this threatened their long-standing use of one of the hacienda buildings. Some may have still been nursing dreams of securing the land in question for the community.

BIBLIOGRAPHY

ARCHIVAL MATERIALS

Archival sources are cited in the text with an asterisk (*) and an abbreviated title and date. These citations are listed here in alphabetical order, together with the expanded title or description of the document and the archive where it is located. Where I have taken the title from the opening words or title found in the document (including titles added later to original documents by archivists or others), the title is given here in italics. Where I identify the document by my own description, the description is not italicized, but words taken directly from the document to aid in identification are placed within quotation marks. I avoid repeating the date in the expanded titles. The following abbreviations are used for the archives:

ACR   Archivo Histórico de la Curia de Riobamba
AIT/R   Archivo de la Inspección de Trabajo de Chimborazo, Riobamba
ANH/Q   Archivo Nacional de la Historia, Quito (Casa de la Cultura)
ANH/R   Archivo Nacional de la Historia, Riobamba (Casa de la Cultura)
APP   Archivo Parroquial de Pallatanga (Convento Parroquial)
APS   Archivo Parroquial de Sicalpa (Convento Parroquial)
CESA   Archivo de CESA, Central Ecuatoriana de Servicios Agrícolas,
             Quito

*Acción Subversiva 1959. Anon. [Misión Andina?]. Acción subversiva entre los indígenas de la provincia del Chimborazo. Mimeo, Riobamba, Nov. 5, 4 pp. ACR.
*Acta 1918. "Copia del acta de la V. Junta Conciliar de Temporalidades, de fecha 19 de enero"; with "Copia de la resolución del V. Capítulo Catedral, por consulta del Rdmo. Sr. Vicario General," Jan. 25. Riobamba. 3 ff. ACR.
*Actas 1961. "Actas Transaccionales/Agrícolas." AIT/R.
*Arreglo 1886. Acta de arreglo/ajuste de cuentas entre Obispo Arsenio Andrade y Miguel Lizarzaburu. Bound with *Fianza 1881. ACR.

*Arrendamiento 1885. "Copia del acta de arrendamientos de 'Monjas-corral' y Llalla en 1885." 8 pp. Bound with *Fianza 1881. ACR.
*Arrendamiento 1895. "Arrendamiento/El Ilmo. Señor Obispo Arsenio Andrade á Cordovez Hos." Escribano Amador Pinto. Riobamba, Jan. 7 ACR.
*Arrendamiento 1902. *Arrendamiento: El Ilsmo. y Rdmo. Sr. Obispo, Dor. Don Arsenio Andrade al Sr. Don Domingo Cordovez Maure.* Escribano Neptalí Vallejo. Yaruquíes, May 30. ACR.
*Arrendamiento 1909. Escritura de arrendamiento, Ob. Andrés Machado a Aurelio Cordovez, suscrita ante el Escribano Neptalí Vallejo, Riobamba, Sept. 26. ACR.
*Arrendamiento 1918. "Arrendamiento/El Ilustrisimo i Reverendisimo Señor Obispo de esta Diócesis Doctor Don Ulpiano Pérez Quiñones al Señor Don Vicente Guevara." Anotador José A. Mancheno L. Riobamba, 12 junio. Copia suscrita por el Escribano Público Neptalí Vallejo, Riobamba, June 13. 4 folios. ACR.
*Arrendamiento 1924. Escritura de Arrendamiento, El Excelentísimo Sr. Dr. Carlos María de la Torre Al Sr. Dn. Vicente Guevara, Riobamba, Oct. 30. ACR.
*Arrendamiento 1931. "Adicional, El Escelentísimo Sr. Dr. Dn. Alberto María Ordóñez C. a favor del Sr. Dn. Vicente Guevara." Riobamba, Nov. 30. ACR.
*Arrendamiento 1938. *Arrendamiento, la Reverendísima Curia de la Diócesis de Bolívar a la Señora María del Cármen Merino de Guevara e Hijos.* Typewritten, Sept. 5, 1938, Notario Alberto A. Dávalos. Included in *Documentos de las haciendas del Seminario.* ACR.
*Barba/Velasco 1873. "Fernando Velasco apoderado de mi hermano, el Sr. Francisco Velasco en el juicio promovido por Don Vicente Barba sobre apeo y deslinde de las haciendas Guangupud, Llalla y Monjascorral . . ." BC No. 34. 1873–1882. Folios are numbered 93–144, 152–156. JsCs 1873. ANH/R.
*Barba-Cárdenas 1879. Escritura de Venta de Monjas Corral y Llalla, Vicente Barba a Vicente Cárdenas. Rejistro de escrituras del vieneio de 1879 i 1880, pp. 31–35. ANH/R.
*Bases 1954. Proaño, Leonidas, Dr. Obispo de Bolívar y Presidente del Consejo Gubernativo. *Bases Generales de la Licitación.* 3 folios, including "Bases Especiales" for La Merced, Monjas Corral, Sta. Cruz. Carpeta "Historia de la Diócesis." ACR.
*Bucheli to Obispo 1917. Pedro María e Ignacio Bucheli al Ilustrisimo, i Rmo. Señor Obispo diocesano, Riobamba, 2 Oct. 1 folio. ACR.
*Cabezas to Vicario 1917. M. Cabezas M. al Presidente del Capítulo Catedral de la Diócesis Bolivarense y Vicario General, [Riobamba], [ca. 1917]. 2 folios. ACR.
*Cacicazgos 1730s. Dⁿ Manuel Lema Sᵉ Cassicasgo de Pallatanga y Ynˢ Guaconas. Ca. 1735–1738 (also contains documents from 1700–1701). 11 folios. Documento No. 19, Caja Cacicazgos, No. 10, Chimborazo 1665–1821. ANH/Q.
*Camino 1668. Pleito, "Don Gerónimo de la Torre cacique de Chimbo con Juan de Silva sobre el camino del Tambillo." Sección Indígenas, Caja 9, ANHQ.

*Cárdenas-Diócesis 1880. Escritura de Venta de Monjas Corral y Llalla, Vicente Cárdenas al Seminario Conciliar de la Diócesis de Riobamba. Registro de escrituras del vienio de 1879 i 1880, pp. 788v–790. ANH/R.

*CFI 1994. "Primer encuentro provincial de servidores de la pastoral indigena." Centro de Formación Indígena—Santa Cruz (Riobamba), Apr. 4–5. Photocopy of typewritten report by Lola Rosero, secretaria del encuentro, 26 pp., author's files.

*Colecturías 1893–1908. Legajo "3, Colecturías, 1893 a 1908." Carpeta "Colecturía, Años 1795–1925." ACR.

*Comparación 1886. Bernardo Larrea. "Plan de comparacion de los inventarios de las haciendas . . . Monjas-corral y Colta, que las ha tenido en arrendamiento el Sor. Miguel Lizarzaburu . . ." Bound with *Fianza 1881. ACR.

*Conciertos 1881. "Lista de conciertos sin documento, entregados al arrendatario de las haciendas 'Monjas-corral,' Llalla y Colta." Firmada por Mariano Prats, Miguel de Lizarzaburu, Manuel Lizarzaburu, 28 mayo. Included in *Lizarzaburu Comparación 1886. ACR.

*Cons. Gub. 1939–1947. *Libro de Actas del Consejo Gubernativo de los Bienes de la Diócesis de Bolívar.* Archive catalogue No. 1.2.1, 0105741. ACR.

*Cons. Gub. 1969–1985. *Actas del Consejo Gubernativo de Bienes de la Diócesis, 1969–1985.* ACR.

*Cordovez to Secretario 1918. Aurelio Cordovez al Señor Secretario de la Curia, Riobamba, Jan. 4. 3 ff. ACR.

*Cordovez to Vicario 1893. Aurelio Cordovez al Vicario Capitular, Riobamba, June 17. 1 folio. In Legajo "3, Colecturías, 1893 a 1908." Carpeta "Colecturía, Años 1795–1925." ACR.

*Cordovez to Vicario 1919. Aurelio Cordovez al V. señor Vicario Diocesano, Riobamba, 16 mayo. Copia hecha por Ángel V. Verdesoto, Secretario de Gobierno Diocesano, Riobamba, May 23. 3 pp. ACR.

*de la Torre 1924. Carlos María de la Torre, Obispo de Riobamba, *Sexta Carta Pastoral . . . con motivo de su viaje a Roma.* Quito: Prensa Católica. ACR.

*Despojo 1862. "Domingo Morocho i socios del comun de Pangor contra Damacio Arze por despojo de terrenos." 1862. JsCs 1862, No. 0061; N94/Civil concluido. ANH/R.

*Diócesis-Tepeyac 1976. "Venta. El Consejo Gubernativo de los Bienes de la Diócesis de Riobamba, a favor de la Asociación de Ex-huasipungueros de 'Tepeyac.'" Riobamba, 20 julio, notario Raúl Dávalos Maldonado, 7 folios. Carpeta "Tepeyac." CESA.

*Dueñas to Ordóñez 1942. J. Nicolás Dueñas Ibarra to Alberto María Ordóñez, Quito, 16 de julio de 1942. 2 pp. In Legajo, *Documentos de las haciendas del Seminario.* ACR.

*Dueñas to Ordóñez 1944. J. Nicolás Dueñas Ibarra to Alberto María Ordóñez, Píllaro, 28 de mayo de 1942. Handwritten, 2 pp. In Legajo, *Documentos de las haciendas del Seminario.* ACR.

*Estado 1918. Anónimo. "Estado de la cuestión entre la Autoridad Eclesiástica y el Sr. Aurelio Cordovez." Riobamba, Mar. 30 2 ff. ACR.

*Estudios 1960. "Estudios de Pastoral," Primera Parte. [Report on the "ejercicios espirituales del clero de Riobamba."] ACR.

*Fianza 1881. Escritura de fianza, Ignacio Lizarzaburu por Miguel y Manuel Lizarzaburu. Escribano Miguel Acevedo. Riobamba, May 4 (copy July 8). 6 pp. ACR.

*Flores and Izurieta to Obispo 1937. Enrique Flores and Rafaél Izurieta [or Zurieta?] to Obispo, "Informe de la Comisión acerca de la Propuesta . . . ," Oct. 4. 2 pp. In Legajo, Documentos de las haciendas del Seminario. ACR.

*Gallegos-Barba 1873. Juicio Civil, seguido por el Sr. Pacífico Gallegos sobre posesión efectiva de los fundos Monjas-corral y Llalla, Juzg. 2º Mpal., Feb. 10. 87 folios. Caja PROT/JsCs 1873. ANH/R.

*Guevara to Vicario 1917. Vicente Guevara al Vicario General, Riobamba, Dec. 7. 2 folios. ACR.

*Iñacoto 1864. "Jose Alulema y otros, solicitando cuentas a su patron Fidel Salvador." Js Civiles, Juzgado 1º Municipal, 1864, 2 folios. ANH/R.

*IERAC (Instituto Ecuatoriano de Reforma Agraria y Colonización) 1965. Acta de liquidación de huasipungos, Tepeyac, 21 julio 1965. Carpeta Hacienda Tepeyac (Monjas Corral), No. 1247 (Haciendas). Archivo del Instituto Ecuatoriano de Reforma Agraria y Colonización, Quito.

*Inventario 1887. "Inventario de entrega de la Hda. de Monjas-Corral y Llalla con dos atos, al arrendador Sor Reinaldo García . . ." Entrega por Dr. Adolfo Granizo. Feb. 10. ACR.

*Jordán to Muñoz Vega 1970. Econ. Fausto Jordán B., Director Ejecutivo de CESA, al Excmo. Sr. Pablo Muñoz Vega, Presidente de la Conferencia Episcopal Ecuatoriana, Quito, Jan. 22, 3 pp. (Copy attached to cover letter, Jordán to Proaño, Jan. 22) CESA.

*Junta Admin. 1937. Rafael Izurieta and Enrique Flores, note on motion headed "En la Junta Administrativa Diocesana de Riobamba, Sesión del 2 de Octubre de 1937." In Legajo, Documentos de las haciendas del Seminario. ACR.

*Legajo 2 bis 1881–1909. Legajo 2 bis. "Escrituras de compra, arriendo, etc." Seminario Conciliar. 1881–1909. ACR.

*León and Dávalos to Vicario 1917. Francisco León G. y Juan B. Dávalos al Vicario General, Riobamba, Oct. 16, con anotación posterior. 3 folios. ACR.

*Liquidaciones 1961. Actas de Liquidación de Cuentas de los Trabajadores, 1961. AIT/R.

*Lizarzaburu to Bishop 1885. Miguel de Lizarzaburu al "Ilmo. Señor" [the bishop?], Riobamba, Apr. 18. 2 folios. Bound with *Fianza 1881. ACR.

*Lizarzaburu to Vicario 1881. Miguel de Lizarzaburu al Vicario Capitular [Mariano Prats] (with a note by Prats, dated in Riobamba, June 3). ACR.

*Morocho/cura 1857. "Domingo Morocho Governador de Indigenas de Pangor, y Pascual Morocho . . ." JsCs 1857, No. 056. ANH/R.

*Observaciones 1886. Miguel de Lizarzaburu, Observaciones hechas al avalúo y descuentos . . . Bound with *Fianza 1881. ACR.

*Ordóñez 1936. Ordóñez Crespo, Alberto María. Por la culturización del indio. Carta Pastoral, Riobamba, Feb. 2. ACR.

*Pangor 1836–1856. *Libro en que se sientan las partidas de los que se bautisan, fcho. en esta nueva Parroq.ª de la Virjen Maria del Rosario de Pangor* . . . APS.

*Pangor 1863. "Manuel Cajilema, Juan Ramos Ortís, Narsiso Guamantaqui, Sebastián Tenemasa y demas indígenas de la Parroquia de Pangor" al Gobernador de la Provincia. JsCs 1863, No. 074, 1 folio. ANH/R.

*Párroco 1915. Párroco de Guano al Obispo. ACR.

*Pérez 1918. Ulpiano Pérez Quiñonez, "Exposición a la V. Junta Conciliar," Riobamba, June 13. 3 folios. ACR.

*Proaño 1917. Proaño, Juan Felix. *Noticia histórica de los bienes del Seminario,* in *Legajo 2 bis 1881–1909.

*Proaño 1958a. Proaño, Leonidas E. "De conversación con mis hijos: Peligros mortales." *Mensaje, Publicación del Obispado de Riobamba* 3(5) (Jan. 19): 1–4. ACR.

*Proaño 1958b. Proaño, Leonidas E. Carta pastoral. ACR.

*Proaño to Castro 1957. Leonidas Proaño a Jesús A. Castro, párroco de Pallatanga, May 13. Carpeta "Comunicaciones Oficiales." APP.

*Prot/EP 1851–1853. Protocolo de escrituras publicas celebradas ante el Escribano Antonio Fraga, Años de 1851, 1852 y 1853. ANH/R.

*Prot/EP 1704. Libro de escrituras, sin título, en carpeta "PROT/EP 1704." Caja PROT/EP 1701–1704. ANH/R.

*Prot/EP 1705. Carpeta "PROT/EP 1705." Caja PROT/EP 1705–1709. ANH/R.

*Rayas 1887–1888. "Libro de rayas y socorros de la gente de Monjas-corral y Llalla, desde la fecha en que tomé en arriendo dichos fundos. Febrero 10 de 1887." ACR.

*Rayas 1898–1902. *Libro de rayas y socorros de los conciertos de la Hacienda Monjascorral siendo su arrendatario el señor Don Reinaldo Garcia echo en 1º de Marzo de 1898 por su Economo Santos Cevallos.* ACR.

*Rayas y Socorros Guacona 1873–1876. *Libro de Rayas y socorros de los consiertos de la hasienda de Guacona del Sor. Luisano [sic] Aviles desde el año de 1873 y de 1876.* ANH/R.

*Rivadeneira al Vicario 188—. José Mariano Rivadeneira, Colector de Rentas del Colegio Seminario, al Vicario General. Riobamba, 22 abr. 188—. [Last digit of date on form letterhead left blank. Probably 1890.] Legajo "3, Seminario Conciliar." ACR.

Romero to Ordóñez 1937. Bernabe Romero to Bishop Alberto María Ordóñez Crespo, Riobamba, Octubre 18 de 1937. 1 p. In Legajo, *Documentos de las haciendas del Seminario.* ACR.

*Rumipamba 1704. Escritura de Venta de Rumipamba, el Sargento Blas Romero Carpio de la Vega a Ana María Ozorio de Santa Rosa. In *Prot/EP 1704.

*Tepeyac 1964. "Diócesis de Riobamba, Hda. Tepeyac, Planilla de Jornales . . ." ACR.

*Tepeyac/CESA 1969–1977. Carpeta "Tepeyac." CESA.

*Terminación 1955. "*MINUTA/*Del contrato de terminación de arrendamiento, levantamiento de gravámenes hipotecarios i de la transacción celebrada entre los señores Antonio Santillán Chávez, Guillermo Novillo Flor [y] el Señor Obispo de la Diósesis [*sic*] de Bolivar." Riobamba, [c. 1955]. [Mistakenly dated in corner by archivist as 1947.] ACR.

*Testamento 1792. In D. Joaquin de Albear, en la causa executiva contra . . . 76 folios. Caja No. 71B, Prot./JsCs, 1792. ANH/R.

*V. de Guevara al Obispo n.d. María del Carmen v. de Guevara al Obispo, Rbb, Oct. 4, 19—. 2 pp. ACR.

*Venta 1918. Neptalí Vallejo, Escribano Público. "Venta e hipoteca: El Ilmo. y Rdmo. Señor Obispo Dr. Dn. Ulpiano Pérez Quiñones al Sr. Dn. Aurelio Cordovez." Riobamba, July 29. 8 pp. ACR.

*Verdesoto to Colector 1920. Carta de Ángel V. Verdesoto, Secretario Episcopal de la Diócesis de Bolívar, al Sr. Colector de fondos de montaña. Riobamba, Jan. 9. 1 p. ACR.

*Visita 1893. Juan Félix Proaño, Informe al Obispo de Visitas Pastorales. ACR.

INTERVIEWS

Amancha, José (JA), Tepeyac Bajo, 9/2/1992.

Amancha, Luis (LA), Tepeyac Bajo, 8/2/1992.

Carguachi, Joaquín (JC), and companion, Riobamba, 7/19/1992.

Condo, Carmelo (CC), Ajospamba, 6/18/1992.

Condo, Carmelo (CC), and Victoria Yumbo (VYu), Riobamba, 7/17/1992 and n.d. (1992, date uncertain).

Condo, Rosa (RC), interviewed by Mercedes Guizado (MG), Tepeyac Bajo, 8/23/1992.

Guailla, Miguel (MG), 8/22/1992.

Guailla, Miguel (MG), and Olmedo Yuquilema (OY), Tepeyac Bajo, 8/10/1992.

Guailla, Virgilio (VG), Tepeyac Bajo, 6/30/1992.

Guerrero, Armando (AG), Riobamba, 2/2 and 5/5/1992.

Llongo, Baltazara (BL), Pangor, 7/1 and 7/24/1992.

Maji, María Manuela (MM), Guangopud, 11/6/1992.

Niamo, Gabriel (GN), Tepeyac Bajo, 8/23, 9/5, and 11/5 1992; 6/16/1995.

Niamo, Joaquina (JN), and Manuel Yépez (MY), Tepeyac Bajo, 6/29/1992.

Niamo, Joaquina (JN), Tepeyac Bajo, 8/22/1992.

Paca, Agustín (AP), Tepeyac Bajo, 11/22/1992.

Pillajo, José María (JMP), Tepeyac Bajo, 7/21/1991 (interviewed by Barry Lyons and Mario Guailla); 9/2/1992; 6/13 and 6/17/1995.

Pingos, Francisco (FP), and Juana Heredia (JH), 12/11/1990.

Sayay, Jacoba (JS), Tepeyac Bajo, 9/4/1992.

Shagñay, Avelino (AS), Tepeyac Bajo, 8/21/1991; 8/29, 9/4/1992; 6/16/1995.

Sisa, Reinaldo (RS), 9/14/1992; 6/15/1995.

Tenesaca, Esteban (ET), Riobamba, 10/4/1992.

Yépez, Andrés (AY), Tepeyac Bajo, 8/22 and 11/22/1992.

Yumbo, Alberto (AYu), Tepeyac Bajo, 7/16/1992; 6/13 and 6/17/1995.

SECONDARY SOURCES

Abercrombie, Thomas. 1998. *Pathways of Memory and Power: Ethnography and History among an Andean People*. Madison: University of Wisconsin Press.

Abu-Lughod, Lila. 1990. The Romance of Resistance: Tracing Transformations of Power through Bedouin Women. *American Ethnologist* 17(1):41–55.

Acosta, Alberto. 1994. *La deuda eterna*. Quito: Libresa.

Aguirre Beltrán, Gonzalo. 1967. *Regiones de refugio: El desarrollo de la comunidad y el proceso dominal en mestizo América*. Mexico City: Instituto Indigenista Interamericano.

Albán, María, and Juan Pablo Muñoz. 1987. *Con Dios todo se puede: La invasión de las sectas al Ecuador*. Quito: Editorial Planeta.

Alberti, Giorgio, and Enrique Mayer, eds. 1974. *Reciprocidad e intercambio en los Andes peruanos*. Lima: Instituto de Estudios Peruanos.

Allen, Catherine J. 1983. Of Bear-Men and He-Men: Bear Metaphors and Male Self-Perception in a Peruvian Community. *Latin American Indian Literatures* 7(1):38–51.

———. 1984. Patterned Time: The Mythic History of a Peruvian Community. *Journal of Latin American Lore* 10:151–173.

———. 1988. *The Hold Life Has*. Washington, D.C.: Smithsonian Institution Press.

Almeida, Ileana, et al. 1992. *Indios: Una reflexión sobre el levantamiento indígena de 1990*. Quito: Instituto Latinoamericano de Investigaciones Sociales, Abya-Yala.

Almeida Vinueza, José. 1990. Luchas campesinas del siglo XX (primera parte). In Enrique Ayala Mora, ed., *Nueva historia del Ecuador*. Vol. 10: Época republicana IV, El Ecuador entre los veinte y los sesenta. Quito: Corporación Editora Nacional/Editorial Grijalbo Ecuatoriana.

Anderson, Perry. 1976–1977. The Antimonies of Antonio Gramsci. *New Left Review* 100:5–78.

Anrup, Roland. 1990. *El taita y el toro: En torno a la configuración patriarcal del régimen hacendario cuzqueño*. Stockholm: Nalkas Boken Förlag, Goteburg University, University of Stockholm.

Arellano Gallegos, Jorge. 1985. *Teología de la liberación: Clericalismo en clave marxista*. Quito: Editorial Voluntad.

Argueta, Manlio. 1983. *One Day of Life*. New York: Vintage Books.

Asad, Talal. 1993. *Genealogies of Religion: Discipline and Reasons of Power in Christianity and Islam*. Baltimore, Md.: The Johns Hopkins University Press.

Ayala Mora, Enrique, ed. 1982–1995. *Nueva Historia del Ecuador*. 15 vols. Quito: Corporación Editora Nacional/Editorial Grijalbo Ecuatoriana.

Barksy, Osvaldo. 1988. *La reforma agraria ecuatoriana*. Quito: Corporación Editora Nacional.

Bastien, Joseph. 1978. *Mountain of the Condor: Metaphor and Ritual in an Andean Ayllu*. St. Paul, Minn.: West Publishing Co.

Bauer, Arnold. 1979. Rural Workers in Spanish America: Problems of Peonage and Oppression. *Hispanic American Historical Review* 59:34–63.

Bernand, Carmen. 1980. Tradition orale, histoire populaire et indianité dans une société paysanne de la *sierra* méridionale. *Cahiers du Monde Hispanique et Luso-Brésilien (Caravelle)* 34:83–98.

Bernard, H. Russell, and Jesús Salinas Pedraza. 1989. *Native Ethnography: A Mexican Indian Describes His Culture.* Newbury Park, Calif.: Sage Publications.

Bonnett Vélez, Diana. 1992. *Los protectores de naturales en la Audiencia de Quito: Siglos XVII y XVIII.* Quito: Facultad Latinoamericana de Ciencias Sociales, Sede Ecuador.

Borchart de Moreno, Christiana. 1980. La transferencia de la propiedad agraria indígena en el corregimiento de Quito hasta finales del siglo XVII. *Cahiers du Monde Hispanique et Luso-Brésilien (Caravelle)* 34:5–20.

———. 1988. Las tierras de comunidad de Licto, Punín y Macaxí: Factores para su disminución e intentos de restauración. *Revista Andina* 6(2):503–524.

Borja, Luis Alberto. 1953. *Cabalgando sobre los Andes.* Buenos Aires: Ediciones Peuser.

Botero V., Luis Fernando. 1992. *Indios, tierra y cultura.* Quito: Ediciones Abya-Yala.

Bourdieu, Pierre. 1977. *Outline of a Theory of Practice.* Trans. Richard Nice. Cambridge: Cambridge University Press.

Brandi, John, ed. 1976. *Chimborazo: Life on the Haciendas of Highland Ecuador.* Trans. Michael Scott and Mal Warwick. Mohawk Nation. Rooseveltown, N.Y.: Akwesasne Notes.

Brumann, Christophe. 1999. Writing for Culture: Why a Successful Concept Should Not Be Discarded. *Current Anthropology* 40 (Supplement):S1–S28.

Burdick, John. 1993. *Looking for God in Brazil: The Progressive Catholic Church in Urban Brazil's Religious Arena.* Berkeley & Los Angeles: University of California Press.

Burgos Guevara, Hugo. 1997. *Relaciones interétnicas en Riobamba: Dominio y dependencia en una región indígena ecuatoriana.* Quito: Corporación Editora Nacional.

Cabildo de Quito. [1577] 1991. Relación de la ciudad de Quito. In Pilar Ponce Leiva, ed., *Relaciones histórico-geográficas de la Audiencia de Quito, S. XVI–XIX.* Colección Tierra Nueva e Cielo Nuevo. Vol. 30, tomo I (S. XVI). Madrid: Consejo Superior de Investigaciones Científicas.

Cancian, Frank. 1965. *Economics and Prestige in a Maya Community: The Religious Cargo System in Zinacantan.* Stanford, Calif.: Stanford University Press.

Cantos, Miguel de. [1581] 1991. Relación para la Real Audiencia de los repartimientos y número de indios y encomenderos que hay en el corregimiento de Chimbo. In Pilar Ponce Leiva, ed., *Relaciones histórico-geográficas de la Audiencia de Quito, S. XVI–XIX.* Colección Tierra Nueva e Cielo Nuevo. Vol. 30, tomo I (S. XVI). Madrid: Consejo Superior de Investigaciones Científicas.

Castillo Jácome, Julio. [c. 1942]. *La provincia de Chimborazo en 1942*. Riobamba: Editorial Progreso.

CEAS, Centro de Estudios y Acción Social. 1971. *La cooperativa agropecuaria "Juan Diego" (Tepeyac)*. Riobamba: CEAS.

Chance, John K., and William B. Taylor. 1985. Cofradías and Cargos: An Historical Perspective on the Mesoamerican Civil-Religious Hierarchy. *American Ethnologist* 12(1):1–26.

Christian, William A. 1981. *Local Religion in Sixteenth-century Spain*. Princeton, N.J.: Princeton University Press.

Cobo, Bernabé. [1653] 1990. *Inca Religion and Customs*. Ed. and trans. Roland Hamilton. Austin: University of Texas Press.

Colloredo-Mansfeld, Rudolf. 1999. *The Native Leisure Class: Consumption and Cultural Creativity in the Andes*. Chicago: University of Chicago Press.

Contreras, Carlos. 1987. La crisis de la Sierra Central y Norte del Ecuador en la segunda mitad del siglo XVIII. *Revista Ecuatoriana de Historia Económica* 1(1):17–40.

Corrigan, Philip, and Derek Sayer. 1985. *The Great Arch: English State Formation as Cultural Revolution*. Oxford: Basil Blackwell.

Coser, R. L., ed. 1964. *The Family: Its Structure and Function* New York: St. Martin's Press.

Costales de Oviedo, Ximena, ed. 1983. *Etnohistoria del Corregimiento de Chimbo, 1557–1820*. [Quito]: Mundo Andino.

Crain, Mary M. 1991. Poetics and Politics in the Ecuadorean Andes: Women's Narratives of Death and Devil Possession. *American Ethnologist* 18(1):67–89.

Crespi, Muriel Kaminsky. 1968. *The Patrons and Peons of Pesillo: A Traditional Hacienda System in Highland Ecuador*. Ph.D. dissertation, University of Illinois. Ann Arbor, Mich.: University Microfilms.

———. 1981. St. John the Baptist: The Ritual Looking Glass of Hacienda Indian Ethnic and Power Relations. In *Cultural Transformations and Ethnicity in Modern Ecuador*, Norman E. Whitten Jr., ed. Urbana: University of Illinois Press.

Deere, Carmen Diana. 1990. Household and Class Relations: Peasants and Landlords in Northern Peru. Berkeley & Los Angeles: University of California Press.

Demélas, Marie-Danielle, and Yves Saint-Geours. 1988. *Jerusalén y Babilonia: Religión y política en el Ecuador, 1780–1880*. Trans. Carmen Garatea Yuri. Quito: Corporación Editora Nacional.

Doughty, Paul L. 1965. The Interrelationship of Power, Respect, Affection and Rectitude in Vicos. *American Behavioral Scientist* (Mar.):13–17.

Duncan, Kenneth, and Ian Rutledge, eds. 1977. *Land and Labour in Latin America: Essays on the Development of Agrarian Capitalism in the Nineteenth and Twentieth Centuries*. Cambridge: Cambridge University Press.

Edelman, Marc. 1994. Landlords and the Devil: Class, Ethnic, and Gender Dimensions of Central American Peasant Narratives. *Cultural Anthropology* 9(1):58–93.

Espinosa, Roque. 1984. Hacienda, concertaje y comunidad en el Ecuador. *Cultura* (Quito) 7(19) (May–Aug.):135–210.

Espinoza Soriano, Waldemar. 1988. *La etnia Chimbo, al oeste de Riobamba: El testimonio de la etnohistoria.* Guayaquil: Museos del Banco Central del Ecuador.

Flores Galindo, Alberto. 1987. In Search of an Inca. In *Resistance, Rebellion, and Consciousness in the Andean Peasant World, 18th to 20th Centuries,* ed. Steve J. Stern. Madison: University of Wisconsin Press.

Foster, George. 1960. *Culture and Conquest.* Chicago: Quadrangle Books.

Foucault, Michel. 1995. *Discipline and Punish: The Birth of the Prison.* New York: Vintage Books, Random House.

Frazier, Lessie Jo; Rosario Montoya; and Janise Hurtig, eds. 2002. *Gender's Place: Feminist Anthropologies of Latin America.* New York: Palgrave Macmillan.

Fuentealba M., Gerardo. 1990. La sociedad indígena en las primeras décadas de la República: Continuidades coloniales y cambios republicanos. In *Nueva Historia del Ecuador,* ed. Enrique Ayala Mora. Vol. 8: Época republicana II: Perspectiva general del siglo XIX. Quito: Corporación Editora Nacional/Editorial Grijalbo Ecuatoriana.

Gal, Susan. 1995. Language and the Arts of Resistance. *Cultural Anthropology* 10(3):407–424.

Gavilanes del Castillo, Luis María. 1992. *Monseñor Leonidas Proaño y su misión profético-liberadora en la iglesia de América Latina: Una aproximación crítica al pensamiento social y acción pastoral del obispo de los indios.* Quito: Fondo Ecuatoriano Populorum Progressio.

Geertz, Clifford. 1973. *The Interpretation of Cultures: Selected Essays.* New York: Basic Books.

Gramsci, Antonio. 1971. *Selections from the Prison Notebooks.* Ed. and trans. Quinten Hoare and Geoffrey Nowell Smith. London: Lawrence & Wishart.

Greenberg, James B. 1981. *Santiago's Sword: Chatino Peasant Religion and Economics.* Berkeley & Los Angeles: University of California Press.

Guaman Poma de Ayala [Waman Puma], Felipe. [1616] 1988. *El primer nueva corónica y buen gobierno.* Ed. John V. Murra and Rolena Adorno; trans. Jorge L. Urioste. Mexico City: Siglo Veintiuno.

Guerrero, Andrés. 1977. La hacienda precapitalista y la clase terrateniente en América y su inserción en el modo de producción capitalista: El caso ecuatoriano. *Anuario Indigenista* 37 (Dec.):65–130.

———. 1983. *Haciendas, capital y lucha de clases andina.* Quito: El Conejo.

———. 1991. *La semántica de la dominación: El concertaje de indios.* Quito: Ediciones Libri Mundi, Enrique Grosse-Luemern.

Haboud de Ortega, Marleen, et al. 1982. *Caimi Ñucanchic Shimiyuc-Panca.* Quito: Ministerio de Educación y Cultura, Pontificia Universidad Católica del Ecuador, ILL-CIEI.

Hall, Stuart. 1988. The Toad in the Garden: Thatcherism among the Theorists. In *Marxism and the Interpretation of Culture,* ed. Cary Nelson and Lawrence Grossberg. Urbana: University of Illinois Press.

Haro Alvear, Silvio Luis. 1977. *Puruhá, nación guerrera.* Quito: Editora Nacional.

Harris, Marvin. 1964. *Patterns of Race in the Americas.* New York: Walker.

Harris, Olivia. 1980. The Power of Signs: Gender, Culture, and the Wild in the Bolivian Andes. In *Nature, Culture and Gender,* ed. Carol MacCormack and Marilyn Strathern. Cambridge: Cambridge University Press.

Harris, Olivia, and Brooke Larson, eds. 1995. *Ethnicity, Markets, and Migration in the Andes: At the Crossroads of Anthropology and History.* Durham, N.C.: Duke University Press.

Harrison, Regina. 1989. *Signs, Songs, and Memory in the Andes: Translating Quechua Language and Culture.* Austin: University of Texas Press.

Horowitz, Maryanne Cline, ed. 1992. *Race, Gender, and Rank: Early Modern Ideas of Humanity.* Rochester, N.Y.: University of Rochester Press.

Howe, Leo. 1998. Scrounger, Worker, Beggarman, Cheat: The Dynamics of Unemployment and the Politics of Resistance in Belfast. *Journal of the Royal Anthropological Institute* 4(3):531–550.

Instituto Geográfico Militar (IGM). 1969. Sicalpa [map]. Serie J721. [Quito]: Instituto Geográfico Militar.

———. 1991. República del Ecuador, Mapa Físico. Escala 1:1'000.000. N.p. [Quito]: Instituto Geográfico Militar.

Isbell, Billie Jean. 1978. *To Defend Ourselves: Ecology and Ritual in an Andean Village.* Austin: University of Texas Press.

Jackson, Jean E. 1995. Culture, Genuine and Spurious: The Politics of Indianness in the Vaupés, Colombia. *American Ethnologist* 22(1):3–27.

Joseph, Gilbert M., and Daniel Nugent, eds. 1994. *Everyday Forms of State Formation: Revolution and the Negotiation of Rule in Modern Mexico.* Durham, N.C.: Duke University Press.

Joyce, Patrick, ed. 1995. *Class.* Oxford: Oxford University Press.

Juan, Jorge, and Antonio de Ulloa. [1747] 1990. *Noticias secretas de América.* Ed. Luis J. Ramos Gómez. Madrid: Historia 16.

Keen, Benjamin. 1985. Main currents in United States Writings on Colonial Spanish America, 1884–1984. *Hispanic American Historical Review* 65: 657–682.

Keith, Robert G., ed. 1977. *Haciendas and Plantations in Latin American History.* New York: Holmes & Meier.

Klaiber, Jeffrey L. 1992. The Posthumous Christianization of the Inca Empire in Colonial Peru. In *Race, Gender, and Rank: Early Modern Ideas of Humanity,* ed. Maryanne Cline Horowitz. Rochester: University of Rochester Press.

Korovkin, Tanya. 1993. Los indígenas, los campesinos y el estado: El crecimiento del movimiento comunitario en la Sierra ecuatoriana. Documento de Trabajo, No. 11. Quito: Facultad Latinoamericana de Ciencias Sociales, Sede Ecuador. (Published in English as Indigenous Peasant Struggles and the Capitalist Modernization of Agriculture, *Latin American Perspectives* 24[3] [1997].)

Kurtz, Donald V. 1996. Hegemony and Anthropology. *Critique of Anthropology* 16(2):103–135.

Lagos, Maria L. "We Have to Learn to Ask": Hegemony, Diverse Experiences, and Antagonistic Meanings in Bolivia. *American Ethnologist* 20(1):52–71.

Langer, Erick D. 1985. Labor Strikes and Reciprocity in Chuquisaca Haciendas. *Hispanic American Historical Review* 65:255–277.

———. 1989. *Economic Change and Rural Resistance in Southern Bolivia, 1880–1930*. Stanford, Calif.: Stanford University Press.

Larson, Brooke. 1991. Explotación y economía moral en los Andes del sur andino: Hacia una reconsideración crítica. In *Reproducción y transformación de las sociedades andinas, siglos XVI–XX*, ed. Segundo Moreno Yánez and Frank Salomon. Movimiento Laicos para América Latina (MLAL), vol. 2. Quito: Ediciones Abya-Yala.

———. 1998. *Cochabamba, 1550–1900: Colonialism and Agrarian Transformation in Bolivia*. Durham, N.C.: Duke University Press.

———, and Olivia Harris, with Enrique Tandeter, eds. 1995. *Ethnicity, Markets, and Migration in the Andes: At the Crossroads of History and Anthropology*. Durham, N.C.: Duke University Press.

Leach, Penelope. 1990. *Your Baby and Child: From Birth to Age Five*. New York: Alfred A. Knopf.

Lentz, Carola. 1986. De regidores a alcaldes: Cambios en la estructura sociopolítica de una comunidad indígena de Cajabamba/Chimborazo. *Ecuador-Debate* 12:189–212.

Lernoux, Penny. 1982. *Cry of the People: The Struggle for Human Rights in Latin America*. New York: Penguin Books.

Levi, Jerome M. 1999. Hidden Transcripts among the Rarámuri: Culture, Resistance, and Interethnic Relations in Northern Mexico. *American Ethnologist* 26(1):90–113.

Lévi-Strauss, Claude. 1964. Reciprocity: The Essence of Social Life. In *The Family: Its Structure and Function*, ed. R. L. Coser. New York: St. Martin's Press.

Levine, Daniel, ed. 1986. *Religion and Political Conflict in Latin America*. Chapel Hill: University of North Carolina Press.

Locke, John. [1690] 1993. First Treatise. In *Two Treatises of Government*. Mark Goldie, ed. London: Everyman.

López de Solís, Luis, Fray. [1594] 1978. Constituciones sinodales fechas por el Ilmo. Sr. D. Fr. Luis López de Solis, Maestro en Santa Teología, Obispo de Quito . . . In *Los sínodos de Quito del Siglo XVI*, ed. Instituto de Historia Eclesiástica Ecuatoriana. Quito: Facultad de Teología de la Pontificia Universidad Católica del Ecuador.

Lyons, Barry. 1994a. Hacienda Expansion and Indigenous Resistance in Alausí (Central Ecuador), 1599–1935. Presented at the 22nd Annual Midwest Conference on Andean and Amazonian Archaeology and Ethnohistory, University of Michigan, Ann Arbor, Feb. 26–27.

———. 1994b. In Search of "Respect": Culture, Authority, and Coercion on an Ecuadorian Hacienda. Ph.D. dissertation, University of Michigan at Ann Arbor.

———. 1999. "Taita Chimborazo and Mama Tungurahua": A Quichua Song, A Fieldwork Story. *Anthropology and Humanism* 24(1):1–14.

———. 2002a. Aurelio's Song. In *Personal Encounters: A Reader in Cultural Anthropology*, ed. Linda Walbridge and April Sievert. New York: McGraw Hill.

———. 2002b. "To Act Like a Man": Masculinity, Resistance, and Authority in the Ecuadorian Andes. In *Gender's Place: Feminist Anthropologies of Latin America*, ed. Lessie Jo Frazier, Rosario Montoya, and Janise Hurtig. New York: Palgrave Macmillan.

———. 2004. The Landowner inside Mt. Tungurahua: A Quichua Song and a Fieldwork Story. In *Quechua Verbal Artistry: The Inscription of Andean Voices/Arte Expresivo Quechua: La Inscripción de Voces Andinas*, ed. John Schechter and Guillermo Delgado. Bonn Americanist Studies series, vol. 38 Bonn: Universität Bonn; Aachen: Shaker.

———. N.d. "Awakening and Resistance: Liberation Theology, Land Reform, and the Indigenous Movement in Central Ecuador."

MacCormack, Carol, and Marilyn Strathern, eds. 1980. *Nature, Culture and Gender*. Cambridge: Cambridge University Press.

MacCormack, Sabine. 1985. The Heart Has Its Reasons: Predicaments of Missionary Christianity in Early Colonial Peru. *Hispanic American Historical Review* 65:443–466.

———. 1991. *Religion in the Andes: Vision and Imagination in Early Colonial Peru*. Princeton, N.J.: Princeton University Press.

Maldonado y Basabe, Rodolfo. 1930. *Monografía de la Provincia del Chimborazo*. Riobamba: Librería e Imprenta Nacional.

Mallon, Florencia E. 1983. *The Defense of Community in Peru's Central Highlands: Peasant Struggle and Capitalist Transition, 1860–1940*. Princeton, N.J.: Princeton University Press.

Maltby, Laura. 1980. Colonos on Hacienda Picotani. In *Land and Power in Latin America: Agrarian Economies and Social Processes in the Andes*, ed. Benjamin S. Orlove and Glynn Custred. New York: Holmes & Meier.

Mangin, William P. 1954. *The Cultural Significance of the Fiesta Complex in an Indian Hacienda in Peru*. Ph.D. dissertation, Yale University. Ann Arbor, Mich.: University Microfilms.

Marchán Romero, Carlos. 1984. El sistema hacendario serrano, movilidad y cambio agrario. *Cultura* (Quito) 7(19):63–106.

———, ed. 1986. *Pensamiento agrario ecuatoriano*. Quito: Banco Central del Ecuador, Corporación Editora Nacional.

Martínez Alier, Juan. 1977. Relations of Production in Andean Haciendas: Peru. In *Land and Labour in Latin America: Essays on the Development of Agrarian Capitalism in the Nineteenth and Twentieth Centuries*, ed. Kenneth Duncan and Ian Rutledge. Cambridge: Cambridge University Press.

Martínez F., Alexandra. 1990. Territorialidad indígena y hacienda a inicios del siglo XIX. In *Nueva Historia del Ecuador*, ed. Enrique Ayala Mora. Vol. 8: Época republicana II. Perspectiva General del Siglo XIX. Quito: Corporación Editora Nacional/Editorial Grijalbo Ecuatoriana.

Mauss, Marcel. 1990. *The Gift: The Form and Reason for Exchange in Archaic Societies*. Trans. W. D. Halls; foreword Mary Douglas. New York: W. W. Norton.

Maybury-Lewis, David, and Uri Almagor, eds. 1989. *The Attraction of Opposites: Thought and Society in the Dualistic Mode*. Ann Arbor: University of Michigan Press.

Mayer, Enrique. 2002. *The Articulated Peasant: Household Economies in the Andes*. Boulder, Colo.: Westview Press.

McKee, Lauris, dir. 1985. *Evil Wind, Evil Air; Mal Viento, Pasmo, Mal Aire*. Serie Etnomedicina y Niños. Museo del Banco Central del Ecuador.

Mintz, Sidney, and Eric Wolf. 1967. An Analysis of Ritual Coparenthood (Compadrasgo). In *Peasant Society: A Reader*, ed. J. Potter, M. Diaz, and G. Foster. Boston: Little, Brown.

Mitchell, Timothy. 1990. Everyday Metaphors of Power. *Theory and Society* 19:545–577.

Monaghan, John. 1990. Reciprocity, Redistribution, and the Transaction of Value in the Mesoamerican Fiesta. *American Ethnologist* 17(4):758–774.

Moncayo Andrade, Abelardo. [1895] 1986. El concertaje de indios. In *Pensamiento agrario ecuatoriano*, ed. Carlos Marchán Romero. Quito: Banco Central del Ecuador, Corporación Editora Nacional.

Moreno, Segundo, and Udo Oberem, eds. 1981. *Contribución a la etnohistoria ecuatoriana*. Otavalo: Instituto Otavaleño de Antropología.

Moreno Yánez, Segundo. 1981. Colonias mitmas en el Quito incaico: Su significación económica y política. In *Contribución a la etnohistoria ecuatoriana*, ed. Segundo Moreno and Udo Oberem. Otavalo: Instituto Otavaleño de Antropología.

———. 1985. *Sublevaciones indígenas en la audiencia de Quito*. Quito: Ediciones de la Pontificia Universidad Católica del Ecuador.

———. 1989. La sociedad indígena y su articulación a la formación socioeconómica colonial en la Audiencia de Quito. In *Nueva historia del Ecuador*, ed. Enrique Ayala Mora. Vol. 5: Época colonial III. Perspectiva General de la Colonia. Quito: Corporación Editora Nacional, Editorial Grijalbo Ecuatoriana.

———, and Frank Salomon, eds. 1991. *Reproducción y transformación de las sociedades andinas, siglos XVI–XX*. Movimiento Laicos para América Latina, vol. 2. Quito: Ediciones Abya-Yala.

Muñoz-Bernand, Carmen. 1986. *Enfermedad, daño e ideología: Antropología médica de los renacientes de Pindilig*. Quito: Ediciones Abya-Yala.

Muratorio, Blanca. 1980. Protestantism and Capitalism Revisited, in the Rural Highlands of Ecuador. *Journal of Peasant Studies* 8:37–60.

Murra, John V. 1962. Cloth and Its Functions in the Inca State. *American Anthropologist* 64:710–728.

———. 1975. *Formaciones económicas y políticas del mundo andino*. Lima: Instituto de Estudios Peruanos.

———. 1978. *La organización económica del estado Inca*. Mexico City: Siglo XXI.

———; Nathan Wachtel; and Jacques Revel, eds. 1986. *Anthropological History of Andean Politics*. Cambridge: Cambridge University Press.

Nader, Laura. 1990. *Harmony Ideology: Justice and Control in a Zapotec Mountain Village*. Stanford, Calif.: Stanford University Press.

Nelson, Cary, and Lawrence Grossberg, eds. 1988. *Marxism and the Interpretation of Culture.* Urbana: University of Illinois Press.

Oberem, Udo. 1981. Contribución a la historia del trabajador rural en América Latina: "Conciertos" y "huasipungueros" en Ecuador. In *Contribución a la etnohistoria ecuatoriana,* ed. Segundo Moreno and Udo Oberem. Otavalo: Instituto Otavaleño de Antropología.

O'Connor, Erin E. 1997. Dueling Patriarchies: Gender, Indians, and State Formation in the Ecuadorian Sierra, 1860–1925. Ph.D. dissertation, Boston College.

———. 2002. Widows' Rights Questioned: Indians, the State, and Fluctuating Gender Ideas in Central Highland Ecuador, 1870–1900. *The Americas* 59(1):87–106.

Orlove, Benjamin S. 1974. Reciprocidad, desigualdad y dominación. In *Reciprocidad e Intercambio en los Andes Peruanos,* ed. Giorgio Alberti and Enrique Mayer. Lima: Instituto de Estudios Peruanos.

———, and Glynn Custred, eds. 1980. *Land and Power in Latin America: Agrarian Economies and Social Processes in the Andes.* New York: Holmes & Meier.

Ortner, Sherry B. 1984. Theory in Anthropology since the Sixties. *Comparative Studies in Society and History* 26:126–166.

———. 1995. Resistance and the Problem of Ethnographic Refusal. *Comparative Studies in Society and History* 37:173–193.

Pallares, Amalia. 2002. *From Peasant Struggles to Indian Resistance: The Ecuadorian Andes in the Late Twentieth Century.* Norman: University of Oklahoma Press.

Parry, Jonathan. 1986. The Gift, the Indian Gift, and the "Indian Gift." *Man* 21(3):453–473.

Paz Maldonado, Juan. [1582] 1991. Relación del pueblo de San Andrés Xunxi para el Muy Ilustre Sr. Licenciado D. Francisco de Aucibay . . . In *Relaciones histórico-geográficas de la Audiencia de Quito, S. XVI–XIX,* ed. Pilar Ponce Leiva. Colección Tierra Nueva E Cielo Nuevo, Vol. 30, tomo I (S. XVI). Madrid: Consejo Superior de Investigaciones Científicas.

Peña Montenegro, Alonso de la. [1668] 1985. *Itinerario para párrocos de indios.* Anuario Histórico Jurídico Ecuatoriano 9. Guayaquil: Corporación de Estudios y Publicaciones.

Pérez Tamayo, Aquiles R. 1947. *Las mitas en la Real Audiencia de Quito.* Quito: Imprenta del Ministerio del Tesoro.

Platt, Tristan. 1986. Mirrors and Maize: The concept of *Yanantin* among the Macha of Bolivia. In *Anthropological History of Andean Politics,* ed. John V. Murra, Nathan Wachtel, and Jacques Revel. Cambridge: Cambridge University Press.

———. 2001. El feto agresivo. *Anuario de Estudios Americanos* 58(2):633–678.

Polanyi, Karl. 1968. *Primitive, Archaic and Modern Economies: Essays of Karl Polanyi.* Ed. George Dalton. Garden City, N.Y.: Doubleday Anchor.

Poole, Deborah A. 1990. Accommodation and Resistance in Andean Ritual Dance. *Drama Review* 34(2):98–126.

————, ed. 1994. *Unruly Order: Violence, Power, and Cultural Identity in the High Provinces of Southern Peru.* Boulder, Colo.: Westview Press.

Ponce Leiva, Pilar, ed. 1991. *Relaciones histórico-geográficas de la Audiencia de Quito, S. XVI-XIX.* Colección Tierra Nueva e Cielo Nuevo, vol. 30, tomo I (S. XVI). Madrid: Consejo Superior de Investigaciones Científicas.

Potter, J.; M. Díaz; and G. Foster, eds. 1967. *Peasant Society: A Reader.* Boston: Little, Brown.

Powers, Karen Vieira. 1995. *Andean Journeys: Migration, Ethnogenesis, and the State in Colonial Quito.* Albuquerque: University of New Mexico Press.

Proaño, Juan Félix. 1915. *Memoria de la Diócesis de Riobamba en los cincuenta años que lleva de existencia, 1865-1915.* Riobamba: Imprenta La Moderna.

Proaño, Leonidas. 1989. *Creo en el hombre y en la comunidad: Autobiografía.* Quito: Corporación Editora Nacional.

Ramón Valarezo, Galo. 1987. *La resistencia andina: Cayambe 1500-1800.* Quito: Centro Andino de Acción Popular.

Rasnake, Roger Neil. 1988. *Domination and Cultural Resistance: Authority and Power among an Andean People.* Durham N.C.: Duke University Press.

Ricciardi, Ramón, and Bernardo Hurault. 1989. *La biblia latinoamericana.* 78th ed. Madrid: Ediciones Paulinas, Editorial Verbo Divino.

Rodseth, Lars. 1998. Distributive Models of Culture: A Sapirian Alternative to Essentialism. *American Anthropologist* 100(1):55-69.

Rose, Nikolas. 1995. Towards a Critical Sociology of Freedom. In *Class,* ed. Patrick Joyce. Oxford: Oxford University Press.

Roseberry, William. 1994. Hegemony and the Language of Contention. In *Everyday Forms of State Formation: Revolution and the Negotiation of Rule in Modern Mexico,* ed. Gilbert M. Joseph and Daniel Nugent. Durham, N.C.: Duke University Press.

Rosero, Fernando. 1990. *Levantamiento indígena: Tierra y precios.* Quito: Centro de Estudios y Difusión Social.

Sáenz, Álvaro, and Diego Palacios. 1992. La dimensión demográfica de la historia ecuatoriana. In *Nueva historia del Ecuador,* ed. Enrique Ayala Mora. Vol. 12: Ensayos generales I. Espacio, población, región. Quito: Corporación Editora Nacional/Editorial Grijalbo Ecuatoriana.

Sahlins, Marshall. 1972. *Stone Age Economics.* Chicago: Aldine Atherton.

Saignes, Thierry, ed. 1993. *Borrachera y memoria: La experiencia de lo sagrado en los Andes.* La Paz: Hisbol/Instituto Francés de Estudios Andinos.

Salazar de Villasante, Lic. [c. 1570-1571] 1991. Relación de la ciudad y provincia de Quito. In Pilar Ponce Leiva, ed., *Relaciones histórico-geográficas de la Audiencia de Quito, S. XVI-XIX.* Colección Tierra Nueva e Cielo Nuevo. Vol. 30, tomo I (S. XVI). Madrid: Consejo Superior de Investigaciones Científicas.

Salomon, Frank. 1981. Killing the Yumbo. In *Cultural Transformations and Ethnicity in Modern Ecuador,* ed. Norman E. Whitten Jr. Urbana: University of Illinois Press.

———. 1983. Shamanism and Politics in Late Colonial Ecuador. *American Ethnologist* 19:413–428.

———. 1986a. *Native Lords of Quito in the Age of the Incas: The Political Economy of North Andean Chiefdoms*. Cambridge: Cambridge University Press.

———. 1986b. Vertical Politics on the Inka Frontier. In *Anthropological History of Andean Polities*, ed. John Murra, Nathan Wachtel, and Jacques Revel. Cambridge: Cambridge University Press.

———. 1988. Crisis y transformación de la sociedad aborigen invadida (1528–1573). In *Nueva historia del Ecuador*, ed. Enrique Ayala Mora. Vol. 3: Época colonial I, Conquista y primera etapa colonial. Quito: Corporación Editora Nacional/Editorial Grijalbo Ecuatoriana.

Sánchez-Parga, José, comp. 1990. *Etnia, poder y diferencia en los Andes septentrionales*. Quito: Abya-Yala.

Santana, Roberto. 1990. El Protestantismo en las comunidades indígenas del Chimborazo en Ecuador. In *Etnia, poder y diferencia en los Andes septentrionales*, comp. José Sánchez-Parga. Quito: Abya-Yala.

Schechter, John, and Guillermo Delgado, eds. 2004. *Quechua Verbal Artistry: The Inscription of Andean Voices/Arte Expresivo Quechua: La Inscripción de Voces Andinas*. Bonn Americanist Studies series, vol. 38. Bonn: Universität Bonn; Aachen: Shaker.

Schroder, Barbara. 1984. Haciendas, Indians and Economic Change in Chimborazo, Ecuador. Ph.D. dissertation, Rutgers University.

Scott, James. 1976. *The Moral Economy of the Peasant: Rebellion and Subsistence in Southeast Asia*. New Haven, Conn.: Yale University Press.

———. 1985. *Weapons of the Weak: Everyday Forms of Peasant Resistance*. New Haven, Conn.: Yale University Press.

———. 1990. *Domination and the Arts of Resistance: Hidden Transcripts*. New Haven, Conn.: Yale University Press.

Silverblatt, Irene. 1987. *Moon, Sun, and Witches: Gender Ideologies and Class in Inca and Colonial Peru*. Princeton, N.J.: Princeton University Press.

Skar, Harald O. 1981. *The Warm Valley People: Duality and Land Reform among the Quechua Indians of Highland Peru*. Oslo: Universitetsforlaget.

Spalding, Karen. 1973. Kurakas and Commerce. *Hispanic American Historical Review* 53:581–599.

———. 1974. *De indio a campesino*. Lima: Instituto de Estudios Peruanos.

———. 1984. *Huarochirí: An Andean Society under Inca and Spanish Rule*. Stanford, Calif.: Stanford University Press.

Stern, Steve. 1982. *Peru's Indian People and the Challenge of the Spanish Conquest*. Madison: University of Wisconsin Press.

———. 1983. The Struggle for Solidarity: Class, Culture, and Community in Highland Indian America. *Radical History Review* 27:21–45.

———, ed. 1987. *Resistance, Rebellion, and Consciousness in the Andean Peasant World, 18th to 20th Centuries*. Madison: University of Wisconsin Press.

Stutzman, Ronald. 1981. *El Mestizaje:* An All-Inclusive Ideology of Exclusion. In *Cultural Transformations and Ethnicity in Modern Ecuador*, ed. Norman E. Whitten Jr. Urbana: University of Illinois Press.

Sylva Charvet, Paola. 1986. *Gamonalismo y lucha campesina (Estudio de la sobrevivencia y disolución de un sector terrateniente: El caso de la provincia de Chimborazo. 1940-1979)*. Quito: Ediciones Abya-Yala.

Taussig, Michael. 1980. *The Devil and Commodity Fetishism in South America*. Chapel Hill: University of North Carolina Press.

———. 1987. *Shamanism, Colonialism, and the Wild Man: A Study in Terror and Healing*. Chicago: University of Chicago Press.

Tedlock, Dennis. 1983. *The Spoken Word and the Work of Interpretation*. Philadelphia: University of Pennsylvania Press.

Thurner, Mark. 1993. Peasant Politics and Andean Haciendas in the Transition to Capitalism: An Ethnographic History. *Latin American Research Review* 28(3):41–82.

Tilly, Charles. 1991. Domination, Resistance, Compliance . . . Discourse. *Sociological Forum* 6(3):593–602.

Tolen, Rebecca. 1995. Wool and Synthetics, Countryside and City: Dress, Race and History in Chimborazo, Highland Ecuador. Ph.D. dissertation, University of Chicago.

Trujillo León, Jorge. 1986. *La hacienda serrana 1900-1930*. Quito: Instituto de Estudios Ecuatorianos, Ediciones Abya-Yala.

Tufiño, Ismael. 1987. *La cantonización de Pallatanga*. N.p.: Ilustre Municipalidad de Pallatanga, Artes Gráficas Arboleda.

Tullis, F. LaMond. 1970. *Lord and Peasant in Peru: A Paradigm of Political and Social Change*. Cambridge, Mass.: Harvard University Press.

Van Aken, Mark. 1981. The Lingering Death of Indian Tribute in Ecuador. *Hispanic American Historical Review* 61:429–459.

Vásquez, Mario C. 1963. Autoridades de una hacienda andina peruana. *Perú Indígena* 24/25:24–36.

Wachtel, Nathan. 1977. *The Vision of the Vanquished: The Spanish Conquest of Peru through Indian Eyes, 1530-1570*. New York: Barnes and Noble.

Walbridge, Linda, and April Sievert, eds. 2002. *Personal Encounters: A Reader in Cultural Anthropology*. New York: McGraw-Hill.

Webster, Steven. 1981. Interpretation of an Andean Social and Economic Formation. *Man* 16(4):616–633.

Weismantel, Mary. 1988. *Food, Gender, and Poverty in the Ecuadorian Andes*. Philadelphia: University of Pennsylvania Press.

———. 2001. *Cholas and Pishtacos: Stories of Race and Sex in the Andes*. Chicago: University of Chicago Press.

Whitten, Norman E., Jr., ed. 1981. *Cultural Transformations and Ethnicity in Modern Ecuador*. Urbana: University of Illinois Press.

Whyte, William Foote, and Giorgio Alberti. 1976. *Power, Politics, and Progress: Social Change in Rural Peru*. New York: Elsevier.

Williams, Derek. 2003. Popular Liberalism and Indian Servitude: The Making and Unmaking of Ecuador's Antilandlord State, 1845–1868. *Hispanic American Historical Review* 83(4):697–733.

Wogan, Peter. 1998. Magical Literacy: Encountering a Witch's Book in Ecuador. *Anthropological Quarterly* 71(4):186–202.

Wolf, Eric. 1955. Types of Latin-American Peasantry: A Preliminary Discussion. *American Anthropologist* 57:452–471.

———. 1982. *Europe and the People without History*. Berkeley & Los Angeles: University of California Press.

———, and Sidney Mintz. 1977. Haciendas and Plantations. In *Haciendas and Plantations in Latin American History*, ed. Robert G. Keith. New York: Holmes & Meier.

Woost, Michael D. 1993. Nationalizing the Local Past in Sri Lanka: Histories of Nation and Development in a Sinhalese Village. *American Ethnologist* 20(3):502–521.

Yánez del Pozo, José. 1988. *Yo declaro con franqueza, Cashnami Causashcanchic: Memoria oral de Pesillo-Cayambe*. Quito: Ediciones Abya-Yala.

Zamosc, Leon. 1994. Agrarian Protest and the Indian Movement in the Ecuadorian Highlands. *Latin American Research Review* 29(3):37–68.

Zuidema, R. Tom. 1989. The Moieties of Cuzco. In *The Attraction of Opposites: Thought and Society in the Dualistic Mode*, ed. David Maybury-Lewis and Uri Almagor. Ann Arbor: University of Michigan Press.

———. 1997. The Wari Songs of the Noble Initiands in Cuzco and Their Possible Content. Quechua Expressive Art International Symposium, University of California, Santa Cruz, Sept. 4–6.

INDEX

Note: Photographs, maps, figures, and other images are indexed in italics.

acude, 79, 137, 144–145

afterlife, 160–163; and blessing, forgiveness, 229; and legitimacy of hacienda system, 128; mountain spirits' warnings of punishments in, 106; soul's journey, 239; of unbaptized babies, 241–242

agrarian reform: Ajospamba, 145–146; Ecuador, 4, 61, 264–265; and memory of hacienda-era suffering, 203–205; and Monjas Corral residents' perceptions of *amos*, bishop, 157–158; Monjas Corral-Tepeyac, 5, 15, 61–62, 263–273; proposals to modify (1994), 255; Reinaldo Sisa on, 200

agriculture: crops and ecological zones, 27, 31–33, 76, 88; planting ritual, prayers, 114. *See also* fiestas: and fertility

Ajospamba (hacienda), 82, 145–146

alcaldes, 106

alcohol: banned in evangelical Protestantism, 207; in fiestas, 108, 110–114, 187; offered by overseers to victims of whipping, 246; in *pascuanchina*, 226–227

Allpa Mama (earth mother), 114

amos, 97–98; as elders, 236–240; and paternalism, 240–245; and racism, 238

archival records: inventory of hacienda residents, debts, 57; limitations of, 10–11, 55; Monjas Corral account books, 131–135, *133*

arrimados, 80; disadvantaged in agrarian reform, 204; and hacienda labor demands, 143

Asad, Talal, 225, 317n11

authority: of catechists, 277, 302–303; of catechists compared to Protestant pastors, 319n11; of chiefs (colonial), 39–40; of chiefs (precolonial), 36; of community officers, compared to landlords, 289–290; of *fundadores*, 116, 121; and hacienda-era respect, discipline, 216–255; hybrid Andean-European, 35; of indigenous catechists and lay ministers compared to priests, 288; parental, as model for rulers', 317n18; and redistribution, 36, 38–40, 50; of religious elders, compared to catechists as modern experts, 298–299. *See also* paternalism; respect

autonomy, 11–16; and base of triangle, 73, 81, 87, 97, 99; and fiesta, 101–102; and resistance, 126

ayuda, 80, 174, 261; laborers disadvantaged in agrarian reform, 204; and post-agrarian reform community, 272

baptism, 241–242; and *compadrazgo*, 83, 85–86; mentioned, 6, 316n10

Baraspamba, 50, 80

Barba, Leandro, 56, 64–65, 88, 192

Barba, Manuela, 55

Barba, Vicente, 49, 52–54

Bible: mentioned, 271; and mountains, 105; role in liberation theology, 5, 22; study and reflection, 5, 272, 277, 282, 295–305, 319n7

bishop (after Proaño), 5–6

bishop(s) (pre-Proaño): in exile after Liberal Revolution, 58; and hacienda rentals, ties to renters, 62–64; on obedience and buying new clothes, 312n10; of Quito, Peña Montenegro, 44, 156–157; on socialists and Indians, 312n8; on worldly poverty, treasures of faith, transience of life, 67

body-mind dichotomy, 222, 228

Bolívar province. *See* Chimbo valley

Bourdieu, Pierre, 222

caciques. See chiefs and chiefdoms: colonial

Cantos, Miguel de, 37

capitalism: agrarian, in Latin America, 18; and hegemony, 19–20, 221; and moral judgment, 127–128; and obligation, 16; and Protestant missionaries, 207; and reciprocity, 91–92, 141. *See also* haciendas: and markets; landlords: as entrepreneurs

Carnival, 92–94; as occasion for ritual exchange, 135–137; saints of, 313n6 (chap. 4)

Castillo, Andrés (*amo* Castillo), 26, 85, 162, 168–170

catechists, 6, 277; authority of, 302–303, 319n11; biography of, 281–282; and conflict resolution, 292; course for, 287; as experts, not elders, 299; on Jesus's color, 238; and sacraments, 300

Catholic Church: agrarian reform period, 33, 61, 124, 264–265; colonial era, 44, 47, 156, 225, 317n17; and festive drinking, 112; and historical narratives, 129; and Liberal Revolution, 55, 58; and nineteenth-century state, 48; and religious subjectivity, 300. *See also* catechists; diocese of Riobamba; fiestas; liberation theology; priests; saints; Vatican II

Centro de Formación Indígena (CFI), 277–278

chiefs and chiefdoms: colonial, 13, 38–42, 44–45, 92, 141; Inca-era, 37; pre-Inca, 36–37

child rearing, 241–245; children's labor on hacienda, 79, 143, 171–172, 178–179, 193; and coercion-persuasion dichotomy, 317n18; contemporary Bible reflections on, 6, 297–298; and domestic life cycle, hacienda debt, 134; and fear of *amos*, 97–98; godparents' role in, 83; instruction in planting prayers, 114; landlord rewarding child for deference, 237; of landowner's daughter by rape, 169–170; parents' moral instruction, 194–195; physical punishment, decline in, 292, 319n5; and post-agrarian reform labor migration, 273; and resistance, 252; respect taught to children, 81, 217. See also *doctrina; pascuanchina;* literacy and schooling

Chimbo (people), 36–38
Chimbo (town), 30
Chimborazo (province), 5, 26, 29, 30
Chimborazo central basin: mentioned, 86; migration from, 51; pasturage arrangements in Monjas Corral, 87; and pilgrimages, 95; precolonial, 36–37
Chimbo valley (and San Ramón), 14, 16–17, 28, 29–30; crime in, 319n6; exchange with Pangor, 89; fictive kinship with Pangor Runa, 86; Inca era, 38; people of, designation, 98; and pilgrimages, 95; ritual whipping of plants, 225–226; whipping by school teacher, 317n15
chuzalungu, 195–196
closed corporate communities, 93
coercion: defined, 223; as element of hegemony, 221; and moral judgment, 127; and persuasion, dichotomy of, 22, 222–223, 235, 253; to retain laborers, 58
colonial period, 38–48
community (post-agrarian reform): as body of Christ, 301; and fiesta, 275–276; and indigenous law, 288–295; as successor to hacienda, 272
compadrazgo. See under kinship
comuna. See community
concertaje, 43, 78; abolition, 58–59; debt and reciprocity, 131; and rental contracts, 57, 65–66
concierto. See concertaje
confession, 190–191, 225–226, 249
conflict resolution: by contemporary community structures, 289–295; in doctrina, 232–235
conflicts (specific incidents): Amanchas vs. Ignacio Lara and renter (1961), 250–252, 259–262; Barba, Manuela, vs. diocese over Monjas Corral, 55; Barba, Vicente, vs. Pacífico Gallegos over Monjas Corral, 52–54; común of Pangor

vs. haciendas, 49–50; detention of suspected animal rustler (1992), 293–295; Paca, Agustín, vs. wife's half brothers over land, witchcraft, 291; Pangor hacienda residents vs. steward over labor demands (1864), 54; Pillajo, José, vs. Ignacio Lara over death of cow, 157, 210–211, 315n10; Sayay, Jacoba, vs. amo over death of sheep under brother's care, 178–179; Sayay, Jacoba, vs. husband, 173–174; Sayay, Jacoba, vs. Ignacio Lara over firewood, 171–172, 213–214; Shagñay, Avelino, vs. Ajospamba steward over potato harvest and gleaning, 154–155; Sisa, Reinaldo, vs. Alonso Guevara in defense of Runa's livestock, 59, 196–199; whipping of Manuel Yépez for incorrectly skinning sheep, 3–4, 255
consent. See persuasion
Cordovez, Aurelio and Domingo, 56, 58, 62, 64–65
Corpus Christi, 93–95
covert appropriation: and conflict over redistribution, 155–157; and Reinaldo Sisa's account of relationship with amos, 184–185, 212
cowhands, 77–78, 156–157, 185, 193, 199
cristiano, 318n2
culture, 8–9; (in)consistencies, 236–237. See also indigenous culture

debt peonage, 12, 14, 18, 43, 49. See also concertaje
deference, 219–220; to God as white man in myth, 216; to landlords, 188; to nuns, 190; to priests, 188; and Protestant conversion, 206; to religious elders and hacienda bosses, 217. See also greetings
development(alism): and historical narratives, 205–208

devil, 9, 17, 97, 159–163, 216; and color symbolism, 238–239

diocese of Riobamba: and haciendas, 62–67, 88; purchase of Monjas Corral, 55; theological outlook, pre-Vatican II, 67. *See also* bishops; Proaño, Leonidas

discipline, 22, 223–224; in child rearing, 241–245, 317n18; in *doctrina*, 231–235; and hacienda labor, 245–248; as sacrament, 224–231. *See also* moral instruction; respect

doctrina, 231–235, 246; Bible reflection as, 297, 303; contrasted with Bible reflection, 300–301; and fiesta sponsorship, 120; García Moreno's promotion of, 312n9; post-agrarian reform decline of, 277

dreams, 123

dress: colonial chiefs' adoption of Spanish, 40; described and terms defined, 318n1; and ethnicity, 28, 33, *34*, 282–284, 302; Proaño's, 5

elders, 81; *amos* as, 235–240; and contemporary Catholic activist discourse, 282–288; contemporary tensions with juniors, 304–305; and *doctrina*, 232–235; and fiestas, 114–124; and hegemonic bloc, forms of domination, 254; and *pascuanchina*, 226–231 *passim*; Quichua term for, and experience, knowledge, 239; religious, contrasted to modern experts, 298–299

encomienda, 41–42, 44–45

ethnicity and race: boundaries as permeable, 9, 23, 25; catechist's commentary on preserving indigenous customs, 301–302; categories and historical origins of, 9, 27, 46–48, 50, 96–98, 313nn6–7; and fiesta sponsorship, 116; hierarchy, solidarity, and contemporary fiestas, 276; and historical consciousness, 52, 130–131; in linguistic conventions, 317n14; literacy as marker of, 239–240, 282; in myth, 130, 216–217, 315n2; precolonial, 36; and resistance as collective tradition, 250–251; of saints, 314n9. *See also amos*; dress; Indians; indigenous; language: and ethnicity; Puruhá; racism

exchange networks, 14, 27; hacienda-era, 87–90; precolonial, 37

exoticism, 28

fieldwork (author's), 5–7, 27–28, 55; author as example in CFI discussion, 318n2; host family, 96, 167; interactions and interviews described, 3–4, 11, 279; meetings with Reinaldo Sisa, 89, 180

fiestas, 100–124; anthropology of, 101; contemporary Catholic activist views of, 287; and elder-junior hierarchy, 81; and fertility, 100–105, 313n1; and fictive kin, 86; and hacienda boundaries and social networks, 92–95; and indigenous autonomy, 101–102; nineteenth-century, 50; post-agrarian reform transformations in, 272–277; Reinaldo Sisa's account of, 186–187; as sacrifice, 313n7; saints' blessings questioned, 281; sponsorship, 106–108; sponsorship as template for community offices, 272; state's, church's, elites' promotion of, 101; and supplements, 132; twenty-first century, 305; in Vicos, 313n4

figures: José María Pillajo's kin, *84*; triangle without a base, *13*. *See also* maps; photographs; tables

fines: in community, 292; on hacienda, 155–157, 176, 193, 243–244

Foucault, Michel, 223
fundadores, 81, 106, 100–124
    passim; and 1960s agrarian con-
    flicts, 254, 261; and community
    social organization, 93; and *doc-
    trina*, 232–235; end of role (1986),
    275; as overseers, and authority
    of, 177–178; and *pascuanchina*,
    230

García Moreno, Gabriel, 50, 68, 103,
    231, 312n9
gender: of catechists, CFI students,
    277–278, 299; and child rear-
    ing, paternalism, 242–243; and
    conflict resolution, hegemony,
    254–255; and domination, defi-
    ance, 212–215, 251; female sexual
    honor and hacienda bosses, 174–
    175; and hacienda labor, 144;
    ideology, 235, 317n12; rape and
    sexual exploitation on haciendas,
    167–170, 172–173, 213, 249–250,
    259; and ritual, 316n7; roles in
    marriage, 193; sexual exploitation
    by priests, 187, 191–192; sexual
    insults, 172, 174; sexual unions
    and racial categories, 47–48; and
    strategic stances toward hacienda
    authority, 211. *See also* marriage
gleaning, 135, 154–155
God: as agent in *pascuanchina*,
    228; and ages of world in oral
    tradition, 130; agrarian reform
    as response to prayers to, 272;
    and agricultural fertility, 102–
    103, 114–115, 123, 185, 216; and
    amos as elders, 236; as angry at
    Runa, 131; baptism and dignity
    of children of, 5–6; catechist's
    view of hacienda-era elders as
    ignorant about, 281; and conflicts
    with landlords, 198, 261; con-
    temporary views of, compared
    to hacienda era, and discipline,
    292; and hacienda production,
    160–161; laborers' appeals to, for

punishment of oppressors, 247;
    and mountains, 106; and origins
    of races, 315n2; as owner of Mon-
    jas Corral, 131; Protestant view of,
    as unrecognized in hacienda era,
    187–190; and respectful greetings,
    219; Tayta Amito as name for,
    97; wandering earth, stories of,
    216–217. *See also* Jesus
good back, 182, 212
Gramsci, Antonio, 19–20, 221,
    315n3, 318n1
greetings: Alberto Yumbo's account
    of learning, 217; and *compa-
    drazgo*, fictive kinship, 83, 87, 89;
    and fiesta sponsorship, 111, 116–
    117, 121; and intergenerational
    tensions (1990s), nostalgia, 224;
    moral instruction in, 190, 232; to
    new renter, 149; and Protestant
    conversion, 206; as public tran-
    script, and God, 219; to renters,
    amos, 188, 237–238; to *virgen-
    citas* (pilgrimage as greeting),
    122
Guaman Poma de Ayala, Felipe,
    233–234, 236, 316n7
Guangopud (community), 279
Guangopud (hacienda), 45, 80, 85,
    162, 168–170, 234; Reinaldo Sisa's
    flight to, 201–202
Guerrero, Andrés, 14, 138, 140
Guerrero, Armando, 26, 264–270
    passim
Guevara family (Vicente, widow,
    sons), 56, 58, 60, 62–63, 65, 196

hacendados. See landlords
haciendas: anthropology of, 7, 10–
    15, 17; colonial origins and de-
    velopment, 38–42; competition
    for *conciertos*, 43; labor regime,
    141–153; labor shortage, 54; and
    markets, 18–19, 49–50, 60–61, 64,
    68; term, 3, 73–74; as unit of iden-
    tity, 95–96; as unit of religious
    life, 92–95; variation among, 7

hegemonic bloc, 20, 254

hegemony, 19–22, 220–223, 241, 253–254

historical consciousness and narratives, 35, 51–52, 69; of awakening, 33, 205–206, 262–263, 270–271, 318n1; and contemporary Catholic activist redefinition of ethnicity, 284–288; and land, 129–131; of resistance, respect as shaping, 250–252

holy earth (*santo suelo*), 202

Holy Week, 53, 249, 316n7. See also *pascuanchina*

household economy: and agrarian reform, 265–267; agriculture, 76; and *arrimados*, 80; and exchange networks, 87–90; and hacienda labor demands, 142–144, 200–201; and hacienda land tenure system, 270; livestock, 76; and marriage, 117–118; post-agrarian reform, compared with hacienda-era, 16, 273; Reinaldo Sisa's account of, 185–186; and supplements, 134–135. See also exchange networks

huasicama, 79, 170–172, 176, 180, 261, 264

huasipungaje, 78, 128–129; and conflict over labor demands, 142

Inca: deities interpreted in theology of inculturation, 288; feast of Citua, compared with Pentecost ritual, 316n7; labor demands, contrasted with hacienda, 145; language, 27; in oral tradition, 103, 130; state, and redistribution, 17, 38; state policies, 37–38, 41

inculturation, 277–278, 288, 296

Indian Hispanism, 220–221

Indians: images of, 9, 27–28, 33–36; term, 36, 200; as thieves, in elite perceptions, 156

indigenous

—culture (as concept in contemporary discourse), 277, 285–288;

community as expression of, 292–293; and fiesta sponsorship, 318n3

—movement, 15–16; and historical narratives, 205–208; mentioned, 269–270

—people (as category), 35–36, 98

—uprising (1990), 15–16, 286, 289

Jesus: color of, 238; as culture hero, 130; and Eucharist, reflection on, 296; and greetings to renters, 188; as Lord of Health, pilgrimage to, 95; and *pascuanchina*, 227; and priest as Christ, 315n6; in Protestantism, 187; Sacred Heart of, 103; wandering earth, stories of, 216–217; as youth, 297–298

kamari, 136–137

kariyana, 213, 251

kinship: among bishop and renter, 62; *compadrazgo* and other fictive forms of, 83, 85–87, 139; among hacienda residents, 82–83, 84, 210–211; and Scott's approach to hegemony, 220

knowledge: and authority of catechist, 299; and/as power, 271, 282. See also literacy

Krueger, José, 26, 170, 175–176

landlords: arrival of new renter, 147–150; as entrepreneurs, 53–54, 64–65, 68; fictional dialogue among, 138; and fiestas, saints, 101–104; land acquisition and hacienda expansion, 40, 45, 49–50; prestige orientation, 53; renters compared to private landowners, 77, 136–137; renters' moral claim to labor, 147; table, renters of Monjas Corral, 56; self-understanding as heirs of Spanish Christianizing, civilizing mission, 237; ties to state and church, 62–63. See also *amos* land reform. *See* agrarian reform

Langer, Erick, 18

language: "bad words," 179, 182; as clue to everyday resistance, 315n9; and ethnicity, 24–28, 46–47; and literacy as ethnic markers, 239–240; of reciprocity, 135, 137, 141–142

Lara, Ignacio, and associates, 26, 65, 78, 152, 249, 315n10. *See also under* conflicts

leftist organizations, secular (communists, socialists), 60, 262, 264, 294, 312n8, 318n2

León, Carlos Arturo, 56, 60–63, 65, 259, 261

Liberal Revolution, 55, 57–58, 94–95, 264

liberation theology, 4–6, 22, 279–309 *passim;* and Bible, 295–297; and fiestas, 116, 274; and historical narratives, 205–208; and inculturation, 277; and indigenous "awakening," 262–263; and modernity, 306

light blood, 182, 212

literacy and schooling: and agrarian reform, 271; and archival record, 10; and "awakening," 33, 188; and Bible reflection, respect, 295–305 *passim;* as ethnic marker, 239–240, 282; and historical consciousness, 130; illiteracy as blindness, 319n8; and physical punishment, 319n5; and power, 147–150, 197–198, 282; and respect, 317n15; Tepeyac Bajo school, 269

Lizarzaburu, Miguel and Manuel, 56, 62–64

Llinllín (hacienda), 167–168, 250

maps: Chimbo and Riobamba basins, 30; Monjas Corral and upper Pangor Basin, 75; Northwestern South America, 29

marriage: colonial chiefs and Span-iards, 40; and dress, 282; as *experiencia,* 239; and fiesta sponsorship as rite of passage, 115–124; hacienda steward and chiefly family, 49–50; interracial, 48; Jacoba Sayay's first, 173–174; and migration, 47; and moral instruction, conflict resolution, hegemony, 194–195, 233–235, 254–255; overseer's wife's pressures on him, 151; and post-agrarian reform land tenure, household economy, 273; Reinaldo Sisa's, 195–196; sponsorship of, 85, 117; and supplements, 132

Martínez Alier, Juan, 13

Mass, 5, 103, 189–190, 296

Mauss, Marcel, 19, 91, 113, 127, 141

memory, 10–11; of hacienda-era discipline as model for contemporary community, 290–291, 294; and interpretation of oral accounts, 203–208; and moral economy, 126; and resentment of hacienda labor demands, 146–147; in ritual, of Liberal Revolution, 94–95

mestizo. *See* white-mestizo

migration, 7, 35, 44, 47, 50–51, 69; contemporary, 273, 282; and identity, 96; and kinship, 83, 84, 85–87; as response to sexual abuse, 250; as weakening sense of ancestral land rights, 131

mita, 41–45, 146

mitayos. See mita

Mitchell, Timothy, 222

modernity, 305–308, 319n8

Monjas Corral (hacienda): administrative structure, 76–80; agriculture, 53–55, 61, 64–65, 76; archival record, 126; demography, 50–51, 57, 80; described in 1873, 52–54, 75–76; as God's hacienda, and fertility of, 131; livestock, 45, 53–55, 58, 64–65, 76; Llalla annexed to, 49; map, 75; origins, 45;

pronunciation, 26; purchased by Diocese, 55; renamed Tepeyac, 5, 263; rental contracts, 56, 58–67; topography and spatial organization, 46, 74–76, 75; as unit of analysis, 7

Monjas Corral-Tepeyac residents (extended discussions or quotations of): Amancha, José, on *doctrina*, 232–233; Amancha, José, on literacy as ethnic marker, 239–240; Condo, Rosa, on parental discipline, 242–243; Condo, Rosa, on reactions to bosses' punishment, 247; Guailla, Virgilio, on learning to venerate saints, 121–123; Niamo, Gabriel, on father as overseer, 151; Paca, Agustín, on conflict resolution and discipline, 234–235, 290–292; Pillajo, José María, kin of, 82–83, *84*; Pillajo, José María, on parents' severity and priests' teachings, 243–244; Sayay, Jacoba, on hacienda life, 167–180, 203–215 *passim*; Shagñay, Avelino, personal history and views of respect, 281–282; Sisa, Reinaldo, on arrival of new renter, 147–150; Sisa, Reinaldo, on hacienda life, 180–203, 203–215 *passim*; Yumbo, Alberto, and Bible reflection, 303. *See also* conflicts; photographs

moral economy, 17–19, 68–69, 125–126

moral instruction, 190–191, 194–195, 226–227, 230, 232–235

mountains: and afterlife, 162–163, 239; anger at trespassers, 27; mythic origins, 103; priest's interpretation of, 288; and saints, ritual, shamanism, 104–106; as source of aid, 313n5; and wildness, 34

niño, 238

nostalgia, 235–236, 282

Novillo, Guillermo, 56, 60, 260

nuns, 190, 274, 279

obedience as virtue, 225, 232, 317n11

obrajes, 39–42

O'Connor, Erin, 254

Otavalo, 29

overseers, 77–78; and conflicts over hacienda's labor demands, 150–151; and *doctrina*, 232–235; and hacienda resources, neighboring Runa, 96; and interpretation of whippings, 246–247; Jacoba Sayay's account of, 176–177; and religious authority, 81; and ritual exchange at Carnival, 137

pachakuti, 313n2

Pallatanga, 29, 30, 32, 36–38, 42, 45, 51, 64, 88, 273, 312n4

Pangor: demography, 46, 54; geography, *29–30*, 29–33; location and coastal markets, 49; precolonial, 36–38; pronunciation, 26; as refuge, 35; town, 32, 286, 313n2

pascuanchina, 224–231; adapted by contemporary priest, 288; and elders' experience, 239

paternalism, 12–13, 81, 240–245; and fiesta, 124; and hacienda violence, Guerrero on, 247–248

Pentecost, 316n7

persuasion, 222–223; and coercion, dichotomy of, 22, 235, 253

photographs: Amancha, José, 227; author, *181*, *286*; Church of Balbanera, *31*; group of villagers, 227; Guailla, Virgilio, *109*; inventory of *conciertos, arrimados*, debts, 57; Monjas Corral, *32*, *46*, *266*, *269*; Monjas Corral account book, *133*; Niamo, Gabriel, *109*, 227; Pangor (town), *32*, *286*; Pangor valley, *32*; procession with image of Saint Rose, *110*; Saint Rose, *109*, *110*; Sayay, Jacoba, *169*; Shagñay, Avelino, *280*; Sisa, Reinaldo, *181*; village music group, *286*; woman spinning wool, *34*; Yépez, Andrés, serving drink to Vicente Yubaillo, *111*; young couple, *285*; youth, *284*; Yumbo, Alberto, *218*

pilgrimage, 95, 122–123

prayer, 8, 114, 272

priests: colonial, 44, 48; contemporary, 5–6, 22, 274–277; and fiestas, 100–101; hacienda-era, 20, 187–192, 239–240; and inculturation, elders, 287–288; mocked, 94; and parental discipline, 244; Redemptorist, 281; and regidor, 106; and ritual discipline, 245–246; as sacred, 315n6

Proaño, Leonidas, 5, 33, 61, 262–263; on *comunas* and leftist leaders, 318n2; and indigenous "awakening," 188, 206; and rental contracts, 66–67

Protestantism, 206–207; conversion of agrarian reform beneficiaries, 264; and fiestas, saints, 124, 274; and historical narratives, 205–208; mentioned, 282, 294, 319n11; and mountains, 105; Proaño on, 318n2; and Reinaldo Sisa's account of hacienda era, 187; and rejection of past, competition with Catholicism, 287

Puruhá: as ancestors in contemporary historical narratives, 284–285; as contemporary ethnonym, 312n5; language, 25, 46–47; pre-Columbian and colonial people, 36–38, 47, 130

Quichua (language), 24–27, 46–47, 311n1; oratorical feature, 319n4; verbal suffix *-shka* and interpretation of oral history, 146

race. *See* ethnicity and race

racism: aesthetic/internalized, 20, 169–170, 238, 270–271, 283–284; in bosses' insults, 142, 149–150,

172, 200, 202, 214, 315n9; of elite, 146. *See also* ethnicity and race

Ramón Valarezo, Galo, 13–14, 134, 138–139

raya, 79–80

rebellions, 40, 159

reciprocity and redistribution, 16–19, 90–92; and agrarian reform, 204; and authority, 36, 38–40, 50; and *concertaje*, 58–59; as enduring principle of Andean social life, 67–68, 125; etiquette of, 135, 137, 141–142; in fiesta, 102, 109–114; hacienda as denying, 141–163; hacienda as fulfilling, 128–137; on hacienda as outcome of struggle, 137–141; and hegemony, 21; and moral judgment, 127–128, 141; and respect, 237–238; and stewards, 151–152; types of redistribution in fiesta, change in, 276; and use intentions, 102; and vertical exchange, 88–89. *See also* exchange networks

reducciones, 43, 312n2

regidores, 81, 106; and agrarian conflicts in 1960s, 254; and *doctrina*, 232–235; obsolete since 1960s, 275; and *pascuanchina*, 230

renters. *See* landlords

resistance, 16–19; and autonomy and reciprocity, 126, 137–163 *passim*; to catechist's authority, 302–303; in discourse of indigenous activists, 285–286; and gender, 212–215, 251; and hacienda formation, decline of chiefdoms, 35, 40, 42; and hegemony (Scott's view of), 218–219; ironic results of, in 1960s–1970s, 271; open, 82; and parental discipline, 244–245; respect complex as shaping meanings of, 250–253; as response to hacienda labor demands, 60, 209; as strategic stance, 208–212; vertical relationships as creating spaces for, 81–82

respect (*respeto*): and child rearing,
81, 217; complex, defined, 21–22,
222; contemporary views, 6, 279–
309; and fear, 237; hacienda era,
216–255; metaphors of deafness,
hearing, 319n9; and speech, 182;
as strategic stance, 208–212
Riobamba (town), 29–30, 42
ritual battles, 93–95
Roseberry, William, 21
Runa, *runa*, 98, 313nn6–7

sacrament, 228–229, 300
sacred places (as concept in contemporary Catholic activism), 286
Saint Rose, 100–124; image, 100, *109*;
official saint, 100; origins, 104;
statue in Monjas Corral chapel, 52
saints, 4–5, 103–106, 314n9. *See also*
fiestas
San Ramón. *See* Chimbo valley
Santillán, Antonio, 56, 60
santo suelo (holy earth), 185
schooling. *See* literacy and schooling
Scott, James: and hegemony, 21–
22, 217–220, 222, 249, 254; and
reciprocity, moral economy, resistance, 17–19, 125
shamanism and witchcraft: and
mountains, 105–106; and ritual
whipping as healing, 316n9; shamanic careers, 299; witchcraft
and devil, color symbolism, 239;
witchcraft and landlords, 159–160;
witchcraft among Runa, 172, 291
sharecropping: in Chimbo valley, 17;
on Monjas Corral, 80, 135, 312n2
Sicalpa, 30
socorro, 89, 132, 135, 153
songs: "Gallegos Runa," 96; "Tayta
Chimborazo, Mama Tungurahua,"
162–163, 285–286, *286*, 314n6
state: colonial Spanish, 38–42, 45,
47–48; Ecuadorian, 1960s, 260–
261; Ecuadorian, late-twentieth
and twenty-first centuries,
288–295, 306–309; Ecuadorian,

nineteenth-century, 48–50; hacienda's judicial role compared
to, 254–255; Inca, 17, 37–38, 41
Stern, Steve, 220–221
stewards: and *doctrina*, 232–235;
as enforcing hacienda labor demands, 144, 151–153; and fiesta
sponsorship, 119; position, 77–78;
sexual advances by, 174. *See also*
Lara, Ignacio
supplement (*suplimento, suplido*),
132–135, 153–154, 261

tables: fiestas, 107; renters, 56
tarea, 54, 79–80, 143
tayta, 13
Tepeyac Bajo: as fieldwork site, 5;
pronunciation, 26
translation, 24
Travolta, John, 28
triangle without base, 12, *13*, 15,
311n4; model critiqued, 73–99

Vatican II, 4, 274, 295, 300
Velasco Ibarra, José María, 188, 197,
315n8
vertical exchange. *See* exchange
networks
violence: anthropology of, 315n4;
everyday, on haciendas, 3–4, 54,
199–200; as making rebellion impossible, 203; symbolic and overt,
222. *See also* coercion, discipline

wanlla(na), 154, 314n5
Weismantel, Mary, 97–98, 311n6,
314n5, 317n16
white-mestizo: as category, 9, 27;
descendants of indigenous *común*,
50; historical origins of categories, 47–48; mythic origins of,
130; terms for, in Quichua, 96–98
witchcraft. *See* shamanism and
witchcraft
Wolf, Eric, 12–13, 35, 73, 124
writing. *See* literacy and schooling

Young People's Organization, 304

"The hacienda experience was a crucial era of injustice and exploitation that set the stage for modern political movements. Lyons has done a remarkable job across the board: obtaining rich autobiographical accounts; offering sensitive, readable translations; recovering the written history; and showing the impact of hacienda experiences and memories on three subsequent decades of community actions and individual lives."
—Rudi Colloredo-Mansfield, Associate Professor of Anthropology, University of Iowa

From the colonial period through the mid-twentieth century, haciendas dominated the Latin American countryside. In the Ecuadorian Andes, Runa—Quichua-speaking indigenous people—worked on these large agrarian estates as virtual serfs. In *Remembering the Hacienda: Religion, Authority, and Social Change in Highland Ecuador*, Barry Lyons probes the workings of power on haciendas and explores the hacienda's contemporary legacy.

Lyons lived for three years in a Runa village and conducted in-depth interviews with elderly former hacienda laborers. He combines their wrenching accounts with archival evidence to paint an astonishing portrait of daily life on haciendas. Lyons also develops an innovative analysis of hacienda discipline and authority relations. *Remembering the Hacienda* explains the role of religion as well as the reshaping of Runa culture and identity under the impact of land reform and liberation theology.

This beautifully written book is a major contribution to the understanding of social control and domination. It will be valuable reading for a broad audience in anthropology, history, Latin American studies, and religious studies.

BARRY LYONS is Associate Professor of Anthropology at Wayne State University. He lives in Detroit with his wife and their two children. He and his family travel frequently to Ecuador, his wife's homeland.

Joe R. and Teresa Lozano Long Series in Latin American and Latino Art and Culture

University of Texas Press

ISBN-13: 978-0-292-71439-7
ISBN-10: 0-292-71439-4

90000

9 780292 714397